SO-BHS-344

CURRICULUM AS CULTURAL PRACTICE:
POSTCOLONIAL IMAGINATIONS

Edited by Yatta Kanu

Although initiatives that deconstruct and challenge the dominance of
Western cultural knowledge in the classroom are gaining momentum,
the effect of these initiatives on curriculum theory and practice have
not been fully explored. *Curriculum as Cultural Practice* aims to revitalize current discourses of curriculum research and reform from a
postcolonial perspective.

In this volume, Yatta Kanu brings together a group of distinguished
scholars to critically examine the implications of Eurocentrism in the
areas of cultural production, representation, and dissemination in
education, and to promote innovative, democratic, and ethical practices in curriculum design. Contributors draw from concepts such as
subalternity, indigenous knowledges and spirituality, critical ontology,
biolinguistic diversity, postnationalism, transnationalism, and globalization to examine and theorize curriculum for postcolonial contexts.
Together these diverse perspectives offer unique insights into the
postcolonial condition and reflect changing educational relations,
practices, and institutional arrangements.

YATTA KANU is an associate professor in the Faculty of Education at
the University of Manitoba.

Curriculum as Cultural Practice

Postcolonial Imaginations

EDITED BY YATTA KANU

REGIS COLLEGE LIBRARY
WITHDRAWN 15 St. Mary Street West
Toronto, Ontario
Canada M5S 2Z5

UNIVERSITY OF TORONTO PRESS
Toronto Buffalo London

LC
196
C87
2006

© University of Toronto Press Incorporated 2006
Toronto Buffalo London
Printed in Canada
Reprinted in paperback 2009

ISBN 978-0-8020-9078-2 (cloth)
ISBN 978-1-4426-1027-9 (paper)

Printed on acid-free paper

Library and Archives Canada Cataloguing in Publication

Curriculum as cultural practice : postcolonial imaginations / edited
by Yatta Kanu.

Includes bibliographical references.
ISBN 978-0-8020-9078-2 (bound) – ISBN 978-1-4426-1027-9 (pbk.)

1. Critical pedagogy. 2. Postcolonialism. 3. Curriculum change.
4. Education and globalization. 5. Nationalism and education.
6. Eurocentrism. 7. Ethnophilosophy. I. Kanu, Yatta, 1952–

LC196.C87 2006   370.11'5   C2006-902577-0

University of Toronto Press acknowledges the financial assistance to
its publishing program of the Canada Council for the Arts and the
Ontario Arts Council.

University of Toronto Press acknowledges the financial support for
its publishing activities of the Government of Canada through the
Book Publishing Industry Development Program (BPIDP).

Contents

Acknowledgments

Curriculum as Cultural Practice: Postcolonial Imaginations would not have been possible without the efforts of the contributors who believed in the need for a book that makes available, in a single volume, a range of ideas about postcolonial/anticolonial curriculum reform that would appeal to the wide range of audiences for whom the book is intended. Their willingness to prepare and revise their chapters, sometimes in the light of new developments in their fields, shows their dedication to this project. Thanks to all of them.

Thanks are also due to the anonymous reviewers whose suggestions contributed to the development of the book.

Special thanks to Stephen Kotowych at the University of Toronto Press for all the advice he gave to help the publication of this book.

Thanks to the authors and publishers for their kind permission to reprint the materials in Chapter 1 and Chapter 9.

CURRICULUM AS CULTURAL PRACTICE:
POSTCOLONIAL IMAGINATIONS

Introduction

YATTA KANU

[Books] let me know firsthand that if the mind was to be the sight of resistance, only the imagination could make it so. To imagine, then, was a way to begin the process of transforming reality. All that we cannot imagine will never come into being.

bell hooks (1991)

Futures in curriculum are not 'out there' waiting for us to arrive. We must visualize them here, now.

Noel Gough (2002)

Setting the Context

The aim of this book is simple: to contribute to and revitalize current curriculum discourses by bringing together a group of curriculum scholars to imagine, that is, to envision/theorize and discuss curriculum reform and research from the perspective of the emerging and often contentious concept loosely known as the 'postcolonial.' Largely as a result of 'post' scholarship (e.g., postmodernism, poststructuralism, post-Enlightenment, postcolonialism), the Western prejudice at the core of virtually all education systems operating in the world today has been exposed, provoking curriculum initiatives that deconstruct and challenge the dominance of Western Eurocentrism in curriculum and making possible the theorization of curriculum from several alternative perspectives, for example, from the perspectives of autobiography, feminism, place, postmodernism, phenomenology, to name but a few. However, although some of the most potent challenges to the dominance of

Western cultural knowledge in education have come from the field of postcolonial theory, the implications of these challenges for curriculum theorizing have not been fully explored. To address this void in the current discourses about curriculum reform and research, the contributors to this book were invited to extend the discussion of the postcolonial to curriculum and pedagogy by exploring ideas that they consider central to understanding and rethinking curriculum as cultural practice in postcolonial educational contexts. In extending such an invitation, my assumption was that multiple modes of theoretical representations would emerge from alternative perspectives on postcoloniality grounded in a dynamic variety of life experiences, thereby adding richness and complexity to the current curriculum discourse of change. The result, as attested to by the chapters in this book, is a rich variety of insights centring around concepts such as hermeneutic pedagogy, hybridity / Third Space, engaged differences, ecological diversity, transnationalism, postnationalism, indigenous knowledges and spirituality, critical ontology, globalization (perceived in a particular way), postcolonial supplement, and the Akan (West Africa) concept of *sankofa* (meaning 'return to the past to move forward'), all of which frame the postcolonial condition and reflect changing educational relations, practices, and institutional arrangements (see also, Burbules & Torres, 2000). While these multiple and diverse insights do not claim to be complete representations of a field as heterogeneous as postcolonial studies, they do comprise a set of interrelated constructs and propositions that spark our imagination and creativity, move curriculum forward into new directions, and suggest that changes can occur in ways that are different, more equitable, and more productive of justice in the public space of education than has been the case to date. They are insights that complicate the conversation about curriculum (Pinar, 2004) and constitute what Keith Morrison has called 'the stuff of the rewired curriculum theoretical brain' (2004, p. 493).

Before remarking further on these shifts and the ideological and cultural forces that have provoked them, I want to articulate the senses in which the expression *curriculum as cultural practice* and the terms *imagination* and *postcolonial* are used in this book. My choice of the expression *curriculum as cultural practice*, both as title of the book and as a lens for examining curriculum, was intended to place culture (i.e., the beliefs, values and meanings on which different groups draw to make sense of their world) at the centre of curriculum analysis and reform, and to emphasize practice as an important context for this endeavour.

To understand social/educational lives and reform, especially as reform relates to social inclusion/exclusion, and to the relations of knowledge and power, culture needs to be one, if not *the*, primary source for radical inquiry, for culture shapes our ways of seeing, and, as Arif Dirlik (1987) argues, it is these ways of seeing that we must question first, if we are to make changes in action at either the micro or the macro level.

The turn towards cultural inquiry in curriculum reform finds rationalization in the works of scholars of cultural politics of education (e.g., Bourdieu & Passeron, 1977; Aronowitz, 1992; Giroux, 1983; Apple, 1993; Popkewitz, 2000) who have deconstructed school knowledge to reveal it as predominantly constitutive of the knowledge and values of particular interest and power groups. According to these theorists, schools function not only to normalize those whose attitudes, norms, cultural values, practices, and behaviours are different from what is constructed as normal, but also to inscribe particular rationalities into the sensibilities, dispositions, and awarenesses of individuals to make them conform to a single set of imaginaries about culture and national citizenship (Popkewitz, 2000). The contention is that the purpose of school is to create a form of consciousness that enables the inculcation of the knowledge and culture of dominant groups as official knowledge for all students, thereby allowing dominant groups to maintain social control without resorting to overt mechanisms of domination (Althusser, 1971; Apple, 1993). These 'politics of official knowledge' work not by coercion but through accords and compromises that favour dominant groups: 'These compromises occur at different levels: at the level of political and ideological discourse, at the level of state policies, at the level of knowledge that is taught in schools, at the level of the teachers and students in classrooms, and at the level of how we understand all of this' (Apple, 1993, p. 10). Power and control, then, become exercised through a corpus of knowledge that the school, in turn, distributes through the school curriculum and rules and regulations. Thus, schools are said to control not only people and meaning but also to confer cultural legitimacy on the knowledge of specific groups (Young, 1971; Giroux, 1983). Because of the important relationship between cultural knowledge and power, any serious engagement with reform in education in the twenty-first century must include a focus on culture. In particular, cultural inquiry needs to be engaged as a means of destabilizing taken-for-granted categories, representations, and truths in educational discourses and practices.

Recent developments in the study of practice theory and situated learning in cultural anthropology (see, e.g., Hoffman, 1999) have high-lighted the importance of *practice* in cultural inquiry. Proponents of practice theory and situated learning have argued that, given the cultural situatedness of all learning and the cultural assumptions that underlie all practices, practice is the most appropriate unit of analysis for understanding education, curriculum, and pedagogy. Accordingly, the concept of curriculum as cultural practice provides an analytical framework both for examining curriculum and curricular practices as they have historically operated, and for rethinking alternatives for the future.

Imagination plays a key role in proposing alternatives for the function of curriculum as cultural practice. As bell hook's quotation at the beginning of this introductory chapter suggests, imagination challenges the banal and the quotidian to open up spaces for re-envisioning alternative social reality. Maxine Greene, too, describes imagination as the cognitive capacity that allows us to break with the taken-for-granted and transcend familiar definitions and distinctions. Imagination is a mode of thinking that 'refuses compliance, that looks down roads not yet taken to arrive at a more fulfilling social order, to more vibrant ways of being in the world' (1995, p. 5). For Greene, then, as for hooks, imagination is the genesis of social transformation, a way of envisioning relations constituted in new cultural practices. The term *imagination* has also been used in recent discourses about globalization and education to help explain how people come to know, understand, and experience themselves as members of a community and citizens of a nation-state. According to Popkewitz imagination functions 'to form individuals into the seam of a collective narrative and help them generate conceptions of personhood and identity' (2000, p. 168). Rizvi expands this conceptual range by defining imaginations as 'the attempt to provide coherence between ideas and actions, to provide a basis for the content of relationships and the creation of categories with which to understand the world around us' (2000, pp. 222–223).

For these theorists, to imagine is to understand the present social order in terms of its historical development, to believe in the possibility of a different and more fulfilling social order, and to harness human agency towards the realization of this possibility. These orientations inform the understanding of imagination that frames the discussions in this book. As used here, imagination provides a framework for understanding how curriculum has been mediated and to what effect; as well, imagination signifies possibilities for alternative constructions of curriculum. In the first instance, imagination is used as an analytical framework for the historical examination of curriculum as cultural practice where the curriculum, mediated by a colonial imagination, has been employed to neutralize difference, assimilate, and establish for the Other a worldview and concept of self and community; in the second, imagination refers to a process proposing reform where curriculum could be reconceptualized/reimagined in ways that are more responsive to the multiplicity, difference, and identity affirmation that condition the postcolonial. Cultural knowledge, curriculum, and imagination co-construct one another as legitimate, coherent, 'commonsense' knowledge in a complex process that is often unarticulated except in moments of crisis such as when change threatens or when public scrutiny intensifies. Of the three, imagination is the most important place to begin the reorganization of the social order.

The term *postcolonial*, as used in its various fields, reflects a heterogeneous set of subject positions, critical enterprises, and a diverse range of experiences pertaining to colony and independent statehood alike (see London, this volume). This diverse use of postcolonial has resulted in a looseness in meaning that has confounded many and occasioned considerable debate about its precise parameters. The postcolonial has been interpreted and explored as 'the scene of intense discursive and conceptual activity characterized by a profusion of thought and writing about the cultural and political identities of colonized subjects' (Gandhi, 1989, p. 5) and as designating a more specific and historically located set of experiences, practices, and cultural strategies (Ashcroft et al., 1995). Within the complex fabric of the field, even this latter view is divided among those who believe that postcolonial refers to not only the period after independence, which marked the departure of the European imperial powers from territories that they had previously occupied and colonized, but also the period prior to colonization where the cultural productions and social formations of the precolonized society are used to better understand the experience of colonization.

Postcolonial is also used as a framework for the study and analysis of the power relations that inscribe race, ethnicity, and cultural production and relations, of which education and schooling – as hegemonic ideological state apparatuses (Althusser, 1971) used by the state in place of repressive force to persuade its citizens to accept the ideological positions of those in power – are components. Additionally, postcolonial is seen as 'a position ... that calls for a major rethinking of given categories and histories, questions assumed, and fixed structures, and brings a greater sense of the political to the interpretation of social and cultural production' (London, this volume). What these different locations have in common is an understanding of postcolonial 'mostly as an object of desire for critical practice' (Slemon, 1995) and the signification of a position against colonialism – the oppression and subjugation of others – of any kind. In this regard, just as desire is at the root of the curricular imagination, so too, does imagination infuse the postcolonial projects in their various guises. At the source of this imaginary is the attempt to see beyond Western Eurocentricism and the dominance of Western knowledge/cultural production, representation, and dissemination. This dominance is interrogated and challenged in this book in an effort to create opportunity for the emergence of subjugated knowledges/cultural productions. From this perspective, postcolonial becomes the site where educational/curricular assumptions and norms are called into question in the struggle for more democratic social relations. In theorizing curriculum alternatives, contributors have drawn on experiences from two groups: (1) former European colonies now experiencing new forms of imperialism through expanding forms of capitalist and cultural globalization and (2) minoritized populations who, according to internal colony theorists (e.g., Fanon, 1963; Barrera, 1979) experience endemic 'savage inequalities' (Kozol, 1991), marginalization, and discrimination in education within dominant-culture societies, forcing them to drop out and reside in 'internal colonies' with little or no hope of upward mobility.

In this book, these three concepts – *curriculum as cultural practice, imagination, and postcolonial* – are the intersecting lenses through which current curricular productions as well as proposals for change are discussed.

Giving the Present a Past

One way to more fully understand and rethink these three concepts in the context of this book is to examine them within a historical framework of colonialism. Such an examination gives the present a past and helps explain, for example, the colonizers' desire to obliterate the identities and indigenous knowledges of the colonized during colonial administration, and why the working class and minority groups in these societies find little of their own culture in schools.

Colonialism, like the postcolonial, has been defined in diverse ways (see, e.g., Spivak, 1990; Nandy, 1983; Willinsky, 1998; Said, 1993; Gandhi,

1989), with each definition linking colonialism with notions of racial and cultural superiority, ideological indoctrination, power and control over others, and greed and violence. An overview of the field suggests that colonialism has been identified both as physical conquest and control of territories, as well as control of the mind of the conquered and subordinated in an imperative to 'civilize' the Other and keep the Other in a perpetual state of psychological subordination. Although the physical occupation and control of territories may end, the processes of colonial cultural production and psychologization persist, a situation that provokes Stuart Hall's (1996) oft-quoted concern: 'When was the postcolonial?' The focus of my analysis here is colonialism as a 'civilizing mission' manifesting as legitimate school knowledge and practice. This civilizing mission is an ideological formation intended to establish for, and impose on, the Other a particular view of the world and a concept of self and community through the production, representation, and dissemination of school knowledge. In this sense, the colonized Other refers not only to the former colonies that comprised the periphery at the receiving end of cultural dispensations from metropolitan centres in Western Europe during the colonial period, but also minority populations in dominant-culture societies whose knowledge and cultural productions have been silenced in the educational space.

For an illustration of how curriculum as cultural practice has worked to the benefit of the colonialists and the disenfranchisement of the colonized I describe, briefly, three cases that depict how the state (here Great Britain, the United States, and Canada), as a privileged entity, contrived and mediated colonial imagination during the process of empire- and nation-building, using curriculum and pedagogy to control the mind of the colonized. The first case is provided by British colonial administration of its territories, and I begin with an analysis of education in Trinidad and Tobago during British colonialism in the nineteenth and first half of the twentieth centuries, drawing mainly on recent insights provided by Norrel London's work on colonial education in that country (see, e.g., London, 2001, and this volume). London discusses how ideology became the primary agent for the internalization and acceptance of British and Western culture, and how education and schooling were used as the medium for developing in the colonized Other the required sense of psychological subordination. The curriculum canvas during the period is described as drawing from the universe of educational ideologies available in the metropolitan arena (Britain), enhanced by thinking prevalent in the United States and parts of Western Europe, which emphasized cultural constructs like mental discipline, humanism, child study, and social efficiency. London argues that 'in each of these traditions the choice of content and of delivery practices was subjugated to the colonial ideal. Congruence with established objectives for domination and acceptance of a defined worldview was a major requirement' (2001, p. 55). For example, because it promoted mindless activities such as drills and rote memorization, mental discipline became an effective tool of the colonial enterprise, reinforcing the colonial desire to suppress creativity and critical thinking in the service of subjugating the Other. Instructive is London's observation of how 'humanism,' the tradition that most emphasized the promotion and maintenance of what was considered the best of Western cultural heritage and values, was put to work as an arsenal of the colonizer in Trinidad and Tobago. Because humanism exemplifies British colonial education almost everywhere during the period of empire-building, London's observation is worth quoting at length here:

> The heroes exalted in the history books, the norms and mores presented for inculcation (the cadence of public holidays established, for example), and the standards of excellence and gallantry paraded for emulation (as depicted in the story of Odysseus and the Cyclops, for example) were contrivances for the colonial purpose. Emphasis on these, to the exclusion of all others, was an attempt to obliterate the existentialist past of the colonized and to present an alternative and preferred view of reality ...The official pronouncement meant that students did not have a voice, nor were they encouraged to develop one. They were the 'voiceless' objects in a socio-political sense, a position which gestures in the direction of Gayatri Spivak's (1988) concern: 'Can the subaltern speak?' (2001, p. 68)

Like Norrel London, I have documented similar foreign-ness of curriculum and voicelessness in curriculum and pedagogy in my analysis of colonial education in another former British colony, Sierra Leone in West Africa (see Kanu, 1993), noting that 'the subject-matter taught was foreign and had no relevance or bearing on students' lived experiences and it was taught in ways that stifled critical thinking and creativity. The main interest of the colonizer was to ensure that the "uncivilized natives" digested the new cultural reality that their official knowledge was imparting ... Students received knowledge but were perceived as incapable of producing or changing knowledge. Teaching was a monological process that lacked any theory about students' capacity to interpret reality and bestow it with multiple meanings' (1993, p. 2).

Kazim Bacchus has described colonial education in the British West Indies in similar words. In his study of colonial education in British Guyana, Bacchus found that 'The curriculum was foreign and aimed at preparing obedient citizens. It was to teach them [students] how not to be critical and question the social (dis)order' (1994, p. 45). Negation of voice, therefore, functioned as a potent force in the colonizer's determination to make 'mimic men' (Bhabha, 1994) of the colonized, the reformed recognizable Other who was almost but never sufficiently the same as the colonizer.

In Sierra Leone, Trinidad and Tobago, and Guyana, the purpose of education was to prepare a small group of people to read and teach the Christian Bible and to fill a limited number of low-waged positions in the African civil service and on the plantations of the West Indies. Bacchus effectively captures the content and character of elementary education in the British colonies when he tells us that 'the primary school curriculum consisted mainly of the 3R's, religious instruction and teaching students "social graces" and "good manners." Religious education, in particular, became a most valuable subject on the curriculum because it was intended to produce pliant and submissive workers and provide them with Christian values to ensure that their moral development had a strong Christian foundation. For this reason, religious education was strongly supported by local authorities' (1994, p. 45). Bacchus refers to a report in which the governor of Tobago suggested that on the Christian and moral instruction of the 'Negro' rests 'the soundness of the fruit to be gathered from the tree of freedom,' while the governor of Jamaica saw religious education as functional in making workers more 'skillful and trustworthy' and to induce them to compete for laboring jobs. Teaching and learning were mainly memorization of passages from the Bible and the catechism, and recitation of sacred poetry and singing of hymns. Postelementary education, when available, was provided by private and endowed schools which later became grammar schools patterned after the famous English 'public' schools that focused on classical studies, history, mathematics, and English composition (Bacchus, 1994).

Overall, the teaching methods employed in the colonial schools were intended to achieve limited, instrumental purposes. They centered on subject matter, were devoid of students' existential realities, and stressed the direct transmission of information by teachers and its reproduction

by students on examinations specifically structured to ensure the digestion of the information. As argued in my analysis of colonial education
in Sierra Leone (Kanu, 1993), the suppression of voice, critical thinking,
questioning, and creativity in the teaching/learning process was an
intentional act by the British colonial administration to repress cultural
self-determination by the colonized and to deny them political agency.
Colonial mimicry also found expression in the imitation of the practices
of English public schools, games, girl guides, boy scouts, and the cadet
corps – which were introduced and often made compulsory because of
their usefulness in shaping the character of students, preparing them
for leadership roles, and helping them to become honest and acquire
greater respect for those in authority (Bacchus, 1994; also in this volume). Through the overt and hidden curriculum, therefore, students
were socialized into English middle-class values and behaviours.

Particularly important are the lessons that might be learned from the
propagation and implantation of the English language as an instrument
of control and civilization in the British colonies. In all of these colonies,
English was accorded primacy as the official language of communication and as a school subject, a pride of place that has persisted despite
the end of British rule in these territories. Through ideological and
hegemonic processes, and through a number of deliberate cultural
strategies (see London, this volume), English came to be accepted, and
continues to function, as the language of communication and opportunity worldwide, in other words, as Seonaigh MacPherson (this volume)
points out, English was and still is made an object of desire. It appears,
therefore, that although recent discourses on education and administration in the former British Empire point to local variations from territory
to territory (Willinsky, 1998), in general the overall intent of colonial
education, as Bacchus has observed, was to instil in the colonized 'a
worldview that would develop in them a voluntary subservience to the
white ruling groups and a willingness to continue occupying their
positions on the lowest rung of the occupational and social ladder'
(1994, p. 308).

Similar observations can be made about the state's use of education
and curriculum to negate identities and impose a new order in the
United States in the nineteenth and early part of the twentieth centuries. American sociologist Randolph Collins (1979), placing the legacy
of homogenization and conformity in education in historical context,
has argued that the impetus for compulsory schooling in the United
States arose from the need to control the socialization of the children of
Southern European immigrants and perpetuate the values of the middle

class and the knowledge base of the traditional Anglo-Protestant culture. Other commentators, for example, Michael Apple, have described the moral mission of the schoolmen of this period as pursuance of a vigorous conformist system that would ensure the cultural hegemony and economic advantages of the English and Protestant middle class who saw their norms, values, and interests under siege by an increasing growth in immigrant populations from Eastern and Southern Europe, and Blacks from the rural South of the United States. Suspecting that these immigrants, with different cultural, religious, and political traditions, would outnumber their 'well-bred' and culturally homogeneous population (thought to be the source of America's stability) this group saw the school as 'the great engines of a moral crusade to make the children of the immigrants and Blacks like "us"' (Apple, 1990, p. 66). Carl Kaestle, writing about the urban centres of eastern United States, tellingly captures this moral superiority attitude in citing from a New York State Assembly report: 'Like the vast Atlantic, we must decompose and cleanse the impurities which rush into our midst, or like the inland lake, we shall receive their poison into our whole national system' (quoted in ibid.). For this pure, native, and embattled population, Kaestle contended, there was only one 'infallible filter' – the school, whose mission was to inculcate submissive and cooperative attitudes among the city's children whatever the vicissitudes of urban life might bring them (ibid.). Thus, schools, largely through curricular selections and the bureaucratization and standardization of these selections and procedures, embarked on vigorous policies of acculturation not only in New York City but also elsewhere in the United States.

Apple informs us, too, that with the advent of the Industrial Revolution the moral mission of education became increasingly coupled with economic ideologies and purposes as the United States expanded its industrial base. Schools, therefore, became charged with the responsibility of producing a 'like-minded' community of people with the norms and dispositions required of industrious and efficient workers. Although this portrait may seem a bit overdrawn – because schools also produce conditions for the possibility of various forms of resistance to this type of social engineering – Apple is largely correct in his argument that schooling in America at the beginning of the twentieth century was driven by concerns that embodied a conservative ideology of preserving the position of the powerful by teaching their values to immigrants and Blacks, and by adjusting these latter groups to existing subordinate economic roles.

It should come as no surprise that this ideological climate pervaded the consciousness and perceptions of the formative members of the curriculum field at the time, for example, W.W. Charters, Franklin Bobbit, E.L. Thorndike, Ross Finney, and David Snedden, to name but a few of the more influential ones, and that they were all Anglo-Saxon, Protestant, 'native,' and middle class. For these early theorists of the curriculum field, response to the immigrant threat lay in defining the social function of the curriculum as fostering social integration through the 'production' of a community of people with 'a large group consciousness,' a process eloquently described by Franklin Bobbit in this way: 'How does one develop a genuine feeling of membership in a social group, whether large or small? There seems to be but one method and that is, *To think and feel and act with the group as a part of it as it performs its activities and strives to attain its ends*. Individuals are fused into coherent small groups, discordant small groups are fused into the large internally-cooperating group, when they *act together* for common ends, with a common vision, and with united judgment' (Bobbit's emphasis; cited in Apple, 1990, p. 70). Clearly, for Bobbit and his associates, like-mindedness in beliefs and standards of behaviour, cultural consensus, and homogeneity, and the imposition of meaning framed the imagination of community. To date, this imagination of what the relationship should be between curriculum and community control continues to mediate curricular conceptions and practices in the United States, as seen in the neo-conservative rightist education reform agenda that focuses on the return to white, middle-class traditional curriculum standards, derails efforts at pluralism, and redefines education as the amassing of specific forms of cultural knowledge (Fairbanks, 2004).

Control and manipulation of the Other through schooling and curriculum was not unique to the United States during its period of nation-building. Like their American counterparts, Canadian scholars (e.g., Axelrod, 1997; Strange & Loo, 1997; Osborne, 1995) have also argued that the enthusiasm for compulsory public schooling in Canada was fuelled by the desire to perpetuate Anglo-Celtic, Protestant, and French Catholic ideals. Athough at the time Canada was struggling with its own identity, wavering between asserting a unique Canadian identity and remaining tied to the majesty and power of Great Britain and the British Empire, Canadian elites showed no uncertainty of purpose when it came to the critical role that they assigned to state institutions like the school in shaping the identity of Canada's citizens (Richardson, 2002). Vincent Massey, the country's first Canadian-born governor general, explicitly laid out the responsibility of schools in the realization of an ideal type of Canadian when he said: 'In a country with so scattered a population as ours and a vast frontier exposed to alien influences, the tasks of creating a truly national feeling must inevitably be arduous but this is the undertaking to which our educational systems must address themselves, for by true education alone will the problem be solved. To our schools we must look for the good Canadian' (Massey, 1926, p. 11). Thus, the state proceeded to build the Canadian nation by regulating the education (and the moral behaviours) of those not considered ideal types. For example, after Confederation, through the Indian Act (1879) and the establishment of the Department of Indian Affairs (1880), the government of Canada became unabashedly involved in transforming the character of all Aboriginals, 'protecting' them on reserves, and civilizing and assimilating the 'savages' into Anglo-Saxon norms. Believing that the best chances for lasting results would be achieved with Indian children, the federal government decided, in 1879, to take a more direct role in their education by setting up residential schools where Indian children could be assimilated from the allegedly corrupting environments of their homes and families (Strange & Loo, 1997). To ensure compliance, in 1930 Ottawa appointed truancy officers, who were empowered to impose penalties to compel all Indian children between the ages of 7 and 16 to attend school.

In the Canadian West, where a massive influx of non-British/non-French immigrants arrived between 1901 and 1921 to settle the 'Last Best West,' the choice between cultural accommodation and cultural change was decided in favour of aggressive assimilationist policies. Richardson reports, for example, that in response to the question of how the diverse cultures of the newcomers were to be accommodated Northwest Territory School Superintendent Arthur Groggin sought to address what he saw as 'the pressing educational problem posed by a foreign and relatively ignorant population' in this way: 'To gather the children of different races, creeds, and customs into the common school and "Canadianize" them ... Though they may enter as Galicians, Doukhobors, or Icelanders, they will come out as Canadians ... A common school and a common language will produce that homogeneous citizenship so necessary in the development of that greater Canada lying west of the Lakes' (cited in Richardson, 2002, p. 85).

Thus, mass schooling and the curriculum were the vehicles through which the accomplishment of the cultural and psychological colonization of the Other was imagined. Despite successive post-1945 immigrations, first from war-torn Europe and, since 1960, from non-traditional sites of immigration such as South Asia, the Caribbean, and more recently Africa, and the subsequent introduction of multiculturalism since the early 1970s, this 'common imagining' of the Canadian nation is still alive in the curriculum of schools across Canada, as documented in recent analyses of homogenizing nationalist discourses in the Kindergarten to Grade 12 (K–12) social studies curriculum in the provinces of British Columbia (McDonald, this volume; 2002) and Alberta (Richardson, this volume).

Theorizing Curriculum for Postcolonial Contexts

As the foregoing historical analyses of curriculum as cultural practice in diverse societies show, curricular encounter with the Other has been unequal, unethical, and anchored in racism and violence. These practices have not always met with the success anticipated because values deemed good by the colonizer and/or nation-state have been constantly repudiated by those on whom they have been imposed. In the former European colonies in Africa, for example, repudiation took the form of nationalist movements that eventually led to independence for these countries. Independence, however, has been followed by the march of neo-colonialism in the guise of modernization and development through globalization and transnationalism. This reinvention of imperialism implies that schools and school curriculum cannot separate themselves from the task of neo-colonization.

In dominant-culture societies with ethnic and other minoritized populations, the refusal of minority groups to become 'carbon copies' of the dominant cultural groups within their countries has meant that the tropes by which the elites have constructed and sustained a single set of national identity are no longer sustainable. Trends in academic scholarship also reveal a vigorous challenge to the dominance of Western traditions parading as pristine truths destined for universal application (Smith, 2002). As mentioned earlier, 'post' scholarship has exposed and questioned the worldwide dominance of Western cultural knowledge and traditions, creating a contemporary crisis that requires creative resolution.

Given these developments, how can democratic, ethical curricular relations be forged? How shall education proceed when its central assumptions about curriculum have been shown to be complicit in the subjugation of many of the world's peoples – peoples now claiming their place as interlocutors equal with anyone bold enough to make proposals about the future (Smith, 2002)? Where does epistemological authority lie, in the wake of the cultural vacuum created by the 'post' critique? How shall knowledge be produced, represented, and disseminated within these new contexts? If intellectual colonization continues, albeit in a neo-colonial mode, how can we interrogate the colonial present and move towards a genuinely postcolonial state of affairs? How must educators attend to issues of equity and social justice in the current context of neo-liberal, neo-conservative, and managerial commitments to market-driven, standards-based education? What is the particular poverty of curriculum and pedagogy within these contexts and what kinds of curricular imaginations are possible in the alleviation of this poverty?

The contributors to this book have attempted to address these and similar questions by exploring several of the concepts/discourses that have given shape to the postcolonial imagination, showing the particular resonance of these concepts with the reconstruction of curriculum and pedagogy as cultural practice. In Part 1 the contributors kick off this process by engaging deconstructive and/or reconstructive moments as they turn a critical and postcolonial gaze towards the school disciplines.

Just over a decade ago Gyan Prakash (1994), in his seminal examination of the foundation of history under British colonialist management in India, reminded us that the critique of the West is not confined to the colonial record of exploitation and profiteering but extends to the disciplinary knowledge and procedures that it authorized. Prakash argued that if the marginalization of sources of knowledge and agency occurred in the functioning of colonialism and its derivative, nationalism, then the weapon of critique must turn against Europe and the modes of knowledge that it instituted. For the contributors of the essays in Part 1 that weapon resides in the deconstructive reading and rethinking of the disciplinary knowledges authorized in the service of colonialism. During empire-building, for example, the English language was made an instrument of domination and was used to regulate and police access to status, authority, and knowledge among colonized peoples. In chapter 1, Norrel London undertakes a postcolonial deconstructive reading of the rise to prominence of the English language in Trinidad and Tabago between 1938 and 1959, the period when the imperial grip on the colony tightened. Using documents kept by the then Department of Education and by individual schools in Trinidad and Tobago, London describes and analyses the intellectual thinking and arguments that might have accorded primacy to English in Trinidad and Tobago, the intervention strategies used by colonial bureaucrats in the schooling enterprise to impose, promote, and establish English among the masses, and the evaluations used by 'managers' to police the English language curriculum that they had put in place. London's analyses are important here because the Trinidad and Tobago scenario was replicated several times in other jurisdictions under British colonial rule in the Caribbean, Africa, and the Indian subcontinent, rendering indigenous languages unprivileged and inferior not only at the time but also for today.

This loss or silencing of other languages in the zeal to promote English as a global language is taken up in chapter 2 by Seonaigh MacPherson, who discusses the pivotal role that English and English-language education continues to play in the current global era. Her central question concerns the relationship between postcolonial education, language, and ecology in the promotion of global biolinguistic diversity and sustainability. She begins by considering the shift in our geographical imaginary from the world as a colonial atlas to the world as a bio-ecological phenomenon embodied in the 'Blue Planet.' She points to the conspicuous absence of a postcolonial period of transition in the shift from colonial English-language education to global iterations of English language teaching in manifold forms and varieties of programs. MacPherson illustrates each type of program using contemporary cases, and concludes by proposing a postcolonial agenda for English-language education as multilingual, multiliterate, intercultural, and grounded in biolinguistic diversity and ecological sustainability.

In chapter 3, John Willinsky elaborates his idea of a 'postcolonial supplement,' first proposed in his eye-opening book, *Learning to Divide the World: Education at Empire's End* (1998), where he analysed the educational legacy of European imperialism. Willinsky's position is that just as schools were an endemic part of empire-building through teaching the order and ideology of empire at almost every turn, so can they play a vital role in directing progressive curriculum efforts towards understanding and critiquing what has come to replace and extend the global force of that earlier era. The postcolonial supplement, Willinsky argues, resides in a series of classroom opportunities for teachers to introduce their students to the historical weight of five centuries of European hegemony. These classroom moments might take the form of practical activities designed to subvert the colonial message and its portrayal of the Other in school curriculum, while helping students to see how knowledge is situated within histories. In Willinsky's chapter, the postcolonial supplement is given life in a Grade 12 English class-room in Vancouver (Canada) where, for three weeks, he and a group of Grade 12 students in a poetry class questioned and critiqued the British colonial themes and images in their prescribed textbook, and success-fully produced an alternative supplementary anthology of poetry that reflected postcolonial Canadian identity and landscape, among other themes.

Chapter 4 considers the contestatory and hybrid nature of postcolonial literary studies in relation to the intellectual engagement and cultural negotiation of curriculum and school reading practices. Taking as a starting point the notion that the postcolonial appears not as a single project or hypothesis but as a set of 'engaged differences,' Ingrid Johnston reflects on how current reading practices in schools are embedded in complex, inherited power relations and contemporary distributions of valuations. Specifically, she questions how such practices are mediated by entrenched and self-perpetuating notions of canonicity and by static understandings of a collective national identity. Johnston exem-plifies the difficulty of challenging these entrenched curricular read-ing practices through the discussion of a research project in which pre-service English teachers attempted to negotiate a postcolonial literary pedagogy.

In chapter 5, Ralph Mason envisions a postcolonial mathematics for the Aboriginal population of Nunavut in northern Canada. Teachers in this newly established Arctic territory are invited to question their adoption of traditional Western mathematics. In that invitation resides the option of adapting curriculum to suit the beliefs of Aboriginal peoples which differ considerably from the dominant culture's tradi-tional beliefs. Positioning curriculum as a representation of what a community believes is worth knowing, Mason recommends a repudia-tion of the idea of one-size-fits-all-cultures mathematics curriculum and points to possibilities of curriculum development which recognize that curriculum/education must empower a people to shape their own future.

In Part 2, contributors explore the recently emerging notion of indig-enous knowledges and spirituality as transformative counter-hegemonic knowledge and as a source of embodied resistance to Cartesian ratio-nalism by which the West measures and validates all knowledge (see, e.g., Dei et al., 2002; Kincheloe, this volume). The chapters in Part 2 explore indigenousness and spirituality as counterpoints to Western knowledge and ways of knowing, and as central to the bricolage that marks the postcolonial condition. In chapter 6, George Dei and Stanley Doyle-Wood pursue a radical analysis of educational and curriculum work as it applies to social inequity and exclusionary practices reproduced and sustained through racialized asymmetrical relationships of power. These authors insist upon a radical contestation of dominant and/or imposing school knowledge discourses and their overt and/or covert claims to cultural supremacy, legitimacy, and normalcy. Working through the lens of curriculum as cultural practice and positioning difference in the form of indigenous knowledges and spirituality, they present an analysis that seeks to challenge and sever the epistemic violence of Western cultural knowledge as it relates to the material exigencies of marginalized subjects and communities. Although their insistence upon the reimagining and repositioning of difference as critical political discourse draws strength from the important work of postcolonial theorizing, nevertheless Dei and Doyle-Wood further insist on an anticolonial agency that enunciates itself in what Stephen Slemon (1995) has referred to as an 'open talk across cultural locations.' They contend that without making such linkages and without taking into account the neo-colonial impact of globalization and global capital interests, we cannot – but we must – fully understand the changing ontology of systemic violence as it impacts us at 'home' when the interests of Western cultural capital feel threatened by the very same bodies 'abroad.'

In chapter 7, Joe Kincheloe develops the notion of indigenousness into what he calls 'critical ontology' which he describes as gaining new understandings and insights about our present state of being in the world and who we can become. Imagining postcolonial teaching and teacher education as a critical ontological undertaking, Kincheloe contends that, too often, studies of teachers' lives, teaching, and learning diminish or marginalize issues of power and privilege in relation to social identities. Becoming a postcolonial teacher-scholar necessitates personal transformation based on an understanding and critique of how and why individuals' political opinions, religious beliefs, gender roles, racial positions, and sexual orientations have been shaped by dominant cultural forces. Towards this end, critical ontology and its relationship to being a teacher and curriculum interpreter in the light of indigenous knowledges and ontologies are delineated and examined. Kincheloe's thesis is that as teachers from the dominant-cultural forces explore issues of indigenousness, they are able to highlight their differences with cultural others and the social construction of their own subjectivities. Through this means, Kincheloe contends, dominant-culture teachers come to understand themselves and how they develop curriculum and pedagogy in postcolonial times. This exploration of indigenous knowledge to renew teacher education and teaching is further taken up in the next two chapters.

In chapter 8, Yatta Kanu turns the postcolonial gaze towards the social and cultural conditions of former colonies and proposes curricular and teacher education processes that would respond more appropriately to these conditions. With her native Sierra Leone as reference, Kanu examines the goals of colonial administration in this former British colony, the educational strategies adopted, and the supporting educational programs instituted during the colonial period. The accompanying demise of indigenous approaches to education and the cultural ambiguity marking the postcolonial condition in Sierra Leone are discussed. Thereafter, Kanu draws on the Akan (West African) concept of *sankofa* to explore curricular and pedagogical reforms based on the retrieval of certain lapsed traditions of indigenous African education. For Kanu, a reappropriation of tradition is necessary not as a nostalgic return to a 'better' past but to bring forward these dismantled traditions in a manner that disturbs and calls into question the norms that currently shape curriculum in Sierra Leone – norms such as rationalization, instrumentalization, erosion of the lifeworld of teachers and students, and a diminished attention to place-conscious education. In her curricular imagination for these postcolonial social and/or cultural conditions, Kanu places teacher education at the centre of reform and highlights the need for preparing teachers committed to critical reflection on not only what they, as educators, might do, but as well, the social visions such practices would support. Kanu's notion of the postcolonial teacher bears affinity to Edward Said's (1996) idea of the intellectual as amateur, someone who raises moral questions about, and problematizes, even the most technical and routine professionalized activity, asking why one does what one is supposed to do, who benefits from it, and how it can be reconnected with a personal project and original thought.

In chapter 9, Glen Aikenhead reclaims and validates Aboriginal indigenous scientific knowledge absent in schools and academic discourses as a result of the perpetuation of a knowledge hierarchy that privileges and fetishizes Western scientific knowledge. Within these politics of scientific knowledge production and dissemination, dismantling this privilege resides in teaching the colonial Western scientific knowledge alongside Aboriginal science in science classrooms. Based on a research project among Canadian Aboriginals, appropriately titled *Rekindling Traditions*, Aikenhead argues that a potential for getting Aboriginal peoples into science careers lies in a postcolonial hybrid curriculum in which Western science content in the school curriculum is integrated into the local community's Aboriginal scientific knowledge. This requires a renegotiation of school science involving a move towards a coexistence of two major science cultures, Aboriginal and Western, within which the Western hegemonic status residing in many schools, communities, university science departments, and in society in general, is seriously questioned. The role of the postcolonial teacher as 'cultural broker' helping students cross the cultural border between Aboriginal science and Western science, so critical to this postcolonial moment in science education in the schools, is highlighted and described in the chapter.

The focus on the teacher and teacher education continues in Part 3, where David Smith and Kazim Bacchus, respectively, locate postcolonial education within some of the conditions and debates surrounding certain forms of globalization, and propose new modes of pedagogy and curriculum within these conditions. In chapter 10, Smith subscribes to two modalities for understanding the phenomenon of globalization: as a form of *human imaginary* 'that serves to organize and mobilize certain forms of action in certain ways,' and as *factity* that names the plans and intentions of the actors. Smith argues that both modalities 'pertain less to any characteristic of the world in its ordinary condition than to what certain people imagine that condition to be.' As such the modalities open up possibilities for critique, creative resistance, and recombination that people undertake in response to these modalities. Herein reside the potential and the space for a new and different form of global reality and, as Smith writes, it is this space that also marks the site for a new understanding of the work of teachers in postcolonial educational contexts. Within this space, Smith explores the preparation of teachers from the perspective of hermeneutics whose mission is to bring about understanding between peoples and groups in ways that are capable of sustaining human welfare in the most creative senses. Because the postcolonial hermeneutic pedagogy requires of teachers, first and foremost, that they be interpreters of culture and curriculum rather than mere transmitters and managers, Smith argues that it is imperative that teachers be educated in such a way as to be able to speak across disciplines, across cultures, and across national boundaries. In this context, Smith continues, it is more appropriate to speak not of receiving an education but 'of constantly being open to the means by which one can be led by life ... into an ever-deepening understanding of the truth of things.'

Bacchus, in chapter 11, defines globalization in terms of the movement and reorganization of modern economic capital which has produced modes of economic restructuring involving budget reductions affecting the welfare state and increased privatization of social services. In terms of education, this neo-liberal version of globalization, especially as implemented by the supranational organizations (e.g., the International Monetary Fund, World Bank, Organization for Economic and Cultural Development, and World Trade Organization, referred to by Bacchus as 'the new colonizers'), is reflected in an educational agenda that directly or indirectly imposes particular policies for educational financing, curriculum and testing standards, and teaching and teacher training. It has led to a reduction of state sponsorship and financing of education while imposing business management and efficiency standards as a framework for making decisions about education (see Burbules & Torres, 2000). Bacchus discusses the effects of this form of globalization on education in the former colonies, almost all of which are in the developing countries, and suggests that the growing importance of the knowledge economy in the realignment of global capital portends educational and curricular changes in these countries for their economic and social survival. The extent to which the standardization entailed in these changes brings forth more cultural homogeneity or produces local forms of resistance remains to be seen. What is clear is that, as Bacchus points out, a major educational challenge for these countries is the training and recruitment of teachers who are able to equip students with the skills, knowledge, and outlook that would prepare them to perceive more incisively the economic opportunities emerging from these global developments.

The chapters in Part 4 raise questions about the viability of the nation and nationalism in postcolonial times, and pose ethical questions about how these two concepts are positioned for teaching and learning about citizenship and national identity in the social studies classroom in Canada. Sociocultural theorists of education have long considered the development of a common national identity and citizenry as one of the essential functions of modern education. However, critics like Benedict Anderson (1991) have argued that that role has been predicated on the notion of a 'common imagining' of the nation, within which the nation is conceived of in terms of a single set of ideas about national identity and citizenship. Renate Salecl explains this common imagining of the nation in terms of the nation-state, faced with the impossibility of incorporating its 'surplus' – that is, those who cannot fit in because they are different – appealing to 'a fantasy structure or scenario through which it perceives itself as a homogeneous entity' (1994, p. 15). Cultural critics Homi Bhabha and Stuart Hall have called attention to the ambivalence of the nation in the production of national identity. In the introduction to his book, *Nation and Narration*, for example, Bhabha refers to 'the impossible unity of the nation as a symbolic force, despite the attempt by nationalist discourses persistently to produce the idea of the nation as a continuous narrative of national progress' (1990, p. 2). Stuart Hall, in turn, locates the attempt to create a sense of nation in discourses that constitute what he calls 'the myth of cultural homogeneity within the nation state,' and assert that '[national cultures] are cross-cut by deep internal divisions and differences, and are unified only through the exercise of cultural power' (1992, p. 297). Today, because of changing migration and demographic patterns and pressures from minority groups within nations, this common imagining of nation and citizenry is being vigorously contested and confronted in a struggle for cultural survival and representation (see Popkewitz, 2000).

In chapter 12, George Richardson extends this criticism into postcolonial education by pointing out that a singular narrative of the nation has come under fire from most postcolonial scholars, who have argued that conceiving of the nation in unitary terms has produced curriculum that privileges Eurocentrism while marginalizing and silencing others. As internal and international migrations increase – and, with it, ethnocultural diversity – it becomes important to problematize the notion of essential nation and pose questions about how to reconceptualize curriculum that does not maintain colonial structures of privilege and dominance. For Richardson, one possibility for doing so is to employ Homi Bhabha's notion of the Third Space in which hybridity replaces essentialism as a founding principle of the nation and in which national identity is seen as a continual process of encounter, negotiation, and dislocation among and between groups. Critical analyses of a recent attempt to reimagine curriculum as a Third Space, along with the difficulties and complexities inherent in this process, are presented.

In the concluding chapter, Kara McDonald explores articulations of nationalist discourses that frame social inquiry in Canadian public schools and many other educational institutions. In particular, she discusses the ways in which these discourses serve to legitimize some students as Canadians, and therefore insiders, and others as not quite Canadians and, hence, outsiders. Nationalist discourses that characterize peoples, priorities, and political and economic actions, and differences are analysed to show how various and intersecting forms of oppression are perpetuated through the production of school knowledge. McDonald acknowledges that understanding how racism and ethnocentrism are mediated through nationalist and globalizing discourses will not transform the imperial legacies of divisions, asymmetries, and exclusions; she does argue, however, that making them visible through critical analysis makes them contestable and that this is necessary for destabilizing their elaborations and moving towards postnationalist discourses.

Taken together, the collection of essays in this volume is an attempt to show the range of perspectives from which the theorization of the postcolonial curriculum is possible, attesting that the postcolonial is a continuing process of contestation and reconstruction fuelled by the desire to escape from dominant-cultural discursive practices that limit the possibility of self-affirmation and self-determination. Undoubtedly, the orientation towards the postcolonial adopted in this book, along with the parameters chosen to explore this concept for curriculum reform, itself constitutes a theoretical position and editorial preference and will not appeal to some who fear that such a diffused use of the term *postcolonial* runs the risk of denying its basis in the material and historical fact of European colonization (see, e.g., Ashcroft, Griffiths, & Tiffen, 1995). However, it must be borne in mind that, as Stephen Slemon observes, postcolonial work 'needs always to remember that its referent in the real world is a form of political, economic, and discursive oppression whose name, first and last, is *colonialism*' (1995, p. 52). Colonialist oppression manifests itself in many different forms and functions, requiring us to take colonial discourse beyond 'its scattered moments of archaeological research' and take it up as 'a general structure of oppression' (ibid., p. 50). In this regard, postcolonial work embraces multiple and sometimes radically different understandings of anticolonial agency. In this book, we consider one form of colonialist oppression, namely, the use of state apparatuses like curriculum in the production of colonialist relation and ask: What kind of curricular imaginations are possible for the formation of democratic, ethical educational relations? In addressing this question our focus is on the notion of curriculum as cultural practice, recognizing that this is only one avenue for exploring this important question but bearing in mind that culture has been a crucial site of struggle in the effort to colonize and decolonize the Other. We hope this book will assist in the re-envisioning of curricular and teaching practices, especially at a time when, as Bill Pinar (2004) reminds us, we educators, besieged by the imperatives of standardization and the business model of education, are losing our ethical commitment to an education that links school knowledge to the subjectivities and identities of students.

Uncommon among recent publications on educational reform, this book makes available, in a single volume, a range of ideas about anticolonial and/or postcolonial curriculum reform that would appeal to the wide range of audiences for whom the book is intended: curriculum scholars and researchers; graduate students of education, curriculum, and cultural studies; researchers and scholars interested in the intricate connection between culture and student learning and in applying postcolonial criticism to education; teachers and teacher educators wishing to investigate ideas not normally addressed in mainstream education; and general audiences interested in curriculum change. For each of these audiences, this book offers critical tools with which to question historical and contemporary practices in curriculum and pedagogy. As well, it offers ideas which help to broaden and deepen understandings of curriculum and curricular engagement, and suggests reform proposals that inform educational policies. Now more than ever the study and teaching of curriculum, such as this book provides, fosters our understanding of the times in which we teach, as well as our ethical and intellectual commitments within these times.

REFERENCES

Althusser, L. (1971). *Lenin and philosophy and other essays*. New York: Monthly Review Press.

Anderson, B. (1991). *Imagined communities: Reflections on the origin and spread of nationalism*. London: Verso.

Apple, M. (1993). *Official knowledge: Democratic education in a conservative age*. New York: Routledge.

Apple, M. (1990). *Ideology and curriculum*. New York: Routledge.

Aronowitz, S. (1992). *The politics of identity*. New York: Routledge

Ashcroft, B., Griffiths, G., & Tiffen, H. (Eds.) (1995). *The postcolonial studies reader*. London: Routledge.

Axelrod, P. (1997). *The promise of schooling: Education in Canada, 1800-1914*. Toronto: University of Toronto Press.

Bacchus, M.K. (1994). *Education as and for legitimacy: Development in West Indian education between 1846 and 1895*. Waterloo, ON: Wilfrid Laurier University Press.

Bacchus, M.K. (2002). *Curriculum, education and globalization, with special reference to the developing countries*. Keynote address at the Conference on Problems and Prospects of Educational Development in Developing Countries. University of the West Indies, Barbados.

Barrera, M. (1979). *Race and class in the Southwest: A theory of racial inequality*. Notre Dame: University of Notre Dame Press.

Bhabha, H.K. (1990). Introduction: Narrating the nation. *The nation and narration*. London: Routledge.

Bhabha, H.K. (1994). The location of culture. London: Routledge.

Bourdieu, P., & Passeron, J.C. (1977). *Reproduction in education, society and culture*. Beverly Hills, CA: Sage.

Burbules, N.C. & Torres, C.A. (Eds.). (2000). *Globalization and education: Critical perspectives*. New York and London: Routledge.

Collins, R. (1979). *The credential society: An historical sociology of education and stratification*. New York: Academic Press.

Dei, G.J.S., Hall, B.L., & Rosenberg, D.G. (Eds.) (2002). *Indigenous knowledge in global contexts: Multiple shadings of our world*. Toronto: University of Toronto Press.

Dirlik, A. (1987). Culturalism as hegemonic ideology and liberating practice. *Cultural Critique, 6*(Spring), 13–50.

Fairbanks, C.M. (2004). Educating the 'right' way: Markets, standards, God, and inequality by Michael Apple. *Journal of Curriculum Studies, 36*(4), 509–514.

Fanon, F. (1963). *The wretched of the earth*. New York: Grove Press.

Gandhi, L. (1989). *Postcolonial theory: A critical introduction*. New York: Columbia University Press.

Giroux, H. (1983). Theories of reproduction and resistance in the new sociology of education: A critical analysis. *Harvard Educational Review, 53*, 257–293.

Greene, M. (1995). *Releasing the imagination*. San Francisco: Jossey-Bass.

Gough, N. (2002). Voicing curriculum visions. In W.E. Doll & N. Gough (Eds.), *Curriculum visions* (pp. 1–22). New York: Peter Lang.

Hall, S. (1992). The question of cultural identity. In S. Hall & T. McGrew

(Eds.), *Modernity and its futures*. Cambridge: Polity Press, in association with Blackwell Publishers.

Hall, S. (1996). When was the postcolonial? Thinking at the limit. In I. Chamber & L. Curtis (Eds.), *The postcolonial question: Common skies, divided horizons* (pp. 242–260). London: Routledge.

hooks, b. (1991). Narratives of struggle. In P. Mariana (Ed.), *Critical fictions* (pp. 53–61). Seattle: Bay Press.

Hoffman, D.M. (1999). Culture and comparative education: Toward de-centering and recentering the discourse. *Comparative Education Review, 43*(4), 464–488.

Kanu, Y. (1993). *Exploring critical reflection for postcolonial teacher education: Sierra Leone*. Unpublished doctoral dissertation, University of Alberta, Edmonton.

Kozol, J. (1991). *Savage inequalities: Children in America's schools*. New York: Crown Publishers.

London, N.A. (2001). Curriculum and pedagogy in the development of colonial imagination: A subversive agenda. *Canadian and International Education, 30*(1), 41–76.

Massey, V. (1926). Introduction. In C.N. Cochrane & W.S. Wallace (Eds.), *This Canada of ours*. Ottawa: National Council of Education.

McDonald, K. (2002). Post-national considerations for curriculum. *Journal of Curriculum Theorizing, 18*(1), 95–110.

Morrison, K.R.B. (2004). The poverty of curriculum theory: A critique of Wraga and Hlebowitsh. *Journal of Curriculum Studies, 36*(4), 487–494.

Nandy, A. (1983). *The intimate enemy: Loss and recovery of self under colonialism*. Delhi: Oxford University Press.

Osbourne, K. (1995). *In defence of History*. Toronto: Our Schools, Ourselves.

Pinar, W.F. (2004). *What is curriculum theory?* Mahwah, NJ: Erlbaum.

Popkewitz, T.S. (2000). Reform as the social administration of the child: Globalization of knowledge and power. In N.C. Burbules & C.A. Torres (Eds.), *Globalization and education: Critical perspectives* (pp. 157–186). New York: Routledge.

Prakash, G. (1994). Subaltern studies as postcolonial critique. *American Historical Review, 99*, 1475–90.

Richardson, G.H. (2002). *The death of the good Canadian: Teachers, national identities and the social studies curriculum*. New York: Peter Lang.

Rizvi, F. (2000). International education and the production of global imagination. In N.C. Burbules and C.A. Torres (Eds.), *Globalization and education: Critical perspectives* (pp. 205–225). New York: Routledge.

Said, E. (1993). *Culture and imperialism*. London: Routledge.

Said, E. (1996). *Representations of the intellectual: The 1993 Reith lectures.* New York: Vintage.

Salecl, R. (1994). *The spoils of freedom: Psychoanalysis and feminism after the fall of socialism.* New York: Routledge.

Slemon, S. (1995). The scramble for post-colonialism. In B. Ashcroft, G. Griffiths, & H. Tiffen (Eds.), *The postcolonial studies reader* (pp. 45–52). London: Routledge.

Smith, D.G. (2002). *Teaching in global times.* Edmonton: Pedagon Press.

Spivak, G. (1990). *The post-colonial critique: Interviews, strategies, dialogues.* New York and London: Routledge.

Strange C., & Loo, T. (1997). *Making good: Law and moral regulation in Canada, 1867–1939.* Toronto: University of Toronto Press.

Willinsky, J. (1998). *Learning to divide the world: Education at empire's end.* Minneapolis: University of Minnesota Press.

Young, M.F.D. (1971). *Knowledge and control.* London: Collier-Macmillan.

PART 1

Rereading the Disciplines Postcolonially

1 Ideology and Politics in English-Language Education in Trinidad and Tobago: The Colonial Experience and a Postcolonial Critique

NORREL A. LONDON

Teaching and learning the English language in Trinidad and Tobago became institutionalized when British colonizers permitted missionaries to engage slaves in a measure of schooling in the territory (Gordon, 1963). English-language education came into sharper focus, however, after emancipation in 1834, and the Negro Education Grant approved by the British Crown was a major provision that leveraged language instruction into place (ibid.). Subsequent formalization of the educational system continued during the nineteenth century, and, as the imperial grip on the colony tightened, teaching and learning English assumed even greater significance in the school curriculum (Bacchus, 1990). Pride of place was accorded to the subject, so much so that some have argued that during this early period of colonization 'school was English and English was school' (ibid., p. 51)

The primacy assigned to English was intended to become a location that would endure for all times. The status was ascribed during the early days of British occupation, became accentuated during the colonial era, and has persisted into the present despite Trinidad and Tobago's displacement from British rule, the agency that historically promoted and privileged English on local soil. The colony acceded to independent nationhood in 1962 and became a republican state within the Commonwealth of Nations fourteen years later. Even so, English, which had been the lingua franca, persisted and has remained what it was under colonialism: the only official language of Trinidad and Tobago. The continuity has endured despite the opportunity provided to adopt other linguistic models (London, 2001b). More importantly, English will in all probability maintain its position of dominance into the foreseeable future in Trinidad and Tobago. Some even contend that the significance of English both as a school subject and the national discourse will increase, a view that supports the observation that, at least in the Commonwealth Caribbean, 'the end of the colonial era has not seen a reversal of the spread of English' despite policy adjustments in some countries to do the opposite (P. Roberts, 1997). Reversal in Trinidad and Tobago is not likely.

The Trinidad and Tobago scenario might be replicated several times in some other English-speaking Caribbean states and elsewhere, but in many ways it is unlike the situation found in some other jurisdictions once colonized by the British.[1] For one thing, all indigenous languages are now effectively defunct, and viable alternatives to English no longer exist in Trinidad and Tobago. The polyglot status that characterized the population during the early days of colonization and experimentation with English-language education has become a thing of the past. Representing a number of languages in Africa from which learners had come, the early students were forbidden through a number of strategies to engage in their native tongues; mother tongue maintenance had been rendered unprivileged through firm policy to propagate and entrench English and to facilitate its use in the emerging diaspora. This policy was important: The understanding was that the imperial language, English, had successfully been promoted as the modality of choice and that this medium was the only variety worthy enough to take root and spread, both as the official language of communication and as the people's language. The politics behind this evaluation were also significant: Central to the move was an attempt to construct socially the role of the English language, and strong ideological and cultural forces were at work to guarantee dominance not only at the time but also for today and most likely in the future.

In this chapter, I excavate the intellectual arguments and thinking that might have accorded primacy to English in Trinidad and Tobago and explain how formal schooling inculcated and imposed English. My primary objective is to critique the Trinidad and Tobago experience, using selected postcolonial constructs, and, in the process, three other objectives are achieved. First, I scrutinize the intervention strategies used by colonial bureaucrats in the schooling enterprise to promote and establish English among the masses; second, I analyse how managers policed the English-language curriculum that they had put in place; and third, I identify the evaluations that managers themselves made about the programs that they had installed. In other words, I put the spotlight on some of the microtechnologies and mundane practices

used by managers as a form of colonial statecraft in the institutionalization of English, and in doing so I disclose for critical and tactical examination some governance modes in the early English-language education
programs.

Rationale, Data Source, and Method

The chapter does not span Trinidad and Tobago's entire past under
British rule but focuses on the late colonial period from about 1938 to
about 1959 (see London, 2001a).[2] This was an era of aggressive empire
consolidation in which the imperial government redirected its energies
to the administration of territory already conquered, instead of attempting to further extend the geographical limits of empire (Evans,
1950). In consequence, emphasis on teaching and learning the English
language, institutionalized during an earlier period, assumed greater
significance, and policies for promoting and entrenching usage were
redesigned. The period stands out, therefore, as an era from which
aspects of colonial linguistic power might be observed but more specifically one from which insights into English-language education in
Trinidad and Tobago might be gained. It provides a good testing ground
from which to integrate the motives and values of colonial administrators in their use of English as a tool in building and consolidating
empire. The period is also significant in that it provides opportunity to
investigate relationships between language education, on the one hand,
and the circumstances of the learner, on the other.

Another rationale for this chapter derives from a recent observation
in the emerging scholarship on language as a medium in colonization
(see, e.g., Ricento, 2000; Canagarajah, 1999; Willinsky, 1998; Phillipson,
1992; Pennycook 1994, 1998). In this connection, Alastair Pennycook has
remarked that there is 'a massive absence of discussion on English-
language teaching and colonialism' despite possibilities that exist for
study in this area as a means of adding important dimensions to our
understanding of how colonialism worked (1998, p. 20). Toward this
end, 'policies about providing or withholding an education in English
were not simple questions to do with the medium of instruction ... but
rather were concerned with different views of how best to run a colony ...
A study of policies around English-language education, therefore, can
give important insights into the more general operations of colonialism.
Such an understanding has considerable significance for understanding
current language policies (ibid.).'

Documents kept by individual schools in Trinidad and Tobago and by the then Department of Education constitute the main data source for this exercise. Chief among these are logbooks that recorded, inter alia, information about the teaching of English. Evaluation reports on the curriculum and on student performance, as well as annual reports on the education system, are also included in the database. The sources used are considered artefacts, a term suggested by Margaret Le Compte and Judith Preissle (1993) to describe the assortment of written and symbolic records kept by participants in situations such as the above education process. The artefacts used in this study are printed material which, according to Walter Borg and Meredith Gall (1989), may be classified into 'intentional documents' and 'unpremeditated documents.' Intentional documents serve primarily as records of what happened, while unpremeditated documents serve an immediate purpose in the recording of an event without any thought having been given to their future use. The log books used, the evaluation reports analysed, and the annual reports consulted fall into the intentional documents category: They contain detailed accounts of English-language teaching and learning in Trinidad and Tobago and indicate the sensations, values, experiences, and emotions that were essential parts of the undertaking.

A recent evaluation explains that in their capacity as unpremeditated and artefactual documents, these above log books constitute a faithful repository of important issues relating to teaching and learning as these transpired at the institutional level of schooling in Trinidad and Tobago (London, 1997). Even so, sources of the type used in this exercise contain both limitations and advantages (Merriam, 1988). They have been generated independently of any research undertaking (including the present study), are often fragmentary, and may not fit the conceptual framework to which the given research applies; nevertheless, as S.R.P. Clarke has pointed out, their independence from the research agenda can also be regarded as an advantage because they are non-reactive. In this sense, they are a product of a given context, and are grounded in the real world (2000). This characteristic imparts the likelihood that analysis of such artefacts will yield insights into the research problem on hand.

The mode of critique adopted in this chapter is postcolonial, central to which is a concern to renarrativize the story of the colonial encounter in a way that gives prominence to issues that have to date been put on the periphery of the education debate as it concerns colonial societies (Hall, 1996). 'There is an immediate need,' contends Linda Tuhiwai

Smith, 'to understand the complex ways in which people were brought within the imperial system, because its impact is still felt,' despite the fact that independence has been gained (1999, p. 23). How the encounter was established, at what cost, and who emerged as the winners and the losers in the experience are questions that have not been fully addressed. The theory of postcoloniality recognizes that the colonial archive preserves some versions of knowledge and agency produced in response to the pressures of the colonial encounter, and, as such, provides an effective dimension for framing the argument in this chapter. Postcoloniality, in context, views the colonial past not simply as a reservoir of political experiences and practices to be theorized from the detached and enlightened perspective of the present but, more importantly, as 'the scene of intense discursive and conceptual activity, characterized by a profusion of thought and writing about the cultural and political identities of colonized subjects' (Gandhi, 1989, p. 5).

The postcolonial probe, therefore, provides some new ammunition and perspectives that might be used to investigate some old themes and, in so doing, helps to revise our understanding of 'the colonial.' The approach has been credited with the capability to impart new prominence to matters relating to colony and to independent statehood alike, and in recent times it has had a major impact on established modes of cultural analysis; this is because postcolonial theory is an approach that has potential to bring to the forefront interconnections among issues relating to race, nation, empire, and cultural production – of which education and schooling are components. In the circumstance, postcolonialism serves as an alternative framework for the study of culture and colonialism, uncovering the many stories of contestation and complicity by getting deep within the colonial archive (Arif, 1994).

Postcolonialism as used in this chapter, therefore, is not conceived in reference to transference of power from colonialist to nationalist bourgeoisie nor to maintenance of colonial institutions and the increase of economic and social power in the former colony. Rather, the chapter adopts the term in reference to a position that goes beyond temporal references and calls for a major rethinking of given categories and histories, questions assumed and fixed structures, and brings a greater sense of the political to the interpretation of social and cultural production. In context, the chapter sees postconialism as 'a political and cultural movement that seeks to challenge the received histories and ideologies of former colonial nations and to open a space for insurgent knowledge to emerge (Pennycock, 1998, p. 49). Bill Ashcroft and his colleagues extend

the conceptual range by adding that postcolonialism is primarily concerned with 'a sustained attention to the imperial process in colonial
and neo-colonial societies, and with an examination of the strategies to
subvert the actual material and discursive effects of that process' (1989,
p. 117). This orientation also forms part of the understanding of
postcolonialism that is used to frame the argument in this chapter, which
proceeds from here in several parts. First, I provide a definition of colonialism used to undergird discussion on the colonial project in English-
language education. Next, some of the main planks in the recent
postcolonial debate are explained. Third, I trace the intellectual argument that ascribed dominance to the English language and indicate how
the issues raised may have had an impact on the English-language education program. The evaluations made by state managers are considered next, and, using selected constructs from the postcolonial framework
just outlined, I provide an interpretation of the English-language education that prevailed at the time. The chapter concludes with a critical explanation of the English-language project within the context of education,
schooling, and culture, and offers a brief evaluation of the appropriateness of postcolonial theory as an effective tool for analysis.

Colonialism

The output of literature on colonialism reached its apotheosis during
the 1960s and early 1970s in the context of the decolonization and
independence movements that had been afoot in Africa, Asia, and
elsewhere, and, in the process, the concept of colonialism became focal-
ized (Prakash, 1995). A classical definition of the term *colonialism*,
offered by French anthropologist Georges Ballandier, is instructive: colonialism refers to 'the domination imposed by a foreign majority, racially and culturally different, over a materially weaker indigenous
majority in the name of racial (or ethnic) and cultural superiority' (1963,
p. 28). David Spurr explains that, in the contact zone, a set of relations
comes into play based on the nature of the two cultures, one of which is
technologically advanced and economically powerful, while the other
lacks technology or a complex economy: 'these relations are antago-
nized by the instrumental role which the colonized society is forced to
play, so that in order to maintain its authority, the colonizing society
resorts not only to force but also to a series of pseudo-justifications and
stereotyped behaviors' (1994, p. 6). The colonial situation is therefore
one of latent crisis, maintained precariously by ideology, representation, and formal administration.

Colonialism as a concept resurfaced more recently in arguments about postcoloniality. Edward Said contends that colonialism 'cannot be identified with only economic gain and political power' but is essentially a state of mind in colonizer and colonized alike (1993, p. 3). Syed Hussein Alatas explains that 'colonialism was not only an extension of sovereignty and control by one nation and its government, but it was a control of the mind of the conquered and the subordinated' (1997, p. 22) In other words, colonialism was a process of cultural production and psychologization, and so, even though the era of decolonization has come to an end, some contenders maintain that colonialism is unfinished business even today (Ghandi, 1989, p. 15). Colonialism begins when colonizers arrive on the scene but does not end when they go home. The resulting interaction is founded on racism and violence (ibid.). The industrialization that took place tells the story of economic exploitation; the democracy that got instituted was splintered by protesting voices; technology combined with warfare; and medicine has been attached to the techniques of torture (ibid.). Colonialism in these circumstances came with two prongs: the seductive narrative of power and a counter-narrative of the colonized 'politely, but firmly, declining the come-on of colonialism (ibid., p. 15).

Two genres of colonialism have been identified. Ashis Nandy (1983), for example, explains that one of these, the first to occur was simpleminded in its focus on physical conquest of territories; the second was more insidious in its commitment to the conquest and occupation of mind, self, and culture. This dichotomy is confirmed by Gandhi, who adds that the former type was of 'bandit-free mode' and as a result, more violent but, in addition, was 'transparent in its self-interest, greed, and rapacity' (1989, p. 15); the second type 'was pioneered by rationalists, modernists and liberals,' who maintained that colonialism was an altruistic harbinger of civilization to the uncivilized world (ibid.). An important dimension is that both depended on force and/or fraud, a characteristic that led Albert Memmi to submit that the colonial condition was one that 'chained the colonizer and the colonized into an implacable dependence, moulded their respective characters and dictated their conduct' (1968, p. 45). An overarching imperative was that colonialism must 'civilize' its Others and fix them into a state of perpetual Otherness.

Selected Postcolonial Constructs

Our understanding of postcoloniality shifts somewhat in each of the above conceptualizations, but collectively the various interpretations provide a weather vane pointing to a common body of constructs. Each component might then be used to probe how English-language education in schools in colonial Trinidad and Tobago proceeded and, as a result, to shed light on the intent of the program as well as on its impact on local participants. The salient constructs are: discourse, power, hegemony, ideology, hybridity and liminality, identity, and discipline. These guideposts are drawn from a perspective of social theory that has gained significant attention in recent years and are based on notions of society and social interaction promoted by commentators such as Anthony Giddens (1985), the late French philosopher Michel Foucault (1970, 1979, 1980), and German social theorist Jurgen Habermas.

Discourse

Saunders describes *discourse* as 'the extended language of a social institution such as the family or a church, or of an institutional practice such as law, medicine or the schooling system' (1990, p. 26) The interpretation here draws on considerations by Foucault, who contends that 'discourses are systematically organized statements which conserve the meanings and enact the power and value of social institutions' (1970, p. 188). Education, like medicine or law, has its own discourse, and in this context might be considered 'the language of a social institution' as Bill Ashcroft, Garath Griffiths, and Helen Tiffin put it (Ashcroft, Griffiths, & Tiffin, 1989). Discourse does not occur independently of the given institution and/or its practices. Such practices, moreover, take place in an organized fashion in accordance with fixed rules, and they encompass the entire conceptional territory on which knowledge is formed and produced. This formulation incorporates not only what is thought or said but also the rules that govern what can be said and what not, what is included and what left out, and what is thought of as insubordination and what is socially acceptable (Loomba, 1989). Discourse, therefore, might be understood as 'a system of possibility for knowledge' (ibid., p. 54).

Power

In a study of language planning James Tollefson argues that power is 'the ability to achieve one's goals and to control events through intentional action' (1991, p. 9). Power is not a characteristic of individuals in isolation, but, instead, individuals exercise power 'as a result of their social relationships within institutional structures that provide meaning to their actions and also constrain them. There is thus a dynamic relationship between structure and power, and power is fundamental to both individual action and social organization' (ibid.) Foucault contends that power does not emanate from some central or hierarchical structure but rather that it flows through society in a sort of 'capillary action' (1980, p. 98).

Whatever the contention, power implies dominance, and individuals in subordinate positions are never completely powerless. Walter Rodney contends, for example, that in the final analysis it is in the masses (whom he describes as those dispossessed of property, wealth, caste, religion, and expertise) in whom power resides in any society (cited in Thomas, 1982). Such groups may carve out specific areas of control over their daily lives and may improve their stock of power from time to time depending on the organizational circumstances. Collaboration of subjects is one of the approaches in which power can best disseminate itself (Foucault, 1980), but even more importantly, at this site power may insinuate itself both inside and outside of the world of its victims (Gandhi, 1989); power may become subjectivized through and within the individual. Furthermore, 'power is employed and exercised through a net-like organization. And not only do individuals circulate between its threads; they are always in the position of simultaneously undergoing or exercising this power. They are not only its inert or consenting target; they are also the elements of its articulation. In other words, individuals are like vehicles of power, not its point of application' (Foucault, 1980).

Hegemony

Antonio Gramsci formulated the concept of hegemony in his attempt to answer two basic questions: Why is it that in every epoch the ideas of the ruling class are always the ruling ideas? How is it that ordinary people come to be persuaded of a specific view of things? These concerns led Gramsci to explain that hegemony is power achieved through a combination of consent or coercions. His argument is that the ruling class achieves domination not by force or coercion alone but by creating subjects who willingly submit to being ruled: hegemony is achieved not only by direct manipulation or indoctrination but by playing on the common sense of people, on what Raymond Williams describes as the 'lived system of meanings' (1977, p. 110). In Gramscian terms, according to Williams, hegemony may be seen as 'a whole body of practice and expectations over the whole of living; our senses and assignments of energy; our shaping perceptions of ourselves and our world. It is a lived system of meanings and values ... which as they are experienced as practices appear as reciprocally confirming. It thus constitutes a sense of reality for most people in the society, a sense of absolute ... It is, that is to say, in the strongest sense a culture, but a culture which has also to be seen as the lived dominance and subordination of particular classes' (1989, p. 57). Hegemony is lived, and it is a realized complex of experiences, relationships, and activities that have specific and changing pressures and limits (ibid.). Hegemony can never be singular; its internal structures are highly complex, and it does not passively exist as a form of dominance. Hegemony must be continually renewed, recreated, defended, and modified; it is also continually resisted, altered, and 'challenged by pressures that are not all its own' (ibid., p. 58). Furthermore, hegemony has kindred links with both power and ideology.

Ideology

Tollefson contends that ideology 'refers to normally unconscious assumptions that come to be seen as common sense' (1991, p. 10); it is connected to power because the assumptions that come to be accepted as common sense depend on the power structure that obtains in society. Ideology shapes behaviour in that it contributes to the manufacture of consent and leads to assumptions about right and wrong. The crucial element is not whether the ideology is true or false but how it comes to be believed in, to be lived out, and it is in trying to understand this feature that our understanding of the concept is enlightened. Ideology, according to Ania Loomba (1998), is the medium through which certain ideas are transmitted and, more importantly, held to be true. French Communist theorist Louis Althusser (1971) notes that ideologies may express the interest of social groups but they work through and on individual persons and subjects, and (according to Althusser) subjectivity or personhood is itself clarified in Gramsci's suggestions about how ideas get transformed via social institutions. In this regard Althusser elaborates that in capitalist societies force or consent provides the leverage. Force is accomplished through the ideological state apparatuses such as the army, the police, and the prison; in the category of consent schools play a dominant role, but other institutions such as the church and the media are used as well. Whether of the ideological or the repressive type, these apparatuses aid reproduction of the dominant culture by creating subjects who become conditioned to accept the dominant value system as given, even divinely sanctioned at times.

Hybridity

Robert Young (1959) reminds us that a hybrid is technically a cross between two different species, and several other observers have engaged the term as a critical element in research relating to the postcolonial. Homi Bhabha's contribution is particularly noteworthy. He defines *hybridity* as 'a problematic of colonial representation ... that reserves the effects of the colonialist disavowal, so that other "denied" knowledges enter upon the dominant discourse and estrange the basis of its authority' (1985, p. 156). Paul Gilroy (1993) explains hybridity as intellectual and political cross-fertilization and shows how, in the process, diasporic cultures generate new and complex identities whose analysis demands some new conceptual tools. Stuart Hall describes hybridity as a 'cut-and-mix' process, and Ania Loomba refers to it as 'a strategy premised on colonial purity and aimed at stabilizing the status quo' (in Hall 1996, p. 18).

Hybridity is an inescapable attribute in any postcolonial critique; it points to the psychic trauma that colonized subjects experience when they come to realize that they could never attain unto the 'whiteness' they have been taught to desire nor shed the 'blackness' that they have learned to devalue. The 'in-betweenity' position, according to Bhabha (1985), produces agony. In the circumstances, the colonized attain the status of 'mimic men,' never able to become 'the real thing' (Naipaul, 1967). This status, according to Benedict Anderson (1983), ensures their domination. Hybridity functions in such a way as to preserve the structures of domination in the colonial situation and is constitutive of a 'process in which the single voice of colonial authority undermines the operation of colonial power by inscribing and disclosing the trace of the other so that it reveals itself as double-voiced (Young 1959, p. 23). One of the important effects of colonial power, therefore, is 'the production of hybridization rather than the noisy command of colonialist authority or the silent repression of native traditions' (Bhabha 1985, p. 148).

Identity

Identity has been described as 'a subjective sense of coherence, consistency and consisting of self, rooted in both personal and group history'

(Henry, Tator, Matis, & TReese, 1995, p. 237). The construct features prominently in the recent postmodernist literature that deals with the cultural politics of difference, and it has direct connections with ideas about the way individuals think of themselves and others. Stuart Hall, drawing on the Enlightenment period, which privileged order and reason, explains the roots of the concept of identity. He argues that identity is 'based on a conception of the human person as a fully centred, unified individual, endowed with the capacities of reason, consciousness and action, whose "centre" consisted of an inner core which first emerged when the subject was born, and unfolded with it, while remaining essentially the same – continuous or "identical" with itself – throughout the individual's existence. The essential centre of the self was a person's identity' (Hall 1992, p. 275).

In the postcolonial sense, identity is understood to be not merely centred and unitary but also decentred subjectivity; it is also continually being made and remade, just as cultures are (Gilroy, 1990). Individuals may see themselves through a variety of lenses in ways that are not always consistent, a view of identity that has consequences for the politics of everyday life. Inherent in the concept of identity is also an understanding of the past, a feature that has direct relevance in a postcolonial theoretical framework. The understanding is that colonialism could not function without the prior existence of an identity of colonized subjects. This is so significant that postcolonialists now argue that the aggressiveness and demoniacal zeal of colonization would have created a prior identity, even in those cases where there was none (Spurr, 1994). Identity has kindred links with 'recognition by others,' is negotiated through dialogue, is partly overt and partly internalized, and above all, identity must be defined against a background of what is considered important and 'what matters,' as philosopher Charles Taylor points out (1991, p. 64).

Discipline

The combination of organized rules and practices in a social institution makes up the discipline of that entity. Foucault defines discipline as 'a domain of objects, a set of methods, a corpus of propositions considered to be true, a play of rules and definitions of techniques and instruments' (1970, p. 188). Furthermore, 'all this constitutes a sort of anonymous system at the disposal of anyone who wants to or is able to use it, without their meaning or validity being linked to the one who happened to be their inventor' (ibid.). Discipline, in Focauldian terms, gets formed and is developed with the passage of time, and institutions such as education, law, psychiatry, and medicine all have their own characteristic forms of discipline (ibid.).

The concept of discipline might be understood in some other ways. Smith suggests that discipline may be thought of 'not simply as a way of organizing systems of knowledge but also as a way of organizing people or bodies' (1999, p. 68). In this mould, discipline conveys a number of meanings as far as a postcolonial critique is concerned. Knowledge, both inside and outside of a school, has been used to impart discipline to the colonized, and contrivances employed in the process have included exclusion, marginalization, liminality, and mere denial. More subtle but far-reaching approaches to discipline were the mechanisms put in place to eradicate or negate alternative epistemologies, obliterate collective identities, and impose a new order. These forms manifested themselves at various levels of colonial society, including the level of the school curriculum, the effect being to silence (forever in some cases) or to suppress relevant or indigenous ways of knowing and living. Reclaiming voices that may have been silenced, occluded, muffled, or submerged is one of the objectives in the contemporary postcolonial debate.

Intellectual Claims for the Dominance of English

As indicated, in colonial Trinidad and Tobago primacy was accorded to teaching and learning English in schools, and the prominence of English drew from notions about the English language both as a medium of communication and as a means of structuring and articulating experience: 'Language is not a nomenclature, or a way of naming things which already exist, but a system of signs, whose meaning is relational. Only a social group can produce signs, because only a specific social usage gives a sign any meaning ... the signs, or words, need a community with shared assumptions to confer them with meaning; conversely, a social group needs signs in order to know itself as a community. On this basis we can think of language as ideological rather than as objective' (Loomba, 1998, p. 35). The ideas that conditioned practice in colonial times drew from what has come to be referred to as the Macaulay Minute (Roberts, 1998). These ideas had a tremendous impact on language education not only in Trinidad and Tobago but throughout the British Empire, 'from Hong Kong to the Gambia' as Edmund King put it (1968).

Pre-eminence of the language was justified on three counts. In 1835

Thomas Babington Macaulay (later Lord Macaulay) expounded on the quality of the literature embodied in the English language, arguing that English abounds with imagination. Second, Macaulay explained that English was a medium for 'useful knowledge.' Third, he rationalized the adoption of English as the language of international communication (Spring, 1998). Macaulay's views were not original. Charles Grant argued in a similar vein, when in 1796 he presented the line that English was the means for communicating 'light and knowledge' and that capability of English usage would prove to be the best remedy for the 'disorders of Asiatic peoples' (in Trautmann, 1997, p. 24).

The ideas of both Macaulay and Grant had seminal influence on language policy throughout the British Empire and were endorsed at the Imperial Conference in 1913 and again in 1923 (Roberts, 1998). The British colony Trinidad and Tobago was part and parcel of the decisional framework and as such could not pursue goals for English-language teaching and learning at variance with those mandated by Whitehall. What was good for Hong Kong, symbolically speaking, had to be good for the Gambia. Robert Phillipson has recently revisited some of the major claims enunciated by Macaulay and noted how the Whig politician had forcefully and eloquently set out his argument: 'Our language ... stands preeminent even among the languages of the West ... Whoever knows that language has a ready access to all the vast intellectual wealth which all the wisest nations of the earth have created and hoarded in the course of ninety generations ... It is likely to become the language of commerce throughout the seas of the East [and around the world]' (1992, p. 136). The arguments came with some additional claims: Race, class, culture, power, and economics were part of the justification, the understanding being that in all of these the British, whose main language was English, were superior.

Another significant feature of the Macaulay Minute was that it established, as well, a hierarchy of languages. At the base were the languages of India; Arabic and Sanskrit were a few pegs up the ladder; the European languages were still higher; and English stood pre-eminent (Roberts, 1998, p. 54). The philological explanation was that English had reached a higher level of evolution than had other languages 'and thus had the status to demonstrate and reinforce the notion that the society which spoke this highly developed language must, per force, be more highly developed than societies which spoke languages that were less advanced' (Trautmann, 1997, p. 89). Some have offered reactions to this thinking, and Gwyneth Roberts in particular reasons that to insist that members of a 'less advanced' society demonstrate knowledge of the 'more highly developed' language as a way of imparting relief to life's circumstances, constitutes a 'benevolent act of altruism' (1998, p. 89). Utilitarianism as a doctrine was also evident in the original claims (ibid.).

Recent commentators admit that the basic tenets of the intellectual argument for English-language dominance became increasingly accepted after the abolition of slavery and with tightening of the reins of colonialism (Crowley, 1998; Kiernan, 1991). Macaulay's approach, in consequence, recommended itself to policymakers not only in the metropolis but also in the colony, and the teaching of English assumed cornerstone status in the curriculum. Thus, the primacy of English had a philological base, reinforced with ideas relating to race, culture, politics, and economics. During the late colonial period, these intellectual claims became significant in Trinidad and Tobago and elsewhere, and proficiency in English became the sine qua non for social, political, and economic advancement. The curriculum of the day was designed to pander to that idea, as we will later see.

Intervention Strategies

The prominence given to English in schools in Trinidad and Tobago was accomplished using several means. The examined records reveal that, during the late colonial period, English achieved the status of an individual subject taught in the school system, that a number of components comprised the subject of English, and that about 80 per cent of officially allocated time in elementary schools was devoted to English. At different levels, the curriculum emphasized what grammarians have sometimes labelled the bones of the subject, comprising fundamentals such as the parts of speech, syntax, rules for agreement, clausal analysis, and so on. Spelling, storytelling, handwriting, reading, and chats were also taught. Specifications for these in regard to content and duration were received from the Trinidad and Tobago Department of Education. Control was tight.

The designation *major subjects* was used to identify the range of teaching-learning components considered under English, and the term *minor subjects* collectively applied to the other, non-English components of the curriculum that were believed to have lower status. Geography, hygiene and nature study, history, civics, drawing, singing, handwork, and sometimes even arithmetic were put in the latter group. The rationale used in the overall packaging is significant: It relates to the strategies and modes used to impart knowledge, and it points to the pre-eminence put on English in schools in Trinidad and Tobago at that time, today, and for years yet to come.

Intervention for prominence had a qualitative dimension. In all subjects (whether those subsumed under English or those categorized elsewhere), one objective was to promote the use of standard official English, and this determination led to what might be described as hypercorrection in the teaching-learning process. Teachers became preoccupied with the use of 'correct' English in the course of evaluation, and students likewise were sensitized to this requirement in written work, as well as in oral communication, particularly within the classroom setting. This preoccupation led to a structure in which form very often took precedence over content, a consideration that might be justified in subjects such as history or geography but that might be deemed suspicious in a subject such as arithmetic. The use of 'correct English,' as it was called, was emphasized ad nauseam and became a bane in the schooling experience of many children. Departmental reports during the 1930s, in particular, are replete with admonishment to 'stamp out bad English' (Trinidad and Tobago Department of Education, 1942).

Methods for teaching English were part of the intervention formula. Teaching aids such as phonogram cards were heavily sanctioned, and the surveillance of such key apparatuses was by no means incidental. Control was relaxed, however, towards the end of colonial rule when it was believed that an acceptable linguistic base had been established. Recitation and rote learning were also important as pedagogical devices, the objectives in their use being acquisition of oral capability rather than comprehension of subject matter.

Regulatory Modalities

The approaches used to regulate, control, and promote the English curriculum were part and parcel of arrangements made to engage the school as a state apparatus in the furtherance of colonial objectives as a whole. Bureaucrats kept a watchful eye on the institution of the school and in particular on the teaching of English. The regulatory models engaged drew from approaches used by His Majesty's Inspectorate in the metropolis and parallelled them in some ways. A chief inspector was in charge, for example, and a hierarchy based largely on experience in inspectoral work was established. M. Kazim Bacchus (1990) notes that in Trinidad and Tobago, as well as in the English-speaking Caribbean in general, the inspectorate was installed towards the mid-1800s consequent upon the emancipation of slavery and disbursement of the Negro Education Grant. The emphasis put on the teaching of English in the schools and the installation of an agency (the Inspectorate) to police progress are by no means coincidental.

Two models were used, based on different styles of management, but they embraced the same objectives: cementing a firm base in the knowledge of English and ensuring the paramount use of English for all times. The 'full inspection' format was the most comprehensive, and it became notorious for the reasons that it struck fear into students and teachers alike. Modelled on functions set out for the Inspectorate in Great Britain at the time, full inspection was executed in Trinidad and Tobago by at least two officers at or above the rank of assistant inspector. As regards English, inspection incorporated every component of the subject: spelling, diction, composition, comprehension, grammar, reading, handwriting, storytelling, and oral expression. The evaluation in each of these areas, together with commendation in the case of outstanding performance and reprimand in the case of poor performance, was sent to the school for the attention of all teachers. When the results were considered substandard, an action plan for remediation accompanied the evaluation.

Inspection was also for the minor type of subject. Whereas full inspection was always scheduled, its minor counterpart was ad hoc. This model was used for a number of reasons, but as far as surveillance of the English curriculum was concerned, the format was applied mainly as a quality-assurance measure. In cases where remediation was required and an action plan specified, unscheduled visits were made for some specific reasons: to ensure compliance, offer expert assistance, and provide a measure of satisfaction that standards were attained as prescribed. The decision to engage the ad hoc approach in tandem with a full inspection is esteemed in retrospect, when it is considered that student performance might not be adequately assessed on the basis of an omnibus comprehensive annual inspection. Interim intervention was essential in the process.

If quality assurance was an objective in the unscheduled visits, then quality control was evidently a primary feature in the scheduled assessments that were conducted annually. Together, the two modes provided a good sense of the direction in which teaching and learning English pointed and of the ground that had to be covered to realize objectives. In other words, the surveillance apparatuses chosen to police the curriculum appeared to be effective. The two approaches are still in use in Trinidad and Tobago, and in many good schooling systems around the world, but the intent during the colonial period and in the given circumstance was different. It was counter-productive rather than productive in that control of the Other for the express purpose of exploitation was the objective, as opposed to liberation, empowerment, and enfranchisement, as is now the aim in the modern application of these tools. Herein lies an example of the distortion that colonialism manufactured and that has become of interest in postcolonial theory.

The Evaluation Reports

Examples of reports on the teaching of English based on the annual scheduled visits are provided in the Appendix for the years 1938, 1948, and 1953. The reports differ somewhat from inspector to inspector, but some umbrella features are identifiable. The language used, the authoritative poise adopted, the sensitive concern for English as a school subject, and the cultural and ideological assumptions expressed and inferred are comparable. What Jacques Derrida (1976) has described as an anthropological war appeared to be waged as inspectors interpreted how students learned the subject and how teachers taught it. The evaluations constituted a confrontation between two cultures, that of the students, on the one hand, and that of the imperial state, on the other, and in that light are reminiscent of Antonio Gramsci's (1971) notion of hegemony and of the power that might inhere in ideas held by a dominant institution in a given society.

The evaluations in the Appendix are characteristic of what inspectors had to say about the teaching of English during the late colonial period. A notable observation is that learners were always referred to as persons who ought to have things done to them by others, rather than as people who did things for themselves, an approach that underscores a factory metaphor in the conduct of teaching, learning, and schooling. The evaluative vocabulary comprised binary or contrasting opposites, for example, 'weak' or 'decidedly weak,' or 'very good,' and conveyed a distinct pattern of before and after images of children that was used to indicate the change that should or would take place as competency in English was acquired. Pronouncement and condemnation came with authoritative force, was complete and final, and imparted a sense that institutional directives constitute the one and only best way. There is the understanding that managers alone could make accurate and fair judgments about teaching and learning the subject of English and its various components.

The rhetoric used in the years considered here remains fairly constant. The lexical choices are similar, and the details highlighted in reporting appear to be indicative of Foucault's panoptic principle and how it might be put to work to accomplish stipulations identified in an authoritative centre. Clear and specific standards are enunciated based on the evaluation outcomes, and persuasion to accept these is demonstrated through the use of the conditional tense. Additionally, only one variety of English was used in reporting, and from the consistency maintained it is believed that the choice was 'natural' (Roberts, 1998, p. 59). There was no other mode.

A Postcolonial Critique

English-language education in Trinidad and Tobago during the late colonial period was designed to equip locals with a linguistic and literacy competence that had been deemed appropriate by the imperial state and was built on a foundation established earlier in the period of colonial contact. This was the obvious objective. A postcolonial understanding of the enterprise, however, reveals some additional, more penetrating and deceptive aims. First, the English-language program and how it was administered constitutes a snapshot of the larger European discourse on Self and the Other. The focus here on Trinidad and Tobago as well as on the given time frame allows a more incisive examination of the concept of discourse that is germane to a postcolonial interpretation of what took place in the schools.

The argument is that what transpired as English-language education was an integral part of 'the language of a social institution' (Foucault, 1970, p. 188). A Foucauldian critique would insist that the program constituted a systematically organized statement imbued with meaning and manifesting the power and value of education and schools as social institutions. This statement might be understood in postcolonial theoretical terms as a cultural, political, intellectual, and ideological process activated for the purpose of promoting a preferred view of colonizer and colonized. That is, the English-language education on offer was a component of the text or discourse of imperial rule, but it had an epistemological dimension as well.

If, as Saunders argues, discourse refers to the extended language of the institution in question, then the epistemology is of further significance (1990, p. 2). Both the knowledge that was made explicit and that which was left out contributed to the discourse. The English-language education offered was intended to inculcate into the colonized masses norms considered socially acceptable, but additionally, the education demonstrated that grassroots variants of English, for example, the 'home speech' that inspectors abhorred and ordered stamped out, were a cultural formulation that conflicted with the colonial project. From their perspective, the pidgin was objectionable, valueless, repugnant, and counterproductive. It did not possess the purity, elan, and esteem of English. But the silencing that greeted the experiment is the type of reaction that would be celebrated as madness in Foucauldian thinking (1979). The reaction demonstrates how culture might be made to intersect with economic, administrative, and sociopolitical ideals to the benefit of a powerful (colonizer) Self, but to the detriment of a weaker (colonized) Other.

The philological assumptions that underpinned decisions to promote the primacy of English in Trinidad and Tobago schools might also be seen in postcolonial terms. The claims to altruism demonstrate the above conceptualization of power as the ability to achieve goals and to control through intentional action. The claims were, in fact, subterfuge and constituted a convenient course of action for the colonizer. So too was the cognate element of utilitarianism, the understanding that the morally correct course of action had to be insistence on English-language acquisition – for the good of the learners themselves. Employment opportunities and chances for social and political advancement, so the colonial state claimed, were the practical benefits, but the root metaphor that determined delivery and oversight of the program was another matter altogether. Internalization of an ethos and appropriation of some seminal values, attitudes, and mores that were critical for colonial exploitation constituted the real aim. Cementation of an English-language base would assure what Memmi (1974) has described as that 'implacable dependence' on the colonizer. The insistence that English was the most important subject, as well as the related administrative requirement that students had to achieve competence in English, was another prescription designed to ensure domination both during the colonial era and after the colonizer had gone home. This persistence reveals how ideology, described above as a body of commonsense knowledge, might be implanted, but, worse yet, people in Trinidad and Tobago have come to believe in the superiority and critical importance of English in their daily lives. They have, in other words, made a former colonial ploy true. Whether true or false, this is the kind of verification mentioned in the above construct of ideology, and it is one of those concepts that, according to postcolonial thinking, has created some serious problems for the future development of former colonial territories.

Valorization of the subject of English led to a strong element of Catch-22. Those who were successful in learning the mechanics of English as prescribed and who had internalized the culture intended came to have little or no interest in maintaining or practising what was by this time left of indigenous linguistic forms. This group included local teachers, functionaries in the government civil service, and persons who served in the ecclesiastical sector of the society. But for those who did not make the grade or who did not show interest in conforming to what was taught as English, the understanding was that there was a long way to go to become cultured, a status for which more education (of the type already provided) would be needed. This thinking had considerable advantage for the colonizing power in both practical and ideological terms when the above goals of colonialism are considered.

A postcolonial appraisal would insist that the above philological rationalization in which the English language curriculum found expression served as an idiom or trope used to establish and sustain colonial authority. A theory of race was central to the conceptualization, and a comment by Sir Henry Maine testifies to the connection: 'The new theory of Language has unquestioningly produced a new theory of Race ... There seems to me no doubt that modern philology has suggested a grouping of peoples quite unlike anything that had been thought of before. If you examine the bases proposed for common nationality ... [y]ou will find them extremely unlike those which are advanced and even passionately advocated in parts of the Continent' (in Trautmann, 1997, p. 1). The philological argument informed the language curriculum in at least two additional ways: It gave rise to the attitude that English was the only acceptable medium for self-expression, and as a result, it justified viewing indigenous experiments with English as retrograde and uncivilized. These two reactions contributed to the esteem accorded to English, but, more importantly, they undermined the essential cross-fertilization that the above concept of hybridity suggests and that some postcolonialists agree is an advantage in the present era.

A similar relationship has been noted in another schooling system in what was then the British Empire. Referring to India, Guari Viswanathan has presented some strong arguments that link the institutionalization and valorization of English as a school subject in the subcontinent during the colonial era and has connected these moves to the above philological reasoning, in explaining that 'British colonial administrators, provoked by missionaries on the one hand and fears of native insubordination on the other, discovered an ally in English literature to support them in maintaining control of the natives under the guise of a liberal education' (1987, p. 17). This comment is reminiscent of a remark by British Parliamentarian William William, who, after the Rebecca Riots in Wales, blamed the disturbances on ignorance of the English language. His thinking was that 'if the [Welsh] people had been acquainted with the English language, had proper instruction provided, instead of being, as they now are, a prey to designing hypocrites with religion on the lips and wickedness in their hearts ... they [the Welsh] would be at this moment ... the happiest as well as the most peaceful and prosperous population in the world' (Roberts, 1998, p. 24). The argument for the establishment and prominence of English in the schools in Trinidad and Tobago was equally cogent, so much so that postindependence attempts to introduce Spanish, argued for on grounds of economic possibilities with and juxtaposition to Latin America, failed abysmally (Trinidad and Tobago Ministry of Education, 1958). The secured location that English held at this point represents a late stage in the development of a hybrid linguistic situation. The pain, agony, and confusion about learning in former years have abated significantly, yielding to a defence of English by those who were once victims in the language transfer process. This is a situation that requires for adequate analysis the mobilization of new tools mentioned above by postcolonial thinkers, some of which might be Durkheimian and Foucauldian insights.

Another line of this critique concerns power. If, as explained above, power is the ability to achieve goals and to control events through intentional action, then the English-language education that was promoted in Trinidad and Tobago is a good example of power demonstrated in a subtle but ruthless manner. This is the civilizational line adopted in the colonial experiment, and the rationalists, modernists, and liberals were the policymakers and administrators who cogently, convincingly, and faithfully argued the case for the supremacy of English (Ghandi, 1989). The rationale in its quintessential and sublime form was that to have competence in English was to acquire the highest form of culture, and learners came to internalize that reasoning. The thinking, however, was a subtle way of furthering dominance of the English language and culture in Trinidad and Tobago and, by extension, in the British Empire. The effectiveness of the approach is reminiscent of the observation that under imperial rule 'the moral power of the schoolmaster' was a more effectual instrument for governing people than was 'the bayonet' (Roberts, 1998, p. 38).

As regards the other side of the coin, ruthlessness is evidenced in the conscious oppression of indigenous culture and personality brought about through the insistence that English (and no other language) had to be learned and mastered. By the late colonial period, this approach served to drive the last nail in the coffin of the linguistic heritage of the people of Trinidad and Tobago. When the colonizer retreated at independence, all the roots of indigenous languages ever spoken in Trinidad and Tobago were effectively dead. They could be found only in the folklore, calypso and Creole being two such sites (London, 2001b). There was also no questioning of the supremacy of English in the education system and in the local society.

A good sense of the application of power and determination that buttressed the English-language education project might be ascertained from a comment by the abolitionist William Wilberforce in 1813: 'Let us [the British] endeavour to strike our roots into the [colonial] soil by the gradual introduction and establishment of our own principles and opinions; our own laws, institutions and manners; above all, as the source of every other improvement, of our religion, and consequently our morals' (in Childs, 1999, p. 38). A postcolonial response would contend that this approach also constituted an application of power in the civilizational sense, the objective being to restructure lives through colonial rule. The English-education project rendered native forms of communication unprivileged and unacceptable and 'civilized' learners to embrace English, the language of imperial rule, as the one best modality for interpersonal and other forms of communication. The intent is summarized by Ashcroft et al., who observe that 'one of the main features of imperial oppression is control over language. The imperial education system installs a "standard" version of the metropolitan language norm, and marginalizes all other variants as impurities' (1989, p. 7).

Movement of power is never unidirectional, from a powerful Self to an impotent Other. Foucault explains that the phenomenon 'circulates between the treads' and in the process empowers those who have been disenfranchised and dispossessed (1979). For example, the colonized students' difficulties with the aspirate *h* cannot be altogether understood as incapability or ineptitude. Presence or persistence of the error must also be seen in terms of the exercise of personal and cultural autonomy and in light of the above understanding that, in the final analysis, the bedrock of power resides with the masses, the dispossessed, and the disenfranchised. The aspirate *h* incapability must also be considered to be an indication of a personal decision to refute something imposed as pure in favour of a mode that was indigenous but that was branded as impure or objectionable by school people. For this reason, some students never came to master the English language as taught, and as a result they could not become serious contenders for the school product and, consequently, success as far as schooling was concerned. Even so, they developed positive self-images and in some cases emerged as thought leaders and social role models in their local communities. This experience sheds light on the nature of purity as far as language is concerned and suggests that this designation is itself subjective and internally derived. As regards colonialism, however, the episode explains an important feature that is very often overlooked in the literature. It clarifies that colonialism was and is not altogether simply an imposition on inert or mindless people. Rather the process, as A. Suresh Canagarajah (1999) reminds us, was and still is met with a degree of opposition, contestation, and struggle. The cases of linguistic ineptitude identified by the inspectors point to the presence of a counterhegemonic backlash at work.

A feature of schooling in general was Anglocentricity, and how this characteristic became operative is instructive. Hegemony, described above as 'a whole body of practices and expectations over the whole of living,' served as the main lever (Williams, 1989, p. 57).[109] It was used to promote English, but in so doing it accomplished another major feat of equal significance: the denial of all other language varieties. This was a draconian approach, now seen in retrospect as poor pedagogy and as an unethical practice by contemporary language educators. Nonetheless, British interest required that the position be taken as a way of locking the masses into the colonial power structure 'exclusively on the colonizers' own terms' (Trautmann, 1997, p. 42). The desire to bring English centre-stage is an act of 'symbolic violence' (Ghandi, 1989, p. 38) demonstrated at several junctures in the teaching-learning process and exemplified in the 1948 concern about 'comprehension of text.' Teachers insisted on the mechanics of English as a language, even at the expense of understanding what was read. Good teachers went the extra mile to enhance student comprehension of what was committed to memory by rote; nevertheless, speaking and writing good English was always an overarching policy objective and became, as well, an important benchmark in the schooling process.

Hegemony as lived was manifested in the sanctions applied and revealed in the system of policing established to commandeer English into prominence. The 1948 call for systematic drill in 'basic speech' and the 1938 directive for more attention to the phonic plan outlined were not merely guidelines that may or may not have been followed. More appropriately they were pronouncements. They came with the understanding that penalty would be the result of non-compliance, and they constituted a coercive measure applied with some degree of finality. Sanctions of this nature, and sometimes more severe, were part of the bigger hegemonic project that was empirewide in scope. Ngugi wa Thiong'o (1981) draws attention to a similar process in colonial Kenya where suppression of a native language, Gikuyu, was enforced. He explains that the practice in that colony led students at the time to associate use of their first language with humiliation, a reaction that evoked the same sentiments in the use of home speech referred to by the inspectors in Trinidad and Tobago.

The response to the hegemonic practice here is instructive on another count. Administrators remained resolute in purpose even after a foundation had been laid (during the earlier colonial period) and continued to impose measures that they considered pedagogically necessary to attain purity of the language acquired and used. Some counterhegemonic forces were at play, nevertheless, and these increased in intensity as closure of the colonial era was formalized, the outcome being a more widespread use of dialect and substandard forms of English (London, 1997). This was the case not only in the wider society but even within the classroom instructional process, and the admixture is evidence of the 'war of positions' to which critical theorists have drawn attention (Gramsci, 1971). It is not only a phenomenon characteristic of language teaching and learning in Trinidad and Tobago during a given past era, but more significantly, it tells a story of the struggle against an imperial linguistic form and about the inroads that the Others might achieve as they are empowered through the liberating forces that they detect and embrace.

When the spotlight is put on the concept of ideology, the postcolonial perspective reveals some other features. The later colonial period in Trinidad and Tobago was characterized by an ideology as regards English-language education, and this was the case despite the turbulence mentioned above. It was commonsensical during this period to accept English as the language of popular choice, and as a result, the language in which oral and written skills had to be perfected if personal economic and political advancement was to be achieved. Mobility in context demonstrates at least three characteristics about ideology: It reveals that the construct might be linked to the prevailing power structure, that it shapes behaviour, and that it contributes to the manufacture of consent. Cementation of English in the school system (and beyond) was, therefore, the result of a colonial administration that was in place and was only partially the result of volition on the part of students to learn the language. Left alone, most students would have made other contrivances for communication.

Ideology worked to instill the understanding that proficiency in English was the advisable route to go even if perfection was not always attained. English, the language of the schooling process as well as a separate subject on the curriculum, enjoyed esteem. As a result, all students at the time came to accept the position that 'if you can't parse, you can't pass' (London 2002, p. 70). More significantly, this understanding serves to sharpen our interpretation about the nature of ideology itself, which is 'a relatively formal and articulated system of meanings, values, and beliefs, of a kind that can be abstracted, as a world view or a class outlook' (Williams, 1989, p. 56). In addition, ideology is a phenomenon that becomes most effective when its workings are least visible (Fairclough, 1989). The recognition in Trinidad and Tobago of the benefits that might accrue through competence in English is a case in point.

The ideological preference for English in schools and elsewhere was the result of some features that remained quiescent. Among these are the issue of language loss (mentioned above), cultural marginalization, and a preference for the foreign over the local, a penchant that by this time had established itself. These outcomes were fundamental but silent in the language education program, and for strategic reasons they could not be made manifest. English had to be fortified for all times. A postcolonial explanation would summarize that if such outcomes were revealed, esteem and legitimacy for English would be vitiated, particularly at a time (the late colonial period) when former instruments of domination such as the repressive state apparatus had been relaxed in the school system (Gordon, 1963). The manipulation here is a good example of ideological engineering, and it became significant because Anglocentricity as a curriculum principle had to prevail.

The microtechnology engaged is significant as regards the ideology that authenticated and valorized English. The approaches to reading and language study, for example, constitute in themselves a process designed to have students appropriate and internalize the presumed status of English. They comprised a technology that directly affected the thinking of students, but teachers too, were targets in the ideological manoeuvre. The microtechnology used demonstrates how subjects and their deepest selves might be interpolated, positioned, and shaped by what lies external to them, in this case the notion that English is the language to be learned and mastered if life chances are to be improved. More significantly, the technology used reveals how subjectivity and personhood of student and teacher alike came to end up as casualties in the Trinidad and Tobago language-education project. These were subordinated to the dominant ideology about language and socioeconomic mobility.

As regards hybridity, postcoloniality maintains that the construct is a 'problematic of colonial representation' (Young, 1959, p. 3). Hybridity, we recall, refers to cross-fertilization and 'in-betweenity,' and the language education program in Trinidad and Tobago at the time demonstrates this idea. The intention was never to make 'Englishmen' out of the boys and girls taught, but to produce a *hybrid class* who would appreciate, respect, and put the highest value on the English language and British culture, the indigenous counterparts having been devalued. The insistence on the use of 'good English' at all times, and the emphasis put on speech and pronunciation in the curriculum, were devices to clone special individuals who would be neither fish nor fowl – and the instructional technologies used in the transformation ensured the intended product. As Ania Loomba (1998) explained in another context, such technologies were contrived with the notion of evolving a new strain of subjects harnessed to the metropolis.

The pedagogical methods used by the teachers emphasized proficiency, but here again, the acquisition of English was supposed to be a cost obliteration and eradication of local Creole. The vision was, as Gandhi metaphorically interprets it, to take on the characteristics of the tiger without having the tiger's nature (1989, p. 30). Excellence in learning the English language sometimes earned the commendation of being 'more English than the Englishman,' with the ironic understanding that the successful local learner could and would never attain fully the 'whiteness' of the English, regardless of the extent to which she or he might have come to devalue local linguistic identity in the process of schooling. In-betweenity is painful, agonizing, and puzzling for the new breed, as Bhabha (1985) explains. It comes with psychic trauma because the real thing (being English rather than speaking or writing perfect English) cannot and will not ever be attained in the circumstance. This is a position of liminality, inherent in the concept of hybridity (Young, 1959).

The goals of hybridity in the Trinidad and Tobago context were not a well-guarded secret. There was deliberate, open, and observable construction of a comprador class through the method of what Anderson describes as 'mental miscegenation' (1983, p. 13). The approach came with empire-building and was enunciated in respect to India in what is now referred to as the infamous Macaulay Minute: 'We must at present do our best to *form a class* who may be interpreters between us and the millions whom we govern; *a class of persons*, Indian in blood and color, but English in taste, in opinions, in morals, and in intellect. To that *class* we may leave it to refine the vernacular dialects of the country, to enrich those dialects with terms of science borrowed from the Western nomenclature, and to render them by degrees fit vehicles for conveying knowledge to the great mass of the population' (in Spring, 1998, p. 16). The objective was the same for those who went to school in Trinidad and Tobago. A postcolonial critique would contend that the underlying aim of the recitation as a pedagogical device, that the inspectors' insistence regarding the aspirate *h*, and that the assignment of chats as a separate, time-tabled subject on the curriculum were measures designed to evolve the new breed of 'mimic' (and not real) men, as Vidaidhar Naipaul (1967) calls them, incapable of ever becoming truly English even though mastery of the language might be attained. The perpetual gap was to ensure subjection of the colonized for all times and to guarantee dependence on the imperial state. The device was imbued with racism.

If, as indicated, hybridity comprehends an element of intellectual cross-fertilization, then the above recommendation for the use of methodology 'based on the common defects in pupils' everyday expression' constitutes one example of how hybridity was supposed to proceed. The local (incorporating indigenous defects) was to be used as a reference point for perfecting use of the foreign (pure) strain of English. In the process a form of linguistic metamorphosis was at work leading to a new hybrid, the distinctive and colourful Creole varieties that are today idiosyncratic of this enclave (Trinidad and Tobago) in the Afro-Indian diaspora (Burchfield 1985; London, 2001a). The local dialect, both in structure and formulation, has evolved, although the above cut-and-mix process constructed culturally, politically, and historically as well as in contemporary times demand some new conceptual tools to unravel.

Identity as a postcolonial construct featured in the language-education program in Trinidad and Tobago, and the critique here draws from an observation in another context. Simon During convincingly makes the point that writing and speaking in an imperial tongue is to call forth a problem of identity (1989). This was the case in Trinidad and Tobago where all languages, except the language of the imperial state, were forbidden in the elementary school system. The problem of identity appears as well in the regulatory modalities identified, in the evaluation reports, and in the intervention strategies used. In all of these, students are never identified by name; they had no identity and were invisible. References were made to 'the pupils,' 'standards,' 'the juniors,' 'the seniors,' and so on. Teachers, too, had no names. The reference was to 'teachers' or to 'the head teacher.' The approach in such instances constitutes a homogenizing principle in which a distancing technique is at work, the purposes being to inject into the educational experience the element of decentred subjectivity (mentioned above) and to throttle any device that would produce the 'new man' (with a distinct identity of his own) of whom Memmi (1974) spoke. In postcolonial rhetoric this new creation is the 'subaltern,' who metaphorically is now learning to speak, but Memmi assures us that the road to effectiveness is long, tortuous, and complex (ibid.).

The inspectors' insistence that any local or indigenous language form was an interference and should be stamped out is also concerned with the question of identity. If, as indicated, identity includes as well a concept of the past, then this insistence is an attempt to discount the cultural and linguistic background of the students concerned. The use of imperfect English by the students was an attempt to engage some of the products of their language communities, an issue that points to a criticism raised by Ashcroft and colleagues (1989) about the way in which British colonials undertook the teaching of English. The approach is said to have generated a measure of amnesia among the subjects schooled, replaced memories of the past with a new myth of the past, and created, as David Grele put it, a past that was now usable (in Gandhi, 1989, p. 84).

The loss of identity among the colonized, and how the process worked in general, have been summed up in Gandhi's interpretation of Hegel's paradigm relating to the slave and his master (ibid.). Gandhi explains that 'initially there is an antagonism and enmity between these two confronting selves; each aims at the cancellation or death and destruction of the Other; hence, and temporarily, a situation arises where one is merely recognized while the other recognizes' (ibid.). English-language teaching in Trinidad and Tobago during the colonial era met these prescriptions. It was an exercise designed to deracinate the identity of the Other and to implant for all times an identity of Self. The method reveals another issue: legitimate authority for language use might be constructed, a rationale that was pivotal in the success that the Trinidad and Tobago language-education program enjoyed. Construction, as postcolonialists see it, is always against what matters or what is made to matter.

Discipline in postcolonialist terms had to become an important principle in the language-education exercise, for the reason that an undertaking that seeks to organize people and put them into preconceived categories (linguistic or otherwise) necessitates the application of certain structures. In the circumstance, creativity and experimentation with linguistic forms as a means towards self-expression would not likely become an option. Standard forms must prevail, as we have seen in the program in Trinidad and Tobago. Moreover, the surveillance system that was established ensured compliance with official policy and provided some assurance that the brand of English approved, together with the ideologies that it conveyed, would be learned and internalized. In other words, only certain ways of seeing were introduced and transmitted to students; other ways were denied. The sum total of the regimentation obtained was, as Linda Smith puts it, the organization of people, their minds, and their consciousness in the interest of colonialism (Smith, 1999).

Conclusion

The English-language program and the way that it was administered and policed in Trinidad and Tobago demonstrates an important issue that has been raised in the critical analysis of education, schooling, and culture. The language of the school – English in its approved form only – constituted both the language to be learned and the medium of instruction. English was a major component of the culture of the institution, but incisive, penetrating, and pervasive as this phenomenon was, it was at variance with the culture that was brought to school by most students of the day and contributed to underachievement in many cases. French sociologists Pierre Bourdieu and Jean-Claude Passeron (1977) have pointed to this type of disjuncture in their discussion of cultural capital and of the reasons for failure in school among certain social classes. Despite the dissonance, in retrospect, colonial adminis- trators and policymakers insisted that English in an approved standard form had to be learned. Many students did not make the grade and fell by the wayside, despite the competencies that they did achieve, or that they had the potential to achieve, in school. The experience is confronta- tional and demonstrates the way in which one culture might come to dominate another in the anthropological war of which Derrida speaks in his discussion *Of Grammatology* (1976). The Trinidad and Tobago case is a good example of the deculturation referred to, and it is constitutive of a process that sought to assimilate the dispossessed from one angle only – structurally through acquisition of the English language. That is, the enculturation provided was limited, the terms and conditions for incorporation into the culture of the colonizer being determined by prevailing epistemologies of Self and the Other and by the political and economic imperatives of the imperial state.

The postcolonial theoretic used in this chapter is by no means unique or inaugural in its concerns about matters relating to colony and em- pire, but the specificity it demands in analysis is insightful. In this chapter, it puts the spotlight not only on a given locale, Trinidad and Tobago, but also on a particular time, the late colonial period. The insights yielded through this approach are reminiscent of the provoca- tive and unsettling disclosures about the colonial condition unearthed in David Johnson's (1996) examination of Shakespeare within the South African context and, in particular, unpack and expose some of the resistances, contradictions, and compromises inherent in the colonial enterprise. A major disclosure here is the way in which an Anglicization project did work in situ, a feature that calls attention to the need for comparative studies in the area. Equally important are the lessons that might be learned about language propagation and implantation under colonialism and in a new diasporic enclave. These insights have impli- cations for social class structure and mobility, as well as for the colonial and postindependence political process.

As regards the contradictions revealed in the colonial enterprise it- self, the Trinidad and Tobago example is particularly illuminating. The primacy accorded to English served, for example, as a means of forging into one the identities of the two major transplanted groups, peoples of Africa and East Indian origins, that make up the population. It is a strategy known to have yielded, at least on the surface, the kind of cultural unification that language planners in many developing nations aspire to achieve, but the net result is different here. Under colonialism in Trinidad and Tobago, the acquisition of competence in English was at the expense of mother tongue competence, a scenario very unlike the situation in many contemporary developing nations, where mother tongue maintenance has been a key feature even in the face of aggressive campaigns to globalize and enroot English.

The Trinidad and Tobago outcome, nonetheless, might in some way be considered a blessing rather than a bane. The draconian, monolingual policy turned out to be a major factor in nation-building during the postindependence years in that the stratagem has yielded at least one big dividend. This is the current English-language base that now provides a special and important glue in the interaction of the above two major groups, originating as they did from a kaleidoscope of linguistic backgrounds, some genres of which were very different from others. Exacerbated by the politics of partisanship that was promoted by aspirants for national control, the local interethnic and cross-cultural landscape has been subjected to unprecedented stress, but the use of a common lingua franca, English, together with widespread use of indigenized variants (Creole) both in speech and in song (e.g., calypso and soca), has provided at least one impregnable bastion against forces that have threatened national unity and cohesion.

The colonial Anglicization schema and the engagement of schools in the process has, therefore, had significant advantages in Trinidad and Tobago, and nation-building is very likely the area of local pursuit that has been the key beneficiary. Despite the advantage, however, this sequel must be understood in postcolonial theoretical terms. It is an unintended rather than a planned and deliberate outcome of colonialism. The cohesion and unity achieved, in other words, was never part of the colonial dream, and so the present gains in ethnic, social, and cultural rapprochement must be understood as a discrepancy or a contradiction in the colonial enterprise, a feature that postcolonial thinkers have seriously enjoined us to consider. This disjuncture calls attention to 'that greater sense of the political' (mentioned above) that must be brought to the interpretation of social and cultural production facilitated by engagement of a postcolonial theoretic. The insight is part of that 'insurgent knowledge' that we must allow to emerge from the received histories and ideologies of the colonial past, and the postcolonial probe ministers to the endeavour (Pennycook, 1998, p. 39).

Appendix: Evaluation Reports (Trinidad and Tobago Department of Education, 1938, 1948, 1953)

1938

Reading was weak in Stage 1A and fair in Stages 2 and 3.[3] The weakness was due to inability of pupils to combine elementary sounds. More attention must be given to the phonic plan as outlined in the Reading B Scheme.

Recitation was very fair but more dramatics should be taken. Chats and storytelling were unsatisfactory. These were affected by one-word answers and inability of pupils to discover and correct faults. Word-building was fair.

Mechanical reading was weak in Std. [Standard] V, good in Std. III and fair in the other classes. In the juniors enunciation and pronunciation were faulty, while in the seniors better fluency and expression were desirable (Gramsci, 1971). Comprehension was poor in Stds. VI–VIII; but very poor in VII; parsing was good in IV. Fair dictation lessons were written in every class.

1948

Pupils need more practice in oral work-conversations, narratives, description – in order to check the influence of their home speech. A literary Group for pupils of Stds. 5, 6, 7 is very desirable.

Generally, reading has shown improvement as regards fluency, but comprehension of text has not received adequate attention. In Stds. 6 and 7 this defect was particularly marked. The objectives of reading being information and enjoyment, every effort should be made to make pupils in every Standard realise this end. It is not the number of lessons read that matters, it is the pupils' broadened mental horizon, ability to understand textual matter, and their whetted taste for reading. This is of paramount importance. Standard I was, however, somewhat below expectation. The class teacher should show more power to stir her pupils to greater self-effort.

Pupils were generally weak in this subject. Letter-writing was extremely poor in Std. 4. Stds. 5, 6, 7 did not show that they know much about paraphrasing. Analysis and knowledge of accidence required attention. Marked papers were returned for the Head Teacher's guidance. More systemic drill in basic speech was evidently needed in Stds.

1, 2 and 3 to improve pupils' speech. These drills should anticipate, or be based on, the common defects in pupils' everyday expressions. Frequent drills in oral composition should supplement the written work if the high incidence of basic grammatical errors is to be reduced or eliminated. Std. 7 was quite satisfactory in this subject.

1953

Reading was satisfactory in Std. 3., but fair in Std. 2 and good in Std. 1. There was too much laboured and faltering reading. Too many pupils had to resort to spelling to recognise words that they should normally know. Mastery of new or difficult words written on the Black Board before the reading proper should help to develop the fluency required to make reading an exercise of pleasure to the pupils.

English was a weak subject in all Stages. It should receive the attention it deserves. Reading in sentences and answering questions in sentences would help to improve the standard of English in the Infant School. Too much emphasis is laid on the single word.

Students had difficulty enunciating the aspirate 'h.' Word-building, chats and spelling were good. Story-telling was fair, there being evidence that the stories were hackneyed and as a consequence the pupils recited them by rote. Writing was good in all but Stds. III–IV, their 'ss' being affected by faulty formation and joining and untidiness. Dictation was good in all classes.

Language study, grammar and written composition were weak throughout; the schemes evidently did not receive sufficient attention.

NOTES

This chapter was first published as an article in *Comparative Education Review* (2003), 47 (3), 287–320. Reprinted here with the journal's permission.

1 In several former colonies, especially those in Africa and Asia, 'the language question' is today a big and sensitive issue. The debate is highly politicized, and state manaters have had to confront the dilemma of which language to promote among many, in attempts to grant legitimacy to claims from diverse language communities within national borders. See, e.g., Brock-Utne (1997).

2 The record explains that Spain surrendered the island of Trinidad to Britain

in 1797 and that in 1802 the island (Trinidad) was ceded to Britain by the Treaty of Amiens. In the same year (1802), the island of Tobago was ceded to Britain, this time by the Treaty of Paris and having passed through the hands of several European nations several times. The two, Trinidad and Tobago were thrown together in political union in 1889 to become the Crown Colony of Trinidad and Tobago under British rule. The colony, however, acceded to political independence in 1962 and 1976 became the Republic of Trinidad and Tobago within the Commonwealth of Nations. See London (2001a).

3 Elementary schools during the colonial period considered in this chapter had an identifiable administrative structure: an infant department (Standards I–III), a primary division (Standards I–V), and a postprimary division (Standards VI–VII). In cases where enrolment figures were large enough, the primary and postprimary divisions were sometimes conceptualized as a single entity for administrative and pedagogical purposes, subdivided into 'juniors' (Standards I–III) and 'seniors' (Standards IV–VII). Students began schooling at age 5 and older, and the norm for progression through the system was on stage or standard per year. Thus, by age 15 students were expected to complete the elementary cycle. Promotion was not automatic, however; it was earned on the basis of academic performance, and both repeating and demotion were common practices in cases where proficiency was not demonstrated.

REFERENCES

Alatas, S.H. (1997). *The myth of the lazy native: A study of the image of the Malays, Filipinos and Javanese from the sixteenth to the twentieth century and its function in the ideology of colonial capitalism.* London: Frank Cass.

Althusser, L. (1971). *Lenin and philosophy.* London: New Left Books.

Anderson, B. (1983). *Imagined communities: Reflections on the origin and spread on nationalism* London: Verso.

Arif, D. (1994). The postcolonial aura. *Critical Inquiry, 20,* 328–356.

Ashcroft, B., Griffiths, G., & Tiffin, H. (1989). *The empire writes back: Theory and practice in post-colonial literatures.* London: Routledge.

Bacchus, M.K. (1990). *Utilization, misuse and development of human resources in the early West Indian colonies.* Waterloo, ON: Wilfrid Laurier University Press.

Ballandier, G. (1963). *Sociologie actuelle de l'Afrique noire.* Paris: Presses Universitaires de France.

Bhabha, H. (1985). Signs taken for wonders: Questions of ambivalence and authority under a tree outside Delhi. *Critical Inquiry, 12,* 156–159.

Borg, W.R., and Gall. M.D. (1989). *Educational research: An introduction* (5th ed.) New York: Longman.

Bourdieu, P., & Passeron J.C. (1977). *Reproduction in education: Society and culture.* Thousand Oaks, CA: Sage.

Brock-Utne, B. (1997). The language question in Namibian schools. *International Review of Education, 43*, 241–260.

Burchfield, R. (1985). *The English language.* Toronto: University of Toronto Press.

Canagarajah, A.S. (1999). *Resisting linguistic imperialism in English teaching.* London: Oxford University Press.

Childs, P. (Ed.) (1999). *Postcolonial theory and English literature: A reader.* Edinburgh: Edinburgh University Press.

Clarke, S.R.P. (2000). Researching enterprise bargaining: A qualitative approach. *Education Research and Perspective, 30*, 1–18.

Crowley, T. (1998). *Language in history.* London: Routledge, 1998.

Derrida, J. (1976). *Of grammatology* (Gayatri Spivak, Trans.). Baltimore: Johns Hopkins University Press.

During, S. (1989). Postmodernism or postcolonialism today. In Ashcroft, B., Griffiths, G., & Tiffin, H. (Eds.), *The empire writes back: Theory and practice in post-colonial literatures* (pp. 125–149). London: Routledge.

Evans, E.W. (Ed.). (1950). *Principles and methods of colonial administration.* London: Butterworths Scientific.

Fairclough, N. (1989). *Language and power.* London: Longman.

Foucault, M. (1970). *The order of things: An archaeology of the human sciences.* New York: Vintage Books.

Foucault, M. (1979a). *Discipline and punish.* Harmondsworth, UK: Penguin.

Foucault, M. (1980). *Power/knowledge: Selected interviews and other writings, 1972–1977.* Hartfordshire, UK: Harvester.

Gandhi, L. (1989). *Postcolonial theory: A critical introduction.* New York: Columbia University Press.

Giddens, A. (1985). *The nation state and violence.* Cambridge: Polity.

Gilroy, P. (1990). The end of anti-racism. *New Community, 17* (1), 71–83.

Giroy, P. (1993). *The black Atlantic: Modernity and double consciousness.* London: Verso.

Gordon, S. (1963). *A century of West Indian education.* London: Longmans.

Gramsci, A. (1971). *Selections from the prison notebooks* (Q. Hoare and G.N. Smith, Eds.). London: Lawrence Wishart.

Habermas, J. (1973). *Legitimation crisis.* Boston: Beacon.

Hall. S. (1992). The question of cultural identity. In S. Hall, D. Held, and T. McGraw (Eds.), *Modernity and its futures* (pp. 268–288). Cambridge: Polity.

Hall, S. (1996). When was the post-colonial? Thinking at the limit. In Iain

Chamber and Lidia Curtis (Eds.), *The Post-colonial question: Common skies divided horizons* (pp. 242–260). London: Routledge.

Henry, F., Tator, C., Mattis, W., and Rees, T. (1995). *The colour of democracy: Racism in Canadian society.* Toronto: Harcourt Brace.

Johnson, D. (1996). *Shakespeare and South Africa.* Oxford: Clarendon.

Kiernan, V. (1991). Languages and conquerers. In Peter Burke and Roy Porter (Eds.), *Language, self and society* (pp. 43–68). London: Polity.

King, E. (1968). *Comparative studies and educational decision.* London: Methuen Educational.

Le Compte, M.D., and Preissle, J. (1993). *Ethnography and qualitative design in educational research.* New York: Academic Press.

London, N.A. (1997). Quality control in a colonial school setting: How it worked and for what purpose. In Keith Watson, Celia Modgil, and Sohan Modgil (Eds.), *Education dilemmas: Debate and diversity*, vol. 4, *Quality in Education* (pp. 88–97). London: Cassell.

London, N.A. (2001a). Curriculum and pedagogy in the development of colonial imagination: A subversive agenda. *Canadian and International Education, 30* (1), 45–76

London, N.A. (2001b). Language for the global economy: Some curriculum fundamentals and pedagogical practices in the colonial educational enterprise. *Educational Studies, 27* (4), 338–423.

London, N.A. (2002). Curriculum convergence: An ethno-historical investigation into schooling in Trinidad and Tobago. *Comparative Education, 38* (1), 53–72.

Loomba, A. (1998). *Colonialism/postcolonialism.* London: Routlege.

Memmi, A. (1968). *Dominated man: Note towards a portrait.* London: Orion.

Memmi, A. (1974). *The colonizer and the colonized.* London: Souvenir.

Merriam, S.B. (1988). *Case study research in education.* San Francisco: Jossey Bass.

Naipaul, V.S. (1967). *The mimic men.* Russell Edition. London: Andre Deutsch.

Naipaul, V.S. (1983). *The intimate enemy: Loss and recovery of self under colonialism.* Delhi: Oxford University Press.

Pennycook, A. (1994). *The cultural politics of English as an international language.* London: Longman.

Pennycook, A. (1998). *English and the discourses of colonialism.* London: Routledge.

Phillipson, R. (1992). *Linguistic imperialism.* Oxford: Oxford University Press.

Parkash, E. (Ed.). (1995). *After colonialism: Imperial histories and postcolonial displacements.* Princeton, NJ: Princeton University Press.

Ricento, T. (Ed.). (2000). *Ideology, politics and language policies.* Amsterdam: John Benjamins.

Roberts, G.T. (1998). *The language of the blue books: The perfect instrument of empire.* Cardiff: University of Wales Press.

Roberts, P. (1997). *From oral to literate culture: Colonial experience in the English West Indies.* Mona, Jamaica: University of the West Indies Press.

Said, E. (1993). *Culture and imperialism.* London: Routledge.

Saunders, W. (1990). Discourse in education. In Stephen J. Ball (Ed.), *Foucault and education: Discipline and knowledge.* London: Routledge.

Smith, L.T. (1999). *Decolonizing methodologies: Research and indigenous peoples.* New York: Zed Books.

Spring, J. (1998). *Education and the rise of the global economy.* Mahwah, NJ: Erlbaum.

Spurr, D. (1994). *The rhetoric of empire: Colonial discourse in journalism, travel writing and imperial administration.* Durham, NC: Duke University Press.

Taylor, C. (1991). *The ethnics of authenticity.* Cambridge, MA: Harvard University Press.

Thiong'o N[gugi wa]. (1981). *Decolonizing the mind.* London: James Currey.

Thomas, C.Y. (1982). Walter Rodney and the Caribbean revolution. In Edward A. Alpers and Pierre-Michel Fontaine (Eds.), *Walter Rodney: Revolutionary and scholar: A tribute* (pp. 119–132). Los Angeles: Center for Afro-American Studies and African Studies Center, University of California, Los Angeles.

Tollefson, J.W. (1991). *Planning language, planning inequality: Language policy in the community.* London: Longman.

Trautmann, T.R. (1997). *Aryans and British India.* Berkeley: University of California Press.

Trinidad and Tobago Department of Education. (1942). *Annual report.* Port of Sapin: Government Printer.

Trinidad and Tobago Department of Education. (1953 [?]). *Log books for selected schools, incorporating data for 1938, 1948, and 1953.* Port of Spain: Government Printer [?].

Trinidad and Tobago Department of Education. (1958). *Primary school supplies.* Port of Spain: Government Printer.

Viswanathan, G. (1987). *The beginning of English literary study in British India. Oxford Library Review, 9* (1/2), 17–31.

Williams, R. (1977). *Marxism and literature.* Oxford: Oxford University Press.

Williams, R. (1989). Hegemony and the selective tradition. In Suzaane de Castell, Allan Luke, and Carmen Luke (Eds.), *Language, authority and criticism: Readings on the school textbook* (pp. 52–72). London: Falmer.

Willinsky, J. (1998). *Learning to divide the world: Education at empire's end.* Minneapolis: University of Minnesota Press.

Young, R. (1959). *Colonial desire: Hybridity in theory, culture and race.* London: Routledge.

2 To STEAL or to TELL: Teaching English in the Global Era

SEONAIGH MACPHERSON

> We are being asked to move out of our containers to enter into the evolutionary conversation to understand the biosphere and the emerging planetary culture as one in which Mankind (and I use the sexist term on purpose) as a defensive collection of competing and warring selves has come to its end.
>
> Thompson (1990)

Where Is Afghanistan?

In 2002, I was living in Edmonton, Alberta, on a short cul-de-sac that bordered the North Saskatchewan River Valley. A Canadian soldier lived with his fiancée across the street in a small house. In the morning, as I wrote by my window, I would watch him as he left for work, a striking lean and muscular figure dressed in camouflage fatigues. Several weeks after 11 September, a taxi driver told me that he had taken the soldier to the airport that very morning to fight in the Afghan war. That's how I learned that my neighbour went to Afghanistan, and that's why I knew six months later that he had died – killed by American 'friendly fire.' That morning, after the names of the three dead soldiers were announced on the radio, cars began to converge on my neighbours' house. The world collapsed that day, as Afghanistan leapt out of newspaper headlines and television images to unravel its tragedy on my short cul-de-sac in real-time images of women bearing pots of food, midnight flower deliveries, a pressed uniform picked up by military jeep, and friends sitting with a grieving woman on the front porch, mourning the loss of love.

Today, Afghani children continue to arrive to grace our neighbour-hoods and schools, where they struggle to fit into English-language lessons and Canadian classroom norms, their mothers, some widowed, lonely and isolated, with husbands dead from wars and families dispersed around the world. Meanwhile, further away, in a neighbourhood on the east coast of Canada, an Afghani teen struggles to adapt to his last-chance high school, having been expelled from all the rest. The struggles of Canada and the world to integrate Afghanistan into the international community is part of the same struggle that we experience in local schools and communities to integrate Afghani children and families into our neighbourhoods. The outcome of both is contingent on the realization that our well-beings are interconnected, that our ability to give a hands-up to their country and their refugees here in Canada, to trust them, to assist them in the pursuit of prosperity, health, and happiness is as much about furthering our own futures as theirs. In this sense, events in Afghanistan are transforming our neighbourhoods, just as our neighbourhoods are transforming Afghanistan. We call these transformations, this collapsing of space and time, *globalization*.

A Global Imaginary: The Blue Planet

If nothing else, the twentieth century has taught us that the places and identities that we inhabit are constituted as much of imaginary constructs as of concrete particles, atoms, and physical space. These imaginary spaces include our experience of distinctions such as here and there, Self and Other, and other designations that function as boundaries ascribing whom we identify with and against. The most recent and compelling imagined boundary to exert its presence in our time is the planet Earth, the *Blue Planet*, whose emergence marks a shift in our imagined location and sense of identification, belonging, and collective presence.

As the prevailing image of the world in our time, the Blue Planet is a metonym for our common life. A deep azure, terra cotta, and white-streaked orb set against the deep-black depth of space, the Blue Planet is the offspring of the geographical (Gregory, 1994), global, and astro-nautical imaginary. As David Smith (this volume) suggests, this imaginary 'pertains less to any characteristic of the world in its ordinary condition than to what certain people *imagine* that condition to be, based on their desire, their theory, their ego-projections, or, say, their religious sensibility.' The image of the Blue Planet is fast becoming the dominant contemporary cosmological archetype, supplanting the mapped, measured, and colour-coded globe of the colonial world. Whereas this earlier image suggested an abstract, geometrically partitioned world with imperial nation-states in charge, the new image is a biological world, more organic, holistic, chaotic, and alive. As an actual photograph rather than a two- or three-dimensional abstract representation, it seems more tangible and real, yet inaccessible, distant, and remote, shrouded under white condensation and the detached impersonality of its scale.

As we come to identify home in this ball of azure water condensing clouds of white over terra-cotta-coloured continents, the Blue Planet is fast becoming a quasi-religious icon, a rallying symbol for ecological action and an image of existential solace and refuge. Constituting more than mere astronomical facts, it heralds an emerging universal, evolutionary, and scientific cosmology and worldview, with a corresponding shift in how we construct our sense of place as well as our individual and collective identities. Voicing the sentiments of many astronauts, Edgar Mitchell describes his first experience of witnessing the blue planet as 'a purposefulness of flow, of energy, of time, of space in the cosmos' (in Kelley, 1988, p. 138). Seeking belonging beyond a particular family, state, nation, religious, moral, or cultural order, more and more people are turning to biology, infinity, and ecological interdependence as sources of spiritual inspiration, with identities and identifications implicated in their life as embodied persons nested in successive biological and ecological niches (Inglehart, 1997; Ray & Anderson, 2000). Nisker suggests that this 'fosters the realization that what defines our individual human life is, first and foremost, life. Secondarily it is human. Only thirdly is it individual' (1998, p. 16). The seeds of this ecological imaginary appear as early as 1962 in the words of U.S. President John F. Kennedy: 'We can help make the world safe for diversity. For, in the final analysis, our most basic common link is that we all inhabit this same planet. We all breathe the same air; we all cherish our children's future; and we are all mortal' (1963).

Whatever Happened to the Postcolonial In-between?

The emergence of the Blue Planet as a new collective human icon signals a dramatic transformation from a colonial to a global worldview. So what happened to the postcolonial in-between? There is dubious evidence of any significant postcolonial adjustments in the transition leading up to this transformation. Although humankind and our societies are passing through accelerated changes marked by the proliferation of transnationalism, from new technologies to blurred ethnic and national identities, migration, multinational corporations, and hybrid cultures, the institutions and discourses in which we conduct and engage in formal education show little if any significant break or deviation from their colonial habits and dispositions from the past (see London, this volume).

A key indicator of the uninterrupted colonial legacy in the field of education is the tendency to segregate the study of education in the so-called developed world (as curriculum studies) from the study of education in the developing world (as international and comparative education). In turn, the emphasis placed on subject area expertise and experience in the hiring of faculty in curriculum studies departments discriminates against those educated in non-modern, alternative institutional and cultural contexts. This bias is exacerbated by the tendency for non-modern, traditional educational systems to be religiously based, which conflicts with the secular biases of modern systems. Some may rationalize that education departments first and foremost need to serve local clientele, that is, those who are dealing with a Western form of modern, secular education. Yet, these same faculty members educate and supervise international graduate students, even when unfamiliar with their local cultures or educational histories. They are the same faculty members who are preparing student teachers, in turn, to travel the world in pursuit of teaching experiences.

The drive by the United Nations, particularly the U.N. Educational, Scientific, and Cultural Organization (UNESCO) and other networks of transnational, national, and local bodies to encourage literacy and basic education are fuelling even further the flight to modern, Western norms. These norms are seeping into all facets of educational experience, ranging from institutional funding and structures, classroom organizations, disciplinary and subject-area contents, epistemology, pedagogies, outcomes, and standards, to the very nature and role of knowledge in a community. This trend towards monocultural norms is not the fruit of some grand conspiracy, so much as of ignorance. People gain positions of leadership in national and transnational organizations because they have succeeded in modern, secular (Western-originated) education. In turn, these people find it challenging to imagine, let alone implement or support, alternative forms of education and knowledge that lie outside their experience.

What Is at Stake? The Unimaginable True Diversity of the Empirical World

More than any other point, I would like to focus on the following questions: How can those of us immersed in the North American modern, secular educational machinery even imagine – let alone know, support, or sustain – the true diversity of the empirical world? What do we know about it? The push towards provincial, national, and now international standards needs to be considered with this limitation in mind: These standards are initiatives to propagate modern Western norms as educational outcomes and best practices that have been arrived at without reference to alternative cultural practices or epistemologies. The ethnocentric failing is to see what is local and relative as universal, and to see what is normative as factual. When this failing combines with power and coercion, it is an error that can perpetrate great harm in the name of good. Shiva describes how such coercive practices begin with the negation of local knowledge, which in turn, erodes local biological and cultural diversity and favours biological and human monocultures: 'The universal would spread in openness. The globalizing local spreads by violence and misrepresentation. The first level of violence unleashed on local systems of knowledge is to not see them as knowledge. This invisibility is the first reason why local systems collapse without trial and test when confronted with the knowledge of the dominant west' (1993, p. 10). I will expand on two points that Shiva makes. The first concerns the relationship between local knowledge and global diversity, a subject that I treat in considerably more depth elsewhere (MacPherson, 2003). In short, although the fate of a single language is difficult to predict, what is clear is that the languages of medium to small communities and cultures are being marginalized from public and educational uses. Does this matter? Does it matter if human linguistic diversity is restricted to personal rather than public uses? After all, linguists tend to emphasize home use as the critical factor in the long-term sustainability of a language (Nettle and Romaine, 2000). Also, *diaspora* or minority communities find it easier to organize less formal, weekend or Sunday heritage language education programs and leave public institutions to make decisions about the language of instruction in more formal educational contexts, which tend to be in English or other dominant languages.

The principal danger in this organization of languages into a few dominant public and educational languages and a plethora of diverse personal languages is the potentially catastrophical loss from the human collective pot of conceptually advanced knowledge. To explain, consider Cummins (1991, 2001) distinction between basic interpersonal communicative skills (BICS) and cognitively academic language proficiency (CALP). While basic interpersonal skills require little formal instruction, perhaps one to two years if any, cognitively or conceptually challenging academic language acquisition (also CALP) requires formal and sustained instruction for up to eight years, full-time. By implication, this known gap between the interpersonal and cognitive academic manifestations of a language suggests that success in conserving the personal, home uses of language does not necessarily safeguard the higher cognitive, conceptual, or cultural manifestations of language. With the erosion of linguistic diversity in formal public and educational contexts, the cultural knowledge embodied in the CALP form of the language is vulnerable to erosion and extinction, even if the language is sustained in its simplified form for interpersonal use. As Mark Abley concludes in his narrative study of threatened languages and their communities: 'What the survival of threatened languages means, perhaps, is the endurance of dozens, hundreds, thousands of subtly different notions of truth. With our astonishing powers of technology, it's easy for us in the West to believe we have all the answers. Perhaps we do – to the questions we have asked. But what if some questions elude our capacity to ask? What if certain ideas cannot be fully articulated in our words?' (2003, p. 277).

The second of Shiva's arguments that I would like to discuss is the connection that she draws between biological and human monocultures. Nettle and Romaine (2000) call this interrelated condition of biological and cultural diversity *biolinguistic diversity*. To ordinary appearances, the relationship between biological and linguistic and cultural diversity may not be apparent. Our conditioned view is to see the causes and conditions of human experience as independent of the causes and conditions of physical, biological or non-human experience. Some of this tendency is culturally conditioned through education by the exaggerated division of knowledge in the West between the arts and the sciences (Capra, 2002; Wilson, 1998; Snow, 1959). Some derives from human arrogance, reinforced by economic and religious myths that suggest we are somehow not a part of, or dependent upon, the biological world (Rees, 1999, 2002; Beattie & Ehrlich, 2001). Some is conditioned by our perceptions, and our tendency to filter out conscious perception of slow or low-level environmental changes, which makes us susceptible to ignore the gradual erosion of biological, linguistic, and cultural diversity altogether (Ehrlich, 2000). Accordingly, knowledge of the erosion of global biolinguistic diversity appears to us as facts or statistics rather than as felt experiences or values, thereby minimizing our ability to respond personally, affectively, and hence appropriately and wholly, to the loss.

Yet, even on their own, the statistics are staggering. The World Conservation Union identified as endangered 11 per cent of bird species and 25 per cent of mammals on the planet (Wilson, 1992), which, by 2000 had increased with 18 per cent of the 11,000 threatened species falling within the most extreme category of 'critically endangered' (Worldwatch Institute, 2002, p. 8). There is considerable public awarenesss of these alarming biological extinctions, but much less is known of the corresponding and interrelated loss of linguistic diversity. Extrapolating from current rates of language attrition, Vines (in Lo Bianco, 2000, p. 98) goes so far to suggest that only 600 of the existing estimated 6,000 human languages will remain by the year 2020, and of those, only a small number will be used by large numbers of people. More conservative figures estimate that more than 50 per cent of the extant human languages will be extinct by the end of this century (Crystal, 2000, pp. 18–19), which does not seem any more comforting. Native speakers of English or other dominant tongues find it very difficult, if not impossible, to understand what this might mean in more personal terms. We have little experience to help us to imagine or empathize with what it might mean to be the last speaker of a language, to know that our language will disappear with us.

Globalization poses significant threats to biolinguistic diversity from two paradoxical extremes: (1) global assimilation and monoculturalism and (2) fundamentalist resistance. Modern educators applaud efforts to bring education and literacy to modernity's hinterlands; there is far less evidence, however, of a reciprocal movement of knowledge about the true extent of the diversity of the empirical world. Well-meaning academics reach out to Africa, China, India, or Tibet with the spirit of sharing pedagogies that we secretly when not openly believe to be advanced, with little knowledge of the indigenous education and knowledge that we are supplanting and suppressing in the process. The threat implicit in the globalization of modern knowledges and cultures, imbued as they are in the history of a local language, culture, and knowledge base (see Gray, 1995), has given rise to what can be an equally insidious strategy of resistance: traditionalism or fundamentalism (Hobsbawm & Ranger, 1983).

Traditionalism or fundamentalism is a stance assumed by some peoples who find themselves marginalized or otherwise threatened by modernization and globalization, and who respond by rigidly conforming to historical relations and traditions (Giddens, 2000; Gross, 1992; Heelas, Lash, & Morris, 1996). It is no wonder that the other significant threat posed by globalization comes from those who resist it. Fundamentalist resistance is a reaction against the perceived threat from unconstrained modernization and development, and it is generating aggressive, even violent, resistance that threatens modernity's promise of enhanced equity for marginalized, disenfranchised, and persecuted groups. Too often women, minority groups, and bordering peoples, not to mention non–human beings and environments, suffer under such traditionalist or fundamentalist resistance strategies. Just as globalization threatens to impose the interests of one group or culture over another, so do most forms of traditionalism and fundamentalism, insofar as they decide which privileged members are included as consenting agents. Those excluded are denied the exercise of free and informed consent, and they become subject to, rather than subjects of, the dominant discourses and discursive communities of a language.

One of the traps of this bifurcated mindset is the construction of exaggerated, if not false, dichotomies between assimilation and fundamentalism and, in a related fashion, between modernity and tradition. Although there are distinct qualities associated with traditional values and households (Ray & Anderson, 2000) such as patriarchal organizations, conservative views of the family, and strong religiosity, Loy (1997) argues that these may not be as different from the modern economic-oriented culture as we think. He claims that the marketplace, monetary values, and corporate and bureaucratic hierarchies propagate their own form of fundamentalism, merely replacing God with profits at the helm. So, the promise of modernity as liberation is itself constrained by colonial cultural and linguistic threats. Ignatieff argues that 'rights talk and Western culture are quite separable. Other cultures want to have rights protection without choosing Western dress, food, or technology' (2000, p. 45).

A genuine postcolonial resolution is to negotiate a way for humanity to move beyond the sense of a narrow choice between the extremes of monocultural assimilation and fundamentalism. Therefore, we might ask: What constitutes a genuine postcolonial in-between in education, that is, an *inter*national, *inter*cultural Third Space, which is neither modern nor non-modern. Such a postcolonial path would be free of the tendency to privilege either the variants of Western education that now serve as global prototypes, or the sentimentalized variants of 'traditional' education reinvented in our imagination to conform with some ideal vision of the past. This is the postcolonial agenda, and at the top of the list of its necessary curricular priorities are multilingualism and interculturalism ways to cultivate the ability to move between and across various cultures (Kim, 2001; Kim, Lujan, & Dixon, 1998a, 1998b; Lo Bianco, 2000). What distinguishes genuine *inter*nationalization and *inter*culturalism from globalization is the presence of choice, the willingness to challenge all norms that are presented as facts, and to engage openly, other cultures and educational lineages.

Lurking in TESOL's Shadow: To STEAL (Surreptitiously Teach English as an Assimilative Language) or Not to STEAL, That Is the Question

I have long been haunted by the spectre of how my language, education, and field of inquiry (English language teaching) may be perceived by future generations. Will they think: Where were *they* when the languages and cultures of the world died? The spread of English and English-language education, principal factors in the loss of biolinguistic diversity (species, languages, cultures, and knowledges), show signs of being the modern equivalents of the comet that wiped out the dinosaurs, spreading dust and residue about the Earth to stifle its light. In 1996–7, after hearing Ngugi wa'Thiongo speak, I was moved to write a review of his work, in which I reflected: 'One question I have wrestled with as a graduate student in the field is whether we are unwittingly serving exploitative multinational corporate interests as missionaries once served conquistadors, weakening the cultural and linguistic resources of people in a manner that makes the carnage of local cultures and economies possible' (MacPherson, 1997, p. 641).

Just as English as a world language is a key feature of globalization, English as a second language (ESL) teachers are key agents of globalization. The plethora of acronyms used to identify the field and the profession (T/ESL, T/ESOL, T/EFL, T/EAL, T/EIL, T/ESP, TEML, TEIMP)[1] betrays the intimate link between TESOL and the technologized, global world of information communications technologies, worldwide webs, and chief executive officers. At times ESL bears more resemblance to technology education ('tech ed') than English-language education, preoccupied as it can be with technique and efficiency over the poetic ruminations of William Shakespeare, Emily Dickinson, Margaret Atwood, Michael Ondaatje, or David Block, say. calls this technologized model of communication promoted by TESOL 'McCommunication' (2002), as a means to draw attention to the misapplication of economic values of efficiency on a language and a form of communication. This is reflected in TESL practices as well, where students are more likely to download information, language, and skill-sets in classrooms (see Horodezsky, 2004) than read and debate ethical meditations in English by the likes of John Stuart Mill or Mary Wollstonecraft, Edward Said, Amartya Sen, Martha Nussbaum, or Ngugi Wa Thiong'o. Indeed, some could go so far as to suggest that TESOL is not fundamentally about teaching a language and culture, at all, but simply an avenue to access a modern technological and a corporate existence that has yet to warrant the label of 'culture.'

Half–tongue-in-cheek, then, I refer to the dark side of the globalization of English as STEAL-ing, that is, taking something from the world that is not freely given. What is at risk of being stolen is diversity, the linguistic, cultural, and biological resources of future generations, the confidence that people derive from knowledge of their local languages, histories, and ecosystems, which when lost, can catapult those affected into the anxiety, insecurity, and doubt of what Bennett calls 'encapsulated marginality' (1993). As many sociolinguists caution, the spread of English as a global language to increasingly remote corners of the world may signal a cataclysmic erosion or outright elimination of human diversity in languages, cultures, and consciousness, which in turn, could accelerate the loss of global biodiversity writ large (Skutnabb-Kangas, 2000; Davis, 2001; Nettle & Romaine, 2000; Crystal, 2000). This sacrifice is not freely given with informed consent: What *free* choice does a student in China have when her access to, and promotion in, post-secondary education is contingent on her performance on an English-language test, in China where English is a foreign language? What *informed* choice does a Cree university student have in Canada when struggling to pass university courses and examinations in an access program, all the while losing track of the language, culture, and community of his upbringing in the North? Even if succeeding within the mainstream English-dominated world, does something inside of these people die? Do they feel broken and lost, and wonder whether it was worthwhile in the end? Or, do such terrible choices lead them to reject success in mainstream society and the opportunities that might afford?

These questions haunt those of us in the field who are willing to bear them, and repel those threatened by the doubts that they inspire. Yet, these are questions that we need to suffer to hold in our awareness without wincing, without fighting or swooning in the dubious bliss of ignorance. The response we do not want to make is to bury our heads in the sand with the hopes that the questions will go away or prove mistaken. Too much is at stake. Although now global in scope, the English language moved to such prominence through Britain's aggressive colonial expansions, occupations, and the migration of its peoples, who sowed the seeds for English to become the *lingua mundi* of the modern global order. That the English language's imperial centre shifted from London to New York has not made the teaching and learning of english any less colonial in effect, although perhaps in name: 'A language becomes an international language for one chief reason: the political power of its people – especially their military power' (Crystal, in Drohan & Freeman, 2000, p. 429). Some would argue that the current flight to English is by choice and demand rather than through colonial occupation or force; this but simplifies the central problem of volition in the global era. Nettle and Romaine (2000) point out that such a distinction between voluntary and involuntary language shift and attrition overlooks the challenges of making an informed choice about the long-term effects of mother tongue attrition on one's family, community, and psychological health when language shift transpires gradually and outside of a sense of conscious control or choice. People respond to what they perceive to be a short-term necessity; they do not go about deciding to lose a native tongue in the conventional sense of decision-making.

TESOL, and the educational industries surrounding the practice of TESOL, are implicated in this pressured flight to monolingual English by the general competitive anxiety of the global period. This anxiety is what encourages local peoples and otherwise well-meaning teachers to become complicit in propagating English and English-language education in contexts and ways that threaten students' affiliations and relationships to first languages, cultures, families, communities, and eco-systems. Evidence of this anxiety-driven flight to monolingual English can be found across diverse groups from Canadian Aboriginals (Norris, 1998, 2004) to immigrants (Kouritzin, 1999), and it lurks behind many public education language policies, whether in Korea, Japan,

China, or the State of California. In the process, TESOL has been and continues to be the most transnational, if not global, of all educational sectors, with an annual international conference (TESOL International) that draws 6,000 to 8,000 participants from forty-five to fifty different countries.

This trend towards transnationalism in English-language education coincides with the emergence of two new forms of transnational citizenship: global economic citizenship and global ecological citizenship. Whereas global *economic* citizenship is neo-colonial, modernist, and materialist with economic systems as common ground, global *ecological* citizenship is postcolonial, postmodernist, and postmaterialist with ecosystems as common ground. These are entangled in the four forms of cultural globalization identified by Peter Berger (2000, pp. 419–427): global economic citizenship in the *Davos culture* (cultural and economic elite); the *McWorld culture* (American popular culture); *Evangelical Protestantism* (Pentecostal); and global ecological citizenship in the *Faculty Club International* (Western intelligentsia, values, and ideological culture): 'The two perhaps most important features of [these four faces of globalization are] their Western, principally American, provenance, and related to this, their relation to the English language' (2000, p. 426). Although the global ecological movement relies on English as a lingua mundi as much as on global economic forces, it involves very different means and ends for TESOL: the search for a more ethical, postcolonial way forward against the exploitative and imperialistic practices and assumptions of the past.

I concede, with Berger, that the old neo-Marxist label of 'imperialism' does not fit well the complex global conditions of today. Nevertheless, the United States is emerging as a de facto economic and cultural empire, and, similar to the British, Chinese, or Roman empires of the past, the United States relies for its imperial outreach, consolidation, and control on the linguistic imperialism of a language, in this case English – and notably, ESOL education (Canagarajah, 1999; Skutnabb-Kangas & Phillipson, 1995). Three troubling manifestations of ESOL education in international contexts speak to its covert place on the U.S. 'imperialist' agenda. These three are named, again, half-tongue in cheek: (1) teaching English as an outsourcing language (TEOL), (2) teaching English for imperial or military purposes (TEIMP), and (3) teaching English as a missionary language (TEML). Under the pretext of providing lessons in language, these programs are transforming the world into a common free market, 'antiterrorist' militarized, and Pentecostal Protestant culture that is coalescing around a decidedly uniform, U.S. prototype of the world. What is troubling is that all three types of ESOL programs flirt with duplicity or deception in the staffing, objectives, curriculum, and/or outcomes of their programs. Therefore, I label them STEAL, for they are involved in STEAL-ing local languages, cultures, and biolinguistic diversity from the world and from future generations by failing to fully inform students and teachers of their intentions or outcomes. To exemplify each of the three types of programs, I offer specific examples that have crossed my path during the past months alone, like strange snapshots or post cards from the edge:

Teaching English as an Outsourcing Language (TEOL)

In an Op-Ed column in the 29 February 2004 issue of the *New York Times*, Thomas Friedman recounts observing an 'accent neutralization' class at a customer service call centre in Bangalore, India. This class trained new Indian recruits in the nuances of the Canadian accent, to help them 'play' Canadian when interacting with Canadian customers on the telephone. Whether the intention is to deceive or merely to cater to the biases of Canadian consumers who might be irritated by non-Western accents, the effect is the same: teaching accent reduction in such a way as to reinforce the continued organization of English speakers into centre-periphery distinctions, which Friedman makes embarrassingly clear in his column: 'The instructor was teaching the would-be Indian call center operators to suppress their native Indian accents and speak with a Canadian one – she teaches British and U.S. accents as well, but these youths will be serving the Canadian market ... Watching these incredibly enthusiastic young Indians preparing for their call center jobs – earnestly trying to soften their t's and roll their r's – is an uplifting experience ... Many have credit cards and have become real consumers, including of U.S. goods, for the first time.'

Teaching English for Imperial or Military Purposes (TEIMP)

Not far behind the (ab)uses of English as an outsourcing language is the teaching of English for imperial or military purposes. Edge has identi- fied and described the dangers of this trend in a fascinating perspective piece entitled, 'Imperial Troopers and Servants of the Lord' (2003), in which he points to the unprofessional, unethical expansion in recent years of TESOL as a tool of U.S. imperialism and Christian conversion. He implores readers to consider what TESOL professional ethics might mean in the wake of 11 September 2001 and the occupation of Afghanistan and Iraq, where increasing numbers of TESOL instructors would soon be recruited to serve. TESOL ethics are, first and foremost, about putting the interests of students ahead of our personal interests as employees of a particular institution, citizens of a particular state, and members of a particular religion.

Shortly after reading this opinion piece, I received a TESL job notice from my automatic, on-line *Chronicle of Higher Education* download. I opened the message to find the following (*www.chronicle.com*, retrieved on 27 February 2004):

Position: English Language Educator
Institution: Military Language Institute
Location: United Arab Emirates
Date posted: 2/27/2004
The Military Language Institute (MLI) is seeking applications from English language teachers and program coordinators for vacancies at its colleges and language centers in the U.A.E. Contract with the U.A.E. Armed Forces includes a salary of US$ ...

The ad went on to say that recruitment would be conducted in Washington, DC, and during the 2004 Annual TESOL International Conference in Long Beach, California. There were multiple positions available, both for teachers and coordinators, indicating that it was a new or growing initiative.

Is it naïve of me to wonder why the United Arab Emirates (UAE) military needs specialized English-language training programs? Surely the programs are for more than job perks or educational access to specialized trade journals. Are they to help coordinate the UAE Armed Forces with the U.S. and British military occupation of the region or, more specifically, with the occupation of Iraq? It is not so much what is said, as what is *not* said in job advertisements like these that make them ethically suspect: a version of TESOL as STEAL. Why should prospective employees not be interested in knowing the ends of the English they are being asked to teach? We would expect professional physicists or engineers to know as much, so why not English teachers?

Teaching English as Missionary Language (TEML)

The final and perhaps most prolific of the STEAL-ESOL programs spreading across the globe are programs for teaching English as a missionary language (TEML) and, in particular, those that are covertly intended to convert students to Christianity. Research by Pennycook and Coutand-Marin (2004) indicates that large numbers of U.S.-based Evangelical Protestant English-language mission schools are being established in remote non-Christian and non-Protestant communities everywhere around the world. They recount how some of these programs pursued their goal of converting local communities to Christianity by first luring unsuspecting and potentially resistant students with the offer of free or affordable lessons in English. In fact, some who publish in the field of TEML explicitly advocate using such intentional deception on the grounds that their desired ends (of religious conversion) justify duplicitous means.

Yet, even if the religious contents and conversion outcomes of such curricula are made explicit to students or their communities, if these programs avail people who have no other choices of education, it is unconscionable to pressure them to choose between their native religion and culture and the intrinsic desire we have as human beings to be educated – in English or any other language. It is no different than providing food to these students during a famine, but insisting that they first take communion and attend a church service. This is the antithesis of an unconditional act of charity or *caritas*, that is, love. Thus, it comes down to a question of informed choice: truly informed, real choice; anything else is an act of STEAL-ing.

This is not to impugn as STEAL-ing all religious-based education in the developing world; indeed, much of the education in these areas is only possible because it is subsidized or administered by religious organizations. For example, informed consent can be implied: (1) where the religion is indigenous or has had a presence in the community for centuries or (2) where English-language education is freely offered as charity, without expectation, pressure, or even, I would argue, hope on the part of teachers and administrators for students to convert. Many Roman Catholic schools in the developing world function as one of these two cases, for example, either as parishioner-sponsored schools in Catholic communities in the Philippines or as charitable mission schools in non-Catholic countries like India, where communities send children (often paying large tuitions fee) for generations without being pressured to convert.

TESOL's Promise: To TELL (Teach English as a Liberatory Language) or Not to TELL, That Is the Question

Across the Himalayas from Afghanistan, where I began this essay, Tibetans are engaged in an equally costly struggle with globalization and modernity. Their struggles too are colonial at root, arising from the Chinese colonization and occupation that began in 1949. Why is a 3-year-old Tibetan refugee child in the Indian Himalayas learning the English script alongside the Tibetan at such an early age, when so few people speak English in her community? What desires and expectations are being implanted by this early exposure to English? Is this a sign of additive, sustainable bilingualism, in which English is introduced to complement her native Tibetan language? Or is it a sign of subtractive bilingualism, and the imminent demise of the Tibetan language and culture? These are important questions to ask and answer, as more and more of these children become our students, overseas or here in Canada.

The key issue remains that individuals, families, and communities are complicit in the spread of English. This young Tibetan girl's parents have taught her the English alphabet alongside the Tibetan alphabet because they believe that it is necessary, that it will help her education and development. Learning English is associated with greater freedom and prosperity; it is a conduit to the 'global,' transnational network of education, justice, economic development, and mobility that is what liberation means to most people in the world. To refugees like the Tibetans, it can mean the difference between a life of underemployment in exile in an isolated Himalayan community or joining a growing number of Tibetan 'urban nomads,' whose English-language skills give them access to a transnational community of people who support their political, activist, religious, ecological, and economic aspirations and needs.

This paradoxical, ambiguous place of the English language in the lives of indigenous and developing world communities forces many TESOL/TEFL teachers and students alike to learn to resist as much as to master the English language in their education. Evidence of such resistance has been documented in South Africa (Norton Peirce, 1989), Sri Lanka (Canagarajah, 1993, 1999), and with Tibetan refugees in India (MacPherson, 2001b, 2003, 2005). I use the acronym TELL to suggest that, if English is to serve as a language of liberation, it needs to be offered and learned under terms of informed, ethical free choice: (1) 'informed' by research and thoughtful reflection, (2) 'ethical' in that students' and the local communities' interests come first, (3) 'free' to the extent that the choice is made on the basis of transparent program objectives and curricular outcomes, and (4) 'choice' in that students and/or their communities have viable options in the languages and curricular contents of their education. High on the list of information relevant to being 'informed' is the consistent call by educational and linguistic researchers for sustainable multilingual and intercultural education as a path to individual (Kim, 2001) and biolinguistic (Nettle and Romaine, 2000) well-being.

Dolma Ling: A Case Study of a Postcolonial, Intercultural Curriculum

When I discuss these issues at TESOL conferences or in classes or casual conversations with colleagues and students, occasionally there are comments on the depressing or discouraging effects of this research or knowledge. I could not disagree more, and find this response puzzling, to be frank. Would anyone say that we should not speak about history because it is depressing, or medicine because it is discouraging? Nevertheless, I realize that it is important to provide constructive cases of successful programs to complement critiques, so that consideration can be given for how to move forward not simply how to move away from past habits. This is the principle behind the identification of 'best practices,' and for this reason, I will illustrate a case of best practices in TESOL as TELL-ing, which demonstrates the kind of sustainable, multilingual ESOL and intercultural curriculum that is required of any effective postcolonial educational agenda.

Dolma Ling is an educational institution in the Indian Himalayas that serves Tibetan refugee and Himalayan Buddhist nuns. I had the good fortune to teach ESOL/EFL at Dolma Ling in 1992 and again in 1997–98 while conducting doctoral research. Most of the nuns who are drawn to live and study at Dolma Ling are interested in both traditional Buddhist and more modern, secular or professional education. Accordingly, a bilingual program was developed and implemented at Dolma Ling that offers comprehensive education in each language and course of study. On the one hand, the nuns follow the exacting curriculum of traditional Buddhist scholastic studies, which women were excluded from until

now. This involves the intensive study of five texts and topics occupying three to five years each in the 15- to 20-year program, including the
fascinating process of peer debating for up to two hours a day to
complement the textual and in-class studies. These studies emphasize
the cultivation of rational thinking, logical language, confidence, and
conceptual clarification. This curriculum relies on the highly specialized, academic form of the Tibetan language that is used to communicate Buddhist philosophy, logic, and debate.

Alongside this traditional Buddhist monastic curriculum is woven a
secular, English language–based modern curriculum that offers courses
in English, geography, world history, mathematics, and science, as well
as the Tibetan language and Tibetan history. Some of these courses are
taught exclusively in English, some in both Tibetan and English, and
some in Tibetan alone. To teach these courses, the administration hires
Tibetan teachers trained in the Indian universities or Tibetan teacher
education programs, and the occasional Western teacher to teach English on a short-term basis. By engaging in the two curricula within a
single academic program, these Tibetan Buddhist nuns have benefited
from the learning of English and Western discourse genres. Rather than
endangering their language and culture, they perceive such moderniza-
tions to be a way to enhance the sustainability of their own language
and culture (MacPherson, 2003). The exposure to English-language
education encourages them to reflect critically on their traditional education to be sure, as is characteristic of modernity.

Yet, the multilingual, intercultural curricular context for the introduction of English and modern subject areas at Dolma Ling cultivated
more than mere reflectivity; it generated the type of reflexivity Beck
asso-ciates with postmodernity, postcolonialism, and what Giddens
calls posttraditionalism (Beck, Giddens, & Lash, 1994). This is characterized by several conditions, including change that 'can quite well
take place without reflection, beyond knowledge and consciousness'
(ibid., p. 177). Therefore, although the two languages, cultures, and
curricula seemed to operate as distinct, unrelated courses of study,
these Tibetan Buddhist women and nuns showed signs of a transforming awareness arising from the intercultural contact. Principal among
these transformations were increased questioning and, as is common
in reflexive modernity, becoming 'ever more free of structure; in fact
they have to redefine structure (or as Giddens puts it, tradition) or,
even more radical, reinvent society and politics' (ibid.). This is not the
result of exposure to the modern curriculum per se, I would argue, but

rather the experience of negotiating a very strong, rational, literate, and structured traditional form of education alongside the modern curriculum. The reflexivity was as much or more the fruit of the Buddhist education as of modern, English education. I attribute this reflexivity arising from intercultural, multilingual curricula to the metacultural awareness that one needs to negotiate when moving across languages, cultures, and systems of knowledge (MacPherson, 2000, 2001a, 2005b).

Conclusion: Towards a Postcolonial Curriculum for the Teaching of English as Multilingual, Intercultural Education

My experiences at Dolma Ling impressed on me the need to move beyond the ideology and politics of teaching the English language (so eloquently discussed by Norrel London in the previous chapter) and promote English-language teaching in the developing world in the context of broader curricular objectives. In particular, it impressed on me the need to advocate for multilingual, multiliterate, and intercultural curricula as central to the postcolonial educational agenda. The language dimension of such an agenda is too readily overlooked by unilingual Anglophones who are accustomed to speaking to the world with insufficient self-awareness of the power and privilege that their language bestows on them. To learn another language is to enter a space of vulnerability, of listening and giving, ever so gradually, of succumbing with time to what can be a radically different worldview. Accordingly, this multilingual and intercultural postcolonial agenda for education is equally relevant to the so-called developed world.

Particularly fruitful are programs that attempt to integrate traditional and modern curricula, as suggested by Kanu (chap. 8, this volume). As in the case of Dolma Ling, the success of such programs is contingent on the indigenous or local peoples themselves having adequate control over the directions and development of the curricula and programs, with students willing and able to participate in forums for debating educational, linguistic, and cultural change. Even more challenging is the need to bring this same postcolonial curricular model home to North America, seat of the new imperialism. This is the ever-present challenge of a postcolonial agenda, which requires that we first: (1) break down centre-periphery distinctions and divides; (2) understand the necessity for reciprocity in all exchanges of culture, language, knowledge, and ecology; and finally, (3) accept as the premise of ethical practice that the diversity of the world is an inherent good. For, in the end, we do inhabit a shared planet, perhaps not the Blue Planet, but a common, interconnected home, nevertheless. Thus, it may very well be that our struggles with globalization, and with English as the language of globalization, ultimately become the struggle to understand our collective place in the universe. Yet, this struggle can lead us home, to appreciate how this collective struggle is entangled in our most intimate, personal lives, that is, our struggles to understand the singular and unique ecologies of the local languages, cultures, and communities that we encounter through the course of an ordinary day.

NOTES

1 These are acronyms used to describe the teaching of English to non-native speakers. There are many other areas in which acronyms are applied in the field as well. These acronyms stand for:

T/ESL: Teaching/English as a Second Language (Canada)
T/ESOL: Teaching/English to Speakers of Other Languages (United States)
T/EFL: Teaching/English as a Foreign Language (where English does not appear in the wider context)
T/EAL: Teaching/English as an Addition Language (Australia, UK, sometimes United States)
T/EIL: Teaching/English as an International Language (to participate in global culture)
T/ESP: Teaching/English for Specific Purposes
T/EML: Teaching/English as a Missionary Language
T/EIML: Teaching/English for Imperial or Military Purposes

REFERENCES

Abley, M. (2003). *Spoken here: Travels among threatened languages.* Toronto: Random House.

Beattie, A., & Ehrlich, P. (2001). *Wild solutions: How biodiversity is money in the bank.* New Haven: Yale University Press.

Beck, U., Giddens, A., & Lash, S. (1994). *Reflexive modernization: Politics, tradition, and aesthetics in the modern social order.* Stanford, CA: Stanford University Press.

Bennett, J. (1993). Cultural marginality: Identity issues in intercultural training. In R.M. Paige (Ed.), *Education for the intercultural experience* (pp. 109–36). Yarmouth, ME: Intercultural Press.

Berger, P. (2000). Four faces of global culture. In P. O'Meara, H. Mehlinger, & M. Krain (Eds.), *Globalization and the challenges of a new century* (pp. 419–27). Bloomington: Indiana University Press.

Block, D. (2002). 'McCommunication': A problem in the frame for SLA. In D. Block & D. Cameron (Eds.), *Globalization and language teaching* (pp. 117–33). London: Routledge.

Canagarajah, A.S. (1993). Critical ethnography of a Sri Lankan classroom: Ambiguities in student opposition to reproduction through ESOL. *TESOL Quarterly, 27*(4), 601–26.

Canagarajah, A.S. (1999). *Resisting linguistic imperialism in English teaching.* Oxford: Oxford University Press.

Canagarajah, A.S. (2002). Globalization, methods, and practice in periphery classrooms. In D. Block & D. Cameron (Eds.), *Globalization and language teaching* (pp. 134–50). London: Routledge.

Capra, F. (2002). *The hidden connections: Integrating the biological, cognitive, and social dimensions of life into a science of sustainability.* New York: Doubleday.

Crystal, D. (2000). *Language death.* Cambridge: Cambridge University Press.

Cummins, J. (1991). Conversational and academic language proficiency in bilingual contexts. In J.H. Hustijn & J.F. Matter (Eds.), *Reading in two languages, AILA Review, 8,* 75–89.

Cummins, J. (2001). *An introductory reader of the writings of Jim Cummins.* Toronto: Multilingual Matters.

Davis, W. (2001). *Light at the edge of the world: A journey through the realm of vanishing cultures.* Vancouver: Douglas and McIntyre.

Drohan, M., & Freeman, A. (2000). English rules. In P. O'Meara, H. Mehlinger, & M. Krain (Eds.), *Globalization and the challenges of a new century* (pp. 428–34). Bloomington, IN: Indiana University Press.

Edge, J. (2003). Imperial troopers and servants of the Lord: A vision of TESOL for the 21st century. *TESOL Quarterly, 37*(4), 701–709.

Ehrlich, P.R. (2000). *Human nature: Genes, cultures, and the human prospect.* Washington, DC: Island Press; Covelo, CA: Shearwater Books.

Giddens, A. (2000). *A runaway world: How globalization is reshaping our lives.* New York: Routledge, Chapman and Hall.

Gray, J. (1995). *Enlightenment's wake: Politics and culture at the close of the modern age.* London: Routledge.

Gregory, D. (1994). *Geographic imaginations.* Cambridge, MA: Blackwell.

Gross, D. (1992). *The past in ruins: Tradition and the critique of modernity.* Amherst: University of Massachusetts Press.

Heelas, P., Lash, S., & Morris, P. (Eds.). (1996). *Detraditionalization: Critical reflections on authority and identity.* Oxford: Blackwell.

Hobsbawm, E., & Ranger, T. (Eds.). (1983). *The invention of tradition.* Cambridge: Cambridge University Press.

Horodezsky, Z. (2004). Animals and vegetables. *TESL Canada Journal, 21*(2) 105–109.

Ignatieff, M. (2000). *The rights revolution.* Toronto, ON: Anansi Press.

Inglehart, R. (1997). *Modernization and postmodernization: Cultural, economic, and political change in forty-three societies.* Princeton, NJ: Princeton University Press.

Kelley, K.W. (1988). *The home planet.* New York: Addison-Wesley.

Kennedy, John F. (1963). Commencement address at American University 10 June 1963. Available at: http://www.jfklibrary.org/ifkquote.htm. Accessed 5 Dec. 2005.

Kim, Y.Y. (2001). *Becoming interculture: An integrative theory of communication and cross-cultural adaptation.* Thousand Oaks, CA: Sage.

Kim, Y.Y., Lujan, P., & Dixon, L. (1998a). 'I can walk both ways': Identity integration of American Indians in Oklahoma. *Human Communications Research, 25,* 252–274.

Kim, Y.Y., Lujan, P., & Dixon, L. (1998b). Patterns of communication and interethnic integration: A study of American Indians in Oklahoma. *Canadian Journal of Native Education, 22*(1), 120–37.

Kumaravadivelu, B. (2001). Toward a postmethod pedagogy. *TESOL Quarterly, 35,* 537–560.

Lo Bianco, J. (2000). Multiliteracies and multilingualism. In B. Cope & M. Kalantzis (Eds.), *Multiliteracies: Literacy learning and the design of social futures* (pp. 92–106). New York: Routledge

Loy, D. Religion and the market. *The religious consultation on population, reproductive health and ethnics.* Available at: www.religiousconsultation.org/ publication.htm. Accessed 5 Dec. 2005.

MacPherson, S. (1997). Ngugi wa Thiong'o: An African vision of linguistic and cultural pluralism. *TESOL Quarterly, 31*(3), 641–645.

MacPherson, S. (2000). *A path of learning: Indo-Tibetan Buddhism as education.* Unpublished doctoral dissertation, Centre for the Study of Curriculum and Instruction, University of British Columbia, Vancouver.

MacPherson, S. (2001a). An alternative enlightenment praxis: Tibetan Buddhist monastic education. *International Journal of Curriculum and Instruction, 3*(1), 97–114.

MacPherson, S. (2001b). A genre to remember: Tibetan popular poetry and song as remembrance. *Language and Literacy: A Canadian Educational e-Journal.* http://educ.queensu.ca (23 pages).

MacPherson, S. (2003). Biolinguistic for biolinguistic sustainability: The ecology of English as a lingua mundi. *TESOL, 20*(2), 1–22.

MacPherson, S. (2005a). Researching liminal English: Identity, resistance, and the 'strange' in TESOL. *Journal of Curriculum Theorizing, 21*(1), 39–56.

MacPherson, S. (2005b). Negotiating language contact and identity change in a bilingual Tibetan/English program. *TESOL Quarterly, 39*(3), 1–16.

Nettle, D., & Romaine, S. (2000). *Vanishing voices: The extinction of the world's languages.* New York: Oxford University Press.

Nisker, W. (1998). *Buddha's nature.* New York: Bantam.

Norris, M.J. (1998). Canada's aboriginal languages. *Canadian Social Trends.* Ottawa: Statistics Canada, cat. no. 11-008, 8–16.

Norris, M.J. (2004). From generation to generation: Survival and maintenance of Canada's Aboriginal languages, within families, communities and cities. *TESL Canada Journal, 21*(2), 1–16.

Norton Peirce, B. (1989). Toward a pedagogy of possibility in the teaching of English International: People's English in South Africa. *TESOL Quarterly, 23*(3), 401–402.

Pennycook, A., & Coutand-Marin, S. (2004). Teaching English as a missionary language (TEML). *Discourse: Studies in the cultural politics of education, 24,* 337–353.

Ray, P., & Anderson, S.R. (2000). *The cultural creatives: How 50 million people are changing the world.* New York: Harmony Books.

Rees, W. (1999). Patch disturbance, ecofootprints, and biological integrity: Revisiting *The Limits to Growth* – Or, why industrial society is inherently unsustainable. The Integrity Project, University of British Columbia, Vancouver.

Rees, W. (2002). Globalization and sustainability: Conflict or convergence? *Bulletin of Science, Technology and Society, 22*(4), 249–268.

Shiva, V. (1993). *Monocultures of the mind: Perspectives on biodiversity and biotechnology.* London: Zed Books; Penang, Malaysia: Third World Network.

Skutnabb-Kangas, T. (2000). *Linguistic genocide in education – or worldwide diversity and human rights?* Mahwah: Erlbaum.

Skutnabb-Kangas, T., & Phillipson, R. (Eds.). (1995). *Linguistic human rights: Overcoming linguistic discrimination.* Berlin: Mouton de Gruyter.

Smith, D.G. (1999). Economic fundamentalism, globalization, and the public remains of education. *Interchange: A Quarterly Review of Education, 30*(1), 93–117.

Snow, C.P. (1998). *The two cultures*. Cambridge: Cambridge University Press. (Originally published in 1959)

Thompson, W.I. (1990). *Imaginary landscape*. New York: St Martin's Press.

Wilson, E.O. (1992). *The diversity of life*. New York: W.W. Norton.

Wilson, E.O. (1998). *Consilience: The unity of knowledge*. New York: Vintage Books.

Worldwatch Institute. (2002). *State of the world, 2002: A Worldwatch Institute report on progress toward a sustainable society*. New York: W.W. Norton.

3 High School Postcolonial: As the Students Ran Ahead with the Theory

JOHN WILLINSKY

Not long ago, I walked into a grade 12 English class in a Vancouver high school as anxious and uncertain as a new teacher showing up at the initial practicum posting. Though away from school teaching for close to two decades, I was about to step up to the front of the room and teach the assembled class what I knew very well in theory but was entirely uncertain about how best to implement over three weeks of daily English classes. This is not, however, the story of my faltering efforts to teach secondary school English. It is rather the story of how much farther the students were able to go with my efforts to introduce them to what postcolonial theory might mean for an English class. It is the story that follows on the teaching of poetry a few years earlier, as I came to realize how far I have still to go in catching up with the lessons students in this class were ready to invoke about a world in which the legacy of European imperialism was so readily made present in their lives. It is about a teacher in theory slowly catching on to, and catching up with, the lessons of practice. It was about the limits of my theory given students' readiness to practise it in the classroom.

Of course, there was nothing new about wanting to teach the young about the age of empire. In history classes, students learn about David Livingstone and Henry Stanley in Africa, of Francis Drake and James Cook in the Pacific. In literature, they may read Rudyard Kipling's poetry for its heroic smugness or William Golding's novel *Lord of the Flies* to expose the savagery ascribed to others that lies beneath the veneer of Western civilization. More daring teachers may take them through colonial themes in Joseph Conrad's *Heart of Darkness* or Shakespeare's *Tempest*. However, what I had come to teach that Grade 12 classroom about was the aftermath of empire. The postcolonial theory I travelled with was all about how we mislead students by teaching such history as if it were past, just as we mislead them by suggesting that the schools were ever idle spectators in this imperial pageant, operating at a safe distance from the unfolding of the great colonial empire.

The postcolonial theory I carried up to that high school was concerned with how, in theory, schooling was an endemic and vital part of empire-building, from the cities of the motherland to the far-flung reaches of the empire. The schools had long been places for learning the order and ideology of empire at almost every turn, from the Euclidean roots of mathematics to the racial taunts flung around the schoolyard. However, nations now stand where there were once only colonies, and the colonizers' great cities are now home to the once-colonized. There may seem little point in going on about colonial legacies. That was then and this is now. What is needed now, some may well say, is to direct progressive curriculum efforts toward understanding the realities of the new empires, driven by economic globalism, knowledge economies, and terrorist resistances.

My interest in creating a deliberately *postcolonial* curriculum is that we do not so easily forget what lives on, out of this history, especially as it bears on education's special role in that history. Many of the prejudices and stereotypes that students suffer from reflect well-schooled lessons from the age of empire about the character of difference, whether difference by culture, language, or race. These prejudices are in the educational air we breath, with trace elements found in *National Geographic* specials, and with levels that approach toxicity in Disney movies, such as *Ali Baba and the Forty Thieves*. Yet that legacy is also radically marked by changes in the student body of the high school where I was headed to teach, in the former 'white settler colony' of Canada.[1]

Yet that is not what had come immediately to mind when Frank Goldman, a high school teacher in Vancouver, proposed that I come into his Grade 12 English class and do something about all that had so concerned me in writing about imperialism in education (Willinsky, 1998). Here I was suddenly confronted by the classic challenge posed by the concerned school teacher to the no-less-concerned theorist and former school teacher. What are *we* going to do about this legacy in the classroom? And more specifically, what are *we* going to do about it this Monday, with a Grade 12 English class that was about to engage in a unit on poetry? What came immediately to mind, when Frank raised the prospect of joining his class, was nothing at all. I was not prepared with ready answers about where exactly one jumps right in with postcolonial lessons, in a classroom which had lessons in poetry, drama, and novels to cover before the Grade 12 provincial examinations were upon them.

English was not the mother tongue of many of the students, and calling the course, as we typically do, 'English,' is misleading, as you already need a good mastery of English to be able to take the class, which is really a study of English literature. It is the study of a relatively narrow band of creative works in English that are taken to define qualities of English culture, imagination, and artfulness. English class is where this work is taught as if to bring the young into what is rightfully theirs or to make it clear that, by dint of class or cultural background, it is a greatness they can at best learn to appreciate. If the imperial legacy lives on in the curriculum of today, then the ways in which it lives on – at the core of the educational experience – needs to be part of what students and teachers explore and learn about, rather than ignore and pretend was never there.

At one level, it does not matter what the poetry is about, since it will be taught as another form of IQ test. Poetry classes often take the form of cognitive-aerobics. 'Alright class, let's puzzle this out together? Reach with me for the conceit in the first line. Stretch for that final metaphor.' This would seem to neutralize any poetic promotion of an English empire based on the delicacy of effect and sensitivity to form in the language of the conquerors. Such ideological effects are displaced in high school English by the attention given to vocabulary quizzes, device-naming and structure-detection. Students are called upon in the literature class to solve the quadratic equation of the quatrain, the calculus of metaphor and anapest (if the rising sun is a metaphor for the glory of found love, then …). It has been transformed from an aesthetic experience into a hard-nosed exercise of pattern recognition in decoding difficult scripts, with all of the gendered implications of such moves. The poem in the classroom resembles for many students nothing so much as computer code running down the page, accompanied by plenty of white space. It is code for a program that continues to effectively discriminate among students.

Yet not only are Edmund Spencer's or John Milton's higher cultural purpose subordinated to a matter of identifying the theme as one of many poetic devices by this approach, but poetry's very claim to being a universal form of expression is obscured by this concentrated attention on the literary canon of one language. Yet if poetry is often taught at a remove from its greater purpose and claim, these other qualities are never entirely absent, which is why the postcolonial curricular moment needs to be realized at some point in the student's education.

After all , the very roots of poetry's place in the school curriculum run back to the colonizing mission of education, headed by such emblematic figures as Thomas Macaulay and Matthew Arnold (which I hope I will be forgiven for introducing once more into my work). In his 1835 Minute to the British Parliament on education for India, the historian Thomas Macaulay made a persuasive case for teaching English and English literature to a certain class of Indian students, 'a class who may be interpreters between us and the millions whom we govern – a class of persons Indian in blood and colour, but English in tastes, in opinions, in morals and intellect' (Macaulay, 1971, p. 190). As Gauri Viswanathan would have it, the teaching of English literature in colonial India served as a 'mask of conquest,' which was worn in the hope that it might convince Indian students how principled, humane and civilized these colonizers were, even as the study of literature was turned by the British 'into an instrument for ensuring industriousness, efficiency, trustworthiness, and compliance in native subjects' (1989, p. 93). Later in the nineteenth century, poet and school inspector Matthew Arnold can be found promoting the teaching of poetry as a necessary bromide for children in the charity schools of Great Britain, for which he was an inspector, as he assured the government of how 'good poetry does undoubtedly tend to form the soul and character; it tends to beget a love of beauty and of truth in alliance together; it suggests however indirectly noble principles of actions, and it inspires emotions so helpful in making principles operative' (1908, p. 60). Of course, this now seems a distant and far-off time, and in its most blatant sense this poetic mask of conquest has passed. English poetry is taught to everyone in English-language schools. Similarly the canon has expanded to include more local representation of poetic expression. My argument is that it is not that all of this history can be undone, as if to recover the true teaching of poetry, but that this pedagogical history can figure in the teaching.

Take the textbook itself that Frank Goldman gave me to use with his Grade 12 class. Entitled *Theme and Image: An Anthology of Poetry / Book II*, it was published by Copp Clark Pitman in Toronto. The late Copp Clark publishing house dated back to a stationery store in the colonial city of Toronto in 1841, and was later owned by the British-based conglomerate Pearson and thus suffered its own form of neo-imperialism. The anthology is designed for the senior grades of high school, and begins its thematic set of chapters with one entitled 'Canadian Identity,' followed by 'Canadian Landscape,' before going on to 'Nature,' the 'Sea,' 'Time' – and you can imagine the rest. The two opening chapters take their own postcolonial stand. The Canadian Literature movement, which broke the spell of the English greats and created a space for Canadian authors, who could then be taught as Canadian Literature (also known as Canlit), was itself a modestly emancipatory product of the 1960s, constituting its own postcolonial move, its own declaration of independence. *Theme and Image* opens with 'Poem on Canada,' by Patrick Anderson:

What are you ...? They ask, in wonder.
And she replies in the worst silence of all her woods:
I am Candida with the cane wind.

Here is the poetic representation of this land's silence, woods, and whiteness (at the root of *Candida*) – 'America's attic ... a cold kingdom' – in which the British expatriate Anderson stayed for a few years, teaching at McGill University before heading off to Singapore and then back to London. So runs the poetry of this Canadian identity theme. There is Earle Birney's 'Canada: Case History,' which begins, 'This is a case of a high-school land / deadset in adolescence,' and F.R. Scott's 'Laurentian Shield,' whose final verse concludes 'O Canada, O Canada, Oh can / A day go by without new authors springing / To paint the native maple.' It is sometimes cranky, self-critical (self-loathing?) stuff, yet this theme of Canadian identity stands, in its way, as a free-verse declaration of independence, running over the first ten pages of this long-standing anthology.

I might well have tried to teach *Theme and Image* to the Grade 12 students of that classroom, just as it might well have been taught to me when it was first published thirty-five years ago while I was still in high school. Given the book's near-historic status, it certainly did constitute its own postcolonial artefact of Canada's development and self-assertion. Where did we turn in those years of independence movements – including the 'quiet revolution' that led to Quebec's linguistic and cultural status as a *distinct society* – to define ourselves, I might well ask the students. Where did we seek to make a name for ourselves: to landscapes of woods and snow, to Andersons and Scotts? Although, to be fair, there is a poem in that first section about a rocking chair which is by A.M. Klein that gives a hint of ethnic diversity in this land.[2] And

Canadian women poets figure in the Canadian landscape section, with Anne Marriott's 'Prairie Graveyard' and P.K. Page's 'T-Bar' with its 'while far behind / etching the sky-line, obdurate and sloe / the spastic T-bars pivot and descend.'

The history which this anthology represents is my own, replete with riding the T-bar up snowy hills, and the integration of Jews into the mainstream of Canadian society. The anthology upholds the educated sensibility present in the European descendents that largely governs this land and its institutions. Yet it is a history that is otherwise unspoken in the teaching of these poems. Poetry anthologies such as this one are not taught as an effort to form Canada. *Theme and Image* might have well served in the teaching of postcolonial lessons, in how its selection of Canadian poets struck out against an earlier educational history. Not that its selectivity was representative then, let alone now, of the contemporary Canadian landscape of these students' lives or the teachers for that matter.

But as teachable as that textbook's historical moment might be, I decided not to teach from it. Instead, having realized that the textbook was itself an issue, and that I, who was stepping into the high school but for a moment, needed to make some larger contribution, to cover my long-standing absence. After all, the very age of the anthology also spoke to a place for new textbooks in the English program. More than that, the school clearly needed an alternative, supplementary anthology of poetry. This was not about the dated quality of *Theme and Image*, nor with its Shakespearean sonnets singing of how 'love's not Time's fool' or Dylan Thomas declaiming that 'death shall have no dominion.' It was about extending the anthology's very project of gathering poetry that reflected Canadian identity and landscape, among other themes.

If the class was not really about *English*, but about the poetic uses of language, and if the class was intended to build on students' experience of language and culture, then it made perfect sense to create an anthology that did a better job of recognizing the global shifts that have accompanied this postcolonial era, most notably creating a recognition of the growing diversity of the community. The school needed another anthology. It needed an anthology that was, first, multilingual, and second, contained the original language and a translation into English. The original languages would need to be present and accounted for, as they constitute a part of both a global and a Canadian linguistic landscape. The languages would represent the school and community as part of a constant global flow of people who constitute at any given moment the nation. It was meant to signal a further moving away from cultural legacies of colonialism that marked this land. After all, in Vancouver, the majority of the students do not speak either of Canada's official languages, English or French, as a mother tongue. This alternative anthology would not need to hold that this land was bound in the imagery of snow and leaf. It would deal in translation and, by analogy, in the translated experiences, perceptions, and places that are so much a part of this city perched on the edge of the Pacific Ocean.

My first class with the students began awkwardly enough, with Frank introducing this stranger from the university who was stepping into the class's well-established routines and expectations. I started with a short lesson on Matthew Arnold's 'Dover Beach' from *Theme and Image*. I did this for continuity's sake, mine and theirs. I found myself trying to find my feet, in exploring what Arnold's poem might be about – 'swept with confused alarms of struggle and flight / where ignorant armies clash by night.' I quickly felt how many years it had been since I had worked with what was, at least initially for the new teacher, the sullen indifference of adolescence. We did little enough with Arnoldean concerns about culture and anarchy (composed, as speculation has it, during the last night of his honeymoon), before I closed the poetry book, having decided to jump right in with the idea for a new anthology.

I told the students how *Theme and Image* had served well enough when I was a high school student. It was one of many attempts for Canada to give a poetic name for itself. However, the country's understanding of itself had changed, and after thirty years, and in response to the need for a new textbook, we were going to create an alternative poetry anthology that spoke in many languages. It would be one small step in righting the misrepresentation that resulted from a lack of money for new books. I played, as well, on the students being in their final year of high school, as I spoke of them leaving behind a legacy, a mark, that had the potential to perhaps change some small part of what went on at their school after they had left.

After three decades of *Theme and Image*, it was time to introduce, at the very least, a supplementary text.[3] Our new anthology would offer an alternative, a supplement, rather than a cultural revolution. It was designed in a careful and calculated way to increase the chances that it would be used by teachers to expand the education of students in this school. How could we expect teachers to begin to use this new collection if it bore no resemblance to the collections they were so accustomed to using? The road to change, I might have said melodramatically, begins with a single step in a still-familiar landscape.

We went briefly back into *Theme and Image* to see what had made it such a long-standing and well-used textbook. There was the poetry, certainly. A poetry anthology indeed had to have its share of carefully chosen poetry, based on the editor's judgment. Each student in this class was going to have to provide just such a poem, in its original language and in translation, or multiple translations, as we talked about literal and poetic renderings of one language into another. And given the newness of much of this work for our intended audience, they would have to present a defence of why it warranted inclusion. *Theme and Image* also had short biographies of the poets, at the back of the book, along with explanations of tricky and archaic vocabulary and concepts in the poems. We would do the same for each poem in our anthology. Was there anything more that makes a textbook a textbook?

One student suggested that there should also be questions at the end of each poem or at the back of the anthology for assigning in class. As it was, *Theme and Image* did not have questions at the back. They may have been in the teacher's guide, which had been lost over the years. We agreed that questions would cinch the deal for many teachers. It would make our anthology something that teachers would seriously consider using to teach. Finally, I suggested that they include some of the ingredients – the critical frameworks and poetic devices, from metaphor to meter – that would be on the provincial examinations in English, which were written in their final high school year. I did want this postcolonial curricular turn to contribute to the more traditional measures of academic success. In this way, we moved in and out of this postcolonial theme, letting it guide the overall project, letting it disappear from view, as with the students' actual choice of poems.

To provide the students with a starting point, I brought in a series of bilingual poetry books. A number of students turned to the Web, as well as their own collections of poetry in the form of lyrics. The result was the forty-two-page, *Word and World: An Anthology of Poetry,* which was 'produced by F. Goldman's English 12 Class.' The anthology consists of seventeen poems with translation into English, accompanied by the students' introductions, interpretations, and questions. The students who produced the anthology included this statement, by way of introduction to the project: 'Although the poetry in Pt. Grey's standard issue Grade 12 anthology is wonderful and immortal, it is not reflective of the place and times in which it is being studied. Thus, we produced this booklet of poems from other cultures to help enrich the poetic experience of future Grade 12 students at the school.'

In finding her contribution to the anthology, Alyssa Mann turned to her parents to translate one of the famous songs by the German poet Heinrich Heine (1827). It begins, in their translation, 'You are like a flower / So sweet and beautiful and pure' (Du bist wie eine Blume / So holt und Schon und rein). 'Since my background is German,' Alyssa explained about her choice of Heine, 'I thought it would be a good opportunity to learn more about him.' And in her interpretation, she offers that the poem's narrator 'becomes filled with sadness because he does not feel that something so perfect could be so real.'

Eunice Chen brought in 'Returning Home,' one of the famous poems by He Zhi-zhang (659–744) from the Tang Dynasty, which schoolchildren in China have been learning for centuries. Although this poem has been translated into English many times, Eunice translated it herself, carefully preserving the seven-syllable line structure:

> Return home at an old age.
> Vernacular did not change.
> Children don't know who I am,
> Asking, 'Where are you from, sir?'

She also provided a Mandarin phonetic translation in her entry in the anthology, which the class followed when she presented the poem orally to the class. She explained to the students the choices that she made in translating the Chinese language characters. The sense of her pride in the lesson she taught us that afternoon may not have been captured all that well in our anthology, although she did include an illustration of a ceramic Ferghana horse from the Tang Dynasty to accompany her entry.

Drawing on the strong Hong Kong–Vancouver connection, another student, Gloria Leung, chose 'Art and Truth' by Andrew Parkin, from a bilingual and bi-national collection of poems by Parkin and Laurence Wong. In their collection *Hong Kong Poems* (1997), Parkin and Wong, both Canadian poets living in Hong Kong, contributed poems in English and Chinese respectively. The book features facing-page translations into the other language, some translated into Chinese by Wong himself, although not vice versa. Gloria picked up on this bi-national and bilingual context, in her choice of Parkin's poem, 'Art and Truth,' for as Gloria explained in her notes on the poem, art 'learns from different cultures and develops its own styles (1997, p. 109). It accepts new ideas readily and changes them to new forms.' She concluded her reading of Parkin's poem with her own algebraic translation-equation of the poem's theme, while playing on its title: 'Art + Truth = Life + Value.'

For his contribution to the anthology, Jason Watkins chose the poem 'Arcadia' by Carmen Rodríguez, a former Chilean who was now living in Vancouver, after being forced into exile in 1973 by the Pinochet regime (Rodríguez, 1992, p. 63). This poem, written in Spanish, introduces the theme of Canada as a home for political refugees who arrive, carrying with them memories of those who stayed behind. Rodríguez's poem, 'Arcadia,' is about the death of a Chilean freedom fighter in 1979: 'The day of your death ... you came at me like gunfire / clamor / chill.' Jason knew no Spanish; nevertheless, he not only included the original Spanish version and the translation (by Heidi Neufeld Raine) from the bilingual volume in which he found the poem, but he went on to provide his own 'literal translation' of 'Arcadia.' It was a move that reflected a further engagement with the poem, as he turned the translated lines, 'The day of your death ... you came at me like gunfire / clamour / chill,' into 'But when you died it shook me I can't comprehend.' In his analysis of the poem, Jason noted how 'Carmen uses fragments of ideas both to emphasize her lack of first hand knowledge of her subject, and also to effectively create strong images of Arcadia's heroism.' Jason was careful to introduce the dictatorship of General Augusto Pinochet as the context of this heroic death. Yet clearly more could have been done in the class to consider the toppling of the democratically elected Allende government in Chile by Pinochet, with American support, which forms its own codicil on neo-imperialism.

A number of students played with this idea of creating a poetry anthology of different languages and cultures by bringing in contemporary song lyrics from their favorite musicians. The student, T.J. Hobbs, for example, selected 'I Used to Love H.E.R.,' by the hip-hop artist Common (1994). As T.J. explained in the comments to the anthology, 'even though this song was meant for the underground rap community, I think Common's message should be shared with everyone.' He also explained to readers that 'whereas 10 years ago rap music was neither respected nor appreciated as a real form of music, now it is considered one of the leading influences in the music world.' T.J. boiled down Common's lines and rhymes to a simple, singular message which is, in T.J.'s words, 'I am going to keep my message alive.' He took Common's sexual references – 'she didn't have a body but she started gettin thick quick' – that turned disturbingly violent and vulgar at times in the poem, and recast them as metaphor: 'Throughout the entire poem,' T.J. wrote, 'Common talks about a lady, however the lady is just a metaphor for hip-hop.' Common's poem does end on just such a note: 'But I'm a take her back hopin that the shit stop / Cause who I'm talkin bout y'all is hip-hop.' T.J. made it clear in his commentary that he recognized that Common's regard for women bears some critical scrutiny, given the traditions of this genre, and his 'translation' was directed at emphasizing just what Common is taking issue with, as T.J. rendered a couple of lines from the poem this way: 'The focus of hip-hop has changed from black culture to shooting guns / selling drugs and making money.'

Another student, Paul Kilinski, also took me at my word about the need for cultural expansion. He chose an excerpt from *The Seventh Octave* by the hip-hop poet Saul Williams (1998). The excerpt begins with: 'I spoon powdered drum beats into plastic bags / sellin' kilos of kente scag' (Paul's translation: 'I place powerful drugs into plastic bags / I sell kilos of drugs'). In providing a series of questions for this poem, Paul asked whether someone unfamiliar with hip-hop culture could understand a poem such as this, and whether the reader was 'in agreement with' his simplified English translation, 'or would you interpret it different?' Paul pointed out how Saul Williams 'constantly travels the country, giving children at schools an introduction to a culture of poetry beyond the usual classroom books dedicated almost exclusively to dead white men.'

In creating this project, I had not foreseen students reaching into their music collection to make 'a poetry book from different cultures,' as T.J. put it in the introduction to his poem. My first thought was that these students were taking the easy path to this idea of creating an anthology of poetry in translation. But such thoughts only reflected, I can now see, my shortsightedness and failure to immediately grasp the African-American contribution to the postcolonial project, both in the very literal sense of slavery's role in empire and in the recognition of the civil rights movement by the U.S. government as part of a cold war ploy in securing the allegiance of the independence movements in Africa. That rap, not to mention jazz, blues, gospel, and rock 'n 'roll, had moved from an initial state of neither respect nor appreciation from the dominant culture, as T.J. pointed out, to recognition as leading influences in the music world, is another indication of a shift in the empire of culture.

Two white students, if not more of the class, were attuned to the 'underground rap community,' in T.J.'s words, or as Paul affirmed, 'I share a passion for the culture of hip-hop and all the elements that surround it.' It is a culture that is no less involved in living out a segment of the history that had inspired this postcolonial class project. The articulate defiance that marks hip-hop's cultural claim was very much in the face of the pervasive history and cultural tradition which I sought to address with the students in that English class. That does not prevent a questioning of the misogyny or drug abuse in hip-hop or in their particular selection of lyrics for this collection, as T.J. foresaw. I might have asked Paul which poems Saul Williams used for his work in the schools, as a way of exploring how hip-hop is represented, outside of its more troubling themes. Still, through their choices, the students had moved far ahead of my original position on what the school needed by way of a new poetry anthology for Canadian schools.

I was only able to catch up with where the students had run with this postcolonial theory well after our work together was over, as I now come to write up and make greater sense of my time in Frank's classroom. Even if T.J. and Paul did not think of hip-hop in anything approaching postcolonial terms, these two students were clearly drawn to what this musical form represented and resisted in a broader sense. They saw hip-hop as having an edge with 'roots ... in urban America in the 1970s,' to draw from Paul's notes. Just as I was tempted initially to write off their choice of song lyrics to translate for the likes of me as youthful rebelliousness, their move had helped me begin to see hip-hop in far more of a historical light. My own education, then, had been extended by the students' curriculum choices, speaking to the worth of this poetry unit that I had not foreseen. It would not be the only time in this project that I would prove too slow on the uptake – if willing to learn at a later point – as the students intuitively moved ahead of me on this postcolonial theme and on what I had imagined for this project.

This leads to me to Sabry Husayn's choice of 'The Martyr,' by Abdelrahim Mahmud (1937) for the anthology, a poem which she found on the Web. The poem, originally in Arabic, and first published in 1937, begins: 'I will carry my soul in my hand / And throw it in the valleys of death.' Sabry explained in her notes how Abdelrahim Mahmud was a professor of Arabic literature at Al-Najah who left his university job to fight against the British Mandate. He went on to take military training, before being killed in a battle 'against the Zionists' near Al-Nasirah (Nazereth) in 1948. She noted the irony of the opening image of the soul carried into battle 'because the soul is an inner-spirit and philosophical belief and not a physical object that can be carried.' Sabry was also taken with the poet's passion to 'protect his land, his people,' as she sought to understand the theme of martyrdom: 'He states that a man has certain duties in life, and without accomplishing those duties has no reason to live and therefore should surrender and give up his life.' Or as Mahmud puts it in his poem, 'The noble man's soul has two goals / To die or achieve its dreams.'

Nowhere is it more clear how, in working with the class on this project, I was capable of missing the full import of the students' selections, even as I was caught up in working with Frank and the class, helping the students, in selecting and setting up the poems. Here, with Sabry Husayn's selection of Mahmud's poem, the force of this postcolonial theory was coming to a head. Here, the project moved out of an abstract poetics and into the bloodied headlines of martyrdom that was very much alive in the struggle between Israelis and Palestinians, as well as elsewhere in the Middle East. The press has certainly carried many reports on how the suicide bombers in Palestine are given a martyr's treatment.[4] Sabry must have given some thought to the martyr question, as she read about Mahmud's predicting, in effect, his own sacrifice in defending the Arab cause a half-century earlier and in light of the Palestinian suicide bombings that were an all-too-regular part of the news at that time, only to increase – including some carried out by young women very close to the same age as Sabry. Yet Mahmud was a soldier who met his 'enemies' on the battlefield, so there are distinctions to be made here that could have been explored within the context of this poem and the public space of the classroom.

In the final section of the accompanying materials Sabry prepared for 'The Martyr,' she posed the question: 'Why do you think the poet used the title "The Martyr"?' Explaining the poet's choice of a title is not an unusual question for a textbook anthology, but in this case the answers are bound to raise troubling issues over the Palestinian struggle. Even if one were to play it academically safe with an etymological explanation, one discovers how the Greek root of the English word refers to *witness*, as the martyr's death, even as it silences this witness, provides its own powerful testimony that turns us all into witnesses to the martyr's beliefs, or as Mahmud states in his poem: 'When I speak, all the world listens.' We have since learned a lot more about how death speaks out of this still unfolding history that holds its own still contemporary chapter in the national self-determination struggles that mark the postcolonial era.

The urgency of that historic struggle was only going to increase with the tragic events of 11 September 2001, which had yet to happen when we worked on the anthology. The impact of Abdelrahim Mahmud's poem has a way of reverberating through a number of the students' selections in this small collection of poems, even as it speaks prophetically to what has become a defining theme of our current post–9-11 age. That horrific event also has a way of giving new meaning to Spanish poet Frederico Garcia Lorca's poem, 'Dawn,' selected by Stephen Forseti for the anthology, a poem which deals with the overwhelming force of New York City on the imagination: 'Dawn in New York grieves / on the towering stairs / ... And staggering there in the suburbs, the insomniacs, / as though lately escaped from a bloody disaster' (Lorca, 1955, p. 63).

It also has a way of adding to a reading of Kahlil Gibran's poem 'Faith,' which Rachel Richter included in the collection.[5] In this poem, Gibran attests to the strength of his beliefs in the face of powerful adversaries. Gibran, who was born in Lebanon of Syrian Christian parents in 1883 and lived in the United States for most of his life, was involved in the political struggle to free Lebanon from the Ottoman Empire prior to the First World War. This selection from Gibran complicates the commonly held idea of him as a spiritual poet by alluding to the postcolonial context that informed his work.

Rachel included a photograph of Nelson Mandela with a child to accompany her commentary on the poem. She sought to turn away from the battle and bullets – 'And bullets able to shatter / My faith / Do not exist' – that figure in the poem and towards the poem's equally strong affirmation of life – 'A joyous thrill / to be alive.' The image of Mandela acts as its own point of postcolonial interpretation of the poem, on Rachel's part, as it securely locates Gibran's faith within the struggle for self-determination and human rights, in the name of a new generation. And this faith – 'My faith / That tomorrow / Life will be finer / Life will be wiser' – is what Rachel ultimately held to as she concluded that the poem is about how 'you must always believe that tomorrow will be finer, wiser and worth the battle.' Of course, it is that sense of battle which has continued to take on no less of a literal sense since Lebanon's struggle against the Ottoman Empire, which so concerned Gibran.

The question that remains for me is how, then, do we begin to talk about the force and passion that Sabry and Rachel spoke of as underwriting this poetry in light of the contemporary historical context? How does the poetry itself provide its own window into what are among the most alarming events of the day? The poems which these and other students gathered gives more than an inkling of the feelings and interpretations that connect and divide people today. They give the faceless struggle, which only encourages our tendency to write people off in easily feared stereotypes, a poetic, human dimension. Mahmud and Gibran are not removed by their poetry from historical struggles, but their poetry keeps those struggles from becoming simplified abstractions. And poetry's way of doing that was clearly part of the lesson I missed sharing with the students.

It might have begun with what is so strongly felt and so clearly expressed by the poet, and moved from those emotions to the historical contexts, to what might seem the reasons and causes, and then back again to their expression in the lines of the poetry. Without trying to arrive at a consensus about the rights and wrongs, or even asking students to take a stand on the issues in their English 12 class, we might have considered the role of poetry in these struggles, in what this particular form of writing was able to express and convey. Creating that sort of open and public space for discussing what we had created with this anthology and what it conveyed about the world would have been the educational challenge and goal, really, for the teacher.

For example, it was also a small step from the history surrounding Abdelrahim Mahmud's 'The Martyr' to Laura Ambrose's contribution to the anthology, when she selected the traditional Yiddish poem 'Little Boy, Little Boy,' translated by Miriam Hartman Flacks (Kohn & Flacks, 1999, pp. 96–8). Laura found this poem in a collection of photographs of children by Roman Vishniac as part of his extensive and poignant photographic record of Eastern European Jewry which he took in the years leading up to the Second World War. Laura included in the anthology a photocopy of one of Vishniac's photos of a young child with the poem ('Little boy, little boy, where did you go ...'), along with the Yiddish in both Hebrew and Roman alphabetic scripts. The historical connections among this small, seemingly chance, selection of poetry makes its own powerful statement. What I can see now that I could not see then is the potential for discussing with the class the elements of history that come into play with this poetry, not with the intent of somehow resolving or deciding the right and wrong of these matters, but of momentarily coming closer to them through the poetry.

Let me offer a final instance, as the students' anthology also contained a poem by the Pakistani poet Ishaat Aafreen from an Urdu collection (Aafreen, 1991, p. 149). Aafreen's poem, 'Dialogue with an Incomplete Man,' forms a further point of connection with Mahmud's 'The Martyr' and Gibran's 'Faith.' As Stephen Glanzberg, who chose the poem for the anthology (from a book which I happened to bring to the class), explained in his notes, Aafreen is identified as part of a feminist resistance to the wave of fundamentalist Islam that arose in the 1980s in Pakistan and through the Persian Gulf region. 'Dialogue with an Incomplete Man' speaks to another form of martyrdom, which is not identified this time by nation or by faith, but by gender: 'You are merely / a boy, for whom / weeping girls ... provide sadistic solace.'[6] Aafreen's poem provides a further commentary on the unfolding of a larger world which had yet to find a place in the schooling of these students, even as that world is both removed from and a part of their lives. It is, perhaps, too easy to see something more than is really there in what the students pulled together with this collection, as the Western world now scrambles to know something more of Islam. It may be enough to say that this history was already part of our lives, long before any single event brought these issues into the headlines.

The defining historical theme of postcolonialism is self-determination, which it shares with feminism and other human rights movements. It began with the spirit of nationalism in India, Africa and Southeast Asia, and the force of that spiritual nationalism, which fires Mahmud's poem, is no less relevant today in thinking about the self-determination of the Palestinian people. Lest anyone object that such nationalist chauvinism has no place in a class on poetry, it is well to recall that the school's official textbook anthology, *Theme and Image*, was making its own nationalistic pitch for Canadian self-determination, with the poems gathered under the two opening themes of Canadian identity and Canadian landscape. The students in Frank Goldman's Grade 12 class, in selecting this set of poems for their own anthology, were engaged in nothing more than providing an additional sense of Canadian identity and landscape to the scope of the curriculum.

Yet *Theme and Image* also has a section entitled 'War,' which begins with Wilfred Owen's poem, 'Dulce et Decorum Est,' which would deny 'the old Lie' that there is any glory to be found in dying for one's country. There would be opportunities aplenty, then, for reading across poems and anthologies; the students' invented textbook, *Word and Worlds*, has a way of making something new of the poems in *Theme and Image*. It demonstrates how poets speak to poets, if only in trying to tell what rings true within, and how anthologies speak to anthologies, in trying to represent the world in a handful of selections. Certainly, the students made it clear through their selections that literature has a larger life that goes on outside the curriculum and the textbook, a life that brings with it both a legacy and urgency no less worthy of honing their critical reading skills on than the collection that it was intended to supplement.

Yet I am very aware of saying all of this after the fact. I only realized the scope of what that class had assembled long after the students had completed their year and gone on to other things. What I have come to see is that the way in which the students were alive to this history represents more than a few missed teachable moments on my part. What the students pulled together in response to this visiting teacher's little return-to-the-classroom unit formed, in itself, a greater lesson for me on postcolonial themes. They had found it easy enough to bring into the class the lived and uncomfortable aspects of this historical legacy, and bring it in with all of the intensity that poetry can muster. The students rightly left it to me to consider how these ideas can be managed and learned from, within the scope of an English 12 course in the high school. The poetry class became, during our few weeks together, a witnessing of what was then and is still now a history of significant differences that the concept of postcolonialism only begins to get at. The very act of assembling this anthology brought us face to face with the quadratic equation, Art + Truth = Life + Value, which Gloria Leung had introduced in her analysis of Parkin's poem, 'Art and Truth.'

Like many a teacher of teachers before me, I had tried to structure a learning experience based on a powerful idea or theory – postcolonialism, in this case – which, while it has not received much attention at the school level, had something important to offer to these students' education. While I had imagined the benefits of bringing greater theoretical sophistication to the schoolroom, I had failed, in the process, to foresee how the students' ability to run with these ideas would test a teacher's ability to build, in this case, an open, collaborative, and earnest atmosphere in the class that could balance poetry and history, that could hear out the celebration of martyrdom and underground culture. Poetry as a source of risk and peril in the classroom may seem a refreshing concept for the English teacher, yet I recognize that it might still take a year or two more teaching in this way to find the right balance in managing the confluence of issues that this approach raises.

For such work might also test the teacher's relations with the school community. Parents might well be concerned about using this anthology in class, following the September 11th terrorist attacks, as well as the continuing Palestinian suicide bombings. They might object that the students were not capable of handling responsibly the deadly themes of Mahmud's 'The Martyr.' They might object to the inclusion of hip-hop lyrics with their drug and sexual references, pointing to how the recordings are sold with 'explicit lyrics' advisory warnings on them. They might more simply and pointedly object to any sort of class project that would, in Grade 12, take even an hour away from the class's study of William Blake and Robert Frost, so clearly do these poets possess well-established poetic grandeur and undeniable examination relevance. And finally, they might remind the teacher, as well, of the incidents of racial violence among high school students which, however infrequent, are nonetheless a serious concern to this community.

In response, it would need to be made clear that the choice of the poetry to read in class is not simply academic. The discussion with concerned parents would need to be based on the explanations that the students provided in the anthology for their choices, as well as in the interpretations, background, and questions that they offered, all demonstrating the literary skills at work in the unit. The works that the students chose were not light verse, as their choices spoke to the social and ethical critiques of Blake and Frost. There was also much room in the project for a close reading of how these poems work among the students. More of this could have been introduced earlier in the project by having an editorial collective, made up of the students, arguing the case for their choices, confronting questions over (to take examples from this collection) whether a song lyric reflects misogyny or a poem jingoism and empty patriotism. At issue here is the value of students, after studying textbook anthologies for eleven years, taking hold of their own education in their final year of high school, and inserting their own historical position in the shape of the curriculum. But, as you can see, I have much still to test with this idea and even more to prove of its educational value.

Our final class together on this project saw the students go in pairs to visit the other English teachers in the school, carrying with them samples of our anthology, just like door-to-classroom-door sales representatives. They pulled the other English teachers in the school out of classroom and staffroom to introduce to them what they, as students, had created for the school. The students pointed out to the teachers the advantages of the anthology, which we had created as a surlock-bound class set for teachers to use in other classes. The students (who clearly liked the prospect of wandering the hallways, ostensibly in search of English teachers) reported at the end of class that the teachers they met with had expressed more than a modicum of interest in using the anthology as a supplement for their poetry teaching.

As much pride as we collectively took from the interest generated in using our work, this project was obviously about more than augmenting the teaching resources of the school. The students had succeeded in moving the school forward, shifting the possibilities of teaching poetry as a matter of 1960s postcolonial Canadian nationalism, with *Theme and Image*, on to a far more global and radical contemporary space. Whether inadvertently or inevitably, the students' anthology, *Words and Worlds*, brought a complex, troubling history into the present moment of the classroom. It then fell to me, as teacher, to turn their efforts into lessons about history and poetry, theme and image, in a way that bears out its postcolonial themes, rather than betrays the passion of the writing.

The students fulfilled their end of the bargain. They had created an anthology to supplement the class, taking the project that extra step with their choices and interpretations. Whether you think of Eunice Chen and Alyssa Mann preparing original translations for the collection, or T.J. Hobbs and Paul Kilinski pushing the translation idea with hip-hop, or Sabry Husayn, Jason Watkins, Rachel Richter and others selecting poetry that resonated with human rights themes, the students had assembled the means to do much more with the history that each of us continues to live, as they ran with the theory. As always, there is much more teaching and learning to be done in realizing the value of what students are capable of within the scope of their, and our, schooling.

NOTES

1 Canada has gradually come to officially recognize and support its cultural diversity through the multicultural policies which began in the 1960s. These policies have played their part in the schools, in a new range of curriculum materials, while failing to provide any historical or present sense of why this recognition should be an issue of some pride and distinction.
2 The anthology editor, Carol Gillanders, addresses the poem's identity theme in the notes this way: 'A.M. Klein's first poetry was predominantly concerned with Jewish culture but was broadened with the writing of the *Rocking Chair*, which contains a French Canadian theme, for which he was awarded the 1948 Governor General's Award for Poetry' (1967, p. 214).
3 The idea of a postcolonial supplement led to a fair amount of criticism for

Learning to Divide the World (Willinsky, 1998). The postcolonial stand should not supplement but displace the colonial legacy of these tired poets and texts. But again, out of who I am and what I cannot help but feel on reading the poetry of *Theme and Image*, I was not ready to retire Keats, Yeats, and Dickinson. Let us, by all means, examine the story their anthologized packaging tells about the education of generations of students in English literature's civilizing mission, even as we may still be given real pause on reading Emily Dickinson when she writes, for example, of how 'A color stands abroad / on solitary hills / that science cannot overtake.'

4 That the English language has been witness to the martyrdom of militant Muslims is now a part of the *Oxford English Dictionary* definition of martyr, in the sense of 'a person who undergoes death or great suffering for a faith, belief, or cause,' with a quotation from the 1990 novel by G. Gordon Liddy, *The Monkey Handlers*: 'It was a tenet of Islamic faith that anyone who died in a jihad would, as a martyr, earn admission to Paradise.'

5 After reviewing many of Gibran's poetry collections, I was unable to locate a bibliographical reference for this poem.

6 This, in turn, might have led back, in terms of Sabry's background, to Hoda Sha'rawi, who was a pioneer of the Egyptian feminist movement, founding the Egyptian Women's Union in 1923 and leading women's demonstrations against British rule, even as she took a public stand against the tradition of the veil for women (Soueif, 2001).

REFERENCES

Aafreen, I. (1991). Dialogue with an incomplete man. In *We sinful women: Contemporary Urdu feminist poetry including the original Urdu* (p. 149). (R. Ahmad, Ed. & Trans.). London: Women's Press.

Arnold, M. (1908). *Reports on elementary schools, 1852–1882*. London: HMSO.

Common. (1994). *Resurrection* (Audio CD). Relativity.

Gillander, C. (1967). *Theme and image: An anthology of poetry* (Book 2). Toronto: Copp Clark Pitman.

He-Zhi Zhang (659–744) Returning home. http://lf-www.he.cninfo.net/wsjx/englishclub/scjp1.htm

Heine, H. (1827). Du bist wie eine blume. In *Buch der lieder.* http://ingeb.org/Lieder/dubistwi.html

Kohn, M.V., & Flacks, M.H. (1999). Little boy, little boy. In *Roman Vishniac: Children of a vanished world* (pp. 96–98) (M.H. Flacks, Trans.). Berkeley: University of California Press.

Lorca, F.G. (1955). Dawn. In *Poet in New York* (p. 63) (Ben Belitt, Trans.). New York: Grove.

Macaulay, T.B. (1971). Thomas Babington Macaulay on education in India (orig. 1835). In P.D. Curtin (Ed.), *Imperialism* (pp. 178–191). New York: Harper and Row.

Mahmud, A. (1937). The martyr. Barghouti.com http://www.barghouti.com/poets/mahmud/shaheed.asp.

Parkin, A., & Wong, L. (1997). *Hong Kong poems*. Vancouver: Ronsdale Press.

Rodríguez, C. (1992). Arcadia. In *Guerra Prolongada: Protracted War* (p. 63). Toronto: Women's Press.

Soueif, A. (2001, 8 December). The language of the veil. *Guardian* http://www.guardian.co.uk/weekend/story/0,3605,614360,00.html

Viswanathan, G. (1989). *The masks of conquest*. New York: Columbia University Press.

Williams, S. (1998). *The seventh octave (early writings of Saul Williams)*. Atlanta, GA: Black Moore Press.

Willinsky, J. (1998). *Learning to divide the world: Education at empire's end*. Minneapolis: Minnesota University Press.

4 Engaged Differences: School Reading Practices, Postcolonial Literatures, and Their Discontents

INGRID JOHNSTON

In this chapter my focus is the contestatory and hybrid nature of postcolonial literary studies in relation to the intellectual engagement and cultural negotiation of school reading practices and curriculum. I take as a starting point the notion that the postcolonial in Canada appears, as Stephen Slemon points out, 'not as a single project or hypothesis, but as a set of engaged differences,' because

> The concept of post-coloniality ... is not one that simply inhabits a text, an individual, or a collective at the level of social *identity*. The postcolonial ... is not a club that issues memberships, not a state that patrols its borders, not an ethos that subtends a literary canon. Rather, the postcolonial ... is an incomplete project; it is colonialism's shadow; it is a dialectic of engagement and not a singular logics. (2003, p. 320)

Such an engagement involves 'a sustained challenge to the dominant in contemporary distributions of valuation and power' (ibid., p. 321). Current school reading practices, I would argue, are embedded in particularly complex inherited power relations and contemporary distributions of valuations. As several other chapters in this volume (e.g., Kanu's introduction, Richardson, McDonald) suggest, schools have tended to reproduce notions of a common culture with narratives about the nation-state, stories told from one dominant perspective with heroes and villains that reflect one particular worldview and marginalize all others.

Literary text selections and school reading practices are mediated by entrenched and self-perpetuating notions of the canon and by static understandings of a collective national identity. English teachers in

Canadian high schools often find themselves perpetuating the teaching of texts that have gained the status of school canonicity. These texts have become familiar to several generations of teachers and students, multiple copies of the texts are available in school bookrooms, and there is a ready abundance of resources written by curriculum designers and teaching colleagues to support the teaching of these particular texts. Robert Eaglestone offers his views of the school canon:

> In English at all levels the same canonical texts come up again and again, year after year. A person who studied English and has become a teacher often teaches the same texts she or he was taught, in part because she or he was taught those texts were the most important. As students, you expect to study texts you have heard of and assume are worthwhile. Many textbooks for English and books on literature in general assume a familiarity with the canon, which stresses its importance ... The canon then is the list of books you expect to study when you do English, and reading the canon is doing English. The subject and the canon in part define each other. (2000, p. 56)

A reliance on a school canon of literary texts often goes hand in hand with a tendency to reinforce the entrenched nature of school reading practices. Teachers are reluctant to open up discussions that move outside the text to focus attention on what they perceive as more 'problematic' issues of race, class, or power. As bell hooks explains,

> The unwillingness to approach teaching from a standpoint that includes awareness of race, sex, and class is often rooted in the fear that classrooms will be uncontrollable, that emotions and passions will not be contained. To some extent, we all know that whenever we address in the classroom subjects that students are passionate about there is always a possibility of confrontation, forceful expression of ideas, or even conflict. (1994, p. 39)

This unwillingness to engage with difficult questions of culture and difference often remains intact even within schools where teachers claim to have an awareness of the increasing ethnocultural diversity of their school population and to support the need to promote multicultural education. The attention to cultural diversity often takes the form of an adherence to static notions of multiculturalism that seek to value pluralism but take little account of the dynamic nature of cultural difference. Homi Bhabha (1994) has pointed to distinctions between the two ways of representing culture. He argues that signifiers of cultural diversity merely acknowledge a variety of separate and distinct systems of behaviour, values, and attitudes, and may entrench ideas that such differences are exotic. Cultural difference, he suggests, moves beyond thinking that cultural authority resides in a series of fixed and unchanging objects and emphasizes the process by which we come to know these objects and bring them into being. Bhabha observes that the concept of cultural difference emerges from poststructuralist thinking and psychoanalysis, and is linked with the radical ambivalence that he sees in all colonial discourse. This ambivalence, he argues, is evident in any act of cultural interpretation, which is never static but is always changing and open to further possible interpretations:

> Cultural diversity is an epistemological object – culture as an object of empirical knowledge – whereas cultural difference is the process of the *enunciation* of culture as "knowedge*able*," authoritative, adequate to the construction of systems of cultural identification ... Cultural diversity is the recognition of pre-given cultural contents and customs; held in a time-frame of relativism it gives rise to liberal notions of multiculturalism ... The concept of cultural difference focuses on the problem of the ambivalence of cultural authority. (1994, p. 34)

Multicultural education in its focus on the more outward and static signs of cultural diversity has become the new North American mantra for paying attention to issues of culture. Multicultural education initiatives in Canada have centred on the need to acknowledge the claims of indigenous inhabitants and to make provision for an increasingly pluralistic immigrant population. In addition, Canada's initiatives have been guided by themes of bilingualism and the safeguard of heritage languages, in an attempt to reconcile the maintenance of so-called British and French cultures with an added commitment to the numerous other cultural groups across the country. Official policies of multiculturalism, issues of human rights, and antiracist teaching philosophies have increased teachers' awareness that changes need to be made in what and how they teach. Yet these policies have done little to help teachers to understand how complex questions of representation are intertwined with issues of culture, race, gender, and ethnicity or to comprehend what it means to initiate new reading practices in their schools. As a result, despite 'official' policies of multiculturalism that have been mandated at both the federal and the provincial levels, changes have largely been ideological rather than structural, and schools continue to function largely as assimilationist agencies.

Ato Quayson argues that in the multicultural classroom context, 'even when attention is paid to the realities of race, class and identity, this is carefully managed so as to delink them from lived experience in order to detonate their potential explosiveness' (2000, p. 184). Similarly, Greg Demetriadis and Cameron McCarthy consider that, in general, multicultural education in North America has resulted in the creation of a discourse of containment about cultural difference, pointing out that

> multicultural education has become the new metadiscipline that is most often deployed to address the current eruption of difference and plurality in social life now invading the school. It has become a set of propositions about identity, knowledge, power and change in education, a kind of normal science, which attempts to "discipline" difference rather than be transformed by it. (2001, p. 113)

According to these critics, while multicultural education in North America has succeeded in focusing more attention on questions of culture, it has done so by petrifying culture as an object of study. Students from 'non-mainstream' cultures are thereby invited to retain and celebrate their nationalist histories and knowledges, while schools continue to resist the need to address complex issues of power relations and subjugated knowledges and practices. Despite paying lip-service to the need for changes in reading practices, high school educators have overwhelmingly resisted any substantial shifts in how they approach literary studies in their classrooms. Most of the well-loved texts that have remained on school reading lists for decades continue to be taught, with little attempt made to deconstruct or address issues of race, class, or gender that might appear in the literature, or to uncover the ideologies of the texts. Often, the introduction of some new multicultural text is presented as an 'add-on' to existing literature and taught as a culture tour of exotic and unknown places. In such classrooms, multicultural education is played out by parading newly represented cultures in what Deborah Britzman et al. have called 'a seamless parade of stable and unitary customs and traditions or in the individuated form of political heroes modeling roles' (1993, p. 189). Knowledge of these cultures, these authors continue, 'is presented as if unencumbered by the politics and poetics of representation' (ibid.).

Postcolonialism, in contrast, offers possibilities for educators to challenge such binaries as 'here-there,' 'white-black,' and 'centre-margin' and to move beyond a discourse of cultural containment towards a more radical engagement of difference. The objective here is less to promote debates over polarized entities and more to consider the intersections of the aesthetic and the political in the study of literary texts. Reading 'in-between' the aesthetic and the political might be a fruitful position from which to consider the fluid boundaries of culture, race, and subjugated knowledges. This form of reading might also avoid oversimplications about cultural difference and plurality in reading practices.

Demetriadis and McCarthy (2001) suggest that 'Thinking in postcolonial terms about the topic of difference and multiplicity in education means thinking relationally and contextually. It means bringing back into educational discourses all those tensions and contradictions that we tend to suppress as we process experience and history into curricular knowledge' (2001, p. 119). These tensions and contradictions may erupt as teachers and students admit historical materialities and historical inequities on the bases of race, class, and gender as valid topics of discussion in the English classroom, alongside the literary analysis of texts. Teachers' sensitivity to considerations of the historical and material contexts surrounding a text means that contemporary problems of political, social, and cultural domination enter the classroom debates alongside discussions of literary allusions, foreshadowing, metaphor, and metonymy.

Postcolonialism challenges any easy understandings of the aftermath of empire and the colonial encounter as it exposes the problematics of literary production within the economies of the international marketplace, and brings to light what Deepika Bahri has termed 'the functional economy and orientation of the postcolonial text' (2003, p. 285). These issues, she claims 'are at least as important for pedagogy as they are for postcolonial theory' (ibid.). Teachers discussing a postcolonial text in the classroom might show how postcolonial writers are striving to write back against the centre. At the same time, they could begin to analyse with their students how and why such authors are writing in the former colonizers' language, being marketed for, and read by Western academia and rewarded by international literary prizes from the West: 'The postcolonial intersects with the complex functioning of the educational institution within a larger context: the world, the text, the critic ... and the teacher and students ... That these sets are also dynamic rather than static makes it the more difficult to discern their boundaries' (ibid., p. 281).

Such complex intersections might include deconstructing literary texts that have achieved particular canonical status within Western schools, in an effort to understand how such texts have been normalized in the classroom and read in particular ways. In Canadian high schools, one of the most canonized of such texts is undoubtedly Harper Lee's novel *To Kill a Mockingbird* (1960). A Canada-wide study of provincially recommended booklists (Gambell, 1982) found that Lee's novel was recommended on booklists in eight Canadian provinces. In the late 1990s, a study of the texts taught in Grade 10 English classes in Edmonton, Alberta (Altmann, Johnston, & Mackey, 1998), reported that *To Kill a Mockingbird* was the novel most frequently offered to students in these classes. A recent study of the texts taught in Grades 10 and 11 classes in two Ontario district school boards (Reed, 2003) revealed that the book still ranks among teachers' top four novel selections.

Harper Lee's novel offers a liberal humanist stance on questions of race and intolerance. Filtered through the perspective of Scout, a young white girl, the story centres around Atticus, her lawyer father, who exposes the racism of Maycomb, a small southern U.S. town, and saves the life of Tom Robinson, an African-American man wrongly accused of rape. Recent critiques of the text and how it is taught (Ricker-Wilson, 1998; Ryan, 1999; Johnston, 2003) have focused on Lee's portrayal of strong, rounded white characters compared with the shadowy, one-dimensional portrayal of the African-American characters in the novel. These critics point to the novel's construction of a righteous white lawyer 'saving' voiceless and marginalized African Americans, a theme also taken up in a number of Hollywood movies such as *A Time to Kill*.

One Canadian teacher and critic, Carol Ricker-Wilson, describing her teaching of Lee's novel in her multiethnic high school, explains that for many of the white students in class, 'their experiential identification with the wise and kindly Atticus and feisty Scout enabled them to close the covers, angered by injustice, but with their racial identities unscathed' (1998, p. 70). In contrast, despite her efforts to frame and mediate the text, her African-Canadian students reacted very negatively to the novel. Written comments from these students suggested that it was the very act of reading, through their identification with the black characters in the novel that caused them to feel demoralized. Ricker-Wilson points out that, although her African-Canadian students had been willing to speak about issues of black identity and slavery during discussions in which 'they were the subjects of their own carefully framed depictions,' they still felt demoralized by their reading experience of a book that they perceived had 'positioned them as objects of a lesson on racism for white students' (ibid.). She surmizes that even though authorial intent might have been to critique marginalization and racism, the novel still positions black readers as Other, while it invites white readers to share in the pleasurable experience of identification with the main characters of the text.

Despite the immense popularity and controversy surrounding canonized school texts such as *To Kill a Mockingbird*, preservice and beginning teachers are rarely offered opportunities to question or deconstruct problematic representations of whiteness or the Other in texts such as this or to challenge singular notions of subjectivity and identity. While increasing numbers of undergraduate students do take courses in world literature and do read postcolonial texts, they are less likely to engage in debates around the potential and limitations of such texts for their teaching or to question what a postcolonial pedagogy might look like.

Recently, in an attempt to raise questions around postcolonial reading practices, I invited a group of preservice English teachers to participate in a small research study. With the encouragement of their English Curriculum and Instruction course instructor, five preservice teachers, one male and four female, all from white European backgrounds, volunteered to meet with me for a series of weekly lunchtime conversations. These audiotaped sessions were held once a week for five weeks preceding their nine-week field experience in high school English classes and once after they had completed their student teaching. Research objectives for the study were to raise participants' awareness of the historically privileged positions of power conferred by 'whiteness'; to discuss postcolonial literary texts and pedagogical strategies; and to challenge them to understand sociocultural values embedded in various Western literary texts and instructional practices and their potential effects on students from historically marginalized backgrounds.

During our first audiotaped conversation, we discussed the wide-ranging field of postcolonial literary studies. We began with Ashcroft, Griffiths, and Tiffin's introductory descriptions of key concepts in the area: '[P]ost-colonial analysis increasingly makes clear the nature and impact of inherited power relations, and their continuing effects on modern global culture and politics ... Post-colonial analysis draws upon a wide variety of theoretical positions and their associated strategies and techniques. Moreover, the field seeks to develop adequate and appropriate approaches to material that is itself diverse, hybrid, diasporic. Its terminology, then, functions in a highly charged and contestatory atmosphere of intellectual exchange and cultural negotiation' (1998, p. 1).

Considering how, as teachers, we might engage in this process of cultural negotiation led to further discussions of the role of literature in the history of postcolonialism. As Ashcroft, Griffiths, and Tiffin explain, 'in its engagement with the culturalist myth of "literature" ... postcolonialism brings to cultural studies its own well-established concepts of diversity, particularity and local difference' (2002, p. 210). Over the five weeks preceding their student teaching, I asked participants to engage with these concepts of cultural difference in particular contexts by reading and responding to the following three postcolonial short stories, written by authors from differing backgrounds and traditions: 'An Afternoon in Bright Sunlight,' by Native Canadian writer Shirley Bruised Head (1990); 'The Boy Who Painted Christ Black,' by African-American writer John Henrik Clarke (1992); and 'The Answer Is "No,"' by Egyptian writer Naguib Mahfouz (1995). Each of these texts, in its own way, challenges Eurocentric ways of thinking and forms of representation. The stories present readers with new possibilities for thinking about race, ethnicity, tradition, gender, class, and power. Our literary discussions were supplemented with five theoretical and pedagogical articles: a reading of Shirley Bruised Head's story in a British school context (Hodges, 1990); an African-American teacher's discussion of the challenges she faced when introducing multicultural literature in a predominantly white school (Jasper, 1998); a white teacher's experiences of introducing postcolonial literature to her students in a large Toronto school (Goldblatt, 1998); a teacher's perspectives on reading *To Kill a Mockingbird* with her African-Canadian students (Ricker-Wilson, 1998), and a teacher-educator's story of reading the novel with preservice teachers (Johnston, 2003).

Comments from the study participants at the end of our five weeks of reading and discussing the postcolonial texts, theories, and pedagogical possibilities indicated that they had reconsidered some previous notions about literature selections and school reading practices. They were enthusiastic about the possibilities offered by postcolonial literary theories and pedagogies for their teaching and more reflective about how to approach teaching canonized texts such as *To Kill a Mockingbird*. One participant in the study described her experience like this: 'Because I am going to be teaching *To Kill a Mockingbird*, it was really useful for me to consider the fact that I am approaching it from a cultural context where I will be the one that feels good at the end. I can see how, socially, maybe justice is not really done, but through Atticus and some of the other people, they take just small steps towards it. I can be the one that will feel good, but there may be students in my class who will really resist some of the material in the book because they're not coming from the same context.' Another participant began to make links between her reading of *To Kill a Mockingbird* and current negative societal views on black people: 'I'm trying to collect my thoughts here, about the whole idea of whiteness being the standard. You have a white lawyer because that gives it legitimacy, right, in the eyes of the population and it had never occurred to me you know, that when we approach, when I approach a text, there are those standards of whiteness. Like it reminds me about the portrayal of blacks as in gangs or all these other negative things. Rodney King is in the news again for being involved with drugs, but it doesn't talk about the fact that most serial killers are white, most union busters are white, all those other things that are just kind of glossed over.'

In their student teaching, three of the five preservice teachers were asked to teach *To Kill a Mockingbird* in a Grade 10 class, but they were also given opportunities by their cooperating teachers to bring in a variety of literary texts alongside this novel and other canonical texts already present in the classroom. The two other study participants were teaching short story and poetry units, and again, had some freedom and encouragement to bring in new texts to their English classrooms. One of these preservice teachers, who had a strong literary background in postcolonial literature and a high level of confidence in her teaching ability, was able to work with her cooperating teacher in adding some postcolonial texts alongside the stories by white-American and British writers for a short story research project. She told us:

> It was good to have the resources you gave us and to think about some postcolonial type stories for the English 30 short story research project ... The students had to work in groups of two or three, select a story, do an author biography, and give some historical context as well as the analysis of the story. My cooperating teacher had given me a list of short stories, and they were all the usual British and American ones, like the 'The Rocking Horse Winner' and 'Young Goodman Brown'; so I started suggesting some other stuff and now we have a chapter by Michael Ondaatje, a story by Zora Neale Hurston and ones by Gabriel Garçia Marquez and

Amy Tan. My teacher was really receptive and the students found them interesting to read.

This was the only participant among the five who felt that she had the confidence to take initiative in the classroom and create some changes in the school reading practices. The other four participants, despite their new insights and teaching opportunities, seemed to revert to what Britzman (1991) has termed the 'commonplaces of teaching' and the 'discourse of conformity.' Their desire to effect curricular changes that might be appropriate for their students' learning was contradicted by their need to fit into the established culture of the school. Although teaching in ethnoculturally diverse classrooms, these preservice teachers were generally reluctant to consider how representations of race, ethnicity, class, and gender in the texts being taught might be problematic for some of their students and, except for the one participant, they lacked the confidence to bring in any texts outside those already in the school. In their teaching, they relied on the outdated curriculum resources available in their school and engaged in the kinds of pedagogical practices that they had previously critiqued in our group conversations. In their discussion following their nine weeks of teaching, they spoke of the specific constrains and tensions that emerged from their teaching experiences, focusing on these as particular forms of school literary practices that mediated questions of identity and subjectivity.

One common theme that emerged from four of the participants' post-teaching discussion was an acceptance that the canonized texts being taught in the school had particular value for them as teachers because they had 'stood the test of time.' As one participant rationalized:

When I got in, they were just finishing off the short story unit. I had a choice of novels and I basically picked *Mockingbird*, not because I particularly liked the issues, but because it's a practical thing. It's been taught by the teacher ten times, you know, over the last ten years. There's tons of resources out there so I wanted to spend my time sifting through resources and trying to find what's good as opposed to trying to find resources or reading stuff up in my book.

Along with their acknowledgment of the staying power of such texts came a belief that 'classroom demographics don't matter; "literature" is universal.' This idea of the universal appeal of canonized school texts emerged again in relation to participants' discussions of teaching *To Kill a Mockingbird*. One preservice teacher commented that she was happy that she had taught the novel because she felt all students loved it:

> I do think it's significant to know that every one that I talk to, if they studied *To Kill a Mockingbird*, they rank it as their favourite so I mean, the kids love it, the kids really enjoy reading it and yeah, I find it a little moralistic for the reasons like I said and ... even cheesy sometimes, but I think it's worth teaching.

Another participant echoed similar sentiments, apparently convinced that the novel was appropriate for and well received by all her students:

> There was actually a very broad diversity of ethnic backgrounds, religious backgrounds. A lot of immigrant children in the class. It was really a great spread of backgrounds. Oh yeah. Yeah. They all loved *To Kill a Mockingbird*. We talked a lot about the themes and characters. We talked a lot about courage and justice and equality and things like that. I think those are pretty universal.

The desire of these student teachers to cling to 'the tried and true' and their unwillingness to acknowledge the different subject positions of their classroom readers can be attributed to their lack of confidence and experience in what and how to teach and their fear of failure in the classroom: 'I would like an alternative to teaching *To Kill a Mockingbird*, but then again, there's that whole issue about having the confidence to know what to teach about a different novel and also "am I getting it?" Is it also grade appropriate? And is it curriculum relevant?' This same lack of confidence led them to select texts with ready-made questions for students to respond to. One participant explained:

> Being beginners in teaching it would be very helpful to have questions or something that we could use, because it's pretty hard to know if we're getting everything from a text when we don't have any other resources to sort of help us out ... as far as if we're catching everything.

And another suggested that she would not consider introducing new texts unless they also included questions for students to respond to:

> I think I would have done the multicultural stories if there were questions

involved with it, because of the way that I do my lesson plans is that I don't pick the story because of the story, I pick how good the questions are afterwards, so I go with 'What are the questions out there relevant with what we're doing?' and then backtrack on the story.

One participant went as far as selecting some postcolonial literature (poetry), but felt too insecure to teach the poems:

> I would have used more poems if I had more background ... like, I took out a book of Langston Hughes poems to use, but I couldn't find one that went well with my material, partly because I didn't know what I was looking for and I'm not familiar enough with his work to feel just, 'Oh I want to use that poem.'

This student teacher's discomfort in his lack of expertise, and his reluctance to teach a text over which he felt he had no control is reminiscent of Reed Way Dasenbrock's reminder that we need to move away from metaphors of 'possession' of a text towards a consideration of each reading experience as 'new scene of learning' (1992, p. 39). In taking such a stance, we view each encounter with an unfamiliar work of art as a learning opportunity, allowing that the text and the author will offer enough guidance to enable us to grow with each encounter. For these student teachers, lacking both teaching experience and a sense of autonomy in the classes they were teaching, it was easier to reaffirm a stance of control over a text rather than making themselves appear vulnerable in teaching an unfamiliar and possibly controversial postcolonial text.

These research participants' conversations around their teaching reflect many of the challenges and dilemmas faced by beginning teachers when encountering cultural difference in the classroom. Feeling too insecure to move outside the school canon of literature, and lacking the confidence to engage students in a non-traditional reading of the canon, they revert to prescriptive teaching strategies that shut out possibilities for a dialectic of engagement with questions of difference, race, gender, and power.

This study points to a number of the complex challenges that we face as educators interested in developing postcolonial reading practices in contemporary classrooms. Thinking in postcolonial terms about the topic of difference in education, as Demetriadis and McCarthy suggest, 'means thinking relationally and contextually. It means bringing into educational discourse all those tensions and contradictions we tend to suppress as we process experience and history into curricular knowledge' (2001, p. 119). Paying attention to this form of educational discourse does not mean becoming what Demetriadis and McCarthy term a *curricular monologist* (ibid., p. 118), who seeks to displace the Eurocentric core of the curriculum with the cultural knowledges and experiences of previously marginalized minority groups. Rather than entrenching such a curricular binary, educators interested in developing an engaged postcolonial pedagogy can create spaces and strategies for rereading existing canonical school texts through the aesthetic and political prism of newer postcolonial literature in ways that open up dialogue on the broader contemporary social issues that are raised by the texts.

Over the past decade, as Ashcroft, Griffiths, and Tiffin explain, 'the term "post-colonial" has experienced one of the steepest trajectories of any theoretical concept; seldom used in 1989, it now raises over 10,000 entries in the Library of Congress catalogue' (2002, p. 219). While debates over the use and application of the concept continue to rage, it is obvious that postcolonial studies have offered new possibilities for reexamining the colonial past and reconfiguring contemporary worldwide cultural concerns. In pedagogical and educational terms, our challenge as educators will be to find ways to bring these complex international and interdependent sensibilities into the lives of students and to recognize how new reading practices can help us to become more engaged with the challenges of living in a world of difference, discontinuity, and multiplicity.

REFERENCES

Altmann, A., Johnston, I., & Mackey, M. (1998). Curricular decisions about literature in contemporary classrooms: A preliminary analysis of a survey of materials used in Edmonton grade 10 English courses. *Alberta Journal of Educational Research, 44*(2), 208–220.

Apple, M. (1999). *Official knowledge: Democratic education in a conservative age.* New York: Routledge.

Ashcroft, B., Griffiths, G., & Tiffin, H. (Eds.) (1998). *Key concepts in post-colonial studies.* New York: Routledge.

Ashcroft, B., Griffiths, G., & Tiffin, H. (2002). *The empire writes back: Theory and practice in post-colonial literatures* (2nd ed.). London: Routledge.

Bahri, D. (2003). *Native intelligence: Aesthetics, politics and postcolonial literature.* Minneapolis: University of Minnesota Press.

Bhabha, H. (1994). *The location of culture.* London: Routledge.

Britzman, D. (1991). *Practice makes practice: A critical study of learning to teach.* Albany: SUNY Press.

Britzman, D., Valles, K.A., Munoz, G.M., & Lamash, L. (1993). Slips that show and tell: Fashioning multiculture as a problem of representation. In C. McCarthy & W. Crichlow (Eds.), *Race, identity and representation in education* (pp. 188–200). New York: Routledge.

Bruised Head, S. (1990). An afternoon in bright sunlight. In T. King (Ed.), *All my relations: An anthology of contemporary Canadian Native fiction.* Toronto: McClelland and Stewart.

Clarke, J.H. (1992). The boy who painted Christ black. In J.H. Clarke (Ed.), *Black American short stories: One hundred years of the best* (pp. 80–113). New York: Hill and Wang.

Dasenbrock, R.W. (1992). Teaching multicultural literature. In R. Trimmer and T. Warnock (Eds.), *Understanding others: Culture and cross-cultural studies and the teaching of literature* (pp. 35–46). Urbana, IL: NCTE.

Demetriadis, G., & McCarthy, C. (2001). *Reading and teaching the postcolonial: From Baldwin to Basquait and beyond.* New York: Teachers College Press.

Eaglestone, R. (2000). *Doing English: A guide for literature students.* London: Routledge.

Gambell, T. (1982). *Canadian learning materials in elementary and secondary education project.* Toronto: Association of Canadian Publishers, Canadian School Trustees Association.

Goldblatt, P.F. (1998). Experience and acceptance of postcolonial literature in the high school English classroom. *English Journal, 87*(3), 71–7.

Hodges, G.C. (1990). One morning's reading of 'An afternoon in bright sunlight.' In E. Bearne & V. Watson (Eds.), *Where texts and children meet* (pp. 71–81). New York: Routledge.

hooks, b. (1994). *Teaching to transgress: Education as the practice of freedom.* New York: Routledge.

Jasper, G. (1998). Multiculturally challenged. *English Journal, 87*(3), 93–7.

Johnston, I. (2003). Reading and resisting silent spaces of whiteness. In W. Hurren & E. Hase-Lubeke (Eds.), *Curriculum intertext: Place, language, pedagogy* (pp. 227–238). New York: Peter Lang.

Lee, H. (1960). *To kill a mockingbird.* New York: Popular Library.

Mahfouz, N. (1995). The answer is no. In J. Borovilos (Ed.), *Breaking free: A cross-cultural anthology* (pp. 214–217). Scarborough, Ontario: Prentice-Hall.

Quayson, A. (2000). *Postcolonialism: Theory, practice or process?* Cambridge, UK: Polity Press.

Reed, B. (2003). *Curriculum decisions about teaching literature in high school.* Unpublished master's thesis, Queen's University, Kingston, Ontario.

Ricker-Wilson, C. (1998). When the mockingbird becomes an albatross: Reading and resistance in the language arts classroom. *English Journal, 87*(3), 67–72.

Ryan, J. (1999). *Race and ethnicity in multi-ethnic schools.* Clevedon: Multilingual Matters.

Slemon, S. (2003). Afterword. In L. Moss (Ed.), *Is Canada postcolonial? Unsettling Canadian literature* (pp. 318–324). Waterloo: Wilfrid Laurier University Press.

5 A Kinder Mathematics for Nunavut

RALPH T. MASON

It is *Atauttimut Havaktugut 2003*, the time of 'Learning Together' for the teachers of the Kitikmeot region of Nunavut, Canada. Politically, Nunavut is Canada's newest territory, created in 1997, spanning three time zones east to west and reaching from the Manitoba border to the North Pole. With 25,000 inhabitants, 90 per cent of them Aboriginal (Boychuk, 2004), the vastness of Kitikmeot provides a hundred square kilometres for every person. For the teachers gathered in Cambridge Bay for a week of professional development, the outside temperature of minus 40° Celsius is just an inconvenience.

Halfway through our session on teaching elementary mathematics, a sincere question changed the conversation completely. We had been looking at different ways that students can visualize the ten-for-one ideas at the heart of place value. In the activities, students would begin with things to count or measure or order, forming images of quantities and actions they have taken concerning quantities. Classroom conversations would enable students to share their mathematical images and procedures. Number lines, hundreds charts, and metre sticks would provide supportive access to the symbols of arithmetic *before* students were required to do arithmetic with those symbols. The momentum of the workshop had been growing, and I was particularly pleased with the increasing participation of the Inuit participants. Some were teachers, some were classroom aides, and some were participants in the Arctic College's one-year teacher certification program. A Grade 3 teacher spoke up: 'I can see these activities really working in my classroom. Some of my students really struggle with adding and subtracting three-digit numbers. They're stuck when I just give them numbers on a page, and these activities will help with that. But I have other kids that aren't coming to school much, and at the end of the year, they'll be moved on to Grade 4 just like the ones that I can help every day. How do I help the ones who don't come to school often enough?' What a challenging question! Why would Grade 3 students not go to school every day? No, it is not the weather. No, their families are completely functional. It is something much simpler. The students don't *want* to come. Their parents will encourage them to go, but, for a variety of reasons, will not force them. And a child who has missed some school knows she will be behind when she returns, and the problem gets worse, not better.

It's not the social environment of the classrooms – the teachers make school inviting, and school is a chance to be with friends. It isn't the literacy program that bothers them, either – reforms in teaching children to read have made learning to read both appealing and rewarding, and for those who are not as successful as quickly there are alternative instructional resources. Even if the home language is not English, teachers or teacher aides in each classroom speak and teach in Inuktitut or Inuinaqtun. Seldom is a student excluded or stuck because of missing understandings or inexperience during literacy instruction. In mathematics, however, the teachers in the workshop agreed that during and even before Grade 3, some students felt anxious when they didn't know the prerequisite concepts for a lesson's arithmetic. Traditional school mathematics is primarily symbolic, not activity and imagery or negotiated understanding, and there are students who don't understand the symbolic code as well as a given lesson requires of them. Traditional instruction was creating winners and losers, just as it does in southern Canada. And when at least one Grade 3 teacher saw the possibility of a curriculum that might engage and appeal to all her students, she didn't want to leave behind those 8-year-olds who were already avoiding school. The teachers in that room wanted the math in their early-years classrooms to be inviting for all of their students, but would such a mathematics curriculum be possible?

That question could be asked on at least two levels – the pedagogical and the political. The teachers' first interest was pedagogical – they wanted the resources and lesson ideas that could be the foundation for reforming their instruction, and they deserve to have access to them. In communities where many students begin school with little experience counting and measuring and manipulating quantities, those resources and ideas will focus first on enabling Nunavut students to build experiences with quantities and numbers. But that leaves a question more suited to the form of address that a book chapter can provide: Is a mathematics curriculum where all children succeed *politically* possible?

I believe that it is not only possible, but inevitable. The instruction that children receive must fit with and suit the society in which they live. The people of Nunavut want all their young people prepared for a future that they recognize to be unpredictable, and as a consequence are, I believe, more willing than their southern compatriots to consider alternatives to the school mathematics that they themselves experienced as children. But standing in the way of change are the practices and traditions of a school mathematics imported from other places and other times. The dissonance between the goals of the people of Nunavut and the mathematics they have innocently adopted for their schools provides the context for this essay.

This chapter invites the teachers of Nunavut to see themselves as entitled, even compelled, to critically question their schools' tacit acceptance of a mathematics program that developed in a society (southern Canada) that is geographically, socially, and *morally* different from theirs. The voices of critical pedagogy will call out in support. As well, the chapter will point to other cultures' pursuits of new visions of school mathematics, and introduce readers to ethnomathematics as a curriculum option. The chapter will suggest that there is potency available in reforming Nunavut's school mathematics as a part of Nunavut's movement towards autonomy, a potency reflected in the ideas of postcolonial educational theorists. Finally, in its Conclusion, this chapter will recommend a strategy for developing an instructional program in mathematics that is more suited to its peoples' goals than any school math imported from the dominant culture to the south: grow their own.

Questioning Traditional School Mathematics

Perhaps the first step for the educators and educational leaders of Nunavut is to recognize that the school mathematics that they now have is not the only choice, and that they are entitled to a role in choosing. Because school enables students in general to become more capable, it is easy to think that school (and its mathematics) is automatically a good thing. Yet, school mathematics clearly convinces many students that they are not as capable as they 'should' be (Wolodko, Willson, & Johnson, 2003). And minority-culture students are more often convinced of their mathematical inability than are students of the dominant culture (Lubienski & Bowen, 2000; Secada, 2000; Tate, 1997).

Indeed, many critical mathematics theorists think that school mathematics is *designed* to create losers as well as winners: 'Mathematics is therefore a tool for selection, possibly to a greater extent than other subjects; a role that is tacitly accepted by many teachers, students and also parents' (Dorfler & McClone, 1986, p. 72). This function of school mathematics is called *gatekeeping* (Silver, 1997), and it refers to the exclusion of students from further involvement in school mathematics, in school, and beyond, based on their lack of success as mathematics learners.

Robert Moses and Charles Cobb (2001) are outspoken about the need to disrupt how school mathematics acts to deny minority students economic opportunity: 'Industrial technology created schools that educated an elite to run society, while the rest were prepared for factory work by performing repetitive tasks that mimicked factories' (2001, p. 11). They suggest that today more than ever, economic, social, and political opportunity depend on students' success in formal mathematics: 'So algebra, once solely in place as the gatekeeper for higher math and the priesthood who gained access to it, now is the gatekeeper for citizenship; and people who don't have it are like the people who couldn't read and write in the industrial age' (ibid., pp. 13–14).

Jones and his colleagues offer similar claims, although their views of teachers' complicity in maintaining traditional disparities should not be considered to include all teachers: 'There is a history of predominantly low-income, minority schools treating mathematics learning as procedural and formulaic and, subsequently, the learning and performance of underrepresented students suffer. As the mathematics specialist helps teachers deepen their mathematics content and pedagogy, she runs up against teachers' assumptions about the capability of URMs [underrepresented minorities] to succeed in mathematics. The act of engaging elementary teachers to think in new ways about what constitutes college-prep mathematics curriculum for underrepresented students is not a simple technical matter; it is infused with cultural beliefs about race and ability' (Jones, Yonezawa, Ballesteros, & Mehan, 2002, p. 9). Put simply, the mathematics chosen for Nunavut schools and the manner in which it is taught will affect how children from different backgrounds succeed.

If school mathematics makes some children feel incapable, then for those children school itself becomes less than inviting. But can we imagine a mathematics curriculum that invites students to attend every day, one that enables them all to succeed? This would mean imagining a school mathematics that does not exclude those with less developed prior knowledge, a school mathematics that does not automatically privilege students with a home environment more aligned with a certain set of values. It would mean envisioning a school that does not casually maintain or reproduce social inequalities. This is the premise of critical or liberatory pedagogy (Frankenstein, 1987, 1997; Skovsmose, 1994). Of course, school as an institution reflects society as least as much as it shapes it – a move towards a kinder and more inclusive mathematics would be a move towards a kinder and more inclusive Nunavut. But can we actually challenge the curriculum we are given? Of course we can! Noss would suggest that we must do so: 'It is most useful to view the curriculum as a site of struggle in which pupils, teachers, parents, as well as voices from industrial, commercial, and other settings have at various times competed in various ways and with varying relative strengths to assert their priorities ... From this perspective, the curriculum is *neither* free from *nor* determined by the economic and political space in which it operates: it makes more sense to ask how mathematical ideas fit with society, how they encourage particular ways of seeing, particular ideologies' (Noss, 1994, p. 7).

These are big words and ideas, but ultimately they mean that if 8-year-olds do not deserve to find mathematics to be cold and forbidding (Stiff, 1990), then teachers can actively pursue curriculum that they do deserve, and get support for their efforts. In the next section, I will suggest that the teachers of Nunavut will not be alone in such a pursuit.

Envisioning a Socially Appropriate Mathematics

Imagine a Grade 4 teacher, who believes that her students deserve mathematics that is connected to their lives, introducing the topic of division. She considers two contexts.

Context 1: A hunter pulls the seal onto the ice. As he cuts it up and packs it on the sled behind the snowmobile, the meat of the seal freezes quickly. Back at the village, the hunter will share, providing two weeks' meat for three households.

Context 2: A case of beef jerky in the co-op store has twenty-four boxes, each with twelve individually wrapped 28-gram sticks. It will keep the display rack full for about ten days.

Both contexts provide opportunities for students to form imagery about division, but the two contexts are not mathematically equivalent. One is full of numerically specific values, and its portions fulfil one of the conditions of mathematical division, which is that the portions are equal. In the other context, the quantities will be carefully determined by the hunter, but they will not be enumerated. The shares for the families, determined more by tradition than by arithmetic, will not be equal. But they will be equitable. The two contexts are not culturally equivalent, either. Not surprisingly, the context that is most aligned with mathematical division is the one most aligned with modern (southern) life. The likelihood that schoolchildren will have personal experiences in either context will depend on the lifestyles of their families. Making mathematics relevant involves more than cultural connections – it involves value judgments, and the choices that are made will differentially affect the children in the classroom.

There is a form of inquiry called *ethnomathematics* that searches for 'the mathematics which is practiced among identifiable cultural groups' (d'Ambrosio, in Gerdes, 1994, p. 19). It suggests that there is more to mathematics than what is now studied in schools. It suggests that the mathematics of different peoples are different not just in form or the context in which it is enacted, but in its nature: 'Ethnomathematics is an idea concerning the cultural meanings and representations of concepts of quantity, relationships and space' (Barton, 1999, p. 34).

What does the ethnomathematics and multicultural mathematics literature have to offer the teachers of Nunavut? One, ethnomathematics theorists can help the teachers ask hard questions of the school mathematics tradition, and their efforts to improve the math that they offer. For example, as we look back on the two contexts that opened this section, it must be asked if their use would be respectful of the traditions that they include: 'How can ethnomathematics be taught so that it is not simply a folkloristic introduction to real mathematics?' (Kitchen & Becker, 1998, p. 361). Two, researchers and practitioners of mathematics education in multicultural environments have documented the effects of traditional practices on minority cultures (and in the broader Canadian framework, Nunavut's cultures are all minorities): 'The mathematics presented in schools is not simply a fragment of the whole, but a biased fragment that is aligned with a predominantly modernist and Western world-view' (Davis, 2001, p. 21). Other writers (e.g., Barton, Fairhall, & Trinick, 1998; Moore, 1994; Pinxten, 1994; and Roberts, 1998) offer glimpses into the complexities and challenges of teaching mathematics across cultural or linguistic chasms. An example might be the caution urged by Adler, who investigated the effects on the mathematics learning of students in South African classrooms, where mathematical communication was highly valued but failed to include all students because of differences in student capabilities in the language of instruction: 'Does meaningful mathematics conversation as a route to mathematical meaning, become, however unintentionally, the preserve of the privileged few? Expressed in more political terms: In whose interests is the dominant construction of *mathematically rich and meaningful communication?'* (2001, p. 142). As the teachers of Nunavut grapple with such issues, they will find value in the experiences of others that look forward to a time when 'education, in particular mathematics education, is involved in building a less unequal world, one with more solidarity present' (Knijnik, 2002, p. 12); chapters in this book (e.g., Kincheloe, Richardson, Johnson, Aikenhead) offer positive examples with subjects other than mathematics.

What might the study of Nunavut's own ethnomathematics offer the teachers of Nunavut, as a source of influences on their school mathematics? At first glance, we might think of the Inuit culture as not very mathematical. As an igloo is shaped, blocks of snow spiral upward and inward to make a dome without need of support. Yet, no one calls the blocks 'trapezoidal prisms,' and no measurements or calculations take place. By those criteria, the same person's building of a hockey net for his children out of plastic piping would be more mathematical. Similarly, hunters' strategies for positioning themselves to maximize the probability of being within range of a surfacing seal are surely not as mathematical as the same hunters' participation in Bingo night, where the odds of winning are precise and can be enumerated. And the artist's precise positioning of the whalebone support for a harp seal carved in soapstone takes place without measure or calculation, even if the finances of the artists' co-op that distributes the carvings involves careful accounting and financial projections. If we take southern mathematics as the standard, we see much more mathematics in those aspects of Nunavut life that are most affected by southern values. The principles of ethnomathematics guide us to set aside our southern prejudices in the search for the mathematics that might enable children to connect with their experiences beyond school; they also lead us to ask hard questions about the relationship between mathematics and our children's cultural experiences.

With hard questions at the ready, let us return to the Grade 4 teacher who must introduce division. She remembers as a child, watching her mother cut up the meat from seal hunts into cooking portions, rocking the sharp, curved blade of the *ulu* back and forth, then passing the *ulu* to her to let her try. And they laughed and talked about the cuts she made. In the co-op store, the teacher watches as the owner's son, only 8 years old, spreads packages of beef jerky among the trays in the display while the father stands by silently. And then they, too, talk about a job well done, and again there is laughter. That night, the teacher designs an activity for her students that involves the sharing of plastic counting cubes in different ways, to be followed by light-hearted conversation about each student's methods. Perhaps there will even be laughter. For the teacher, her consideration of ethnomathematics to find ways to teach division has escaped the consideration only of context, and includes attention to the learning that already goes on in the culture (Sharp, 1999). Students will learn about division using the same processes that she saw in the lived mathematics of their cultures: doing with guidance, expressing, and enjoying. Returning to the cultural practices of the past as a way to go forward (Kanu chap. 8, this volume) could help us reconstruct school mathematics to begin with tactile and visual experience, scaffolded through watchful encouragement rather than critique. When progressively getting better at something of value is celebrated through conversation and laughter in math class, as well as in the child's life with her or his parents, we will have a mathematics that reflects Nunavut's natural and effective ways to teach and to learn.

Envisioning a Mathematics for Nunavut's Future

The mathematics that children of Nunavut need is as hard to declare as Nunavut's future is to predict. For example, consider whether Nunavut mathematics should approach geometry as traditional southern programs do, as a formal deductive system that traces back to Euclid more than two thousand years ago (Romberg, cited in Parker, 1993, p. 6). Should a foreign and ancient terminology (e.g., isosceles triangle, perpendicular bisector) be taught and learned by children whose fathers are able to navigate without tools and whose mothers can make caribou-hide *mukluks* that fit their children's feet perfectly without using numerical measurement? A decade ago, many people said no. Now, in a time when land claims and mining claims require precise surveying practices depending on global positioning systems, and the growth industry of the next few decades is likely to be diamond cutting and polishing, geometric skills both formal and conceptual are gaining in curricular prestige. A curriculum for children must necessarily prepare them for their lives to come. But when those lives are changing more quickly than curricula can be adapted, what are curriculum designers to do? More and more, curriculum is being reshaped to be framed around successful learning experiences, rather than content: 'Rather than accepting the modernist assumption that schools should train students for specific labor tasks, it makes more sense in the present historical moment to educate students to theorize differently about the meaning of work in a postmodern world. Indeterminacy rather than order should become the guiding principle' (Giroux, 1999, p. 102). In other words, the content and skills that we provide for children must be justifiable for their utility in relation to the fundamental goals that we know will be relevant tomorrow, and for their flexibility in relation to specific contexts that at present cannot be determined.

We cannot prepare the children of Nunavut for a traditional life on the land, or for a life of employment in specific commercial and government endeavours, for the simple reason that the future of Nunavut is not clear. Nor is the future of each individual child clear. Davis gives the same idea a cultural orientation: 'It is time to shift our attentions in school mathematics away from the current emphasis on concept competency and toward anthropological interpretation' (2001, p. 23). In other words, the children of Nunavut deserve a mathematics that prepares them to define themselves, to determine their relations with the land, and to negotiate their relations with the rest of Canada and the world. Such a curriculum does not need to be based on the particular content needs that could be listed if we could see students' future life-roles. Instead, it needs to be based on who the children are now, and what kind of persons we want them to become. Curriculum for Nunavut needs to be matched to the character of Nunavut that its citizens want to enact.

The above paragraph recommends three shifts in curriculum structure, all of which are generally considered *postmodern*, or *poststructuralist* (Walshaw, 2001; see also Kanu's introduction, this volume.) One, curriculum designers cannot presume to know the future and prescribe a specific list of knowledge and skills based on their foresight. Two, curriculum needs to be based not on universal truths, but on the local and specific realities of particular communities and cultures. Three, curriculum is becoming less a definition of what should be learned, and more of a consideration of what students are and could become. As such, it is a disruption of the centrality of the teacher in the classroom as a politically conserving force in the mathematics classroom. Freire describes student-based curriculum this way:

> I believe that a fundamental concern, not only of mathematicians but of all of us, mainly educators, who are responsible for deciphering the world, should be this one: to propose to youth, students, pupils, farmers, at the same time as they discover that four times four is sixteen, they also discover that there is a mathematical way of being in the world ... We start from what the learner knows in order that he or she can know better, know more and know what he or she does not know yet. I believe that what we do, to start from the world-view of the teacher, shows disrespect, which is an elitist disrespect. (Freire, in Freire, d'Ambrosio, Mendonca, & do Carmo, 1997, pp. 7–8)

There is a word that incorporates the different kinds of curriculum thinking that I have proposed for the teachers of Nunavut. First, I suggested *caution* regarding any assumption that a mathematics curriculum from a dominant and different culture would automatically be appropriate. I suggested *suspicion* regarding the appropriateness of the power relations implicit in any curriculum that is derived within the traditional gatekeeping mentality of traditional southern schools. I have recommended that the process of designing a mathematics curriculum for Nunavut *privilege* the strengths and beliefs of the culture and people which the curriculum must serve. In this section, I have suggested that anyone choosing or designing any curriculum today cannot presume to know the future towards which that curriculum must be aimed. Sumara, Davis, and Laidlaw identify the same three shifts more succinctly: 'In Canada, the moment one raises issues of identity, knowledge, and history – the subject matters of curriculum – one enters the realm of the contextually dependent, the negotiated, and the compromised' (2001, p. 150). If the curriculum processes of Nunavut reflect these principles, the word that would describe their curriculum stance would be *postcolonial*.

Knijnik exemplifies a postcolonial orientation for mathematics curriculum development in recommending that we 'examin[e] mathematics education from its connections with cultural difference as a field shaped by power relations, i.e. a political field' (2002, p. 12). Such an examination would reveal as a power relation the southern mathematics tradition of leaving behind the many students who do not learn successfully in a primarily symbolic mathematics: 'The expression *the cultural heritage of humankind* is very often only identified with academic mathematics. It is precisely this identification that masks power relations that, in turn, legitimize one very specific way of producing meaning – the Western, white, male urban and heterosexual one – as the cultural heritage of humankind' (ibid., p. 12). For Nunavut's own version of school mathematics to escape the shadows of the more dominant and dominating traditional forms of school mathematics, the postcolonial educational literature may be useful (see, e.g., Tejeda, Espinoza, & Gutierrez, 2003; see Aikenhead, this volume, for a parallel example in school science).

Bishop (1994) describes five approaches to teaching mathematics with cultures in conflict. Each approach is identifiable by its assumptions, its curriculum, the manner of teaching, and its use of language. The *culture-blind approach* would adopt traditional school mathematics practices. *Assimilation* would draw examples from the children's culture, and *teaching* would be caring, but the language of mathematics would remain formal and traditional. *Accommodation* would allow some influence upon instruction from the child's culture and language, although the formal curriculum would still be dominant. In the fourth option, curriculum is determined by negotiation between cultures, and the languages of both cultures are used. That choice is called *amalgamation*. Finally, when curriculum is totally that of the children's community, and instruction is by and about that community, Bishop offers the term, *appropriation*. The citizens of Nunavut will see in their school system's approaches to language of instruction and the adoption of alternate pathways to teacher certification elements spanning all five of these categories.

What Should Nunavut Take from Southern Mathematics Education?

It is unjust to leave the image of the mathematics curriculum of southern North America as a homogeneous and generally traditional force. There are many voices from the south who hope to end the colonial nature of their schools' relationships across social groups, or just reform their school mathematics to be empowering for all students rather than categorically selective among those students. I find that many of these academic voices are in harmony with the caring voices of Nunavut educators. I offer a sample of those voices below.

Education might be best organized around centers of care: care for self, for intimate others, for associates and acquaintances, for distant others, for nonhuman animals, for plants and the physical environment, for the human-made world of objects and instruments, and for ideas. (Noddings, 1992, p. xiii)

I recommend a way of knowing that moves away from treating race, gender, class, and ability as *categories* designating different and separate domains of social life, to discovering how they are features that arise in human interactions. That is, they are *relational properties* located in time and space. (Ng, 2003, p. 209)

If children are to become mathematically powerful ... then the educational community must find ways to ensure that these children, and others, have ongoing opportunities to do mathematics: to conjecture, invent, ponder, describe, represent, communicate, solve, create, and search for the patterns and relationships that surround them. They must have ongoing opportunities to learn that mathematics is a powerful tool for making sense of and for impacting their world. (Parker, 1993, p. 142)

Given voices such as these, if school mathematics determines that school must be a hostile and forbidding landscape for some (or many) students, why do we tolerate it? In southern Canada and in the United States, perhaps the answer is straightforward: it has always been so, and tradition is such a powerful force that even when traditional goals – of training and privileging an elite few and subjugating and streaming the rest towards lesser options – are no longer acceptable, the mechanisms that pursued those goals carry on. As much as listeners might resonate with the central values heard in the voices of reform-oriented educators, in the south we are not ready to risk the *destruction* of schools, our last universal social institution, to allow the *deconstruction and reconstruction* of schools' central identity. The sequence of quotes below shows the variation in voices across a deconstruction-reconstruction gradient:

As for curriculum, get rid of it ... Postmodern teachers will construct pedagogy out of local interests and concerns where worth and value is set within a narrative in which its players have a stake and a voice.' (Parker, 1997, pp. 151–152)

Changing the meaning of 'school.' We must come to understand that a school is not a school unless all learn. (Tharp & Gallimore, 1988, p. 272)

> Surely the central task of education today is not to confirm what is but to equip young men and women to meet change and to imagine what could be, recognizing the value in what they encounter and steadily working it into their lives and visions. (Bateson, 1989, p. 74)

The choices facing the educators of Nunavut about the nature of school mathematics are *not* constrained or predetermined by traditions emanating from school's historical responsibility to categorize students to prepare them for roles in an inequitable society. The schools are free to adopt the traditions of the south by allowing and participating in the unquestioned adoption of school mathematics that has already begun – or they may choose otherwise. So far, I believe, they have not chosen. They have not asked themselves the two tough questions I am raising: One, do we want all students as unique individuals to succeed in personally meaningful ways in Nunavut's schools – or do we want school mathematics to sort the students, predetermining their range of participation in the future to come? Two, based on the first answer, what do we want our children's experiences in mathematics (i.e., in schools) to be?

So Where Could Nunavut Mathematics Educators Begin?

In 1997, when the territorial government of Nunavut was first established as a separate entity from the Northwest Territories, the government was determined that it would escape some of the baggage that seemed to limit other governments. Towards that end, it approved a set of beliefs that are directly in synchrony with the autonomous development of a kinder and empowering mathematics: the beliefs set out first in the *Inuit Qaujimajatuqangit*, and second in the *Bathurst Mandate Pinasuagtavut*. The people of Nunavut know these government statements of principle well. The first one, known as IQ, is a commitment by the government of Nunavut 'to incorporate Inuit values and practices into all government operations. This includes schools. Some of these practices include consensus decision making and shared leadership' (Nunavut Department of Education, 2003, p. 3). The second document was written by the government in 1999 to set priorities and principles for all its endeavours. It specifies four sets of principles, each accompanied by a set of priorities. Below are some of the statements that are potentially relevant to the construction of a kinder and more inclusive school mathematics

1 Healthy Communities ... People come first ... Nunavut needs to provide options and opportunities which build the strengths of individuals, families and communities.
2 Simplicity and Unity ... By developing programs and services which are fair, understandable and easy to access we will encourage public participation and create accountability ... Cooperation will be the operating standard at every level.
3 Self-Reliance ... We will incorporate traditional activities and values into new strategies ... We will build on our strengths, respecting and highlighting the unique elements of our residents, communities, and the environment and economy in Nunavut.
4 Continuing Learning ... Equal opportunity and equal access across Nunavut is fundamental to our success ... Our education system needs to be built within the context of Inuit Qaujimajatuqangit ... Respect for individuals is the basis of effective learning. (ibid.)

Now it is up to teachers' imagination, along with the support of members of the mathematics education community in southern North America. Imagine a school mathematics program that consisted primarily of activities that all students could enter, because 'equal opportunity and equal access across Nunavut is fundamental' (quotes are all from the above IQ statements). Imagine a curriculum where content was secondary, because 'people come first.' Activities for the classroom would be designed or selected because of their inviting and inclusive nature. Such activities would have tactile and visual engagements with quantities and measures, to 'build on our strengths,' as people who *do* and *imagine* before they symbolize formally. Imagine a feedback system that reports to students what they are doing well, without comparative descriptions that foster competition, because 'cooperation will be the operating standard at every level.' Imagine a classroom based on conversation and collaboration, because 'Inuit values and practices [and] consensus decision making' make it unconscionable to leave any one student behind.

Of course, imagination is only a beginning. Any imaginative endeavour requires planning, enactment, evaluation, and refinement. This document provides only a starting point, an expression of belief and faith in the ideals expressed by teachers one year ago. The literature in mathematics curriculum reform, critical theory, ethnomathematics, and postcolonial theory was brought into action to amplify the basic principles of universality, inclusion, and equitable opportunity at the heart of the teachers' beliefs. If the educators of Nunavut act on their beliefs, their experiences could help mathematics educators everywhere with the curriculum reforms taking place in their schools.

Conclusion

There is one more asset that is at the disposal of the educators of Nunavut, should they decide to reform their school mathematics to reflect their values and the values of their people and government. To point to that asset, I return to the storytelling mode that opened this chapter. In a blizzard, when a hunter's snowmobile will not start, it is more than an inconvenience. It is not life or death: the hunter has strategies for staying alive until he is found. He can build a snow shelter, depending on the snow, and he carries a small stove for heat. He carries home-dried arctic char or shrink-wrapped beef jerky from the South to eat. Chances are, though, it's a clogged fuel line (any water content in the fuel will crystallize in the line at these temperatures), or the spark plugs are fouled. The hunter, whose father ensured that his son knew how to deal with unforeseen events when travelling by dogsled, will diagnose the problem. Then, even though he can only operate bare-handed for seconds at a time before rewarming his hands, he will deal with the problem. And the snowmobile will start. He will be back in town for his shift at the airstrip on Monday morning. An Inuit hunter is, by necessity, a snowmobile mechanic.

At home, supper for the rest of the family is on the stove. Sometimes it is traditional food: caribou, seal, arctic char. Sometimes, it is food from the co-op store. The mother's mother had ensured that her daughter knew how to keep an igloo warm and cook meals with a seal-oil burner, and how to keep the family well-clothed in home-sewn caribou parkas with wolverine-fur trim. Now, the mother knows how to do all that, and she is teaching her two children (aged 8 and 12) to decorate caribou mittens with traditional beadwork. But she also knows how to balance a household budget, work part-time in the community health office, and get the kids to school, three things her mother did not know, and did not teach.

The people of Nunavut are learners.

They deserve a school mathematics they can all learn.

REFERENCES

Adler, J. (2001). *Teaching mathematics in multilingual classrooms*. Dordrecht: Kluwer.

Barton, B. (1999). Ethnomathematics: A political plaything. *For the Learning of Mathematics, 19*(1), 32–35.

Barton, B. & Fairhall, U., & Trinick, T. (1998). Tikanga reo tatai: Issues in the development of a Maori mathematics register. *For the Learning of Mathematics, 18*(1), 3–9.

Bateson, M.C. (1994). *Peripheral visions: Learning along the way*. New York: Harper Collins.

Bishop, A.J. (1994). Cultural conflicts in mathematics education: Developing a research agenda. *For the Learning of Mathematics, 14*(2), 15–18.

Boychuk, R. (2004). The road from Bathurst Inlet. *Canadian Geographic, 124*(2), 38–56.

D'Ambrosio, U. (1997) Where does ethnomathematics stand nowadays? *For the Learning of Mathematics, 17*(2), 13–17.

Davis, Brent (2001). Why teach mathematics to all students? *For the Learning of Mathematics, 21*(1), 17–24.

Dorfler, W., & McLone, R.R. (1986). Mathematics as a school subject. In B. Christiansen, G. Howson, & M. Otte (Eds.), *Perspectives on mathematics education* (pp. 49–97). Boston: Reidel.

Frankenstein, M. (1987). Critical mathematics education: An application of Paulo Freire's epistemology. In I. Shor (Ed.), *Freire for the classroom: A sourcebook for liberatory teaching* (pp. 180–210). Portsmouth, NH: Boynton and Cook.

Frankenstein, M. (1997). In addition to the mathematics: Including equity issues in the curriculum. In J. Trentacosta & M.J. Kenney (Eds.), *Multicultural and gender equity in the mathematics classroom: The gift of diversity* (pp. 10–22). Reston, VA: National Council of Teachers of Mathematics.

Frankenstein, M., & Powell, A.P. (1989). In C. Keitel (Ed.), *Mathematics, education and society* (pp. 157–159). Paris: UNESCO.

Freire, P., d'Ambrosio, U., & Mendonca, M. (1997). A conversation with Paulo Freire. *For the learning of mathematics, 17*(3), 7–10.

Gerdes, P. (1994). Reflections on ethnomathematics. *For the Learning of Mathematics, 14*(2), 19–22.

Giroux, H.A. (1999). Border youth, difference, and postmodern education. In M. Castells, Flecha, R., Freire, P., Giroux, H.A., Macedo, D., & Willis, P. (Eds.), *Critical education in the new information* (pp. 93–115). Lanham, MD: Rowman and Littlefield.

Government of Nunavut. (2004). http://www.gov.nu.ca/Nunavut/English/departments/bathurst/ Accessed 20 March 2004.

Jones, M., Yonezawa, S., Ballesteros, E., & Mehan, H. (2002). Shaping pathways to higher education. *Educational Researcher, 31*(2), 3–11.

Kitchen, R.S., & Becker, J.R. (1998). Mathematics, culture, and power. *Journal for Research in Mathematics Education, 29*(3), 357–363.

Knijnik, G. (2002). Ethnomathematics: Culture and politics of knowledge in mathematics education. *For the Learning of Mathematics, 22*(1), 11–14.

Lubienski, S.T., & Bowen, A. (2000). Who's counting? A survey of mathematics education research, 1982–1998. *Journal for Research in Mathematics Education, 31*(5), 626–633.

Moore, C.G. (1994). Research in Native American mathematics education. *For the Learning of Mathematics, 14*(2), 9–14.

Moses, R.P., & Cobb, C.E., Jr. (2001). *Radical equations: Civil rights from Mississippi to the Algebra Project*. Boston: Beacon Press.

Ng, R. (2003). Toward an integrative approach to equity in education. In P.P. Trifonas (Ed.), *Pedagogies of difference: Rethinking education for social change* (pp. 206–219). New York: Routledge Falmer.

Noddings, N. (1992). *The challenge to care in schools: An alternative approach to education*. New York: Teachers College Press.

Noss, R. (1994). Structure and ideology in the mathematics curriculum. *For the Learning of Mathematics, 14*(1), 2–9.

Nunavut Department of Education. (2003). *Join team Nunavut!* Iqaluit, NU: Author.

Parker, R.E. (1993). *Mathematical power: Lessons from a classroom*. Portsmouth, NH: Heinemann.

Parker, S. (1997). *Reflective teaching in the postmodern world: A manifesto for education in postmodernity*. Buckingham: Open University.

Pinxten, R. (1994). Ethnomathematics and its practice. *For the Learning of Mathematics, 14*(2), 23–25.

Roberts, T. (1998). Mathematical registers in Aboriginal languages. *For the Learning of Mathematics, 18*(1), 10–16.

Secada, W.G. (2000). *Changing the faces of mathematics: Perspectives on multiculturalism and gender equity*. Reston,VA: National Council of Teachers of Mathematics.

Sharp, J.M. (1999). A teacher-researcher perspective on designing multicultural mathematics experiences for preservice teachers. *Equity and Excellence in Education, 32*(1), 31–42.

Silver, E.A. (1997). 'Algebra for all' – Increasing students' access to algebraic ideas, not just algebra courses. *Mathematics Teaching in the Middle Schools*, 2(4), 204–207.

Skovsmose, O. (1994). Towards a critical mathematics education. *Educational Studies in Mathematics, 27*, 35–57.

Stiff, L.V. (1990). African-American students and the promise of the Curriculum and Evaluation Standards, In T.J. Cooney & C.R. Hirsch (Eds.), *Teaching and learning mathematics in the 1990* (pp. 152–158). Reston, VA: National Council of Teachers of Mathematics.

Sumara, D., Davis, B., & Laidlaw, L. (2001). Canadian identity and curriculum theory: An ecological, postmodern perspective. *Canadian Journal of Education, 26*(2), 144–163.

Tate, W.F. (1997) Race-ethnicity, SES, gender, and language proficiency trends in mathematics achievement: An update. *Journal for Research in Mathematics Education, 28*(6), 652–679.

Tejeda, C., Manuel, E., & Gutierrez, K. (2003). Toward a decolonizing pedagogy: Social justice reconsidered. In P.P. Trifonas (Ed.), *Pedagogies of difference: Rethinking education for social change* (pp. 10–40). New York: Routledge Falmer.

Tharp, R.G., & Gallimore, R. (1988). *Rousing minds to life: Teaching, learning, and schooling in social context.* Cambridge: Cambridge University Press.

Walshaw, M. (2001). A Foucauldian gaze on gender research: What do you do when confronted with the tunnel? *Journal for Research in Mathematics Education, 32*(5), 471–492.

Wolodko, B.L., Willson, K.J., & Johnson, R.E. (2003). Metaphors as a vehicle for exploring preservice teachers' perceptions of mathematics. *Teaching Children Mathematics, 10*(4), 224–229.

PART 2

Indigenous Knowledges as
Postcolonial/Anticolonial Resistance

6 *Is We Who Haffi Ride Di Staam*: Critical Knowledge / Multiple Knowings – Possibilities, Challenges, and Resistance in Curriculum/Cultural Contexts

GEORGE J. SEFA DEI AND STANLEY DOYLE-WOOD

The intent of this chapter is to pursue a radical analysis and inquiry of educational and curriculum work as it applies to social inequity and exclusionary practices reproduced and sustained through racialized asymmetrical relationships of power. To this end this chapter insists upon a radical contestation of dominant and/or imposing school knowledge discourses and their covert and/or overt claims to cultural supremacy, legitimacy and normalcy. Working though the lens of curriculum as cultural practice, and positioning difference in the form of indigenous knowledges and spirituality as a source of embodied resistance and transformative counter-hegemonic knowledge, the analysis seeks to challenge and sever the epistemic violence of Western cultural knowledge as it relates to the material exigencies of marginalized subjects and communities. Although our insistence upon the reimagining and repositioning of difference as critical political discourse draws strength from the important work of postcolonial theory, we nevertheless, further insist upon an anticolonial agency and anticolonial curriculum that enunciates itself in what Stephen Slemon has referred to as an 'open talk across cultural locations' (1995). Without making such linkages and without taking into account the totalizing neocolonial impact of globalization and global capital interests, we (as marginalized bodies in the North) cannot (but we must) fully understand the changing ontology of systemic violence as it impacts us at 'home' when the interests of Western cultural capital feels threatened by the very same bodies 'abroad' (in the South). As the Black British poet Linton Kwesi Johnson has rightly observed, referring to Britain under Prime Minister Margaret Thatcher and the subsequent intensification of minoritized subjugation and repression, in such times *'is we who haffi ride di staam'* (it is we who have to ride the storm).

As we write this chapter we recall, a story shared by a colleague. It is of Paulo Freire giving a talk at our academic institution shortly after returning from Africa, where he had been engaged in organizing literacy classes. A member of the audience asked him what he liked best in the revolutionary setting that he was working in, and Freire replied: 'The joy of working with people whose only illiteracy is with language.' This is more than simply a sarcastic response on the part of Freire. It is a statement that alludes to the power of language and how it becomes (for us all) an essential challenge and responsibility to be able to hear each other's embodied cultural knowledge as part of the project of promoting social and educational transformation. In keeping with this framework, then, we position this chapter as a sort of conversation with educators, drawing on a sense of collective 'we' to make our point regarding the necessity to rethink our teaching, instructional, and curricular practices in order to make our work more effective. We devote a large portion of the discussion specifically to addressing issues of difference, pedagogy, curriculum as cultural practice, and the roles of educators in bringing about educational change. We begin by raising some key questions: (1) What do we see as the role that education can play in the creation of a socially cohesive society? (2) What do we see as the crisis of public education today? (3) How do we allow our schools to do what they do best? (4) How do we achieve the characteristics of a healthy school system? And lastly, (5) Do we believe that we have some consensus on what we see as the urgent and most enduring task of public education? (See Ungerleider, 2003.)

We have no definite answers to any of these questions. But we will say this. If race, gender, class, dis/ability, sexuality, and other forms of difference are not central to our discussions of the answers, then we are heading towards failure. We say this because the long-endured systemic marginalization of minoritized peoples has constituted the two most powerful poisons crippling our school systems today, namely, those of race and poverty. And yet it is ironic because our schools are the true meeting place of diverse bodies, a place where people hang together for lengthy periods hoping to acquire knowledge for self and collective advancement. Unfortunately, as is often the case, race and class work together to produce alienation for many of these bodies. The marketization of educational systems has not helped the situation, either. In fact, because of this we see an increased production of tensions and divisions reinscribed in ways that threaten to tear the very fabric of society. The bodies in our school systems, for example, are demarcated on the lines of race and poverty. How do we avoid race and poverty tearing down the success of our public school system? We submit that the answer does not lie in wishing away race, class, and other forms of social difference, but in openly confronting the challenges that they pose for us as educators, learners, policymakers, parents, communities, and organizations.

The success of the public school system today calls for sacrifices, honesty, and a collective desire to 'do the right thing' for all our students, as much as it calls for the infusion of resources. Schooling is too important to be left in the hands of educators alone. Communities, parents and/or families, and social workers, all have roles to play. Quite often we expect parents to make the first move, to be involved in schooling, perhaps rightly so. But then educators must play their part by supporting local communities. This becomes clearer when one thinks that cutbacks in education to frontline services (e.g., school community advisers and equity departments, in the case of Ontario; Dei, 2003) have meant that under-resourced and underfunded community organizations have been forced to step in and fill the gap to ensure that the needs of children from racialized communities are met. Yet, many of these community organizations spring from marginalized communities that themselves already have limited resources (Zine, 2003).

Thus, we are speaking here of how difference is significant and imperative to discussions of schooling. By *difference* we include broad questions of identity and power, and in broaching difference we would like to implicate and start with the self. The tensions and contradictions that take place in our lives as we pursue intellectual and political work in many ways speak to the complexities of difference, whether in terms of standpoints or personal identities. In our work to bring about educational change we are often confronting the question of how we each navigate the moments that complicate the self as a multiple, differentiated subject. No doubt, the self is not just one thing. Each self has different layers that define its multiple and sometimes competing expectations, desires, and ambitions. Unfortunately, there are moments and spaces in everyday life when we are more apt to deny difference in the name of a shared commonality, as if the recanting of difference is in itself a problem. It is this realization that propels us to write about difference in the context of Canadian schooling, and how schooling practices around critical cultural curricular instruction and classroom pedagogy offer possibilities for delivering education to a diverse group of learners. We are motivated by intellectual and political desires to speak about the nature and complexity of *difference*, how it is understood, imagined (and reimagined), and how these challenges cannot be decontextualized from minority engagements with schooling in Canada and the postcolonial and/or neo-colonial global tensions in which they are set. Part of the commonsense talk about difference revolves around the calls for respect and tolerance. But what does it mean to tolerate someone? Not only is this discourse patronizing; it is also very abusive. 'Tolerance' allows one to maintain a hold on power and respectability. It places the violent onus on the Others to ensure that they do not overstep their boundaries or risk the penalty of being disliked and abjectified.

The postcolonial and/or anticolonial tapestry is a call for action. It is a call for educators to anchor their pedagogy in a critical interrogation of the structures for education delivery, that is, structures for the teaching, learning, and administration of education. Our educational projects must continually serve as a bridge to students who are often considered 'at the margins.' We use the term *margins* here not simply to typify particular (racial) bodies but to gesture to all who do not fit into conventional definitions of what constitutes 'success and excellence.' Students who may not be marked and designated as 'high achievers' in the conventional, narrow, Western sense of academic scores and grade point averages are quite often 'high impact' persons in the communities in which they live. Partly, this is because they make practical usage of their education just like anybody else does. It is also because the students themselves are committed people to begin with. We must allow all our students to impact on some form of social justice. It is not only what our students want; perhaps all of us who consider ourselves progressive educators want this as well. We also need a broader view of the educational process that encompasses personal satisfaction, achievements, significance, and happiness in our collective endeavours.

In a postcolonial and/or anticolonial context, schools must be open spaces that give opportunities to people from non-traditional backgrounds, from the margins, and from the most disadvantaged segments of our communities to realize their goals and dreams. The physical presence of different bodies in our school systems is a great thing to see, but equally significant is unpacking how we get to this position and – this is crucial – what happens to these bodies in relation to the dissemination and interrogation of the knowledge production that they face. In addition, we need to ask why our current crop of students and teachers does not always reflect the racial, ethnic, class, gender, and sexual diversity that characterizes our larger communities. We must allow students to come to school to *learn*. This is not a cliché or trite statement that we are enunciating here: It seems to us that there is no point in claiming open access to *all* students, if in reality not *all* the students have the means or resources to make use of the opportunities for learning and succeeding well in society, both socially and academically. Educators must not only help shape students' career trajectories; they must also become facilitators of a sense of community where intellectual work can flourish. As we undertake our tasks, we must provide critical education that allows students to question the absences, omissions, and negations and, in turn, be rewarded for their resistance. If we give our students anything less than a critical education, we are shortchanging them not just metaphorically but literally. In concrete, material terms we run the risk of murdering their dreams and imaginings before they are barely conceived.

Re-articulating Difference

How do we begin to discuss and theorize critical education within curriculum and/or cultural contexts? In reimagining and repositioning difference, questions of who gets to define and speak of difference(s) are critical: What are the spaces, political positions, textual locations, discourses, and moments from which particular voices speak? When and how do they speak? Whose voice is assigned legitimacy or illegitimacy (Spivak, 1988)? What forms of knowledge and/or power allows the particular ways of articulating and re-articulating difference in relation to the nation-state (Shohat, 1995). What are the discursive effects of colonial power in this form, and how is this power disseminated through difference and cultural practice? Is difference conceptualized and/or constituted by authority as a deficit or lack? If so, what then are the possibilities for resistance and spiritual transformation beyond or within (and in opposition to) the space of oppressive authority? Finally, what forms does embodied indigenous and/or spiritual knowledge take in the context of minoritized resistance to imposed colonial and neo-colonial dominance? These are just some of the theoretical questions that we hope to shed light on as we continue further into this conversation.

As an entry point into the discussion we are reminded of three interrelated incidents or experiences that occurred some years ago while one of us was participating in a lengthy observation and work study project in a Canadian public school Senior Kindergarten program. Seen by the children largely as an outsider and not part of the school institution, this author was able to experience childhood culture in a way that is often not accessible to official authority figures. The first incident involved a 6-year-old boy (we will call him Toni) hitting a girl of similar age on her arm during recess. The girl began to cry and called for help, causing this author, who was close by, to intervene. After the intervention, which drew an apology from Toni, the young boy left the scene to play in another area of the playground. It seemed (at least from the author's perspective) that this was the end of the matter, until a short while later Toni approached the author to explain to him in a confidential way why he had hit the girl. According to Toni, it was because he is black. In the words of that 6-year-old, 'that's what you do when you're black. You see that guy in Scarborough who raped that woman?' said Toni. 'He was black, see that's what you do when you're black. And you swear too, see that's what you do when you're Jamaican.' In the second experience, the author overheard a verbal exchange in the classroom between two Asian-Canadian boys (we shall call them Jay and Phil). In the course of a visual arts activity Jay made a comment to Phil in his first language. Phil immediately remonstrated with Jay in their second language (English), by asking, 'Don't you know we're not supposed to speak our language in here?' Heeding the warning, Jay reverted to English in continuing his conversation. The third experience saw the author observing and participating in a group reading, writing, and drawing session at a table with four students. One of them, Asian-Canadian (we shall call her Mia), asked the author to pronounce the word *volcano*, which was written in the book that she was reading. The author did so phonetically, in English. Mia then looked at the word and the accompanying picture of a volcano and asked the author, 'Do you want me to show you how to write that in Chinese?' The author nodded, signalling his willingness to be taught. Mia then proceeded to write in Mandarin the word characters for both fire and mountain, explaining to the author that when the two are put together they become 'fire-mountain' which is (explicitly expressed by Mia) another way of saying and thinking, 'volcano.'

As we invoke these stories it is important to emphasize our belief that the lived realities of students such as Toni, Jay, Phil, and Mia cannot be abstracted from the racialized sociopolitical discourses from which they ultimately emerge. As such we seek to contextualize these incidents and experiences and stories within a dominant discursive paradigm that formulates learning and education towards the path of institutionalizing student bodies to the 'natural' social order of things in ways that decontextualize difference from the asymmetrical power relationships that underpin their social environment. Chandra Talpade Mohanty has rightly argued that classrooms are not only sites of instruction, 'they are fundamentally political and cultural sites that represent accommodations and contestations over knowledge by differently empowered social constituencies' (1997, p. xvi); thus, the 'struggle over representation is always a struggle over knowledge' (ibid.). The struggle for the students, therefore, in all three vignettes is the struggle – as living embodiments of knowledge – to be heard, recognized, acknowledged as human, and the struggle to maintain a sense of agency in face of the normalizing systems of power. All four children enunciated, in their actions and words, a politics of diasporic belonging that is either denied or occluded by the processes and structures of 'official' knowledge systems.

To hear a 6-year-old like Toni equate his body, group, and community, and thus his embodied cultural knowledge with that of rape is, no doubt, a disturbing aspect – particularly from a dominant liberal standpoint that fears and is horrified by the supposed criminality of black male bodies. The fear is of an inchoate deviant body that someday may be loose in 'our' neighbourhood, threatening 'our' streets and families. And yet to position Toni as violent in this form propounds the violence that draws him to such positionings. The violence of a classroom and educational setting that negates a student's daily social experience of navigating the intensity and terror of dominant knowledge's racialized signifying practices is what we should be condemning. Toni's positionings, we would argue, arise from his struggles to resist and subvert the dominant (mis)reading of his body. In this particular period Toni's daily experience witnesses day-to-day racism that permeates his (and his family's and community's) life in both systemic and cumulative ways. From birth, Toni has navigated a world of images, signals, discourses, and messages where black bodies are seen to not count. This is a world where whiteness dominates at every turn, a world where backlash and antipolitical-correctness politics lends respectability and dominant consensus to the racialization of crime, circulating inherently racist discourses of 'black on black' crime, while denying 'white on white.' This is a period in time when mainstream newspapers project, on their front pages, sensationalized photographs of black bodies in handcuffs or in situations related to violent criminal acts – and whether they are innocent or not, the image condemns them as guilty. This is where Toni's knowing comes from. This is a world in which the saliency of racism produces 'rejection, exclusion, underestimation, and inequities and impediments [that are so] regularly infused into "normal" life that they appear unquestionable' (Essed, 1991, p. 146).

In part it is that unquestionability and the contradictions of these discourses that Toni appears to be questioning when he says to the author, 'That's what you do when you're black.' He gives the author a lesson in the daily struggles he is faced with. The author did not believe the phrase was uttered in any pathologized sense. It did not appear in any form that Toni actually believed that this is (really) what you do when you're black. Rather, the enunciation was delivered in an almost ironic sense that said to the perceived outsider white figure, 'Isn't this who you say I am? Isn't this what you think of me ... isn't this whom I'm supposed to be ... a rapist? Isn't this what you tell me every day?' It appeared to the author that Toni knew full well that this is not what you do when you're black, but the question had to be picked up by the perceived dominant figure. When the author (despite his light skin) was able to evoke his own Afro-Caribbean ancestry, his father, his uncles, his aunties, and say to Toni, 'No that's not what you do when you're black,' when he was able to bring his own indigenous knowledge to bear, to give Toni alternative ways of seeing, and to let Toni know that he never wanted to hear him say that again, 'ok.' The answer was 'ok' back. Yet that 'ok' was a powerful 'ok.' It was an 'ok' that carried reciprocal love and respect. Toni seemed to be looking for that same response from the dominant systems of power within his learning environment, a response in opposition to his daily experience that would say through the curriculum, 'No that's not what you do.' But in his institution of learning that answer never came. Every shred of white Eurocentric knowledge was a reinforcement of his sense that they believe 'that's what you do in this body.' Like Phil, Jay, and to a certain extent Mia, Toni was forced to engage in the double consciousness of policing his body and embodied knowledge while probematizing and resisting his social reality.

Within his classroom and the school itself there was certainly no overt rules telling the students that they could not express their first language or bring to bear their indigenous or local knowledges and cultural knowings to the centre of the learning environment. There were no posters on the walls (such as 'one should never start a sentence with a preposition') that spoke of their knowledges as invalid or forbidden. But there did not need to be. Corrigan points out that it is in the school routines of normalization that 'deny, down value, distort, and dilute' the embodied knowledges, voices and lived experiences of marginalized students that invalidation is enforced (1990, p. 160); moreover, such routines are productive of 'active wounds' (ibid.). These active wounds in different ways and to various extents are seared in the struggles of students such as Toni, Phil, Jay, and Mia. They are *active* in their accumulative capacity to despiritualize, disempower, disengage, and shut out the students from their schooling environment.

The violent dissemination of the wound is further bolstered by a Cartesian-Newtonian teaching approach that is based on cause and effect, and Western empiricism and deductive reasoning that completely disregards the asymmetrical relations of power that shape people's lives. In *Rethinking Intelligence*, Joe Kincheloe et al. (1999, p. 2), noted the dangerous implication of Western cognitive and/or educational psychology in schooling methodologies of this nature. Grounded on a culturally specific post-Enlightenment theoretical foundation, Western educational psychology as a field 'measures' and seeks out traits of intelligence with which it is culturally familiar (for more on this point, see Kincheloe, this volume). As a result 'unknown attributes of intelligence' that cannot be measured by psychology are ignored, in terms of intelligence quotients (IQs) and standardized testing methods, 'only a culturally specific set of indicators of aptitude is sought. In this way the intelligences of individuals from cultures different from [the norms set by the field, including] unique thinkers from any sociocultural background are dismissed' (ibid.). This clearly has profound consequences for brilliant students such as Toni, Jay, Phil, and Mia who exercise different knowledges and who, in their own way, are already engaged in an analysis and theorization of power relationships. At issue here is whether educational professionals, including cognitive and/or educational psychologists, engage the type of critical ontology put forward by Kincheloe (this volume) which would enable them to gain insights and understandings alien to their own worldviews.

Hegemonic messages proclaiming what is culturally and/or racially legitimate and what is not are pervasive in discourses of normalization. They are structurally grounded in the hidden culture of the schooling institution itself. They become explicit and/or implicit in forms that project a 'deep curriculum' (Dei, Mazzuca, McIssac, & Zine, 1997, p. 144), that is, those formal and informal aspects of the school environment that intersect with both the cultural environment and the organizational life of the school. As a result white and Eurocentric neo-colonial dominance is spoken loudly and unequivocally in the forces of such normalizing routines that are institutionally supported. Minoritized students are constrained into disembodied silence, and their capacities of expression and communication that are severely regulated by cultural and/or racially charged discourses of what is considered, acceptable, appropriate, or what is approved. It is the educator and more accurately the 'deep curriculum' that determines which bodies should speak and which should not, what is considered *speech* and what is not, what should be spoken, for how long, in what form, and in what language. Critical here is the question of *voice* (implying cultural agency, as opposed to mere speech) that Yatta Kanu raises in her analyses of British colonial education in Sierra Leone and in Trinidad and Tobago (see her introduction to this volume). As Kanu crucially implies, the question is whose voice is allowed expression in a colonial approach to education? What counts as voice? The colonizer's imperative need to *give* (conceptualized in colonial power relations as a gift in the same manner that the slave master bestows freedom upon the slave, thus re/constituting an imagined sense of deified racial superiority) the colonized speech cannot be underestimated here. It is the Robinson Crusoe discourse, which, as Gayatri Spivak (1999, p. 187) reminds us, is premised on the colonial desire to give speech to the native. As Spivak has observed it is in the very first encounter between Crusoe and Friday that Crusoe claims: 'I began to speak to him [Friday], and teach him to speak to me.' As Spivak points out, 'Crusoe does not need to learn to speak to the racial inferior. [He] knows savages have a language' (ibid.), but this is to be ignored. Crusoe needs the racial Other to speak back to him in mimetic fashion, thereby possessing and domesticating the native as a body of mimic through the violent denial and negation of her or his voice. Colonial mimicry in this form is thus 'the desire for a reformed recognizable Other, as a subject of a difference that is almost the same but not quite' white (Bhabha, 1994, p. 86). Homi Bhabha has noted further, however, that within such spaces of instabilities of power and not quite-whiteness there lie ambivalences and ambiguities that offer sites for resistance to colonial power which we shall touch upon later in the discussion. For now it is important to continue to interrogate the dominant discursive practices and formations that do violence to students such as Toni, Jay, Phil, and Mia.

The response from the teachers at least in the case of Toni, when the incident was brought to their attention, was surprise – then to blame and pathologize Toni's family. The teachers did not see that the school as an institution and its curriculum could be implicated. Indeed, it was taken for granted that inclusion existed because all the students were learning in a multicultural classroom and in an environment in which cultural diversity was 'celebrated.' Indeed, the classroom and school were a popular destination for student teachers primarily because of its 'cultural diversity' and 'inner city' character. Yet, we would suggest that it is precisely the dominant conceptualization of 'multicultural' that lends itself to the accumulation of oppression and/or repression that is experienced by minoritized students. In other words, a culturally diverse space does not necessarily promote the expression of cultural difference. As McClaren points out, multiculturalism particularly in its liberal democratic form, is based primarily on the notion of sameness, whereby social inequality is derived not from systemic oppression, but rather from a lack of opportunity within the existing Eurocentric capitalist system (1954). The resulting calls for modification of the status quo are predicated on the belief that racialized, Enlightenment, universalistic, and Eurocentric norms should remain intact. Cultural difference is conceptualized as an exoticized, fixed entity, devoid of heterogeneity, history, agency, and power, and one that is tacked on to the white norm. The 'multicultural' in this sense becomes a code for the non-white and results in ghettoization. It is a paradoxical relationship, however, because while at specific moments the presence of difference threatens the cultural norm, it is also needed in its form of essential difference. As Trin T. Minh-ha has pointed out, 'if you cannot locate the other you cannot locate yourself' (1991, p. 73). Moreover, as Chatterjee has noted, 'for Enlightenment itself to assert its sovereignty as the ideal universal ideal [it] needs its other: if it could ever actualize itself in the real world as the truly universal it would in fact destroy itself' (1986, p. 17). This needing of the racial Other through which raced-dominant systems of power constitute themselves, has profound implications for bodies such as Toni, Phil, Jay, and Mia: because when difference is fixed in the dominant imagination in ways that serve the constitution of dominance it becomes situated on what Rinaldo Walcott has referred to as a 'continuum that runs from the invisible to the hyper-visible' (1997, p. 36).

We saw the experiences and positionings of Toni, Jay, Phil and Mia as instances of resistance. An enacted resistance that is anticolonial in its nature. As Slemon argues, citing Jenny Sharp's article entitled 'Figures of Colonial Resistance,' resistance itself is never easily located (1995, p. 108). Resistance is ambivalent, ambiguous, and 'always in some measure an "effect of the contradictory representation of colonial authority" [thus, it is] never simply a "reversal" of power ... never simply there in the text or in the interpretive community, but ... always necessarily complicit in the apparatus it seeks to transgress' (ibid.). Resistance, in the form of all four of the embodied oppositional knowledges of the children highlighted here, points towards alternative pedagogical pathways of seeing and doing, and these represent spaces of subversion within an arena of dislocating political oppression that constitutes for some of its citizens the notion of 'home' and 'nation' but denies these spaces to others (see Kara McDonald, this volume, for elaboration of this point).

Phillip Corrigan has made the crucial observation that schools historically not only teach subjects, they also teach, sustain, and constitute subjectivities (1990, p. 156). Dominant subjectivities formed out of a discourse of exclusionary universalism support, sustain, and reconstitute the discourse of the nation-state when placed against a diasporic backdrop personified in the bodies and communities as represented by Toni, Jay, Phil, and Mia. However, if the discourse of nation-state rests on notions of homogeneity, boundedness, essential differences, and a racial and/or cultural 'unifying force, then the presence of diasporic bodies such as Toni, Phil, Jay, and Mia, can be seen to represent what Sayyid (2000) has referred to as an 'anti national' and anti-globalization presence.

In evoking diaspora as a political formation, Sayyid contends that diaspora (unlike the nation-state) suggests heterogeneity, porousness. It is anti-nation and anti-global because it interrupts the imaginative and/or material racial and/or cultural (en)closure of nation, as it is conceptualized in Western Enlightenment discursive thinking. Sayyid argues that nations define home, whereas diaspora is a condition of homelessness. In the nation the territory and people are fused in one but in the diaspora the two are disarticulated. The diaspora, however, is not the Other of the nation precisely because it is constructed from the antithetical elements of the nation. The existence of a diaspora prevents the closure of the nation since a diaspora is by definition located within another nation. The relationship of diasporic bodies to the nation, therefore, is paradoxical and ambivalent. In one sense they point towards the possible strength of nation 'in their attempt to maintain the sense of nationhood in the context of territorial dispersion and, on the other hand, they point towards the inability of a nation to be completed by making it difficult to erase difference'; it is in this latter form where difference, as embodied knowledge, cannot be and refuses to be erased that Sayyid conceptualizes the notion of diaspora as the 'antithesis of the nation' (Sayyid, 2000, p. 42).

Here we find connections with Paul Gilroy's notion of the Black Atlantic that asserts a similar 'reinterpreting [of] the cultural core [of the so called] "authentic national life"' (1993, p. 11) through a political black hybridity that is both intercultural and transnational. Both Gilroy and Sayyid seek to move beyond ontological essentialist standpoints that are both imposed and internalized, and by doing so they challenge the psychological and material racial and/or cultural (en)closure of the Western nation space. In this form they point towards the creation not only of a 'counter-culture of modernity' (ibid., p. 29) and space that transcends the closed boundaries of Western nation-conceptualizing, but also a rupturing of the entire 'global hegemonic order.' The consequences for failing to reconceptualize hegemonic nation-state discourses in this manner will mean increased oppressions and repressions on marginalized bodies both in the South and in the North, as Euro-American global capital and global capitalist interests continue to constitute their cultural and/or racial material identity and needs, by and through, the bodies of minoritized difference.

Difference, thus, points to oppositional agencies and diasporic knowledges that have profound consequences for the reimagination of state and nation. Mia showed us that critical and/or transformative pedagogy is a collaborative process in which indigenous and/or local knowledge, lived experiences and/or lived crisis, cannot be decontextualized from schooling practices, nor indeed can they be relegated to the margins or cracks of the educational centre. We are reminded here of the important work undertaken by Homi Bhahba in which he argues for a Third Space of resistance in the very fissures, cracks, 'contradictory and ambivalent space of enunciation' (1994, p. 37) to which Toni, Jay, Phil, and Mia are consigned. However, in the context of our discussion of schooling as cultural practice we are mindful of what Gilroy has described as the dazzle of whiteness that dislocates (1993), particularly its psychological impact and colonial hold on knowledge production. As Vandana Shiva reminds us, 'colonialism has from the very beginning been a contest over the mind and the intellect. What will count as knowledge? And who will count as expert or as innovator' (2000, p. vii).

It has been argued elsewhere that 'school systems in their production of Eurocentric practices continue to impose colonial/imperial control on the processes of knowledge production, interrogation, validation and use. Although knowledge resides in the body and cultural memory, the Eurocentric gaze has influenced and shaped what we see and what not to see as valid knowledge. Specifically, the dominance of Eurocentric knowledge is evident in the limits that have been set on what can be critiqued, how the critique is conducted, and who does the critiquing' (Dei, 1999, p. 404). What then do we mean when we speak of acknowledging and *re*thinking difference from a transformative, anticolonial standpoint? What do we mean when we speak of the need to accentuate difference and individual agency?

First, we see *difference* as both a site of personal identity and a site of asymmetrical power relations based upon race, class, gender, sexuality, and other forms of social difference. Centring difference in anticolonial work means resisting and challenging what has traditionally and oppressively been constructed and valorized as normal. It means understanding that 'all representations are the result of social struggles over signifiers and signified' (McLaren, 1994, p. 58); it means acknowledging the power of individual agency and collective action (ibid.). Rethinking difference means understanding how difference can become a strategic way of constructing oneself and a source of radical social action. In this form it is no longer a site of exclusion and repression but a site of resistance. In this form the terms of existence and self-actualization are determined not by the centre but by those on the periphery. In this form race and difference become a 'way of self-definition, of self-naming, a way of fighting back' (Arber, 2000, p. 50). In understanding difference one must deal with what Edward Said has referred to as the 'nexus of knowledge and power' that underpins the creation of the Other and 'in a sense obliterating him as a human being' (1979, p. 27).

Educators must take 'critical discourse' seriously in terms of broadening our knowledge of what it means to 'transform' – through activism and creativity – knowledge from the mundane to a more spiritual engagement and/or connection with the discursive practices so that we can move away from a preoccupation with 'limitation' to 'possibilities' of pedagogy. The possibilities of pedagogy include educators being bold to acknowledge and respond to difference and diversity within the schooling population; this means ensuring that curriculum, pedagogy, and texts reflect the diverse knowledges, experiences, and accounts of history, ideas, and lived experiences and struggles. Such possibilities require that educators enact and apply their agency in their classrooms. There must be accountability in terms of how educators can evoke power to address issues of minority schooling. Indeed, in the contexts of schooling in Canada and elsewhere in North America there are multiple sites of power and accountability. Educators are urged to frame educational 'praxis' in terms of agency and deliberation, as well as a constant confrontation of the varied forms of domination and subjugation in the schooling lives of youth. The implications of radical scholarship in Euro-Canadian/American contexts today, therefore, are to theorize inclusive schooling work beyond the boundaries of adherence to the sacredness of educational activity. We must all develop an anticolonial awareness of how colonial relations are sustained and reproduced in schooling practices. To have a decolonized space requires a decolonized mind: Colonialism is situated in the psyche and we cannot create decolonized schools without decolonizing the minds that run them. We believe in political action for change. Consequently, there is power in working with resistant knowledge. Resistance starts by using received knowledges to ask critical questions about the nature of the social order. Resistance also means seeing small acts as cumulative and significant for social change (Abu-Lughod, 1990). It will, for example, require shifting away from Eurocentric/Western theorizing and discursive practices towards a radical lens that interrogates hegemonic discourses and centres the exigencies of the marginalized. It will mean embracing the epistemologies of anticolonial agency. We should then look towards different ways of theorizing identity, difference, and nation-state in terms of schooling curriculums, making connections to notions of 'home,' of belonging and multiple knowings, or, what we might call (to borrow from Mia), rupturing the volcano with fire-mountain.

Anticolonial Agency and Indigenous Knowledge

In our continuing reflections on difference and agency in the anticolonial discursive sense we draw upon the revolutionary work of anticolonial thinkers such as Albert Memmi (1991), Frantz Fanon (1963, 1967), and Aimé Césaire (2000) among others. We define and contextualize our critique, therefore, through the lens of a radical field of scholarship that has exposed and analysed the violent impact and contradictions of the asymmetrical power relations embedded in the nexus of colonizer and colonized. Such writings assert resistance to the dehumanizing effects of colonial systems of power as they emerge from dominant knowledge production, education, and learning. Knowledge production, and thus education disseminated in regions of the geopolitical south such as the Caribbean, Africa, and Latin America, has been essential to the process of colonialism in terms of institutionalizing the colonized to the social order. As Memmi observed that 'it is not enough for the colonizer to be the complete master ... he must also believe in its legitimacy. [At the same time] it is not enough for the colonized to be a slave, [she or] he must also accept this role' (1991, 88–89). Thus, the process of dehumanization is the process of objectification. At the end of the day, the colonized body should exist not as a human being but as an object of 'the colonizer's supreme ambition.' She or he 'should exist only as a function of the needs of the colonizer, i.e., be transformed into a pure colonized' (ibid., p. 86).

Colonial language disseminated in the form of education has played a key role in this project. Ngugi wa Thiong'o, speaking of colonial education in African contexts has noted the insidious power of colonial language in its knowledge productive form, citing it as the 'most important vehicle through which [European/colonial] power fascinated and held the soul prisoner. The bullet was the means of the physical subjugation, language was the mean of the spiritual subjugation' (1995/1986, p. 287).

Like Ngugi Wa Thiong'o, who long ago challenged the primacy of English literature and culture in African academies and called for the abolition of the University of Nairobi (1972), Eric Williams has castigated the colonial education system in the Caribbean in the same vein (1976, p. 76). Focusing particularly on the curriculum for Caribbean students wishing to enter university, Williams notes that the Caribbean student was forced to take English political history, followed by a *special* period of English political history, for example, European history, Greek history, English colonial history, or English economic history; study Latin textbooks, translation, and composition, as well as Roman history; French textbooks, translation and composition; Spanish textbooks, translation and composition; two plays by Shakespeare, one play by Chaucer; and produce two papers on English Literature. The examinations were set by English examiners in England. In one instance the subject of an assigned essay was entitled 'A Day in Winter.' Needless to say, few students had ever seen a European winter's day outside of colonial textbooks. As John Willinsky (this volume) points out in reference to the public school literature curriculum, if we switch to the twenty-first century Canadian public school curriculum, we find that little has changed. Subjects are taught and dominant/subaltern subjectivities are still being constituted.

The study of literature, arts, economics, world history, Canadian history, social sciences, and humanities all place Europe and white normative middle-class values and perceptions at the forefront and centre, to the erasure of all other knowledges. Where there is 'inclusion' it is usually in the form of limited, 'optional' texts such as Harper Lee's *To Kill a Mockingbird*, which serves primarily to reconstitute white dominance through the essentialized positionings of blacks and minoritized bodies as simple-minded victims in binary opposition to whites as their intellectual saviours and superiors. How many of those who defend and 'love' the Atticus Finch character and the part played by Gregory Peck can, for example, give the black 'central' character's fictional name (Tom Robinson) or even the actor (Brock Peters) who played him in the film? Long ago the epistemic, material, and spiritual violence of colonial and neo-colonial knowledge production as it applies to colonized bodies and marginalized communities was vividly captured in the words of the Cuban scholar José Marti: In conditions of colonialism and imperialism where local and/or indigenous histories, identities, and experiences are (mis)appropriated and negated, it is as if the 'head of a giant is being placed on the body of an ant. And every day ... the head is being increased and the body decreased' (Marti, cited in Williams, 1976, p. 76).

With these thoughts of Marti in mind we conceptualize agency as a site of liberation and the practice and/or theorization of resistance by colonized and marginalized peoples to systemic oppression and/or repression. We view agency as a site of empowerment and active resistance formed by the oppressed within specific social and spatial asymmetrical relations of political power. To borrow from Grossberg, we define agency as the 'articulation of subject positions into specific places (sites of investment) and spaces (fields of activity) on socially constructed territorialities. Agency is the empowerment enabled at particular sites and along particular vectors ... it points to the existence of particular formations of practices as places on social maps, where such places are ... potentially involved in the making of history. Agency as a site is ... realized [when] specific investments are enabled and articulated' (1993, pp. 100–101). To speak of anticolonial agency, then, is to know our political self. It is to resist, rupture, and renounce the giant's head in counter-hegemonic ways. It is to refuse its violation and despiritualization of our collective minds, bodies – and souls. It is to know and see the giant's head for what it is, not for what it *claims* (Eurocentrically/universally) to be. Anticolonial agency arising from an anticolonial discourse (Dei, Hall, & Rosenberg, 2002, p. 7) places stress on power that is held and sustained through practice in local and/or social spaces to survive colonial and colonizing encounters. It argues that power and discourse are not the exclusive terrain of the colonizer. The power of resistance and discursive agency reside in and among colonized and marginalized groups. Subordinated and/or colonized peoples had a (theoretical and practical) understanding of the colonizer that 'functioned as a platform for engaging in political/social practice and relations' (ibid.). The notion of 'colonial' is, therefore, grounded in power relations and inequities that are imposed and engendered by tradition, culture, history, and contact. Anticolonial agency and/or theorizing, however, 'rises out of alternative, oppositional paradigms, which are in turn based on indigenous concepts, analytical systems and cultural frames of reference' (ibid.) that are vital in reclaiming our sense of self and spirituality.

In arguing for Western educational curriculums to open up space to indigenous knowledges and anticolonial agency we are not seeking simply to replace one centre with another, nor are we seeking to (re)create and sustain the false dichotomies of conventional and/or colonial and/or external knowledge as bad and non-Western or marginalized or indigenous knowledges as good (ibid., p. 4). Rather, we are calling for diverse ways of knowing that are dynamic and continuous and that represent a multiplicity of centres. Moreover, we view anticolonial agency and indigenous knowledges not as romantic, static or fixed entities but rather as collaborative, liberating, and fluid. Our conceptualization of indigenous knowledge refers to a body of knowledge derived from the long-term occupancy by a people (not necessarily indigenous) of a specific locale or place (ibid., pp. 6, 72). From this situatedness in-depth understandings and/or knowledges encompassing particular, norms, traditions, and values are accrued. Mental constructs born from lived and learned experiences serve as guides to regulate and organize ways in which people and communities live and make sense of their world; they become the means through which decisions are formed in the face of challenges that are both familiar and unfamiliar (ibid., p. 6). We view indigenous knowledges as differing from conventional knowledges in the sense that colonial and/or imperial hegemonic impositions are absent.

Like Kincheloe (this volume), we would argue that *indigenousness* is central to power relationships, global knowledge, and ways of acting, feeling, and knowing. Indigenous knowledge acknowledges the multiple, collective, collaborative origins and dimensions of knowledge, with the belief that the interpretation or analysis of social reality is subject to different perspectives that are oftentimes oppositional. We see indigenousness, then, as emerging from an indigenous knowledge system that is based on cognitive interpretations and understandings of the social, political, and physical and/or spiritual worlds. Indigenous knowledges include beliefs, perceptions, concepts, and experiences of local environments, both natural and social: As articulated elsewhere To speak of 'indigenousness' in African contexts, for example, is to enunciate questions related to local culture and social identities (Dei, 2002, p. 72). Different forms of knowledge represent different points on a continuum. As such they are dynamic, building upon each other in accumulative ways that allow different ways for people to perceive and act upon their world. In the contexts of Western (mis)education systems, indigenous knowledges intersect with anticolonial agency to enable students to arrive at different ways of seeing and articulating both community and individual experiences of marginality and resistance within their space of learning. Students, whose lives consist of explicit and implicit daily confrontations with poverty, discrimination, and alienation, accumulate through their families, elders, and communities diverse cultural knowledges of political and/or spiritual resistance to oppression that demand inclusion in the curriculums of their schooling. It is through the lens of oppositional epistemologies, emerging as they do through local and/or global human connectedness, that we argue for a reconceptualization and reimagining of the Eurocultural, absolutist nature of the Western school curriculum as a site of possibilities – rather than limitations – that are both multiple-centred and expressive of anticolonial agency.

Writing of Hawaiian indigenous philosophies of knowledge, Leilani Holmes has described a 'grounded epistemology' centred on 'heart knowledge,' 'blood memory,' and the 'voice of the land' (2002). Within this indigenous conceptual space knowledge is passed to future generations first from a 'higher power' and then through the 'relationships and deep feelings of connection' with family and *Kapuna* (elders). In this form it is 'lodged in the heart of the listener' and thus becomes 'heart knowledge.' In Holmes's words, 'knowledge is given through the relationships and for the purpose of furthering relationships. It surpasses the intellectual realm, and lodges itself in the emotional realm, so I have called it "heart knowledge"' (ibid., p. 41). As knowledge flows through the bodies of successive generations the 'continuum of time is collapsed into and manifests out from the bodies of humans.' Thus, younger generations exist relationally as opposed to in the abstract. Moreover, as the legacy or idea of knowledge is further transformed into claims about human relatedness to the environment, inseparable links are made between knowledge and the cosmos (ibid.). Through interviews with *kupuna* and *makua* (parent generations) Holmes reveals the importance of blood in the context of *blood memory*. Here, Holmes does not refer to 'blood quantum,' the code of eugenics used to define (by U.S standards) who is indigenous and who is not for the express purpose of dispossessing indigenous peoples from their lands 'officially' (Churchill, 1996, p. 26), nor to the notion of *jus sanguinis* (Sassen, 1999, p. 61) in which citizenship and nation status is based on biological inheritance. On the contrary, blood memory is conceptualized and evoked in ways that challenge and speak back to the destructiveness of these very same discourses through connections made among Hawaiians with each other. As one member of the parent generations, Kalo, reveals in Holmes's interviews, 'it does not matter where Hawaiians live. They can live all over the world ... when you say that you are Hawaiian, we never say "how much Hawaiian do you have?" which is a total ... *alien* concept, but the fact that you are Hawaiian and you are "ohana" (family) and that we eat out of the same ... bowl ... And that we come from the same roots. And that's the connectedness that ... brings all Hawaiians together, no matter how much Hawaiian they have by blood quantum' (2002, pp. 41–42). This represents an immensely powerful and liberating source for spirituality and decolonizing agency for, 'wherever you live, if you are Hawaiian, you are Hawaiian. You are accepted into the "ohana." Unconditionally. There are no ... restrictions, no limitations, no obstacles, no barriers' (ibid.).

Where the sense of identity and of belonging is an experience of dislocation and alienation both in marginalized bodies and communities of the South, and those very same bodies struggling with crisis of identity, belonging, dislocation, and alienation emanating from Western cultural knowledge production in the North, indigenous philosophies of this nature speak to an anticolonial pedagogy that stands in opposition to the cultural curriculums of Western schooling and, in doing so, reveals possibilities for transformative change. 'Blood memory' points to human connections that transcend Western notions of identity, fixed to racialized conceptions of nation-state, and Englightment notions of space and time. As Holmes points out, blood memory is a genealogical connection flowing through God, family, and land. It is thus, 'a circle of love' grounded on blood and roots. 'Central to the idea of blood and roots is the notion that experience is crucial to knowledge. If one does not have the experience, knowledge must come through the experience of the *kapuna.*' *Kapuna* are, therefore, conceptualized as 'containers of memory.' Thus, in the knowledge passed down through stories from families and from the *kapuna*, knowledges are 'validated not through the notion of "truth value" but rather through connection. The memories that are passed down through connection are inviolable' (2002, p. 42). Spirituality is anchored in values that are related to the land and memories of living on the land. In what Holmes refers to as the 'voice of the land' knowledge of the land is passed down through stories told by the *kapuna* in ways that articulate an indigenous cosmology.

In a further enunciation of Indigenous epistemologies that moves us beyond simply a critique of Western cultural knowledge and nation-state, Marlene Brant Castellano reveals the knowledge systems of First Nations people in Canada as emanating from multiple overlapping and interacting sources that include the 'traditional teachings, empirical observation, and revelation' (2002, p. 23). Much like Yatta Kanu's description of indigenous African knowledge (this volume) traditional knowledge, according to Castellano, comprises knowledge that has been handed down from previous generations. Varying from nation to nation it tells stories of 'the creation of the world,' 'the origin of clans in their encounters between ancestors and spirits in the form of animals' (ibid.). Genealogies and ancestral rights to territories are recorded along with the memorialization of battles, boundaries, and treaties. Traditional knowledge 'instills attitudes of wariness or trust toward neighbouring nations.' Moreover, it reinforces values and beliefs through heroic and cautionary tales that in turn 'provide the substructure for civil society. In some of its forms, it passes on technologies refined over generations' (ibid.) As Castellano explains, the elder generations and the wisdom they carry is held in high regard and as such it is the elders who are assigned the major responsibility for the teaching of the young. Empirical knowledge is conceptualized as 'a convergence of perspectives from different vantage points accumulated over time' (ibid., p. 24). This, of course, is in direct contrast to the Western conception of 'empirical' which valorizes methods of quantitative analysis in controlled settings through repeated observations. *Revealed knowledge*, as Castellano points out, 'is acquired through dreams, visions and intuitions that are understood to be spiritual in origin' (ibid.). Such knowledge, she reveals, can play an important role in healing and reclaiming indigenous spirituality: 'In times past, youths of many nations undertook vision quests during which they made the transition to adult roles and responsibilities. In contemporary times it is often adults of mature years – many of them in troubled circumstances – who seek out the help of elders to discover their identity and purpose through fasting and ceremonies' (ibid.). The belief in knowledge as holistic is of central importance in indigenous epistemologies. As Castellano asserts, the most powerful tool for the conveyance of the holistic character of Aboriginal knowledge and experience is that of the medicine wheel. She describes the medicine wheel as a circle representing the 'circle of life' in which there is contained 'all experiences, everything in the bio-sphere – animal, vegetable, mineral, human spirit – past, present and future' (ibid., p. 30). As Castellano further reveals, the Aboriginal teachings of the circle at first seemed to alienate her from her roots, however, 'at some point an elder elaborated on the flags at the ends of the intersecting lines. They signify the winds that blow and move the wheel, reminding us that nothing is fixed and stagnant, and that change is a natural condition of life. I remembered that learning and growth in each of the quadrants had taken precedence in various stages of my life. It dawned on me then that the medicine wheel is not a model of rigid categorization or racial division; rather, it is a model of balance' (ibid.). The medicine wheel, therefore, teaches counter-hegemonic ways of seeing and knowing in global, political, and spiritual contexts. As Castellano points out, the circle is a 'model of the world,' of 'people unitied in a circle.' It is a model of embodied knowledge that decisively ruptures the universalizing intellectual slave ship that many of us are forced to sail upon.

If we can agree that knowledges reside in bodies and cultural memories (Dei, 1999, p. 406) then knowing about race and racism through experience, feelings, and social practice represents a form of 'indigenized knowledge within the spiritual realm.' Research undertaken by Dei and colleagues (1997) in the Toronto public school system has shown that within the African-Canadian student populations, indigenous knowledges and indigenous knowings are often manifested in critical understandings, readings, and theorizings of racialized power relationships that transcend in complexity and analytical clarity the thinking and conceptualizing of dominant authority. As Philomena Essed has pointed out, 'without general knowledge of racism one cannot understand the reality of racism' (1991, p. 72). It is crucial, therefore, that the embodied knowledges in our school systems that experience multiple oppressions of poverty, racism, classism, gender discrimination, and homophobia on a regular basis must have a significant say in the formation of curriculum and learning; anything less is an assault upon the spirit. When we speak, therefore, of the epistemic and/or material violence of colonial systems of power, we are also speaking of the violence of despiritualization that historically has been a crucial tool for colonial oppression. To speak spirituality, then, is to speak of decolonizing resistance.

Spiritual Resistance and Decolonizing Knowledge

Our conceptualization of anticolonial agency and indigenous knowledge as decolonizing educational practice represents a liberatory form of spiritual resistance. When we speak of anticolonial agency and counter-hegemonic epistemologies and practices as forms of spirituality, however, we are speaking of an action-oriented, revolutionary spirituality and not simply one that is aesthetic. We are speaking of an inner spirituality that allows emotional and intellectual paradigmatic shifts. While recognizing that there are multiple articulations and readings of spirituality, our understanding of spirituality here is not necessarily an ascription to a high religious or moral order, but rather an understanding of the self-hood or personhood and culture as a starting point in our engagements with education and learning. As Dei has argued elsewhere (2004), education is anchored in a broader definition that encompasses emotional and/or spiritual dimensions and cultural knowledge. An identification with the learning process that is personalized and subjective makes it possible for learners to become invested spiritually and emotionally in their education.

Spirituality and spiritual knowing can be pursued in schools as a valid body of knowledge to enhance learning outcomes. Spirituality encourages and engages in the sharing of collective and personal experiences of understanding and dealing with the self. A great deal of what is 'universal' in spirituality is related to aspects of knowing and asserting who we are (in relation to dominant knowledges that tell us something else), what our cultures are, where we come from, and the connections of the Self to the Other. Research by Dei shows that spiritual knowledge and spirituality have important implications for reconceptualizing African education, and the education of the learner. Critical educators in Africa today are teaching youth to be spiritually informed and to think of themselves as both Africans and as global citizens. Learning proceeds through the development of the African self and identity. Critical teaching allows the learner to stake out a position as African, a position that is outside and oppositional to the identity that has been, and continues to be constructed in Euro-American ideology (ibid.). Spirituality in this respect, therefore, is an implicit antithesis to the Western concept that the learning of curriculum is ever solely 'universal,' where universal means neutral and common to all. We argue that spirituality as a form of resistance allows for identification with ourselves and the universal that, in turn, provides an implicit means through which we can assert ourselves collectively and individually. In this form spirituality becomes a powerful tool for resisting (mis)education, domination, and discriminatory forces. When spirituality is occluded in classrooms, school curriculums, and systems of education as a whole, the resulting assault can have destructive consequences, particularly for the development of self and identity in minoritized individual and/or community contexts. If nurtured and respected, spirituality can be utilized to involve and energize both schools and local communities.

The ways in which people have understood and seek to further understand their world necessarily includes place, time, and many other critical aspects that such as, among others, the world of the material, of the social, of ideas, and of the spirit. This is the case regardless of how individual groups may perceive or define 'spiritual' (Dei, 2004). The spiritual development of the learner is, therefore, a crucial dimension of learning and of education as a whole. The blurring of specificities and experiential connections of places to people is counter to the spiritual connection of the individual and community. The ways in which knowledge is being produced, consumed, marketed, disseminated, and disposed of is antithetical to the time required for individualized reflection, collective discussion, and integration into ways of thinking, living, and being a part of a people. Time, place, and human connectedness are essential for social communication that moves beyond the superficial depositing and marketing of information into people and communities.

Spirituality, for many peoples of the world, is a crucial dimension of human existence. It is how we come to know and make sense of our worlds. This process of coming to know is not always predicated on the acquisition of what one does not know. Each of us has knowledge that may not easily manifest itself in terms of how we come to understand our social existence and the sociopolitical constructions that come with it. Spirituality and spiritual knowledge, however, represent a critical counter-hegemonic space through which this understanding of subjectivity, self, and identity can be navigated. The self as identity and subjectivity, is itself linked to knowledge production and schooling. Being aware of this makes knowledges positional, situational, and contextual.

It is important to note that the call for spirituality to be viewed as a legitimate aspect of students' learning and knowledge stands as a site of contestation in Western-dominated social arenas. As Butler (in-class presentation, 2000) has noted, in the knowledge economies of Western cultural systems of education, spirituality can fall prey easily to commodification and as a result be rendered as individualistic and solipsistic rather than as arising from a community and/or human struggle for justice and dignity. Strategies in approaching spirituality, therefore, need to be critical and also respectful of different religious traditions, including secular thought, or we run the risk of making the theorizing of spirituality in schooling fundamentalist, laissez-faire, or basist. We believe at the moment that there is greater potential for students to develop a sense of spirituality and strength from their local communities rather than from the school itself. Therefore, if spirituality is to be fostered in schools there must be teachers present who acknowledge and understand the value that spiritual and emotional development represents for the learner. Our searches to understand questions of spirituality must not steer away from interrogating issues of power. We need, for example, to examine how certain spiritual values come to dominate others. Consequently, educators must avoid liberal understandings of spirituality that separate material from the non-material existence. Approaches and strategies for empowering students in our schools should open up spaces for spirituality and spiritual knowledge to be centred in the school curriculum. Spirituality and spiritual discourse give rise to ideas and ontologies that emphasize connections, belonging, identification, love, well-being, compassion, and peaceful coexistence with people and with nature.

Conclusion

In summation, then, we are calling for a curriculum that is multiple-centred and anticolonial. As Fanon has noted, the process of decolonization represents a calling into question (and ultimately a changing) of the entire colonial social order of things (1963, p. 35). Dei and Asgharzadeh have argued that Fanon's process of revolutionary questioning is highly important, 'not as a resting place, but in order to make the connection between what is and what ought to be' (2001, p. 4). In this discussion we have spoken at length of 'what is and what we believe ought to be.' We have broached upon issues of difference, marginality, the political sense of 'home,' the nation-state, diasporic positionings, anticolonial agency, indigenous knowledges, and spiritual resistance in decolonizing contexts as they apply to curriculum as dominant cultural practice. What we would like to argue further, however, is for a bringing together of these issues within an anticolonial curricular space. In arguing for such a space we are drawing on the work undertaken by Dei and Asgharzadeh who assert an anticolonial discursive framework as providing a 'common zone of resistance in which oppressed and marginalized groups are enabled to form alliances in resisting various colonial tendencies' (2001, p. 4). Within this decolonizing space, *colonial* is conceptualized not simply as alien or foreign, but rather as dominating and imposed (ibid., p. 4). Thus, an anticolonial curriculum problematizes and critiques all forms of dominating and oppressive relationships (embedded in social relations and marked by race, class, gender, sexuality, and dis/ability, as well as other forms of social difference) that emerge from structures of power and privilege. Moreover, anticolonial 'interrogates the power configurations embedded in ideas, cultures, and histories of knowledge production, validation, and use' (ibid.).

Alan Bishop (1995), for example, has critiqued the cultural imperialism inherent in the Western conceptualizing of mathematics as a neutral, universal truth (1995). Noting that in Papua New Guinea alone there are more than 600 systems of counting, 'containing various cycles of numbers, not all base ten' (ibid., p. 72), Bishop has revealed the destructive implication for indigenous communities when Western mathematics (denying its appropriation of other indigenous knowledges and 'convinced of its superiority to any indigenous mathematical systems and culture') is imposed in ways that educate students 'away from their culture and away from their society' (ibid., p. 73); for similar criticism in relation to mathematics education among Canadian Inuit in Nunavut, see Ralph Mason (this volume). As Bishop explains further, 'to decontextualize, in order to be able to generalize, is at the heart of western mathematics and science; but if your culture encourages you to believe instead that everything belongs and exists in its relationship with everything else, then removing it from its context makes it literally meaningless' (ibid., p. 74). Within an anticolonial curriculum spirituality, agency, and critical consciousness emerge through resistance knowledge that 'examines our understanding of indigeneity, pursuit of agency, resistance, and subjective politics' (Dei and Asgharzadeh, 2001, p. 4).

A key aspect of anticolonial pedagogy lies in the understanding that institutions and their structures of power are sanctioned by the state 'to serve the material, political, and ideological interests of the state and the economic/social formation.' However, an anticolonial framework also recognizes the power of 'local social practice and action in surviving the colonial and colonized encounters' (ibid.). Thus, power and/or discourse resides not only in its entirety with the dominant and colonizing forces, it is also held by the colonized. In this sense the colonized themselves, as students, adult individuals, and communities, posses, the 'power to question, challenge, and subsequently subvert the oppressive structures of power and privilege' that underpin the Western hegemonic articulation and/or invention of the nation-state and its global interests (ibid.).

Notions of colonial and anticolonial are clearly embedded within the narratives of nation-building and the political projects of national identity. The focus on commonalities and common identities may allow citizens to feel a sense of collective purpose and shared political destiny; however, practices that efface difference can end up sweeping tensions under the carpet in the name of community-building. Such practices of avoiding difference become detrimental especially when difference and sameness are pitted against each other. A critical discourse of differences as connected and intertwined to produce a community of difference is more powerful to ensure a collective sense of belonging. As Dei has argued, when differences are negated and commonality is forced, the ensuing politics can itself be colonizing, for the community is never 'unitary' (2004); if it is projected as such, then it becomes exclusive (Anderson, 2000, pp. 381–391). Similarly, we cannot abandon the presence of diverse bodies into a dominant view of an imagined 'community of sameness.' Usually what are said to be the characteristics of such a community are the values, ideas, and aspirations of the most dominant members of society (Furniss, 1999). Ultimately, as Shiva has rightly observed, 'the future of indigenous knowledges will not simply determine whether the diverse cultures of the world evolve in freedom or are colonized; it will also determine whether humanity and diverse species survive' (cited in Dei, Hall, & Rosenberg, 2002, p. ix). In this sense if we do not transform sooner or later *all of we are going to haffi ride de staam* (Johnson, 1980). The implications for curriculum, pedagogy, and learning are crucial. If we do not begin the change now we become directly implicated in Shiva's poignant assessment. We owe it to Toni, Jay, Phil, and Mia, and we owe it to their children – and to our children – to transform and transcend the status quo.

REFERENCES

Abu-Lughod, L. (1990). The romance of resistance: Tracing transformations of power through Bedouin women. *American Ethnologists, 17*(1), 41–55.

Anderson, K. (2000). Thinking 'positionally': Dialogue across multicultural, indigenous and settler spaces. *Annals of the Association of American Geographers, 90*(2), 381–391.

Arber, R. (2000). Defining positioning within politics of difference: Negotiating spaces 'in between.' *Race Ethnicity and Education, 3*(1), 50.

Bhabha, H.K. (1994). *The location of culture.* New York: Routledge.

Bishop, A.J. (1995). Western mathematics: The secret weapon of cultural imperialism. In B. Ashcroft, G. Griffiths, & H. Tiffin (Eds.), *The post colonial studies reader* (pp. 71–6). New York: Routledge.

Castellano, M.B. (2002). Updating aboriginal tradions of knowledge. In G.J.S. Dei, B.L. Hall & D.G. Rosenberg (Eds.), *Indigenous knowledge in global contexts: Multiple readings of our world* (pp. 21–36). Toronto: University of Toronto Press.

Césaire, A. (2000). *Discourse on colonialism.* New York: Monthly Review Press. (Original work published 1952)

Chatterjee, P. (1990). *Nationalist thought and the colonial world: A derivative discourse.* New York: Zed Books.

Churchill, W. (1996). *From a native son: Selected essays on indigenism, 1985–1995.* London: South End Press.

Corrigan, P. (1990). *Social forms / human capacities.* New York: Routledge.

Dei, G.J.S. (1999). Knowledge and politics of social change: the implication of anti-racism. *British Journal of Scociology of Education, 20*(3), 395–409.

Dei, G.J.S. (2002). African development: The relevance and implications of 'indigenousness.' In G.J.S. Dei, B.L. Hall, & D.C. Rosenberg (Eds.), *Indigenous knowledges in global contexts: Multiple readings of our world* (pp. 70–86). Toronto: University of Toronto Press.

Dei, G.J.S. (2003). Communicating across tracks: Challenges for anti-racist educators in Ontario. Special Issue. *Orbit, 33*(3), 2–5.

Dei, G.J.S. (2004a). Dealing with difference: Ethnicity and gender in the context of schooling in Ghana. *International Journal of Education Development, 24*(4), 343–359.

Dei, G.J.S. (2004b). *Schooling and education in Africa: The case of Ghana.* Trenton, NJ: Africa World Press.

Dei, G.J.S., & Asgharzadeh, A. (2001). The power of social theory: The anti-colonial discursive framework. *Journal of Educational Thought, 35*(3), 297–323.

Dei, G.J.S., Hall, B.L., & Rosenberg, D.G. (Eds.). (2002). *Indigenous knowledges in global contexts: Multiple readings of our world*. Toronto: University of Toronto Press.

Dei, G.J.S., Mazzuca, J., McIssac, E., & Zine, J. (1997). *Reconstructing dropout: A critical ethnography of the dynamics of black students' disengagement from school*. Toronto: University of Toronto Press.

Essed, P. (1991). *Understanding everyday racism: An interdisciplinary theory*. Thousand Oaks, CA: Sage.

Fanon, F. (1963). *Wretched of the earth*. New York: Grove Press.

Fanon, F. (1967). *Black skin, white masks*. Grove Press. (Originally published in 1952)

Furniss, E. (1999). *The burden of history: Colonialism and the frontier myth in a rural Canadian community*. Vancouver: UBC Press.

Gilroy, P. (1993). *The black Atlantic: Modernity and double consciousness*. Cambridge, MA: Harvard University Press.

Grossberg, L. (1993). Cultural studies and/in new worlds. In C. McCarthy & W. Crichlow (Eds.), *Race, identity and representation in education* (pp. 89–105). New York: Routledge.

Holmes, L. (2002). Heart knowledge, blood memory, and the voice of the land: Implications of research among Hawaiian elders. In G.J.S. Dei, B.L. Hall, & D.G. Rosenberg (Eds.), *Indigenous knowledges in global contexts: Multiple readings of our world* (pp. 37–53). Toronto: University of Toronto Press.

Johnson, L.K. (1980). Independent Intavenshan. In *Inglan Is a Bitch* (p. 11). Loncon: Race Today Publications.

Kincheloe, J.L., Steinberg, S.R., & Villaverde, L.E. (1999). *Rethinking intelligence*. New York: Routledge.

McLaren P. (1995). White terror and oppositional agency: Towards a critical multiculturalism. In D.T. Goldberg (Ed.), *Multiculturalism: A critical reader* (pp. 45–74). Oxford: Blackwell.

Memmi, A. (1991). *The colonizer and the colonized*. Boston: Beacon. (Original published in 1957)

Minh-ha, T.T. (1991). No master territories. In *When the moon waxes red: Representation, gender and cultural politics* (pp. 215–218). New York: Routledge.

Mohanty, C.T. (1997). Dangerous territories, territorial power and education. In L.G. Roman & L. Eyre (Eds.), *Dangerous territories: Struggles for difference and equality in education* (pp. ix–xvii). New York: Routledge.

Said, E. (1979). *Orientalism*. New York: Vintage.

Sassen, S. (1999). *Guest and aliens*. New York: New York Press.

Sayyid, S. (2000). Beyond Westphalia: Nations and diasporas – the case of the Muslim Umma. In B. Hesse (Ed.), *Un/settled multiculturalism: diasporas, entanglements, transruptions* (pp. 35–50). New York: Zed Books.

Sharp, J. (1995). Figures of colonial resistance. *Modern Fiction Studies, 35*(1), 137–155.

Shiva, V. (2002). Cultural diversity and the politics of knowledge. In G.J.S., Dei, B.L. Hall, & D.G. Rosenberg (Eds.), *Indigenous knowledges in global contexts: Multiple readings of our world* (pp. vii–x). Toronto: University of Toronto Press.

Shohat, E. (1995). The struggle over representation: Casting, coalitions and the politics of identification. In R. De La Campa, E.A. Kaplan, & M. Sprinkler (Eds.), *Late imperial culture* (pp. 166–178). London: Verso.

Slemon, S. (1995). The scramble for post-colonialism. In C. Tiffin & A. Lawson (Eds.), *Descrambling empire: Post-colonialism and textuality* (pp. 15–32). New York: Routledge.

Spivak, G.C. (1988). Can the subaltern speak? In C. Nelson & L. Grossberg (Eds.), *Marxism and the interpretation of culture* (pp. 271–313). London: Macmilliam.

Spivak, G.C. (1999). *A critique of postcolonial reasons: Toward a history of vanishing present.* Cambridge, MA: Harvard University Press.

Thiong'o, N. (1972). On the abolition of the English department. In *Homecoming essays on African and Caribbean literature, culture and politics* (no pp. nos. available). London: Heinemann. Also in B. Ashcroft, G. Griffiths, & H. Tiffin (Eds.), (1995), *The postcolonial studies reader* (pp. 438–442). New York: Routledge.

Thiong'o, N. (1986). The language of African literature. In *Decolonising the mind: The politics of language in African literature.* London: James Currey (pp. 4–33). Also in B. Ashcroft, G. Griffiths, & H. Tiffin (Eds.), (1995), *The postcolonial studies reader* (pp. 285–290). New York: Routledge.

Ungerleider, C. (2003). *Public lecture on Canadian public schooling.* Presented at the Seminar Series of the Department of Theory and Policy Studies, Ontario Institute for Studies in Education, University of Toronto (OISE/UT).

Walcott, R. (1997). *Black like who?* Toronto: Insomniac Press.

Williams, E. (1976). *The negro in the Caribbean.* New York: Greenwood Press.

Zine, J. (2003). *Personal conversations with George Dei.* Department of Sociology and Equity Studies, Ontario Institute for Studies in Education, University of Toronto (OISE/UT).

7 Critical Ontology and Indigenous Ways of Being: Forging a Postcolonial Curriculum

JOE L. KINCHELOE

Mainstream teacher education provides little insight into the forces that shape teacher identity and consciousness. Becoming educated, becoming a postcolonial teacher-scholar-researcher, necessitates personal transformation based on an understanding and critique of these forces. In this context this chapter develops a notion of critical ontology (ontology is the branch of philosophy that studies what it means to be in the world, to be human) and its relationship to *being* a teacher in light of indigenous knowledges and ontologies. As teachers from the dominant culture explore issues of indigenousness, they highlight both their differences with cultural others and the social construction of their own subjectivities. In this context they come to understand themselves, the ways they develop curriculum, and their pedagogies in postcolonial educational contexts. Such issues become even more important at a time when new forms of economic, political, and military colonialism are reshaping both colonizing and colonized societies. This chapter makes three basic points:

- Critical ontology is grounded on the epistemological and ontological power of difference.
- The study of indigeneity and indigenous ways of being highlights tacit Western assumptions about the nature and construction of selfhood.
- A notion of critical ontology emerges in these conceptual contexts that helps us push the boundaries of Western selfhood in the twenty-first century as we concurrently gain new respect for the genius of indigenous epistemologies and ontologies and explore them for envisioning curriculum.

What Is Critical Ontology?

In this context we engage in the excitement of attaining new levels of consciousness and 'ways of being.' Individuals who gain such a critical ontological awareness understand how and why their political opinions, religious beliefs, gender role, racial positions, and sexual orientation have been shaped by dominant cultural perspectives. A critical ontological vision helps us in the effort to gain new understandings and insights as to who we can become. Such a vision helps us move beyond our present state of being – our ontological selves – as we discern the forces that have made us that way. The line between knowledge production and being is blurred, as the epistemological and the ontological converge around questions of identity. As we employ the ontological vision we ask questions about ethics, morality, politics, emotion, and gut feelings, seeking not precise steps to reshape our subjectivity but a framework of principles with which we can negotiate. Thus, we join the quest for new, expanded, more just, and interconnected ways of being human.

An important dimension of a critical ontology involves freeing ourselves from the machine metaphors of Cartesianism. Such an ontological stance recognizes the reductionism of viewing the universe as a well-oiled machine and the human mind as a computer. Such colonial ways of being subvert an appreciation of the amazing life force that inhabits both the universe and human beings. This machine cosmology has positioned human beings as living in a dead world, a lifeless universe. Ontologically, this Western Cartesianism has separated individuals from their inanimate surroundings, undermining any organic interconnection of the person to the cosmos. The life-giving complexity of the inseparability of human and world has been lost and social and/or cultural and/or pedagogical and/or psychological studies of people abstracted – removed from context. Such a removal has exerted disastrous ontological effects. Human beings, in a sense, lost their belongingness to both the world and to other people around them.

The importance of indigenous (Semali & Kincheloe, 1999; Steinberg, 2001) and other subjugated knowledges emerges in this ontological context. With the birth of modernity, the scientific revolution and the colonial policies they spawned, many premodern, indigenous ontologies were lost. Ridiculed by Europeans as primitive, the indigenous ways of being were often destroyed by the colonial conquerors – not only the military ones but the political, religious, and educational variety as well. While there is great diversity among premodern worldviews and ways of being, there do seem to be some discernible patterns that distinguish them from modernist perspectives. In addition to developing systems of meaning and being that were connected to cosmological perspectives on the nature of creation, most premodern viewpoints saw nature and the world at large as living systems. Western, often Christian, observers condescendingly labeled such perspectives as pantheism or nature worship and positioned them as an enemy of monotheism. Not understanding the subtlety and nuance of such indigenous views of the world, Europeans subverted the sense of belonging that accompanied these enchanted understandings of nature. European Christomodernism transformed the individual from a connected participant in the drama of nature to a detached, objective, depersonalized observer.

The Western modernist individual emerged from the process alienated and disenchanted. As Edmund O'Sullivan puts it, Cartesianism tore apart 'the relationship between the microcosmos and the macrocosmos' (1999, p. 18). Such a fragmentation resulted in the loss of cosmological significance and the beginning of a snowballing pattern of ontological imbalance. A critical ontology involves the process of reconnecting human beings on a variety of levels and in numerous ways to a living social and physical web of reality, to a living cosmos. Of course, in this process Westerners have much to learn from indigenous educators. Teachers with a critical ontological vision help students connect to the civic web of the political domain, the biotic web of the natural world, the social web of human life, and the epistemological web of knowledge production. In this manner, we all move to the realm of critical ontology where new ways of being and new ways of being *connected* reshape all people.

The Power of Difference

The concept of difference is central to a critical ontology. Gregory Bateson uses the example of binoculars to illustrate this point. The image of the binocular – a singular and undivided picture – is a complex synthesis between images in both the left and right side of the brain. In this context a synergy is created where the sum of the images is greater than the separate parts. As a result of bringing the two different views together, resolution and contrast are enhanced. Even more important, new insight into depth is created. Thus, the relationship between the different parts constructs new dimensions of seeing (Bateson cited in Newland, 1997). Employing such examples of synergies, critical ontologists maintain that juxtapositions of difference create a bonus of insight. This concept becomes extremely important in any cognitive, epistemological, social, pedagogical, or self-production activity.

Deploying Difference: Using Subjugated and/or Indigenous Knowledges in Critical Ontology

Cartesian rationalism has consistently excluded subjugated and/or indigenous knowledges from validated databases in diverse disciplines. These local, unauthorized knowledges are central to the work of the bricolage. As Dei and Doyle-Wood (this volume) have observed in their analysis of cultural supremacy and exclusionary practices, too often in Western colonial and neo-colonial history Europeans have viewed the knowledges and ways of seeing of the poor, the marginalized, and the conquered in a condescending and dismissive manner. Many of these perspectives, of course, were brimming with cosmological, epistemological, and ontological insight missing from Western perspectives. Western scholars were often simply too ethnocentric and arrogant to recognize the genius of such subjugated and/or indigenous information. Critical ontologists unabashedly take a hard look at these perspectives – not in some naive romantic manner but in a rigorous and critical orientation. They are aware that Western scientific thinking often promotes contempt for indigenous individuals who have learned about a topic such as farming from the wisdom of their ancestors and a lifetime of cultivating the land. Many of the subjugated knowledges critical ontologists employ come from postcolonial backgrounds. Such ways of seeing force such scholars and teachers to account for the ways colonial power has shaped their approaches to knowledge production while inscribing the process of self-production.

Starting research and pedagogy with a valuing of non-Western knowledges, critical ontologists can spiral through a variety of such discourses to weave a multilogical theoretical and empirical tapestry. They can even juxtapose them with Western ways of seeing. For example, using a Hindu-influenced ontology that delineates the existence of a non-objective, purposely constructed reality, a critical theory that traces the role of power in producing this construction, a Santiago cognitive theory that maintains we bring forth this constructed world via our action within and upon it, and a poststructuralist feminist theory that alerts us to the ways patriarchal and other structures shape our knowledge about this reality, we gain a more profound understanding of what is happening when human beings encounter the world. The insights we gain and the knowledges we produce with these concepts in mind move us to new levels of both epistemological and ontological awareness. Such an awareness may be similar to what the Vajrayana tradition of Buddhism calls 'crazy wisdom.' Critical ontologists seek the multilogical orientation of crazy wisdom in their efforts to push the envelope of knowledge production and selfhood (Thomas, 1998; Parmar, 2003; Progler, 2001; Berry, 2001; Capra, 1996; Varela, 1999).

With these insights in mind scholar-teachers can operate in a wide diversity of disciplines and use an infinite number of subjugated and indigenous forms of knowledge. Ethnomathematical knowledges can be used to extend understanding of and knowledge production about math and math pedagogy (Appelbaum, 2003). Organic African-American knowledges of grandmothers, beauticians, and preachers can provide profound insight into the nature of higher order cognition (Dumas, 2003). Hip-hop musicians can help educators working to develop thicker and more insightful understandings of youth cultures and their implications for pedagogy (Parmar, 2003). Ancient African epistemologies and ontologies can help shape the theoretical lenses one uses to study and teach about contemporary racism and class bias.

Feminist understandings are important as they open doors to previously excluded knowledges. Such knowledges often point out the problems with the universal pronouncements of Cartesianism. The presence of gender diversity in this context reveals the patriarchal inscriptions on what was presented as universal, always true, validated knowledge about some aspect of the world. Indeed, this psychological pronouncement about the highest form of moral reasoning may apply more to men than it does to women – and even then it may apply more to upper-middle-class men than to lower-socioeconomic-class men or more to Anglo men than to Asian and African men. With these feminist insights in mind, critical ontologists find it easier to view the ways the knowledges they produce reflect the cultural, historical, and gendered contexts they occupy. In this context universality is problematized. Indeed, the more we are aware of those different from us on a variety of levels, the harder it is to produce naive universal knowledges. In our heightened awareness, in our crazy wisdom, we produce more sensitive, more aware modes of information (Burbules & Beck, 1999). Once the subjugated/indigenous door is open the possibilities are infinite.

The Bricolage, Difference, and Self-awareness in Research

When researchers, for example, encounter difference in the nature of the other, they enter into symbiotic relationships where their identity is changed. Such researchers are no longer merely obtaining information but are entering a space of transformation where previously excluded perspectives operate to change consciousness of both self and the world. Thus, research in a critical ontological context changes not only what one knows but who one actually is. In this process the epistemological and ontological domains enter into a new relationship that produces dramatic changes. Lev Vygotsky was on the right track as he documented the importance of the context in which learning takes place – the zone of proximal development (ZPD). Difference in the sense we are using it here expands the notion of the ZPD into the domain of research, drawing upon the power of our interactions in helping shape the ways we make meaning. In the new synergized position ontologically sensitive researchers construct new realities where they take on new and expanded roles.

Aware of the power of difference, these researchers develop a new consciousness of the self: (1) the manner in which it has been constructed; (2) its limitations; and (3) a sense of immanence concerning what it can become. Self-awareness is a metacognitive skill that has historically been more valued in Eastern traditions such as Buddhism, Taoism, and Yoga than in the West. Time and again we see the value of pluralism manifest itself in this discussion of difference and the bricolage. A pluralistic epistemology helps us understand the way we are situated in the web of reality and how this situatedness shapes what we see as researchers. Such an awareness reveals the limited nature of our observations of the world. Instead of researchers making final pronouncements on the way things are, they begin to see themselves in a larger interdisciplinary and intercultural conversation. Critical ontologists attuned to this dynamic, focus their attention on better modes of listening and respecting diverse viewpoints. Such higher order listening moves them to new levels of self-consciousness (Williams, 1999; Newland, 1997; Lepani, 1998; Thayer-Bacon, 2000).

Of course, difference does not work as an invisible hand that magically shapes new insights into self and world. Humans must exercise their complex hermeneutic abilities to forge these connections and interpret their meanings. In this context critical ontologists confront difference and then decide where they stand in relation to it. They must discern what to make of what it has presented them. With this in mind these critical scholar-educators work hard to develop relationships with those different from themselves that operate to create new meanings in the interactions of identity and difference. In this interaction knowledge producers grow smarter as they reject modernist Cartesian notions that cultural conflicts can be solved only by developing monological universal principles of epistemology and universal steps to the process of research. Too often, these scholars/cultural workers understand that these 'universal' principles simply reflect colonial Western ways of viewing the world hiding in the disguise of universalism. Rigorous examination of the construction of self and society are closed off in such faux-universalism. Indeed, it undermines the development of a critical self-consciousness.

In the face of a wide variety of different knowledges and ways of seeing the world, the cosmos human beings think they know collapses. In a counter-colonial move critical ontologists raise questions about any knowledges and ways of knowing that claim universal status. In this context they make use of this suspicion of universalism in combination with global, subjugated, and indigenous knowledges to understand how they have been positioned in the world. Almost all of us from Western backgrounds or non–Western-colonized backgrounds have been implicated in some way in the web of universalism. The inevitable conflicts that arise from this implication do not have to be resolved immediately. At the base of these conflicts rest the future of global culture as well as the future of research and pedagogy. Recognizing that these are generative issues that engage us in a productive process of analyzing self and world is in itself a powerful recognition. The value of both this recognition and the process of working through the complicated conceptual problems are treasured by critical ontologists. Indeed, they avoid any notion of finality in the resolution of such dilemmas (Richardson Woolfolk, 1994; Degenaar, 1995; Howley, Pendarvis, & Howley, 1993; O'Sullivan, 1999; Fenwick, 2000).

Indigeneity and the Construction of Selfhood

Always looking for multiple perspectives, insight in diverse places, the power of difference, critical ontologists examine human interconnectedness via the lens of indigenous knowledges. Many systems of indigenous knowledge illustrate the *enaction* of interconnectedness and raise profound questions about the ways Western scholars have constructed knowledge, scientific methods, and the scholarly disciplines. While there is great diversity in these indigenous knowledges, most assume that humans are part of the world of nature. Extending this holism many indigenous scholars maintain that the production and acquisition of knowledge involves a process of interactions among the human body, the mind, and the spirit (Dei, 1995; Dei & Doyle-Wood, this volume). Sambuli Mosha (2000) writes that among the East African Chagga peoples knowledge that is passed along to others must further the development of morality, goodness, harmony, and spirituality. Indeed, he continues, in the Chagga worldview it is impossible to separate these domains. Such fragmentation simply does not make sense to the Chagga. Embedded in every Chagga child is a part of the divine dimension of reality, illustrating the interconnectedness of all aspects of reality. Thus, knowledge production and the construction of selfhood cannot take place outside this intricate web of relationships.

In Cartesian-Newtonian modes of colonial science the interrelationships cherished by the Chagga are not as *real* as their individual parts. For example, in Cartesian psychology consciousness is often reduced to neural and chemical dynamics. Researchers in this context often study nothing outside the narrow confines of brain chemistry from graduate school to retirement. The notion that the understanding of human consciousness might be enhanced by anthropological, theological, or philosophical investigations rarely, if ever, occurs to such researchers over the decades of their research.

Making use of indigenous knowledges and the theological insights of Buddhism in this domain, cognitive theorist Francisco Varela develops a dramatically different concept of consciousness. Understanding the indigenous notion that the individual cannot be understood outside the community of which she is a part, Varela posits that human consciousness *emerges* from the social and biological interactions of its various parts. This understanding may over the next couple of decades revolutionize the fields of cognitive science, psychology, and even pedagogy. When scholars grasp the multilogical, interrelated nature of these possibilities dramatic changes in the ways scholars and educators operate begin to take place. Using the indigenous metaphor, knowledge *lives* in the cultures of indigenous peoples. As opposed to the disciplinary knowledges of Cartesian-Newtonianism, which are often stored in archives or laboratories, indigenous knowledges live in everyday cultural practices (Woodhouse, 1996; Dei, 1995; Maurial, 1999).

Critical ontologists ask hard questions of indigenous knowledges.

They know that folk knowledges – like Western scientific knowledges – often help construct exploitation and oppression for diverse groups and individuals. With this caution and resistance to essentialism in mind, ontological scholars study the ways many indigenous peoples in Africa construct the interrelationships of their inner selves to the outer world. This indigenous tendency to avoid dualism that when unacknowledged undermines the balance of various relationships is profoundly important. For example, the dualism between humans and nature can wreck havoc in an indigenous social system. In many indigenous African conceptions humanness is viewed as a part of nature, not separate from it. Unlike for scholars in the Cartesian-Newtonian disciplines, the world was too sacred for humans to study and dominate or conquer. Once humanness and the environment were viewed as separate entities, forces were unleashed that could destroy the delicate eco- and social systems that sustained the indigenous culture. Thus, to accept the dualism between humanness and nature in the minds of many African peoples was tantamount to committing mass suicide.

Another example of indigenous culture whose knowledges critical ontologists deem valuable is the Andean peoples of South America. Everyone and everything in traditional Andean culture is sentient, as, for example, the rivers and mountains have ears and eyes. Acting in the world in this cultural context is a dimension of being in relationship to the world. In one's actions within the physical environment, an Andean individual is in conversation with the mountains, rivers, trees, lakes, and so on. This language of conversation replaces in Andean culture a Western traditional scientific language of knowing. A profound epistemological shift has taken place in this replacement. In Andean culture the concept of knower and known is irrelevant. Instead humans and physical entities engage in reciprocal relationships, carrying on conversations in the interests of both.

These conversations have been described as mutually nurturing events, acts that enhance the ontological evolution of all parties involved via their tenderness and empathy for the living needs of the other. Thus, the epistemology at work here involves more than simply knowing about something. It involves tuning oneself in to the other's mode of being – its ontological presence – and entering into a life generating relationship with it (Apffel-Marglin, 1995). Critical ontologists take from this an understanding of a new dimension of the insepa- rable relationship between knowing and being. Those working in the academic disciplines of Western societies must enter into ontological relationships with that which they are studying. Such relationships should be enumerated and analyzed. How am I changed by this relationship? How is the object of my study changed or potentially changed by the relationship?

Great change occurs as a result of the Andean peoples' conversation with nature. Nature's voice is heard through the position and brilliance of planets and stars; the speed, frequency, color, and smell of the wind; and the size and number of particular wild flowers to mention only a few. Such talk tells Andeans about the coming weather and various dimensions of cultivation and they act in response to such messages. Because of the overwhelming diversity of ecosystems and climates in the Andes mountains and valleys, these conversations are complex. Interpretations of meanings – like any hermeneutic acts – are anything but self-evident. Such conversations and the actions they catalyze allow the Andean peoples to produce an enormous variety of cultivated plant species that amaze plant geneticists from around the world. As Frederique Apffel-Marglin (1995) describes this diversity: 'The peasants grow and know some 1,500 varieties of quinoa, 330 of kaniwa, 228 of tarwi, 250 of potatoes, 610 of oca (another tuber), and so forth. The varieties differ according to regions, altitude, soils, and other factors. Such incredible diversity cannot only be due to ecological diversity. The manner in which peasants converse with plants and all the other inhabitants of the world, be they animate or inanimate, with not only an infinite attention to detail but with a receptive, open, and direct or embodied attitude is at the heart of such diversity' (p. 11).

The Andeans actually have a word for those places where the conversation between humans and the natural world take place. *Chacras* include the land where the Andeans cultivate their crops, the places where utensils are crafted, and the places where herds and flocks live and graze. According to the Andeans these are all places where all entities come together to discuss the regeneration of life. The concept of interrelationship is so important in the Andean culture that the people use the word, *ayllu*, to signify a kinship group that includes not only other human beings but animals, mountains, streams, rocks, and the spirits of a particular geographical place. Critical ontological scholars adapt these indigenous Andean concepts to the rethinking of the ways they study, as they identify the methodologies, epistemologies, ontologies, cultural systems, social theories, ad infinitum that they employ in their multilogical understanding of the research act. Those who research the social, psychological, and educational worlds hold a special responsibility to those concepts and the people they research to select critical and life affirming logics of inquiry. A critical hermeneutics demands that relationships at all levels be respected and engaged in a ways that produce justice and new levels of understanding – in ways that regenerate life and, central to our ontological concerns, new ways of being.

Thus, critical ontologists are able to make use of the power of difference in the context of subjugated and/or indigenous knowledges. The power of difference or 'ontological mutualism' transcends Cartesianism's emphasis on the thing-in-itself. The tendency in Cartesian-Newtonian thinking is to erase mutualism's bonus of insight in the abstraction of the object of inquiry from the processes and contexts of which it is a part. In this activity it subverts difference. The power of these synergies exists not only in the cognitive, social, pedagogical, and epistemological domains but in the physical world as well. Natural phenomena, as Albert Einstein illustrated in physics and Humberto Mataurana and Francisco Varela laid out in biology and cognition, operate in states of interdependence. These ways of seeing have produced perspectives on the workings of the planet that profoundly differ from the views produced by Western science.

What has been fascinating to many is that these post-Einsteinian perspectives have in so many ways reflected the epistemologies and ontologies of ancient non-Western peoples in India, China, and Africa and indigenous peoples around the world. Thus, critical ontology's use of indigenous knowledge is not offered as some new form of postcolonial exploitation – as in pharmaceutical companies' rush into indigenous locales to harvest plants that indigenous peoples have known for millennia possess medicinal qualities. In this context such products are then marketed as culturally sensitive postcolonial forms of exotica. The hipness of such entrepreneurial diversity provides little benefits for the indigenous people watching the process – they are not the beneficiaries of the big profits. Instead, a critical ontology *uses* indigenous peoples as teachers, as providers of wisdom. In their respect for indigenous knowledges and indigenous peoples, critical ontologists use such indigenous teachings to create a world more respectful and hospitable to indigenous peoples' needs and ways of being.

Constructing a Critical Ontology

Making use of our concept of difference and the insights provided by indigenous knowledges and ways of being, we are ready to construct our critical ontological postcolonial curriculum. In a critical ontology the teaching, learning, and curriculum development processes emerge as profoundly exciting enterprises because they are always conceptualized in terms of what we can become – both in an individual and a collective context. In our socio-ontological imagination we can transcend the Enlightenment category of abstract individualism and move toward a more textured concept of the relational individual. While abstract individualism and a self-sufficient ontology seem almost *natural* in the Western modernist world, of course, such is not the case in many indigenous cultures and was not the case even in Western societies in previous historical eras. In ancient Greece, for example, it is hard to find language that identified 'the self' or 'I' – such descriptions were not commonly used because the individual was viewed as a part of a collective who could not function independently of the larger social group (Allen, 2000). In the 'common sense' of contemporary Western society and its unexamined ontological assumptions this way of seeing self is hard to fathom.

Enlightenment ontology discerns the natural state of the individual as solitary. The social order in this modernist Eurocentric context is grounded on a set of contractual transactions between isolated individual atoms. In other works I have referred to Clint Eastwood's 'man with no name' cinematic character who didn't need a 'damn thing from nobody' as the ideal Western male way of being – the ontological norm (Kincheloe, 1993). Operating in this context, we clearly discern, for example, cognitive psychology's tradition of focusing on the autonomous development of the individual monad. In our critical complex ontology a human being simply can't exist outside the inscription of community with its processes of relationship, differentiation, interaction, and subjectivity. Indeed, in this critical (and complex) ontology the relational embeddedness of self is so dependent on context that psychologists, sociologists, and educators can never isolate a finalized completed 'true self.' Since the self is always in context and in process, no final delineation of a notion such as ability can be determined. Thus, we are released from the rugged cross of IQ and such hurtful and primitive colonial conceptions of 'intelligence.' In this context it is interesting to note that famed psychometricians Richard Herrnstein and Charles Murray (1994) in *The Bell Curve* noted without any data that the average IQ of the African is probably around 75 – epistemological/ ontological neo-colonialism in a transparent form.

One can quickly discern the political consequences of a Cartesian ontology. Human beings in Western liberal political thought become abstract bearers of particular civic rights. If individuals are relational, context-embedded beings, however, these abstract rights may be of little consequence. A critical ontology insists that individuals live in specific places with particular types of relationships. They operate or are placed in the web of reality at various points of race, class, gender, sexual, religious, physical ability, geographical place, and other continua. Where individuals find themselves in this complex web holds dramatic power consequences. Their location shapes their relationship to both dominant culture and Western colonialism and the psychological and curricular assumptions that accompanies them. In other words the intelligence that mainstream psychology deems these individuals to possess profoundly depends on this contextual, power-inscribed placement. A prime manifestation of ontological alienation involves a lack of recognition of the dramatic effect of these dynamics on everything that takes place in the psychoeducational cosmos.

In the context of our critical ontology the autonomous self with a fixed intellectual ability becomes an anachronism. As an effort to appreciate the power of human beings to affect their own destinies, to exercise human agency, and to change social conditions, critical ontologists study selfhood in light of the sociological, cultural studies, cultural psychological, and critical analytical work of the last few decades. Much of what dominant psychology and education consider free will and expressions of innate intelligence are simply manifestations of the effects of particular social, cultural, political, and economic forces. We can make decisions on how we operate as human beings, but they are never completely independent of these structuring forces. This is true whether we are Diane Ravitch or Michel Foucault – neither person can operate outside of society or free from cultural, linguistic, ideological influences.

It is important to note here that neo-positivist educational policy makers contend that their work takes place outside of the influence of these dynamics. They claim that their work avoids cultural values and morally inscribed issues and because of such diligence, they have presented us the truth about how students learn and how teachers should teach. In the critical ontological context developed here, such researchers must take a closer look at who they are and the structuring forces that have shaped their views of the world, mind, and self. Their inability to discern the effects of these forces reflects ontological alienation. Such alienation undermines their ability to imagine new and better ways of being human both for themselves and for the teachers and students their knowledges and policies oppress.

A postcolonial curriculum informed by a complex ontology asks the question: how do we move beyond simply uncovering the sources of consciousness construction in our larger attempt to reconstruct the self in a critical manner? Critical teachers must search in as many locations as possible for alternate discourses, ways of thinking and being that expand the envelopes of possibility. In this context teachers explore literature, history, popular culture, and ways of forging community in subjugated/indigenous knowledges. In this context teachers develop their own and their students' social and aesthetic imaginations. Here we imagine what we might become by recovering and reinterpreting what we once were. The excitement of curriculum as ontological quest is powerful.

The Infrastructure of a Critical Ontology

Employing an understanding of complexity theory, Humberto Maturana and Francisco Varela's Santiago Enactivism as the process of life, a postcolonial appreciation of indigeneity, critical theoretical foundations, the critique of Cartesianism, and poststructuralist feminist analysis, we can lay the conceptual foundations for a new mode of selfhood. Such a configuration cannot be comprehensively delineated here, but we can begin to build theoretical pathways to get around the Cartesian limitations on the ontological imagination. With Maturana and Valera's concept (1987) that living things constantly remake themselves in interaction with their environments, our notion of a new self or a critical ontology is grounded on the human ability to use new social contexts and experiences, exposure to new knowledges and ways of being to reformulate subjectivity. In this context the concept of personal ability becomes a de-essentialized cognition of possibility. No essentialized bounded self can access the cognitive potential offered by epiphanies of difference or triggered by an 'insignificant' insight.

As we begin to identify previously unperceived patterns in which the self is implicated, the possibility of cognitive change and personal growth is enhanced. As the barriers between mind and multiple contexts are erased, the chance that more expanded forms of 'cognitive autopoiesis' – self-constructed modes of higher-order thinking – will emerge is increased. A more textured, a thicker sense of self-production and the nature of self and other is constructed in this process. As we

examine the self and its relationship to others in cosmological, epistemological, linguistic, social, cultural, and political contexts, we gain a
clearer sense of our purpose in the world especially in relation to justice,
the indigenous-informed notion of interconnectedness, and even love.
In these activities we move closer to the macro-processes of life and
their micro-expressions in everyday life.

A key aspect of the life processes is the understanding of difference
that comes from recognition of patterns of interconnectedness. Knowing that an individual from an upper-middle class European background living in a Virginia suburb will be considered culturally bizarre
by a group of tribespeople from the Amazon rainforest is a potentially
profound learning experience in the domain of the personal. How is the
suburbanite viewed as bizarre? What cultural practices are seen as so
unusual? What mannerisms are humorous to the tribespeople? What
worldviews are baffling to them? The answers to such questions may
shock the suburbanite into reorienting her view of her own 'normality.'
The interaction may induce her to ask questions of the way she is
perceived by and the way she perceives others. Such a bracketing of
the personal may be quite liberating. This interaction with the power
of difference is another example of Maturana and Valera's structural
coupling that creates a new relationship with other and with self. In
Maturana and Varela's conceptualization (1987) a new inner world is
created as a result of such coupling (see also Varela, 1999; Sumara &
Davis, 1997).

Such explorations on the ontological frontier hold profound curricular implications. As students pursue rigorous study of diverse global
knowledges, they come to understand that the identities of their peer
groups and families constitute only a few of countless historical and
cultural ways to be human. As they study their self-production in wider
biological, sociological, cultural studies, historical, theological, psychological and counter-canonical contexts, they gain insights into their
ways of being. As they engage the conflicts that induce diverse knowledge producers to operate in conflicting ways, students become more
attuned to the ideological, discursive, and regulatory forces operating
in all knowledges. This is not nihilism, as many defenders of the Euro-
canon argue; this is the exciting process of exploring the world and the
self and their relationship in all of the complexity such study requires.

The processual and relational notions of self structurally couple with
the sociocultural context and can only be understood by studying them
with these dynamics in mind. These characteristics of self hold pro-

found implications politically, psychologically, and pedagogically. If our notion of the self emerges in its counter-colonial relationship with multiple dimensions of the world, it is by its nature a participatory entity. Such an interactive dynamic is always in process and thus demands a reconceptualization of the concept of individualism and self-interest (Pickering, 1999). The needs of self and others in this context begin to merge, as the concept of self-reliance takes on new meanings. Notions of educational purpose, evaluation, and curriculum development are transformed when these new conceptions of the personal domain come into the picture. In the first decade of the twenty-first century we stand merely on the threshold of the possibilities this notion of selfhood harbours.

Enactivism as a Way Out: Exploring the Ontological Possibilities

A critical ontology understands that the effort to explain complex cognitive, biological, social, or pedagogical events by the reductionistic study of their components outside of the larger processes of which they are a part will not work. It will not move us to new levels of understanding or set the stage for new, unexplored modes of being human. The social, biological, cognitive, or the curricular domain is not an assortment of discrete objects that can be understood in isolation from one another (Pickering, 1999). The fragmented pieces put forth in such studies do not constitute reality – even if commonsense tells Westerners they do. The deeper structures, the tacit forces, the processes that shape the physical world and the social world will be lost to such observers. As I argue in the Introduction to *The Stigma of Genius: Einstein, Consciousness, and Education* (1999), Albert Einstein's General Theory of Relativity could not have been produced without this ontological understanding of connectedness, process, and the limitations of studying only things-in-themselves.

For 250 years physicists had been searching for the basic building block of gravity – some contended it was a particle (a graviton), others argued it was a gravity wave. Einstein pointed out that it was neither, that it was not a *thing* at all. Gravity, he maintained, was a part of the structure of the universe that existed as a relationship connecting mass, space, and time. This insight, of course, changed the very nature of how we conceptualize the universe. It should have changed how we conceptualize epistemology, cognition, pedagogy, and ontology. Of course, it did not – and that's what we are still working on. The emphasis on studying and teaching about the world as a compilation of fragmented things-in-themselves has returned with a vengeance, of course, in recent educational reforms and mandates for the use of only positivistic forms of educational research.

In this context the work of Humberto Maturana is instructive. Maturana and Varela's Santiago Enactivism employ the same ontological concept of interconnectedness that Einstein used in the General Theory of Relativity to explain life as a process, a system of interconnections. Indeed, they argue, that the process of cognition is the process of life. In Enactivism mind is not a thing-in-itself but a process – an activity where the interactions of a living organism with its environment constitute cognition. In this relationship life itself and cognition are indelibly connected and reveal this interrelationship at diverse levels of living and what are still considered non-living domains. Where mind ends and matter begins is difficult to discern, a situation that operates to overturn the long-standing and problematic Cartesian separation of the two entities. In Maturana's and Varela's conception mind and matter are merely parts of the same process – one cannot exist without the other. A critical ontology seeks to repair this rupture between mind and matter, self, and world. In this reconnection we enter into a new phase of human history, new modes of cognition, and dramatic changes in pedagogy and curriculum.

According to the Enactivists perception and cognition also operate in contradiction to Cartesianism, as they construct a reality as opposed to reflecting an external one already in existence. The interactive or circular organization of the nervous system described by Maturana is similar to the hermeneutic circle as it employs a conversation between diverse parts of a system to construct meaning (for a discussion of how this conversation and/or interconnectedness sustains human life in its most creative senses, see David Smith, this volume). Self-construction emerges out of a set of relationships between simple parts. In the hermeneutic circle the relationships between parts 'self-construct' previously unimagined meanings. Thus, in an ontological context meaning emerges not from the thing-in-itself but from its relationships to an infinite number of other things. In this complexity we understand from another angle that there is no final meaning of anything; meanings are always evolving in light of new relationships, new horizons. Thus, in a critical ontology our power as meaning makers and producers of new selfhoods is enhanced. Cognition is the process in which living systems organize the world around them into meaning. With this in mind critical ontology creates a new era of immanence – 'what could be' has never implied so much.

Specifically, Maturana and Varela argue that our identities do not come with us into the world in some neatly packaged unitary self. Since they 'rise and subside' in a series of shifting relationships and patterns, the self can be described using the Buddhist notion that the 'self is empty of self-nature.' Understanding this, Francisco Varela (1999) maintains, self-understanding and self-change become more possible than ever before. The self, therefore, is not a material entity but takes on more a virtual quality. Human beings have the experience of self, but no self – no central controlling mechanism – is to be found. Much is to be gained by an understanding of the virtual nature of the self. Such knowledge is an important dimension of a critical ontology. According to the Enactivists this knowledge helps us develop intelligent awareness – a profound understanding of the construction and the functioning of selfhood. Intelligent awareness is filled with wisdom but devoid of the egocentrism that undermines various notions of critical knowing. In such a context intelligent awareness cannot be separated from ethical insight. Without this ontological understanding many pedagogies designed to empower will fan the flames of the egocentrism they attempt to overcome. If nothing else a critical ontology cultivates humility without which wisdom is not possible.

Enactivism and the Development of the Relational Self

From Maturana and Varela's perspective learning takes place when a self-maintaining system develops a more effective relationship with the external features of the system. In this context Enactivism is highlighting the profound importance of *relationship* writ large as well as the centrality of the nature and quality of the relationships an organism makes with its environment. In a cognitive context this is an extension of Vygotsky's notion of the zone of proximal development to the ontological realm – it is our assertion here that indigeneity should become a part of Westerners' ZPD. In the development of a critical ontology we learn from these ideas that political empowerment vis-à-vis the cultivation of the intellect demand an understanding of the system of relationships that construct our selfhood. In the case of a critical form of curriculum development these relationships always involve students' connections to cultural systems, language, economic concerns, religious belief, social status, and the power dynamics that constitute them. With the benefit of understanding the self-in-relationship teachers gain a new insight into what is happening in any learning situation. Living on the borderline between self and external system and self and other, learning never takes place outside of these relationships (Pickering, 1999). Such knowledge changes our orientation to curriculum development and pedagogy.

Thus, a critical ontology is intimately connected to a relational self (Noddings, 1990; Thayer-Bacon, 2000). Humans are ultimately the constructs of relationships, not fragmented monads or abstract individuals. From Varela's perspective this notion of humans as constructs of relationships corresponds precisely to what he is labeling the virtual self. A larger pattern – in the case of humans, consciousness – arises from the interaction of local elements. This larger pattern seems to be driven by a central controlling mechanism that can never be located. Thus, we discern the origin of traditional psychology's dismissal of consciousness as irrelevant. This not only constituted throwing out the baby with the bath water but discarding the tub, the bathroom fixtures, and the plumbing as well. In this positivistic articulation the process of life and the basis of the cognitive act were deemed unimportant. A critical ontology is always interested in these processes because they open us to a previously occluded insight into the nature of selfhood, of human being. The autopoiesis, the self-making allows humans to perpetually reshape themselves in their new relationships and resulting new patterns of perception and behaviour.

There is no way to predict the relationships individuals will make and the nature of the self-(re)construction that will ensue. Such uncertainty adds yet another element of complexity to the study of sociology, psychology, and pedagogy, as it simultaneously catalyzes the possibilities of human agency. It causes those enamored with critical ontology yet another reason to study the inadequacies of Cartesian science to account for the intricacies of the human domain. Physical objects *do not necessarily* change their structures via their interaction with other objects. A critical ontology understands that human beings do change their structures as a result of their interactions. As a result the human mind moves light years beyond the lifeless cognitivist computer model of mind – a psychological way of seeing that reduced mental activity to information processing (Lepani, 1998).

The human self-organization process – although profoundly more complex than the World Wide Web – is analogous to the way the Web arranges itself by random and not-so-random connections. The Web is an autopoietic organism that constructs itself in a hypertextual mode of operation. Unanticipated links create new concepts, ways of perceiving, and even ways of being among those that enter into this domain of epistemological emergence. Such experience reminds one that a new cultural logic has developed that transcends the mechanical dimensions of the machine epistemologies and ontologies of the modernist industrial era. Consider the stunning implications that when numerous simple entities possessing simple characteristics are thrown together – whether it be websites on the Internet or individuals' relationships with aspects of their environments – amazing things occur. From such interactions emerge a larger whole that is not guided by a central controlling mechanism. Self-awareness of this process of creation may lead to unanticipated modes of learning and new concepts of human being. Students of critical curriculum have no choice; they must deal with these ontological issues. When they are considered within the context of our understanding of the power of difference and the specific benefits of indigeneity, a postcolonial curriculum begins to take shape that is truly global in its scope, its concerns and its influences. Such a curriculum is transformative in ways that other 'transformative' curricula have not been in its connection to a plethora of knowledges and ways of being. Employing interconnectedness with difference to push the boundaries of the Western alienated self, this postcolonial curriculum sets off an autopoietic process energized by the interplay of multiple forms of difference – cultural, political, epistemological, cognitive, and, of course, ontological. It will be fascinating to watch where a critical ontology can take us in the coming years.

REFERENCES

Allen, M. (2000). Voice of reason. Available at http://www.curtin.edu.au/ learn/unit/10846/arrow/vorall.htm

Apffel-Marglin, F. (1995). Development or decolonization in the Andes? *Interculture: International Journal of Intercultural and Transdisciplinary Research*, *28*(1), 3–17.

Appelbaum, P. (2003). Mathematics education. In D. Weil & J. Kincheloe (Eds.), *Critical thinking and learning: An encyclopedia* (pp. 307–312). New York: Greenwood.

Berry, K. (2001). Standards of complexity in a postmodern democracy. In J. Kincheloe & D. Weil (Eds.), *Standards and schooling in the United States: An encyclopedia*. Santa Barbara, CA: ABC-Clio.

Burbules, N., & Beck, R. (1999). Critical thinking and critical pedagogy: Relations, differences, and limits. In T. Popkewitz & L. Fendler (Eds.), *Critical theories in education* (pp. 45–65). New York: Routledge.

Capra, F. (1996). *The web of life: A new scientific understanding of living systems.* New York: Anchor Books.

Degenaar, J. (1995). Myth and the collision of cultures. *Myth and Symbol, 2,* 39–61.

Dei, G. (1995). Indigenous knowledge as an empowerment tool. In N. Singh & V. Titi (Eds.), *Empowerment: Toward sustainable development* (pp. 93–117). Toronto: Fernwood Press.

Dumas, M. (2003). Critical thinking as black existence. In D. Weil & J. Kincheloe (Eds.). *Critical thinking and learning: An encyclopedia* (pp. 155–158). New York: Greenwood.

Fenwick, T. (2000). Experiential learning in adult education: A comparative framework. http://www.ualberta.ca/~tfenwick/ext/aeq.htm

Herrnstein, R., & Murray, C. (1994). *The bell curve: Intelligence and class structure in American life.* New York: Free Press.

Howley, A., Pendarvis, E., & Howley, C. (1993). Anti-intellectualism in U.S. schools. *Education Policy Analysis Archives, 1,* 6.

Kincheloe, J. (1993). *Toward a critical politics of teacher thinking: Mapping the postmodern.* Westport, CT: Bergin and Garvey.

Kincheloe, J., Steinberg, S., and Tippins, D. (1999). *The stigma of genius: Einstein, consciousness, and education.* New York: Peter Lang.

Lepani, B. (1998). Information literacy: The challenge of the digital age. Available at http://www.acal.edu.au/lepani.htm

Maturana, H., & Varela, F. (1987). *The tree of knowledge.* Boston: Shambhala.

Maurial, M. (1999). Indigenous knowledge and schooling: A continuum between conflict and dialogue. In L. Semali & J. Kincheloe (Eds.), *What is indigenous knowledge? Voices from the academy* (pp. 59–78). New York: Falmer.

Mosha, S. (2000). *The heartbeat of indigenous Africa: A study of the Chagga educational system.* New York: Garland.

Newland, P. (1997). Logical types of learning. Available at http://www. envf.port.ac.uk/newmedia/lecturenotes/EMMA/at2n.htm

Noddings, N. (1990). Review symposium: A response. *Hypatia, 5*(1), 120–126.

O'Sullivan, E. (1999). *Transformative learning: Educational vision for the 21st century.* London: Zed Books.

Parmar, P. (2003). The pedagogy of KRS-One. In D. Weil & J. Kincheloe (Eds.), *Critical thinking and learning: An Encyclopedia* (pp. 175–183). New York: Greenwood.

Pickering, J. (1999). The self is a semiotic process. *Journal of Consciousness Studies, 6*(4), 31–47.

Progler, Y. (2001). Social studies – Social studies standards: Diversity, conformity, complexity. In J. Kincheloe & D. Weil (Eds.), *Standards and schooling in the United States: An encyclopedia*. Santa Barbara, CA: ABC-CLIO.

Richardson, F., and Woolfolk, R. (1994). Social theory and values: A hermeneutic perspective. *Theory and Psychology, 4*(2), 199–226.

Semali, L., and Kincheloe, J. (1999). *What is indigenous knowledge? Voices from the academy*. New York: Falmer.

Steinberg, S. (2001). *Multi/intercultural conversations: A reader*. New York: Peter Lang.

Sumara, D., & Davis, B. (1997). Cognition, complexity, and teacher education. *Harvard Educational Review, 67*(1), 75–104.

Thayer-Bacon, B. (2000). *Transforming critical thinking: Thinking constructively*. New York: Teachers College Press.

Thomas, G. (1998). The myth of rational research. *British Educational Research Journal, 24*(2), 141–161.

Varela, F. (1999). *Ethical know-how: Action, wisdom, and cognition*. Stanford, CA: Stanford University Press.

Williams, S. (1999). Truth, speech, and ethics: A feminist revision of free speech theory. *Genders, 30*. Available at http://www.genders.org

Woodhouse, M. (1996). *Paradigm wars: Worldviews for a new age*. Berkeley, CA: Frog.

8 Reappropriating Traditions in the Postcolonial Curricular Imagination

YATTA KANU

History is a clock that people use to tell their political and cultural time of day. It is also a compass that people use to find themselves on the map of human geography. The role of history is to tell people what they have been, where they have been, what they are, and where they are. The most important role that history plays is that it has the function of telling a people where they still must go and what they still must be.

John Henrick Clarke, African historian (1987)

This chapter draws on the Akan concept of *sankofa* – meaning 'return to the past to move forward' – to theorize curriculum and pedagogy for postcolonial educational contexts in Africa. Sankofa is derived from the Akan people of West Africa, and its literal translation means: 'retrieving the past is no taboo, thus say the ancestors.' Sankofa teaches that we must go back to our roots in order to move forward, that is, we should reach back and gather the best of what our past has to teach us, so that we can achieve our full potential as we move forward. As a measure of time, sankofa looks at history as a circular process (rather than the linear construct of time prevalent in Western culture) where we think of the past not as events frozen in time, but rather as occurrences that are at one with the present and the future (Aldridge, 2003). Sankofa implies that to initiate a progressive civil social existence, one that preserves our humanity, we would have to *reconcile* the best in the wisdom of our ancestors – the best of our tradition – with the changing realities of the present.

Such an appeal to tradition is itself controversial in our modern world, where the charge is that tradition is disappearing, that 'it is simply no longer able to provide the thread needed to keep the fabric of social life from unraveling' (Gross, 1992, p. 3) and that, therefore, its demise should be seen as an opportunity for newness, creativity, and modes of individualism hitherto impossible and unimaginable. Karl Marx, writing in 1852, dramatically expressed this attitude towards tradition, in 'The Eighteenth Brumaire': 'The tradition of all the dead generations weighs like a nightmare on the brain of the living ... The social revolution cannot draw its poetry from the past, but only from the future. It cannot begin with itself before it has stripped off all superstition in regard to the past. Earlier revolutions required world-historical recollections in order to drug themselves concerning their own content. In order to arrive at its content, the revolution of the nineteenth century must let the dead bury their dead' (1978, p. 596). My position is that this is not a productive way of thinking about tradition. There certainly are dangers inherent in retreating to an allegedly better past rather than responding to the world as it comes to us; however, it would be foolish, indeed, to ignore whole realms of experiences and meanings that have been nourished for generations, and on which we can draw for insights about nourishing our own lives.

In this chapter I argue for a return to tradition. More specifically, I call for a return to what was deemed and still is deemed to be valuable in indigenous African education that can inform how we conceptualize educational curriculum and practices in contemporary postcolonial Africa. These indigenous practices are among what David Gross (1992) refers to as 'substantive traditions,' that is, those long-standing modes of thought or practice that for centuries have organized social and cultural life. In proposing a reappropriation of tradition I do not mean a restoration of an earlier set of norms, or a 'heimisch' (home) to which we nostalgically return, as articulated by traditionalists. Rather, like Gross, I propose a reappropriation of tradition in order to gain access to what is Other, foreign, and alien – what Gross calls the 'unheimisch' (that which is non-home). My assumption is that a reappropriation of traditional African curricular and pedagogical values is necessary not simply to recover what has receded into the past and is now regarded as unheimisch because it seems strange, but also to bring these traditions forward in a manner that will disturb and challenge the complacencies of present-day curricular conceptions and educational practices. An embracement of sankofa in this process is proposed not as some nostalgic return to earlier traditions but for the 'creatively disruptive effects' (Gross, 1992, p. 88) of these traditions – disruptive because they call into question the norms that have shaped and continue to shape curriculum development in Africa, norms such as technical ratio-nalization, instrumentalization, erosion of the life-world of the African peoples, disintegration of subjectivity, and absence of place-conscious education.

The term *African peoples* is used here to highlight the diversity of African societies with regard to social and political experiences and processes, as well as aspirations for the future. Across this diversity, however, there is a shared history of the colonial imposition of external ideas and knowledge that was instituted to erode indigenous African beliefs, customs, traditions, and historical experiences (Dei et al., 1998). In the traditional life and thinking of the various African peoples, we can discern features sufficiently common to offer a reasonable basis for the reconstruction of curricular and educational practices anchored in African values and traditions overall (Gyeke, 1995).

I present a brief discussion of the meaning of tradition and the pos-sible attitudes that teachers might adopt in rethinking tra-dition. My primary objective is to re-establish tradition as a means of understand-ing and critiquing the present. Three substantive traditions in indig-enous African education prior to colonization – and negated during the process of asserting colonial ideology – are described and juxtaposed with educational practices during and after colonization. I draw ex-amples from the part of the world that I know best, namely, Sierra Leone, a former British colony in West Africa. My intent is to return to the cultural productions and social formations of Sierra Leone before colonization in order to better understand colonial educational policies and practices. Drawing, in particular, on the concept of sankofa and insights from Homi Bhabha's notion of hybridity, I reappropriate cer-tain dismantled indigenous-African traditions of education to make curriculum proposals that would be responsive to the ambiguous cul-tural contexts that characterize conditions in postcolonial Africa.

Defining Tradition, Rethinking Tradition

Tradition is an existing set of beliefs, practices, teachings, and modes of thinking that are inherited from the past and that may guide, organize, and regulate ways of living and of making sense of the world. Accord-ing to Gross (1992), the term comes from the Latin verb *tradere*, meaning to transmit or to give over; the noun *traditio* indicates the process by which something is transmitted or handed down. Gross depicts the cen-tral responsibility involved in *traditio* as (1) receiving something valu-able or precious, (2) preserving it, and (3) passing it on to those who come after. Gross argues that tradition is not, however, merely preserved and passed down intact to subsequent generations. As traditions are handed down consecutively over time, they undergo changes because the relations that encompass a receiving generation are never exactly the same as those of the transmitting generation: 'As social and cultural changes occur, so do ways of confronting and organizing experience. And as experiences change, so do modes of perception, including perceptions of what a tradition is and means. When needs and perceptions shift, no matter how slightly, the inherited traditions cannot help but be apprehended and assimilated differently. Hence, no tradition is ever taken over precisely as it was given, or passed on precisely as it was received. Rather it is always adapted to a situation' (ibid., p. 14).

In the past, tradition provided the cohesion that held social life together, and by indicating what was culturally normative, tradition established a framework for meaning and purpose (Gross, 1992). As human beings, we are embedded in our cultural traditions; therefore, tradition cannot be treated as something purely external which can be simply accepted or rejected on the basis of rational analysis or something which is wholly Other, 'as if one could continue to be a person even if it [tradition] were entirely rejected' (Fay 1987, p. 160). The relationship between personal identity and tradition would seem to be far more intimate than implied in Karl Marx's (previously quoted) statement. People understand and construct their identities in terms of the traditions that are a part of them, and 'coming to be a person is in fact appropriating certain material of one's cultural tradition, and continuing to be a person ... means working through, developing, and extending this material and this always involves operating in terms of it [tradition]' (ibid., p. 162). An appreciation of the importance of tradition in shaping identity enhances our understanding of how tradition imposes limits on the change that is possible in a society. No matter how revolutionary the change, some continuity will remain in the form of certain modes of thinking, perceiving, relating; certain habitual ways of behaviour will survive as important ingredients in the identities of the people 'who are what they are because they so deeply share them' (ibid., p. 163).

Gross (1992) postulates three forms in which all earlier traditions exist today. There are traditions that have been destroyed or dismantled as active processes, but continue on as fragments of value or behaviours in the periphery of their original contexts. There are traditions that persist at the centre of social life, but at the cost of being rationalized by the state or commercialized by the market. There are traditions that endure more or less intact, but primarily on the margins of society and within a greatly diminished sphere of influence. Of the three forms in which traditions currently find themselves, my concern is with the first, that is, those social and cultural traditions that colonial administration dismantled as part of the educational processes of African children, but which continue on as valuable fragments of indigenous child-rearing practices. In rethinking traditions such as these, one could bury lapsed or dismantled traditions and move on to opportunities for newness and creativity; reject present realities and engage in a coercive restoration of lapsed traditions under the assumption that they were simpler, better, or morally healthier than what we now have (traditionalism); or bring lapsed traditions into the modern world, not to escape into them, but to reclaim them as an opportunity for understanding the present (Gross, 1992). The last attitude and relation to tradition is the most compelling because it salvages outmoded traditions that can contribute significantly to solving contemporary problems. Precisely because they are lapsed or defeated traditions, our sense of connectedness to them has lapsed, and so they represent something other than what they represented to preceding generations. Now they embody something strange or Other – the *unheimisch* that disturbs our present-day sensibilities and raises doubts about many of our hitherto protected illusions. Rethinking lapsed traditions in this way not only makes possible a better understanding of the present, but 'it also lays the groundwork for something just as important, namely, a critique of modernity from outside' (ibid., p. 87). Through this critical leverage, tradition ceases to be an obstacle to progress and becomes a way forward in history. I draw on this reconsidered sense of tradition and the past, in the spirit of sankofa, to reconceptualize postcolonial curriculum and pedagogy.

In the next section, I describe three traditions of indigenous educational tradition in Sierra Leone that were dismantled under colonialism and juxtapose them with education during and after British colonization. Through their 'strangeness' these dismantled traditions raise questions about British colonial education and its legacies and, thus, provide us with a broader and deeper perspective on current educational practices in that former colony.

Indigenous Education versus Education during and after Colonization

Indigenous approaches to education in Sierra Leone emerged from indigenous knowledge systems based on understandings of the physical, social, and spiritual environments (see also, Dei & Doyle-Wood this volume). These approaches are grounded in norms, values, and traditions that were developed over several generations, and they are characterized by many features. Here I focus on three features that did not become part of the processes of formal education during British colonial administration but which did survive as fragments of informal education, especially in Sierra Leone 's rural communities. These features are (1) interwoven theory and practice, (2) communalism, and (3) multilayered understanding transmitted through stories, anecdotes and proverbs.

Interwoven Theory and Practice

In Sierra Leone , indigenous education is for an immediate introduction into society and preparation for adulthood. It emphasizes job orientation, social responsibility, religion, moral values, and community participation. These aims are interwoven with the content, derived from the needs and purposes of the society, and instructional strategies, making it easy to transfer theory to practice in this system. If the aim of the indigenous curriculum is to teach farming, for example, children do not receive elaborate theoretical discussions about farming from adults. Instead, from an early age, they simply accompany adults to the farms where they participate by observing and imitating what adults do. Because every education is for entering adulthood, even in their games, the work and ways of adults provide the material for the play of children. Objective or abstract knowledge is not imparted as such because it is not believed that people first develop theoretical understanding of things and events and then apply this knowledge in making judgments and decisions; rather, the quest for understanding is conditioned and constituted by reflection upon how to act wisely in concrete situations (Bernstein, 1986). Hans-Georg Gadamer's argument for an inextricable connection of the theoretical and practical in all understanding (1984) holds true in the Sierra Leonean philosophy of education. Any theory emerging from such a system is grounded in practice, and knowledge is practice-based.

Unfortunately, school curriculum during the British colonial era was far removed from this indigenous view of education. Similar to Kazim Bacchus's description of education in the West Indies during colonial administration (this volume), the aim of British colonial education in Africa was short term – to produce Africans who could read and teach the Bible and fill in the few clerical positions that existed in the colonial civil service. Curriculum content and teaching methods employed in the schools were intended to achieve these limited instrumental purposes. Curriculum content was alien, divorced from students' and teachers' culture and lived experiences, and transmitted through didactic teaching and assessment methods that ensured its digestion without reflection, challenge, or questions. The main interest of the colonizers was to ensure that the 'uncivilized natives' were assimilated into the new cultural reality that their official knowledge was imparting. A relatively recent study of British colonial administration captures well what some postcolonial nations in Africa inherited by way of institutions and agencies, including those of education: 'The formal agencies transferred to African hands were ... alien in derivation, functionally conceived, bureaucratically designed, authoritarian in nature, and primarily concerned with issues of domination rather than legitimacy' (Chazan, 1989, quoted in Appiah, 1992).

Since independence, education in Sierra Leone has been characterized by the same instrumental, technical, and human capital approach prevalent in the Western countries that largely fund education in these former colonies. Human capital theory rests on the assumption that formal education is highly instrumental in improving the productive capacity of a population. In short, human capital theorists believe that an educated population is a productive population, and their views have had tremendous influence on, and indeed determined, education policies not only in Western countries but also in the former colonies through funding agencies and organizations such as The World Bank, the United Nations Educational, Social, and Cultural Organization (UNESCO), and the Organization for Economic Cooperation and Development (OECD). The belief in human capital theory as a key agent for the development of a society has produced an explosion in educational enrolments and expenditures in both the industrialized and the developing countries. This expansion has been followed by increasing demands (by the funding agencies) for state interventions in education through bureaucratized and controlled curricular practices that plan, implement, and evaluate education in ways that are similar to the values of business culture. This has led to widespread acceptance of the technical model of curriculum development which frames curriculum and teaching questions in terms of technical management focusing around specified objectives, identification, and organization of learning experiences to obtain the objectives and the most effective means of evaluating the achievement of the objectives. The model lends itself well to the bureaucratic management of education where the aim is to control and rationalize education so that the best economic dividends are reaped from educational investments. However, from my foregoing description of indigenous education in Sierra Leone, it can be seen that the technical-rational approach carries constraints for curriculum development in that country. The chief constraint is that indigenous education is not based on such a model. In indigenous education, educational ends are not separated from means, as they are in the technical model; aims, content, methodology, and evaluation are all merged, which makes for education that is effective and functional for the society. There is, therefore, a complete disconnect between the sociocultural experiences and backgrounds of teachers and students from such a culture and the school environment, and this accounts for much of the curriculum failure reported for Sierra Leone (e.g., the 1972 social studies project called 'Man in His Environment,' which was financed by the International Development Agency and the British Council, and planned by British and American consultants and a few Sierra Leonean curriculum experts).

Communalism in African Social Thought and Practice

African social philosopher Kwame Gyekye describes communalism as the doctrine that the group (society) constitutes the main focus of the lives of individual members of that group and that an individual's involvement in the interests, aspirations, and welfare of the group is the measure of that individual's worth. The doctrine of communalism emphasizes the activity and success of the wider society rather than, although not necessarily at the expense of, the individual. Implicit in communalism is the view that the success and meaning of the individual's life depend on identifying with the group. This identification is the basis of the reciprocal relationship between the individual and the group: 'It [identification] is also the ground of the overriding emphasis on the individual's obligation to the members of the group; it enjoins upon him or her the obligation to think and act in terms of the survival of the group as a whole ... Since this sense of obligation (responsibility) is enjoined equally upon each member of the group – for all the members are expected to enhance the welfare of the group as a whole – communalism maximizes the interests of all the individual members of society' (Gyekye, 1995, p. 156). Communalism as a social philosophy is given institutional expression in the social structures of many African societies. Because it is participatory and characterized by social and ethical values such as solidarity, interdependence, cooperation, and reciprocal obligations, the material and other benefits of the communal social order are likely to be available to all members of the society. Furthermore, the community's intricate web of social relations will tend to ensure individual social worth, thus making it almost impossible for an individual to feel socially insignificant (Gyeke, 1995).

Communalism used to be an active component of indigenous education in Sierra Leone because community development was an important objective in the indigenous curriculum. Among the Mende tribe of Sierra Leone this objective was instilled into the young from a very early age, and certain activities were undertaken to encourage and nurture it. For example, youngsters between the ages of 10 and 16 were divided into groups known as 'age grades,' and they could be required to perform specific tasks to contribute to the community effort. Thus, in a village community, all young men belonging to the 16-year 'age grade' might be assigned the task of building a courtroom house for the use of the community, or asked to help a community member with the harvesting of his or her crops. Girls in the 16-year age grade might be assigned the task of cooking *kondoi* (food) for the young men while the work was in progress. Assignments were carried out under the supervision of adults and performed with great enthusiasm, accompanied by community work songs rather than by competitiveness and selfishness. This social structure is a marked contrast to the competitive individualism introduced during British colonization which has continued as a legacy of colonial education in Sierra Leone. The Western value of distinguishing oneself from others and claiming one's autonomy to affirm one's basic originality has produced classroom arrangements, teaching and learning processes, and assessment strategies that have all left students with the belief that their originality and full potential can only be developed through the rejection of communal learning values such as interdependence and cooperation.

Stories, Anecdotes, and Proverbs

Stories, anecdotes, and proverbs are primary ways through which a great deal of African philosophical thought, knowledge, and wisdom have been taught. Preliterate African culture was characterized by an oral tradition that found expression in stories, folktales, anecdotes, proverbs, and parables that provoked a great deal of reflection. As there were no written records of the ancient past of the people, all that has been preserved of their knowledge, myths, philosophies, liturgies, songs, and sayings has been handed down by word of mouth from generation to generation. These oral media preserved, more or less accurately, the history of the people, their general outlook on life, and their conduct and moral values, and they have continued on in communities as forms of indigenous knowledge which play an important role in the education of the young. In remote rural communities in Sierra Leone adults are known to gather youngsters around a fire in the evenings and tell them great stories and legends about the tribal past that help the youngsters grasp the prevailing ethical standards of their tribe. Stories that personify animal characters are often told, and these stories, while explaining the peculiar trait of each animal, also transmit the virtues valued by the society – for example, stories about *Ananse* (the spider), ubiquitous in West African societies, always teach youngsters about the unwanted consequences of characteristics such as greed, egotism, or cunning.

Proverbs and anecdotes are particularly useful as powerful tools that teach without being intrusive. While a great deal of traditional wisdom and folklore is expressed through proverbs, anecdotes have the ability to reveal the characteristics and qualities of situations, times, and persons in a way that is hard to capture in clear language or in a direct manner. For this reason, anecdotes and proverbs are used in indigenous education in Sierra Leone to teach moral values and appropriate behaviours without directly or overtly moralizing and criticizing the individual. Anecdotes and proverbs can be understood as metaphors to guide moral choice and self-examination because, when reflected upon, these pithy sayings act as mirrors for seeing things in a particular way and their concreteness, more than any theoretical discussion or philosophical writing, throws light on the concrete reality of lived experience; they serve as important pedagogical devices because they provide experiential case material on which pedagogical reflection is possible (Van Manen, 1990). As learners break into (analyse) proverbs and anecdotes (or stories), they are able to reflect on the meanings and implications embedded in the experiences. Indigenous educators drew on these teaching devices to informally structure an educational program that encouraged learners to listen to stories, anecdotes, and proverbs and reflect on them to derive meanings that informed and guided conduct and behaviour. Furthermore, these devices brought together the learners and the community since the elders, as the sources of the stories, songs, and proverbs and as experts in oratory, were charged with the responsibility of teaching them to the young.

These powerful traditional teaching and learning tools were, however, negated in colonial education in much of Africa, despite the fact that their usefulness as sources of African wisdom and cultural knowledge had been well documented by nineteenth-century scholars and missionaries like J.G. Christaller (1879), who collected and published well over three thousand Akan stories and proverbs. The utilization of these tools would have also addressed the problem of the separation between the school and the community that was introduced during colonial administration. This negation of indigenous knowledge can be explained by the fact that colonial education was an ideological process in which education and schooling were used as agents for the internalization and acceptance of Western cultural values, and as vehicles for developing in the colonized the preferred sense of psychological subordination. Cameron McCarthy and Greg Dimitriades have categorized these practices of negation as *ressentiment,* after Nietzsche, which they describe as 'the specific practice of identity displacement in which the social actor consolidates his identity by a complete disavowal of the merits and existence of his social other' (2000, p. 193). With Linda Tuhiwai Smith (2002), I argue that the negation of indigenous views constituted a critical part of the colonial strategy mostly because these views challenged and resisted the mission of colonization.

The Past, the Present, and the Postcolonial Curricular Imagination

In this section I attempt to creatively address the tensions and contradictions inherent in some of the traditions of indigenous African education, and integrate what is recoverable about the past into the logic of the present and the needs and interests of the future. The intent is to make curriculum proposals that are responsive to the postcolonial condition in an African country like Sierra Leone.

The recent addition of curriculum internationalization to the educational discourses of reform and research should be thought of not only as exhortations of change but also constructions of imaginaries that potentially embody 'a deep reshaping of the images of social action and consciousness through which individuals are to participate' (Popkewitz, 2000, p. 172). Underlying the new discourse of internationalization is curriculum imagination that 'denotes a collective sense of a group of

people, a community that begins to imagine and feel things together'
(Rizvi, 2000, p. 223). This imagining of ourselves as a community participating, interpreting ourselves, and creating knowledge together is
critical to curriculum reform in a postcolonial context. *Hybridity* becomes crucial in the formulation of the agenda of reform, for its politics
of intellectual and political cross-fertilization embody multiple power
relations which make possible the subversion of colonial authority.

Postcolonial theorist Homi Bhabha contends that one of the consequences of colonialism and, more recently, the accelerated migration of
former colonial subjects into the metropolitan centres of the West has
meant that, intellectually and politically, the colonizer and the colonized have been brought together in identity formation that is continually in a process of hybridity. Bhabha (in an interview published in
Rutherford, 1990) describes hybridity as the Third Space where heterogeneous lifestyles and practices coexist with homogenizing scenarios of
everyday life both at the centre and at the margin. Postcolonialism is
constitutive of the cultural logic of this mixture and the multilayered
forms of interactions between the civilizations of the colonial powers
and those of the colonized. The postcolonial Third Space is where the
meaning of cultural and political authority is negotiated without eliding or normalizing the differential structures in conflict. Elsewhere, I
have referred to Bhabha's Third Space as the place for the construction
of identities that are neither one nor the other (Kanu, 2003). I have
argued that, because of centuries of Western European impact on Africa
– from missionary and trade activities to outright colonization and now
globalization – it is no longer possible to postulate a unitary Africa over
and/or against a monolithic West, as a binarism between a distinct
Self (as African) and Other (as European). There is no longer in Africa
a single set of discourse about progress and change; rather, there is a
hybrid – a Third Space – where local and global images meet in a
weaving that has its own configurations and implications. This overlay
is best expressed in Gayatri Spivak's response to critics who have
faulted her on not seeking possibilities of discovering and/or promoting indigenous theory: 'I cannot understand what indigenous theory
there might be that can ignore the reality of nineteenth century history
… To construct indigenous theories, one must ignore the last few centuries of historical involvement. I would rather use what history has
written for me' (1990, p. 69).

Indeed, education itself in the former colonies occurs within an overlay of discourses that move in the interstices of the colonial and the

colonized. The rapid movements and collision of peoples and media images across the world have further disrupted the traditional isomorphism between Self, place, and culture. The Eurocentric (e.g., Bennett, 1994) and Afrocentric (e.g., Asante, 1993) debates that have emerged in discourses about curriculum reform are themselves driven by nostalgia for a past in which Europe and Africa are imagined without what McCarthy and Dimitriades call 'the noise of their modern tensions, contradictions and conflicts' (2000, p. 195). These debates refuse the radical hybridity that is the reality of today's major metropolitan societies everywhere.

Curriculum reform as postcolonial imagination, grounded in the reality of hybridization, would allow the influences of history and global migration to inform new responses to teaching, and it would invite curriculum workers to rethink the production, representation, and circulation of knowledge so that these do not remain the monopoly and privilege of one group. This way dismantled traditions, as well as the subjugated memories and histories of those who have hitherto been marginalized can become part of the curriculum conversation. Thus imagined, curriculum reform does not involve posing Western culture against the cultures of the non-West, but it is, instead, founded on the principle of the heterogeneous basis of all knowledge and the need to find abiding links that connect groups across ethnic affiliations, geographical origins, and locations; McCarthy would describe the knowledge that results from such interaction as an alloy of racial, cultural and ethnic metals (1998). This emerging approach to knowledge production is already being recognized in the field of medicine, where greater efforts are being made to explore the value of multiple sources of knowledge; for example, traditional health practices such as acupuncture and chiropractic remedies (now known as alternative medicine) are increasingly being utilized in Western societies, while pharmacologists (in developing new drugs) are seeking traditional cures that have been used in different societies (Bacchus, 2002). More of this 'alloyed' approach to knowledge production and dissemination could be embarked upon in postcolonial curriculum work. As indicated earlier, the technical-rationale approach that currently pervades curriculum development in many African countries has produced implementation nightmares unanticipated by the Western countries where the model was conceived. In Sierra Leone, for example, the approach has resulted in teachers perceiving their role as limited to what Pinar calls 'a postal service' (2004), wherein teachers define themselves as deliverers of other people's mail, that is the curriculum for students to learn. The sources, purposes, and relevance of the curriculum are not questioned, and teaching and learning are shaped largely by teachers' concerns over the cultivation of 'effective' technical skills by which to deliver and/or transmit the curriculum.

These problems of rationalization, instrumentalization, and erosion of students' and teachers' life-world from curriculum could be addressed by drawing on the Sierra Leonean indigenous practice of interweaving curricular aims, content, and methodology to enable successful curriculum implementation and to make education more functional and relevant to the places where students live their lives. This approach would place curriculum firmly within a cultural framework, viewing such a framework as a means whereby teachers facilitate the development of students' identities, self-understandings, and understandings of the world by providing them with insights into the cultural values and the tools that they need for interpreting the ambiguous cultural contexts in which they are now living. The situational and/or contextual analysis preceding the development of such curriculum would take into account the needs and goals of the society, the values and attitudes considered to be important and desirable, and the cultural resources available in the society – including any existing parallel learning systems such as religious and/or spiritual education. This process would facilitate the selection of content and methods based on an analysis of the environment in which the curriculum is developed and used – and not on learning objectives as defined by outsiders. This approach would be flexible enough to accommodate local values such as communal approaches to learning and the use of stories and proverbs as tools for teaching and learning. It would also be adaptable and open to further interpretation and renewal in light of changing circumstances and specific contextual needs and aspirations, and it would, perhaps, be more effectively handled by teachers and students who are the users of the curriculum.

Postcolonial imagination questions authority and destabilizes received traditions (Dimitriades & McCarthy, 2001); therefore, African indigenous education itself needs to be interrogated for its inherent limitations for addressing contemporary educational problems. For instance, a crucial objective of indigenous education among the men in Sierra Leone is the preservation of the tribal or community heritage, which is accomplished through the transmission of tribal values such as unquestioned respect for and acceptance of moral values, religious beliefs, and the views of elders as authoritative. The successful transmission of these values requires obedience and conformity. But, while this approach may have helped to sustain tribal values and hold the community together, it has been criticized by some contemporary African educators as transforming African children into submissive youngsters who, although biologically equipped with the same keen interests and imagination as their counterparts from other cultures, quickly come to lack the spirit of initiative, creativity, and critical thinking. Thus, there is a need to question whether the tradition of instructing children to accept authoritative teachings simply out of deference to authority figures serves them well for survival in today's world. An intimate connection does exist between personal identity and particular traditions, which, if rejected, reduces our 'personness' as human beings; yet, I have to argue that humans are not passive in the way that traditions define identity or destiny. Human beings can affirm some of their inherited traditions, cultivate and transmute them, embrace them or recombine, and recreate them in novel ways (Fay, 1987). Indeed, being a person means continuously revisiting tradition and upholding certain elements of it while rethinking others. Hoy quotes Gadamer on the issue of tradition and change: 'Tradition is not merely what one knows to be and is conscious of as one's own origin ... Changing the established forms is no less a kind of connection with the tradition than defending the established forms. Tradition exists only in constant alteration' (1982, p. 127). I interpret Gadamer here to mean that, in addition to having a past which affects us in innumerable and complex ways, we have a present that to some extent always differs from the past and that is animated by concerns and interests driving it towards the future. The past shapes us, but we contribute to its outcome by responding to it in light of our current or contemporary needs (Wachterhauser, 1986). Confronted with new situations that we seek to understand, we are forced to re-examine our traditions in relation to emergent realities and meanings. The real issue, it would seem, is the political will and preparedness to read tradition as an open-ended text rather than as a closed entity.

Cumulative events, such as the European infiltration into Africa, the subsequent colonization of the African continent, the Western-style education that colonialism brought, and the current forces of economic and cultural globalization have all led to a present that differs from our past and to changed and changing concerns that are shaping our future. This invites questions about how to educate students so that they become able to function meaningfully and effectively in these new contexts (a point reiterated by Bacchus, this volume). The situation involves channelling of reflection towards certain aspects of traditional educational practices (e.g., the uncritical acceptance of authoritative teachings) that may have served well to hold the community together, but that now need to be examined critically vis-à-vis incoming authoritative ideas about curriculum, teaching, and education for development. Upon such critical examination depends the survival of African cultures amidst the juggernaut of Western modernity that at present threatens every non-Western civilization. We must appreciate that indigenous educational experiences that discourage critical questioning are likely to shape and mediate how the African child experiences Western-style education. Having learned early in their own culture(s) not to question, challenge, or disobey authority, children come to extend these values to school authorities like teachers, the curriculum, and textbooks, and then take these authoritative sources for – and as – granted. But children can be taught to assume a critical voice towards authority without necessarily devaluing, disrespecting, or destroying authority altogether. A critical voice (rather than merely destructive criticism) attempts the delicate work of rearticulating the tensions within practices, constraints, and possibilities, even as it questions the taken-for-granted knowledge that shapes everyday life (Britzman, 1991).

Critical thinking about education most certainly needs to be nurtured in teacher preparation because teachers play a pivotal role in educational change. Improved educational practices have to begin with an emphasis on the preparation of teachers as critical inquirers who, through offering themselves as models, will eventually pass the habits of critical inquiry on to their students. This involves preparing teachers who are committed to and have the desire to think, not only about what they as educators might eventually do but also about the social visions such practices would support. To think, in this sense, is related to Michel Foucault's understanding of it as 'the motion by which one detaches oneself from what one does, establishes it as an object, and reflects upon it as a problem' (cited in Greene, 1988, p. 2).

Since independence, there has been much rhetoric in African countries about the functioning of education to genuinely emancipate people and improve the quality of their lives. In realizing these emancipatory goals, the tradition of educating students for cultural assimilation needs to be questioned for its usefulness. What is needed is the preparation of teachers who can critically question current educational practices and strive towards innovative curriculum strategies that will enable students to utilize their acquired skills and knowledge in changing their own lives and their societies for the better. Emancipatory education begins with teachers who possess the capacity to surpass the given in curricular practices and approach things as if they could be different. The preparation of such teachers has to be grounded in critical reflection that is driven by four moments linked to a series of questions (Freire, 1973): Teachers must learn to describe (what do I do?), inform (what does this mean?), confront (how did I come to be this way?), and reconstruct (how might I do things differently?).

In *describing*, teachers would attempt to articulate adequately, in their own language, the principles and assumptions behind current curricular practices in order to gain understanding of the knowledge and values that are embedded in curriculum and in teaching practices, and how these limit situations for development in their postcolonial society. *Informing* would consist of unravelling and explaining the contradictions that emerge from the descriptions, the nature of the forces that cause teachers to operate in the ways that they do, and the steps through which to move beyond description to concrete action for change. *Confronting* involves re-evaluating the taken-for-granted ideas and practices, their origins, the social visions embedded in them, and the instruments used to maintain them as constraints on what is possible. In *reconstructing*, the three preceding moments are galvanized towards action for change. Reconstructing involves teacher preparation processes that help teachers see current curriculum and teaching practices not as immutable givens but as constructions that are contestable. By constructing portrayals of curriculum and teaching within their own societal needs and sociocultural realities, teachers become able to: demystify what hitherto was apparently inexplicable, take control of what they do, and act to achieve desirable ends. In short, this process will prepare teachers for critical engagement with the curriculum and with pedagogy in a postcolonial context.

My imagination of postcolonial curriculum based on retrieving some of the past – *sankofa* – and combining it with the realities of the present in a process of hybridization is inspired by Immanuel Kierkegaard's argument (in Caputo, 1987) that no matter how much is subtracted from the individual there is always a remainder that could embrace the task of reconstituting the self. This reconstituting process involves repetition, which, for Kierkegaard, is a forward movement that is cognizant of the past. Through the process of repetition the individual becomes able to press forward, 'not toward a sheer novelty which is wholly discontinuous with the past, but into the being which he himself is ... Repetition is that by which the existing individual circles back on the being which he has been all along, that by which he returns to himself' (cited in Caputo, 1987, p. 12).

The experience of colonization diminished the colonized in many ways, and different forms of neo-colonialism continue to influence and determine decisions and practices in the former colonies. In the midst of such incessant dispersal of the Self, people have the need to define themselves in terms of new memories through which they come to know, understand, and experience themselves – memories that are thereby dissociated from monolithic identities and reimagined within new collective narrative (Balibar & Wallerstein, 1991). Thus, as Priscilla Wald has put it: 'Older identities are estranged and one's "home" [identity] is no longer located where one thought it was' (cited in Popkewitz, 2000, p. 170). If, indeed, we are serious about the construction of another – new – narrative, then curriculum reform needs to be based in imagined communities (Anderson, 1991), where relations are no longer unidirectional or univocal, flowing from the colonialist to the colonized or vice versa. The challenges of the twenty-first century transcend national boundaries and single sets of discourses – we could call them 'supranational or transnational challenges' (Parker, Ninomiya, & Cogan, 1999). Addressing these challenges requires hybrid and/or multinational curriculum thinking and acting, consisting of overlays of multiple discourses, as well as plural assumptions and strategies (see Kanu, 2003).

REFERENCES

Aldridge, D. (2003). The dilemmas, challenges, and duality of an African-American educational historian. *Educational Researcher, 32*(9), 25–34.
Anderson, B. (1991). *Imagined communities: Reflections on the origins and spread of nationalism.* London: Verso.
Appiah, K.A. (1992). *In my father's house: Africa in the philosophy of culture.* Oxford: Oxford University Press.
Asante, M. (1993). *Malcolm X as cultural hero and other Afro-centric essays.* Trenton, NJ: Africa World Press.
Bacchus, M.K. (2002). *Curriculum, education and globalization, with special reference to the developing countries.* Keynote address at the Conference on Problems and Prospects of Educational Development in Developing Countries, University of the West Indies, Barbados.

Balibar, E., & Wallerstein, I. (1991). *Race, nation, class: Ambiguous identities* (Chris Turner, Trans.). New York: Verso.

Bennett, W. (1994). *The book of virtues*. New York: Simon and Schuster.

Bernstein, B. (1986). From hermeneutics to praxis. In B.R. Wachterhauser (Ed.), *Hermeneutics in modern philosophy* (pp. 87–110). New York: SUNY Press.

Britzman, D.P. (1991). *Practice makes practice: A critical study of learning to teach*. New York: SUNY Press.

Caputo, J. (1987). *Radical hermeneutics: Deconstruction and the hermeneutic project*. Bloomington: Indiana University Press.

Christaller, J.G. (1879*). A collection of 3,600 Tshi (Twi) proverbs and stories*. Basel: Evangelical Missionary Society.

Clarke, J.H. (1987). Why Africana History? Available at www.africawithin.com/clarke/why_africanahistory.htm   Retrieved 20 September 2004.

Dei, G.J.S., Hall, B.S., & Rosenberg, D. (Eds.), (1998). *Indigenous knowledge in global contexts: Invisible readings of our worlds*. Toronto: University of Toronto Press.

Dimitriades, G., & McCarthy, C. (2001). *Reading and teaching the postcolonial: From Baldwin to Basquiat and beyond*. New York: Teachers College Press.

Fay, B. (1987). *Critical social science*. Ithaca: Cornell University Press.

Freire, P. (1973). *Education for critical consciousness*. New York: Seabury Press.

Gadamer, H.G. (1984). *Truth and method*. New York: Crossroads.

Greene, M. (1988). *The dialectic of freedom*. New York: Columbia University Teachers College.

Gross, D. (1992). *The past in ruins: Tradition and the critique of modernity*. Amherst: University of Massachusetts Press.

Gyekye, K. (1995). *African philosophical thought: The Akan conceptual scheme*. Philadelphia: Temple University Press.

Hoy, D. (1982). *The critical circle*. Berkeley: University of California Press.

Kanu, Y. (1993). *Exploring critical reflection for postcolonial teacher education: Sierra Leone*. Unpublished doctoral dissertation, University of Alberta. Edmonton, AB, Canada

Kanu, Y. (2003). Curriculum as cultural practice. *Journal of Canadian Association for Curriculum Studies*, 1(1), 67–81.

Marx, K. (1978). The Eighteenth Brumiere of Louis Bonaparte. In R.C. Tucker (Ed.), *The Marx and Engels reader* (pp. 595–597). New York: W.W. Norton.

McCarthy, C. (1998). *The uses of culture: Education and the limits of ethnic affiliation*. New York: Routledge.

McCarthy, C., & Dimitriades, G. (2000). Globalizing pedagogies: Power, resentment, and the re-narration of difference. In N.C. Burbules and C.A.

Torres (Eds.), *Globalization and education: Critical perspectives* (pp. 187–204). New York: Routledge.

Parker, W.C., Ninomiya, A., & Cogan, J. (1999). Educating world citizens: Toward multinational curriculum development. *American Educational Research Journal, 36*(2), 117–145.

Pinar, W.F. (2004). *What is curriculum theory?* Mahwah: Erlbaum.

Popkowitz, T. (2000). Reform as the social administration of the child: Globalization of knowledge and power. In N.C. Burbules & C.A. Torres (Eds.), *Globalization and education: Critical perspectives* (pp. 157–186). New York and London: Routledge.

Rivzi, F. (2000). International education and the production of global imagination. In N.C. Burbules & C.A. Torres (Eds.), *Globalization and education: Critical perspectives* (pp. 205–225). New and London: Routledge.

Rutherford, J. (Ed.) (1990). The third space: Interview with Homi Bhabha. In J. Rutherford (Ed.), *Identity, community, culture and difference* (pp. 301–307). London: Lawrence and Wishart.

Smith, L.T. (2002). *Decolonizing methodologies: Research and indigenous peoples.* London: Zed Books.

Spivak, G. (1990). The postcolonial critique. In S. Harasym (Ed.), *The postcolonial critique: Interviews, strategies, dialogues* (pp. 67–70). New York: Routledge.

Wachterhauser, B.R. (1986). Introduction: Language and history in understanding. In B.R. Wachterhauser (Ed.), *Hermeneutics in modern philosophy* (pp. 3–43). New York: SUNY Press.

Van Manen, M. (1990). *Researching lived experience.* New York: SUNY Press.

9 Cross-Cultural Science Teaching: Rekindling Traditions for Aboriginal Students

GLEN S. AIKENHEAD

Canadian science educators find themselves in a fairly unusual position. Knowingly or unknowingly, they stand between two diverse knowledge systems: Western and Aboriginal ways of describing and explaining nature. On the one hand, a Western-scientific perspective on nature harmonizes with the worldview of science educators (Cobern, 2000), while on the other, Aboriginal perspectives likely do not harmonize with a science teacher's point of view (Aikenhead, 1997; Semali & Kincheloe, 1999). Conversely, for many students, particularly many Aboriginal students, a Western scientific perspective on nature does not harmonize with their own worldview (Aikenhead, 1997); consequently, Western science seems like a foreign culture to these students (Brandt, 2001; Kawagley, 1995; Sutherland, 1998).

A type of cognitive imperialism pervades school science whenever students, particularly Aboriginal students, are assimilated (some would say 'colonized') into thinking like a Western scientist in their science classes (Aikenhead, 2001; Battiste, 1986). This chapter focuses on science education for Canadian Aboriginal students. Readers may, however, find that some ideas and findings expressed here transfer to other contexts familiar to them, including science education for Euro-Canadian students, Maori students, Anglo-American students, or Zulu students.

Worldwide, the Aboriginal academy has argued that colonization under the guise of 'science for all' undermines students' self-identities as Aboriginal people, identities that are essential to the economic development, environmental responsibility, and cultural survival of Aboriginal peoples (Battiste, 2000b; MacIvor, 1995; Mosha, 1999; Purdie, Tripcony, Boulton-Lewis, Fanshawe, & Gunstone, 2000). Canadian educators can either colonize students by attempting to enculturate them into Western science, or they can begin to embrace a decolonizing approach to school science that gives Aboriginal students access to Western science and technology without diminishing their Aboriginal identities. We can adopt a decolonizing approach to science teaching by enculturating students into the students' community (Battiste, 1998), a community increasingly affected by Western science and technology. This shift in the enculturation of students, from Western science to the community, suggests a postcolonial approach to science teaching (Battiste, 2000b).

The purpose of this chapter is to describe a modest project that was inspired by the call/need to decolonize school science through curricular activities that are compatible with the postcolonial notion of Third Space, where Western-scientific knowledge resides side by side with Aboriginal science without either science eliding the cultural and political authority of the other, or 'normalizing' the differential structures in conflict. The project, *Rekindling Traditions: Cross-Cultural Science and Technology Units* (Aikenhead, 2000a), developed culturally sensitive teaching strategies and materials for Aboriginal students in science classes. This project challenges science educators to understand a scholarly Aboriginal perspective on nature, while providing science educators with a political opportunity to make a significant difference to the school experiences of Aboriginal students.

Background

The issue of bridging the two knowledge systems (Western science and Aboriginal science) for the benefit of Aboriginal students is not new (Maddock, 1981; Pomeroy, 1994). One proposed bridge is a field called 'traditional ecological knowledge' or TEK (Johnson, 1992). Snively and Corsiglia have described TEK this way: 'Especially during the last 25 years, biologists, ecologists, botanists, geologists ... have labored to develop approaches that are improving our ability to understand and mitigate the impact of human activity upon the environment. By extending their enquiry into the timeless traditional knowledge and wisdom of long-resident, oral peoples, these scientists have in effect moved the borders of scientific inquiry and formalized a branch of biological and ecological science' (2001, pp. 7–8).

TEK is usually associated with resource management of lands populated by Aboriginal peoples. However, Snively (1990, 1995) has shown that TEK can also become part of school science, to the advantage of Aboriginal students in those classrooms. Some scholars, for example, Battiste and Henderson, have identified TEK even more closely with Aboriginal science, thereby changing the definition of TEK somewhat: 'The traditional ecological knowledge of Indigenous peoples is scientific, in the sense that it is empirical, experimental, and systematic. It differs in two important respects from Western science, however: traditional ecological knowledge is highly localized and it is social. Its focus is the web of relationships between humans, animals, plants, natural forces, spirits, and landforms in a particular locality, as opposed to the discovery of universal "laws"' (2000, p. 44).

In any field of inquiry, knowledge is power by virtue of the way it is put into action (Foucault, 1980; Rodriguez, 1999). McGregor (2000) has defined traditional ecological knowledge in terms of the way it has been practised in Canada, and her critique of TEK reveals the power relationships inherent in TEK. Interest in TEK often originates outside an Aboriginal community (see Snively & Corsiglia, 2001), and consequently, non-Aboriginal scientists end up setting the agenda, which 'perpetuates the same pattern of "discovery" and investigation that has characterized colonial history in North America. TEK, therefore, is symptomatic of the relationship that Aboriginal people have with their colonizers' (McGregor, 2000, p. 439). Because it was Western academics who created the concept of TEK in the first place, TEK tends to be pervasively imbued with a Western perspective.

This hegemonic power of Western thinking (cognitive imperialism) was revealed by Nadasdy (1999) when he studied several cases in which Aboriginal people who were knowledgeable in TEK participated with government Western scientists in resource management and environmental impact assessment studies. Nadasdy examined the act of integrating both knowledge systems, focusing on the power relations underlying the process of integration. His analysis showed, in support of McGregor's concerns, how TEK was used by government scientists to *avoid* a two-way integration of the two knowledge systems and to reinforce a Western cultural bias that controlled decision-making over local land and animal issues (i.e., colonization continued). A more authentic integration of TEK with Western science would share decision-making power, in addition to sharing the knowledge itself. The lack of power-sharing and the subsequent marginalization of Aboriginal participants became evident in each case that Nadasdy investigated (e.g., two boys charged with shooting a musk ox out of season; how the reductionism of Western science systemically controls bureaucratic structures; and how managing a population of Dall sheep can revolve around respect, or lack of respect, for animals and their social relationships).

Because of such systemic and hegemonic power relationships, McGregor concludes that we should not integrate or bridge Western and Aboriginal sciences, as TEK attempts to do but should, instead, actively support a postcolonial model that she calls coexistence, which 'promotes functioning of both systems side by side ... The model of co-existence encourages equality, mutual respect, support, and coopera-tion' (2000, p. 454). This view is embraced by Battiste (2000a), MacIvor (1995), Sainte-Marie (2000), and Urion (1999): 'Creating a balance be-tween two worldviews is the great challenge facing modern edcuators' (Battiste, 2000a, p. 202). This is a major intellectual and political chal-lenge for Canadian science educators today.

Aboriginal students bring the worldviews, which they have learned at home, in contact with a Western science worldview presented at school. Many students experience this as a cross-cultural event (Cajete, 1999; Maddock, 1981; Sutherland, 1998). To balance the two cultures, school science should be cross-cultural in nature (Aikenhead, 1997). In Australia and Aotearoa/New Zealand, the balance is often called 'two-way learning' (Ritchie & Butler, 1990), and in the United States, 'bi-cultural instruction' (Cajete, 1999; Kawagley, 1995, 2000). Central to a cross-cultural approach to science teaching is the tenet that Aboriginal children are *advantaged* by their own cultural identity and language, not disadvantaged. Aboriginal students have the potential to see the world from at least two very different points of view, more so than many of their Euro-Canadian counterparts.

Based on the expectation that future science teaching will need to become postcolonial and cross-cultural in nature (i.e., helping students move from their everyday culture into the culture of Western science – cultural border crossing; Aikenhead, 1997; Aikenhead & Jegede, 1999), and based on the need to understand teachers' views on this topic before cross-cultural science teaching can be implemented, Aikenhead and Huntley (1999) conducted a research study into science teachers' conceptions of (1) the connection between the culture of science and the culture of Aboriginal students, (2) the possible assimilation of these students in their science classes, and (3) the degree to which teachers saw themselves as *culture brokers* (Arhchibald, 1999; Stairs, 1995) who could smooth students' cultural border crossings into school science. The teacher participants (both Aboriginal and non-Aboriginal) taught

Aboriginal students across northern Saskatchewan in Grades 7 to 12. The research identified barriers to student participation in science: while the science teachers tended to blame various inadequacies (a lack of this and a lack of that), Aboriginal educators clearly pointed to the vast differences between Aboriginal culture and the culture of science – differences that made science a foreign and forbidding world to most students. Several recommendations emerged from that study, two of which are relevant here:

1 Knowledge of nature learned in school science should combine both Aboriginal and Western knowledge systems.
2 A group of teachers who are already fulfilling some of the principal roles of a culture broker should be identified, and they should form a working network with other educators who could facilitate their collaborative efforts. Together, they should develop (a) an array of culturally responsive instruction and assessment practices; (b) a culturally sensitive science curriculum; and (c) specific lessons, units, or modules for other teachers to use.

The study also found great diversity in cultures from community to community across the north. This means that teaching materials developed in one community are *not* necessarily transferable to another community. Teaching materials must fit into the meaningful cultural context of the local community; otherwise, many students will find the science curriculum inaccessible (Cajete, 1999; Stairs, 1994). Northern Saskatchewan schools needed cross-cultural science units that convey the local communities' Aboriginal view of nature and convey Western science as *another* way of understanding nature – a way that expresses a Western-scientific worldview and a Western set of values about nature (MacIvor, 1995). No such units existed.

What does this type of cross-cultural science teaching look like in a classroom? This key question became the research question for the present investigation. In the sections that follow, the study is described and its results presented. The chapter concludes with a brief discussion on the decolonization of school science.

Methodology

To ameliorate the deficiency in cross-cultural science teaching materials and strategies noted above, a research and development (R&D) study was initiated. This was a two-year collaborative effort between the author and six teachers (Grades 6 to 11), conducted in communities across northern Saskatchewan.

An R&D methodology is usually associated with the natural sciences, where scientific inquiry informs, and is informed by, engineering design in a context bounded by everyday exigencies (Ziman, 1984). In other words, R&D is a combination of science and technology. In the social science domain of education, an R&D study differs from the typical educational research normally reported in the literature. In an educational R&D study, data are not collected to inform a theoretical model or to be interpreted to convey a participant's lived experience, or to assess a program in any summative way. In an R&D study, research is undertaken and data are collected to be fed directly into improving the product of the study or into initiating practice related to the product. This goal resembles formative assessment. R&D studies were employed, for example, to improve a product in science education in the 1970s and 1980s by a Dutch physics project that produced science-technology-society (STS) modules (Eijkelhof & Lijnse, 1988). Aikenhead (1983, 1994) describes using R&D methods to produce high school curriculum materials, in *Science: A Way of Knowing* (Aikenhead & Fleming, 1975) and in an STS textbook, *Logical Reasoning in Science and Technology* (Aikenhead, 1991). A different genre of R&D studies dedicated to improving science classroom practice, called action research (Keeves, 1998), is illustrated by Pedretti and Hodson's (1995) research with teachers who were introducing STS science into their classrooms; by Bencze and Hodson's (1998) research with teachers implementing inquiry-oriented science instruction; by Nyhof-Young's (2000) gender research into group work in science classrooms; and by McVittie's (2002) action research into teaching a chemistry unit in Grades 6 and 7 guided by two constructivist positions.

In a recent critique of research in science education, Jenkins (2001) underscored the need for research into innovative classroom practices, research not normally undertaken by university science educators. R&D is an emerging methodology that can yield useful curriculum materials and instructional practices for classroom use. This methodology was used to produce *Rekindling Traditions*. Salient details follow.

Participants

A number of teachers were nominated by the directors of two school divisions in northern Saskatchewan as possible participants in the study. Each teacher was contacted by telephone by the author. Seven volunteer teachers were selected to participate in the study; one withdrew midway through the first year. The teachers taught science or technology courses in five isolated communities spread over a distance of about five hundred kilometres. The collaborative R&D team of six teachers (two of whom were Aboriginal) had a personal interest in developing their cross-cultural science teaching further. Their teaching experience ranged from two to twenty-five years, and they currently taught classes composed mostly of Aboriginal students. These teachers were highly involved in school activities and related projects, and they were particularly busy people.

On the advice of the Northern Lights School Division (a major school jurisdiction in northern Saskatchewan), the author approached Elder Henry Sanderson of the La Ronge Indian Band, to ask him to be the project's guide. At a meeting in La Ronge with the author, Elder Sanderson accepted a gift of jams and teas, thereby agreeing to enter into a relationship with the author and become the project's Elder. At the first collaborative meeting with the teachers in La Ronge in January 1999, Elder Sanderson gave the team the vision to care for Mother Earth. He continued to provide guidance throughout the project at key decision points. Other Elders kindly provided knowledge and wisdom from time to time in the various communities.

A number of consultants and advisers assisted the R&D team: for example, translators helped write key words and phrases in Cree, Dëne, and Michif; computer experts provided technical support; an Aboriginal artist provided drawings; and many competent people in the teachers' communities identified authentic Aboriginal science to be included in school science and helped students and teachers learn it.

Research Objectives

Guided by the work of Aboriginal and international educators (Cajete, 1986; Casebolt, 1972; Ermine, 1995; Hampton, 1995; Jegede, 1995; Kawagley, 1995; MacIvor, 1995; Mckinley, 1996; Nelson-Barber, Trumbull, & Shaw, 1996; Ogawa, 1995), by research findings (Aikenhead, 1997; Aikenhead & Huntley, 1999; Allen & Crawley, 1998; Baker, 1996; Deyhle & Swisher, 1997; Fleer, 1997; Harris, 1978; Snively, 1990, 1995), and by the practical knowledge of teachers, the following objectives were formulated for the R&D investigation:

1 To develop *a prototype process* for producing culturally sensitive instructional strategies and curriculum materials that support student learning within any particular community.

2 To produce teaching strategies and materials that exemplify culturally sensitive science teaching for Aboriginal students (Grades 6 to
11), and to make them available electronically through CD-ROM
and Web site sources.
3 To inspire others to continue the practice of cross-cultural science
teaching.

As a consequence, the project *Rekindling Traditions: Cross-Cultural Science and Technology Units* (Aikenhead, 2004a) emerged. The results of
our R&D study are reported in the next three sections of this chapter,
organized around its three objectives.

Result: To Develop a Prototype Process

Our first objective was to develop a prototype process for producing
culturally sensitive instructional strategies and curriculum materials.
Our experiences in this development are documented in two documents, 'Teacher Guide to Rekindling Traditions' and 'Stories from the
Field' (in Aikenhead, 2000a). These documents, along with the individual units themselves, convey a prototype process for others to follow. The following summary describes key aspects to this process,
designed, piloted, and implemented during the R&D study.

Throughout the first six months of the project, teachers received up to
eight days of release time for research, writing, and working with the
local experts in their unit's topic. This release time was essential to the
success of the project. In addition, the R&D team conducted six two-day
planning meetings away from the schools, usually attended by an
Elder. Minutes of these meetings were posted on the project's Web site.
The focus of each meeting changed as time went on. We began by
becoming familiar with past work in cross-cultural science education
(see the 'Teacher Guide' for details). Then we went on to identify
themes for our units. Next we found and piloted appropriate resources,
activities, and teaching methods to suit the units. Time was taken
during the later meetings to edit the units, to polish the lesson plans,
and to plan professional development workshops for other teachers.
Some units developed faster than others. Those that related to specific
seasons (e.g., 'Snowshoes,' 'Trapping,' and 'Wild Rice') could not be
piloted until the season was right.

Significant progress in developing individual units was always
achieved when the teachers interacted face to face away from their
school setting. The R&D team needed uninterrupted time to share

ideas, reflect on the units, and consider how to involve community members in the school science curriculum. The synergy from people interacting around a table with a common purpose proved very powerful. The face-to-face meetings led directly to initiatives being taken by each teacher. Our face-to-face meetings could not have been replaced by e-mail discussion lists, chat rooms, telephones, or faxes. These modes of communication do not allow for the synergetic interaction needed by such a project. In the culture of most schools, there are hourly demands on teachers to interact with students to obtain academic, social, personal, institutional, and parental results. These demands wrap teachers up in a whirl of responsibilities that usually leave them with neither the time nor the energy to interact with the Internet, telephones, or faxes.

Although these pilot schools in northern Saskatchewan were connected to the Internet, the schools were not socially structured to facilitate Internet communication. To ensure such communication, schools will need to change the time demands placed on teachers and to acquire reliable and compatible technology (a very rare commodity in the profit-dominated world of computers and software). The project could not have progressed without the face-to-face meetings. Future projects should follow this traditional pathway rather than the 'information highway.'

Another major facet of the study's successful progress can be attributed to the time that I, as facilitator and coordinator, spent on the project interacting with the teachers in their communities. I was released from all teaching responsibilities at my university during the autumn of 1999 (when the communities were implementing the units), and part-time in the spring of 2000 (when the units were edited and electronically designed for desktop publishing on CD-ROM). Progress would not have been smooth without a facilitator and coordinator to organize meetings, follow up on teachers' suggestions, visit teachers in their schools, write, research, or courier when needed, negotiate computer software problems as they arose, and keep everyone focused on the project's goals as defined by our Elders.

Key community members were essential to the process of developing lessons sensitive to the students' unique community. At first it was a challenge for each teacher to involve people from the community. The challenges were very different from community to community. These challenges, and our advice on how to overcome them, are found in our document, 'Stories from the Field' (in Aikenhead, 2000a). Knowing the politics of the community was always the first step towards success.

Result: To Produce Some Teaching Strategies and Materials

In Alaska, Native American students' standardized science test scores uniformly improved over four years, to meet the national averages, in classrooms where there was a strong cultural fit among the instruction, the curriculum, and the context in which students learned the science (Barnhardt, Kawagley, & Hill, 2000). Our *Rekindling Traditions* project aimed to accomplish such a cultural fit. The project's teaching strategies are described first, followed by an overview of the curriculum materials.

Teaching Strategies

The first strategy that made a world of difference was teaching outdoors. Students reacted very positively when immersed in nature away form the school building, even when this was the case for only one or two lessons in a unit. It was as if these students were sensing their natural place in the world. This inference coincides with one of Hampton's twelve standards of education for First Nations students, namely, *a sense of place*: 'Indian education recognizes the importance of an Indian sense of place, land, and territory' (1995, p. 40). Kawagley and Barnhardt (1999) also describe the importance of place to the Alaskan Yupiaq First Nations and how science educators can be sensitive to that sense of place when planning instruction. The power of Aboriginal science rests with its validity for a particular place; a teacher connects with this place by expanding the walls of the school into the community (MacIvor, 1995; Snively & Corsiglia, 2001).

Another culturally sensitive instructional strategy discovered by the R&D team was the involvement of students in gaining local Aboriginal knowledge related to the unit. Students learned that their community was rich in knowledge, as rich as the Internet and print materials that they worked with at school. To gain access to local knowledge, students were taught the proper protocol for approaching people who possessed that knowledge. For this purpose, students were taught how to conduct interviews. Most of the *Rekindling Traditions* units contain a lesson dedicated to gaining local knowledge appropriately. Interview questions were composed by the class and then used by groups of students to interview people in the community. The local knowledge that was gained by students was shared and synthesized in class. In other words, Elders and other knowledgeable people in the community taught local content to students, who, in turn, recorded the knowledge in a way appropriate to the wishes of the person who gave it to them in the first place (some stories are not to be repeated, and some may only be reported orally). When feasible, students recorded events with recyclable cameras, following procedures suggested by Meadows, Settlage, and Allen (1999). Some of these photos were placed in the units, augmenting the students' pride in their work and connecting the culture of the community with the culture of school science.

After helping students synthesize the local Aboriginal knowledge, teachers verified the validity of this knowledge by talking with people in their community. This procedure established a personal contact between the teachers and people in the community. Some teachers invited Elders or other local experts into the classroom. Students and teachers usually learned the Aboriginal-science content together. In some cases, the Elders or other experts helped the teacher conduct a field trip with the students – for example, a trip to a wild rice stand, to a trap line, or to where certain plants with healing powers grow. These instructional methods showed students how to gain access to their community's knowledge and wisdom. But, more importantly, they taught students to value and respect their own Aboriginal heritage. This tends to develop stronger cultural identity and self-esteem in Aboriginal students (Battiste, 2000a; Cajete, 1999; McKinley, McPherson, Waiti, & Bell, 1992; Ritchie & Butler, 1990).

The various activities described above illustrate one central theme of *Rekindling Traditions*: respect for local knowledge is *foundational*, not a token add-on. Aboriginal knowledge found in each of the *Rekindling Traditions* units creates a context for instruction that most Aboriginal students relate to. It is also a context into which Western-science instruction can logically fit. In other words, Western-science content is taught in the context of the local community's Aboriginal science, a context that creates an Aboriginal framework for the unit. A *Rekindling Traditions* unit uses Western science to learn more about students' Aboriginal worlds, rather than using an Aboriginal world to learn Western science. The approach of *Rekindling Traditions* celebrates the coexistence of both sciences, a condition essential to culturally sensitive instructional strategies and to a postcolonial science education.

When students were introduced to Western science content in a unit (as described in more detail below), this was done with respect for the authentic knowledge that had been shared by the community. Consequently, students could learn Western science without feeling the need to discredit the Aboriginal science that they had learned. Assimilation was consciously avoided. Teachers noted that students became more interested in their science course and no longer approached it as content to be memorized. In one case, two students exclaimed: 'This isn't science; it's too much fun.'

Although we consciously avoided teaching science in an assimilative way, students were nevertheless expected to see the world through the eyes of a Western scientist, just as we would expect students to understand another point of view on an issue. *Understanding* Western science, however, did not necessary mean *believing* in its content and technique. Similarly, when we dealt with spirituality in Aboriginal science, students were expected to understand it, not necessarily to believe it. This distinction was most important to parents who lived a fundamentalist Christian faith. Our approach to teaching has been called 'anthropological instruction' (Aikenhead, 1997) because it puts students in the position of anthropologists: learning the content of another culture.

The integration of Aboriginal science and Western science, according to McGregor's coexistence model (2000), was another culturally sensitive instructional strategy that proved successful. It had a noticeable motivational effect on many students in our study. According to their teachers, students tended to become more involved in science classes, even staying after school to complete projects when necessary. Voluntarily staying after school was normally almost unheard of in the pilot schools of northern Saskatchewan.

A common pattern of integration found in the *Rekindling Traditions* units is the Aboriginal framework established at the beginning of each unit. This introductory Aboriginal content takes the form of practical action relevant to a community, for example, going on a snowshoe hike, finding indigenous plants that heal, listening to an Elder, interviewing people in the community, or assisting in a local wild rice harvest.

Values are particularly salient in Aboriginal cultures (Cajete, 1999). Central to cross-cultural strategies of teaching science is making students aware of the different cultural ways in which one can describe and explain nature. Not only is the science content different in each culture, but the values attached to that content differ. Both Western-scientific and Aboriginal values are made explicit in *Rekindling Traditions* lessons. The introduction to any unit clarifies key values that Elders expect students to learn (e.g., harmony with nature). This practice of making values explicit is then extended to the clarification of values that underlie Western science when scientific content is studied in a unit (e.g., power and domination over nature). This happens to be a requirement of the Saskatchewan science curriculum, defined by one of its seven dimensions of scientific literacy – 'values that underlie science' (Saskatchewan Education, 1991, p. 28). Each lesson plan in a *Rekindling Traditions* unit specifies either a Western-scientific value or an Aboriginal value to be conveyed by the lesson. Key Western-scientific values became the topic of a classroom discussion. During such discussions, Western-scientific values were expressed and then critiqued. As the value structure of Western science became more apparent to Aboriginal students (e.g., the mathematical idealization of the physical world), students became freer to appropriate Western knowledge without embracing Western ways of valuing nature. This process of appropriation has been called 'autonomous acculturation' (Aikenhead, 1997); it is an alternative to trying to assimilate or enculturate students into Western science or getting students to memorize the content covered.

After the unit is firmly grounded in an Aboriginal framework (accomplished in one to three lessons), the next move is to introduce students to relevant Western-science content from the Saskatchewan science curriculum. An introduction to Western science is an explicit border-crossing event into a different culture. This cultural-border crossing is acknowledged by *consciously* switching:

1 Values, e.g., from harmony with nature to power and domination over nature
2 Language, e.g., from *mahihkan* to *Canis lupis*
3 Conceptualizations, e.g., from 'Who is that animal?' to 'How is it classified?'
4 Assumptions about nature, e.g., from the observer being personally related to what is observed to the observer being objectively removed
5 Ways of knowing, e.g., from holism to reductionism

An effective culture-brokering teacher (Archibald, 1999; Stairs, 1995) clearly identifies the border to be crossed, guides students back and forth across that border, and helps them negotiate cultural conflicts that may arise (Aikenhead, 1997; Jegede & Aikenhead, 1999). Each unit differs slightly in terms of where this border crossing first occurs.

Western science can powerfully clarify one small aspect of Aboriginal science. For example, in the units 'Snowshoes,' 'Trapping,' and 'Wild

Rice,' the technologies associated with these topics were originally studied from the historical, technological, and cultural perspectives of the local community. Then the class took a closer, Western-scientific look at the pressure exerted by snowshoes on snow, the play between potential and kinetic energy in animal traps, and the habitat of wild rice and the pH of the water in that habitat. By understanding the Western-scientific stories about pressure, energy, habitat, and pH, students learned to predict more accurately the effects of variations in the technology associated with snowshoeing, trapping, or producing wild rice. Although the Western-science concepts may not improve students' know-how for snowshoeing, trapping, or growing wild rice, the concepts clarify one small aspect of the overall topic. Western science did not replace Aboriginal science; rather it enriched an aspect of it. As various topics in Western science and technology are studied within our units, additional Aboriginal content is introduced from time to time. This is easy to do because the unit already has a framework for that content.

The teaching strategies found in the units nurture the enculturation of Aboriginal students into *their community's* culture (Aikenhead, 1997, 2000b; Casebolt, 1972), an enculturation that engenders a strong self-identity (Battiste, 2000a; Commonwealth of Australia, 2000; MacIvor, 1995; Mosha, 1999; Purdie et al., 2000). This approach differs dramatically from attempts to enculturate students into *Western science,* the goal of the so-called reform movements in, for example, the United States (NRC, 1996), the United Kingdom (Millar & Osborne, 1998), and Ontario (McNay, 2000). The 'reform' goals seem like assimilation or colonization to many of those who reside in an Aboriginal community.

As students brought their community's Aboriginal knowledge, language, and values into the classroom, new relationships between teacher and student tended to replace the conventional colonizing hierarchy, characterized by teachers transmitting what they know to students (Battiste, 1998). This new relationship tended to enhance the cultural sensitivity of any instructional strategy used in a classroom. By teaching a *Rekindling Traditions* unit, teachers learned from students who had recently learned valid Aboriginal science from people in their community. By learning from students and community members, teachers demonstrated how an educated adult learns new knowledge. Teachers, of course, shared their own expert knowledge with students. Teachers were facilitators, cultural tour guides, and learners – in short, culture brokers (Aikenhead, 1997; Archibald, 1999; Jegede & Aikenhead, 1999; Stairs, 1995).

Table 9.1: The six units in *Rekindling Traditions*

English title	Authentic title	Teacher developer
Nature's Hidden Gifts	Iyiniw Maskikiy (Cree)	Morris Brizinski
Snowshoes	Asâmak (Michif or Cree)	David Gold
Survival in Our Land	Kipimâcihowininaw ota Kitashinahk (Cree)	Earl Stobbe
The Night Sky	Tth ën (Dëne)	Shaun Nagy
Trapping	Ḷts'usi Thëlai (Dëne)	Kieth Lemaigre
Wild Rice	Manomin (Algonkin or Cree)	Gloria Belcourt

Teaching Materials

The teaching materials developed in the R&D study include six teaching units, a teacher guide, and a document describing the team's experiences in involving the local community in determining what should count as valid school science content.

The main teaching materials for *Rekindling Traditions* are the six units (Aikenhead, 2000a), listed in Table 9.1 with the English title, the authentic title, and the teacher developer for each. Our units were written by teachers to give fellow teachers the necessary background information, resource materials (including links to Internet materials), and other practical assistance lesson by lesson. Each lesson has the same organization: time required, goals (objectives), values to be conveyed (Aboriginal or Western scientific), instructional strategies used, procedural outline, integration with other subjects, resources, and practical teacher notes. The computer files for these units are very large, between 5,000 and 12,000 megabytes (MB), because each unit has many colour photographs, and several units have substantial teacher resources placed in appendices. The units are available in two formats: (1) Microsoft Word, software compatible with all schools across northern Saskatchewan, and (2) PDF, a format that reduces the size of the computer files considerably but does not allow a teacher to edit the files. Only the units' PDF files are on the project's Web site (http://www.usask.ca/education/ ccstu). Both the PDF and Microsoft Word files are on the CD_ROM (Aikenhead, 2000a). Our units are most valuable when teachers can easily copy and modify them to suit the needs of the local community. For this reason, our copyright was written to allow this to happen as long as no one makes a profit.

Another teaching material developed was the 'Teacher Guide' to *Rekindling Traditions* (Aikenhead, 2000a). It serves as a professional support

Table 9.2: Table of contents for 'Teacher Guide' to *Rekindling Traditions*

Chapter 1: Introduction

Chapter 2: Teaching science In Saskatchewan schools

Chapter 3: The need for cross-cultural science teaching

Chapter 4: The *Rekindling Traditions* project

Chapter 5: Background
 Western Science versus Aboriginal Knowledge of Nature
 A Cross-Cultural Approach to Teaching and Learning
  Cultural-Border Crossing
  Coming to Knowing
  Culture Brokering
 Different Relationships between Western and Aboriginal Sciences
 Resolving Cultural Conflicts between Western and Aboriginal Sciences
  Collateral Learning
 Translation Is Not Enough
 Treating Aboriginal Knowledge with Respect
 Standards of Education for Aboriginal Students

Chapter 6: Integration of Western and Aboriginal sciences

Chapter 7: An overview of units
 Wild Rice
 Nature's Hidden Gifts
 Survival in Our Land
 Trapping
 Snowshoes
 The Night Sky
 Summary

Chapter 8: Culturally sensitive student assessment
 Principles of Assessment
 Written Tests
 Assessment Rubrics
 Checklists
 Portfolios

Chapter 9: Conclusion
References

---

for cross-cultural science teaching and as a general guide to the six units. The 'Teacher Guide' presents background information and ideas that guided our own work. The ideas are from several sources: Aboriginal educators from around the world, Aboriginal educators and Elders in Saskatchewan, and our own experiences and perspectives. The 'Teacher Guide' discusses the integration of Aboriginal science and Western science in much greater depth than can be done in this chapter. It draws upon the six units in detail to illustrate this integration. The Teacher Guide's table of contents (Table 9.2) clearly indicates the topic for each section. For example, the section 'Treating Aboriginal Knowledge with Respect' lists nine principles that guided us during the R&D study.

In 'Stories from the Field' (Aikenhead, 2000a), we convey our experiences and advice related to contacting community people to learn their knowledge, involving them with the school, and gaining support from the community at large. This document takes some of the mystery out of becoming involved with Elders and other people in the context of Canadian Aboriginal communities. It should make Canadian teachers feel more comfortable crossing the cultural border between their personal cultural identities and the culture of Elders and others in the community. This border crossing is an essential teaching strategy in *Rekindling Traditions*.

Results: To Inspire Others

Our third objective, to inspire others to implement cross-cultural science teaching, has involved disseminating our project at teachers' professional meetings. It is premature at this time to describe consequences of the *Rekindling Traditions* project. The project is such a departure from the status quo in science teaching that it will require several years to be implemented by teachers who are capable of becoming culture brokers. However, some preliminary information may be of interest to the reader. Preservice science teachers at the University of Saskatchewan have begun to benefit from *Rekindling Traditions* in their science methods courses because the project concretely illustrates how teachers can integrate Aboriginal science with Western science. At in-service teacher workshops, the reaction has been positive. We consistently hear, 'This is what I've been looking for. There isn't any material like it.'

A different type of outcome has given us more confidence in the cross-cultural teaching strategy called 'border crossing.' As described earlier, the strategy responds to the difficulties that students encounter when they try to learn Western science but are confronted by a foreign culture (Aikenhead & Jegede, 1999; Costa, 1995). For many students, there is a cultural border to cross between their everyday world and the world of Western science. Evidence from cultural anthropologists Phelan, Davidson, and Cao (1991) and Leavitt (1995) has shown that a reasonably smooth border crossing is a central strategy for cross-cultural science instruction (Aikenhead, 1997). This strategy was adopted by American-Indian science educator Gregory Cajete in his book *Igniting the Sparkle: An Indigenous Science Education Model* (1999). Although this endorsement from a revered Aboriginal leader is most encouraging, experience and future research will tell how effective this strategy is for various teachers and teaching situations. Its applicability in urban multi-cultural classrooms remains to be tested. Research into students' border crossing into school science should be fruitful for understanding how students learn in ways highly meaningful to them (i.e., ways that enhance their self-identities), and such research should be useful in designing teaching materials in future R&D studies.

Discussion

Worldwide, there is growing interest in decolonizing school science and addressing the under-representation of Aboriginal peoples in careers related to science and technology (Aikenhead, 1997; Battiste, 2000b; Battiste & Henderson, 2000). Success in school science depends, of course, on a student's interests in succeeding, and it is highly correlated with Aboriginal students' cultural self-identities (Purdie et al., 2000).

One response to this state of affairs was to design models of curriculum development (Cajete, 1999; McKinley, 1998). Another response was to develop instructional strategies and teaching packages that integrate Aboriginal science with Western science (Alaska Native Knowledge Network, 2001; Allen & Crawley, 1998; Linkson, 198; Michie, Anlezark, & Uibo, 1998; Read, 1998; Sainte-Marie, 2000). The *Rekindling Traditions* project goes one step further: science teachers collaborate with local experts to modify a teaching unit (electronically stored), or create a new unit, to meet the unique needs of an individual community. It is antici-pated that a teacher will print out a *Rekindling Traditions* unit from our CD-ROM or Web site (Aikenhead, 2000a), take it to some people in their community who know the topic well, and then ask, 'How could *we* modify this unit so it fits our community?' These local people become a major resource for modifying the unit (or developing a new one). They can also interact with students in the school or on a field trip, thus strengthening students' cultural self-identity and helping them cross the cultural border between Aboriginal science and Western science. This is an important feature of the *Rekindling Traditions* units. It is one response to Battiste's invitation: 'Creating a balance between two worldviews is the great challenge facing modern educators' (2000a, p.

202). It is also the challenge that Kanu (this volume) and Richardson (this volume) refer to in their discussions of teaching amidst the cultural ambiguity that marks the postcolonial condition.

Our project shows that culturally responsive teaching strategies and materials, integral to postcolonial school science, worked well for Aboriginal students in the pilot schools. Teachers modelled successful border crossing between the teachers' life-worlds and the culture of the community. Innovation in other science classrooms, however, represents an intellectual and political challenge for Canadian science educators. Culturally responsive teaching requires us to renegotiate the culture of school science (Aikenhead, 2000b). The negotiation towards a coexistence of two major cultures, Aboriginal and Western, seriously questions the Western hegemonic status quo residing in many schools, communities, university science departments, and society in general (Battiste, 1998; Fensham, 1998; Hodson, 2001). Encouragingly, Friedel (1999) discovered that when the Aboriginal community was involved in an Edmonton public school, the culture of the school changed appreciably, although the administrator and teachers had to change as well. Without a change in the culture of school science, Aboriginal students will not likely respond to curriculum innovations in the way a science teacher might hope they will.

A community's Aboriginal knowledge enjoys a respected place in the *Rekindling Traditions* units. Some students in the R&D study discovered that they already possessed this Aboriginal knowledge because it had been taught to them at home, but they had not valued it as legitimate knowledge for school science. Other students in our study learned this Aboriginal knowledge for the first time in their science class. Either way, Aboriginal knowledge was given voice in the classroom, in the sense described by O'Loughlin (1992) and Brandt (2001) as involving both the speaker and the listener in mutual respect. Each of our units validated the ways of knowing that students brought to school by grounding the curriculum in those ways of knowing – the students' voices and lives.

By giving Aboriginal knowledge a respected voice in science classrooms, teachers learn from students and from people in the community, and students' Aboriginal identities tend to be nurtured (Kawagley & Barnhardt, 1999; McKinly et al., 1992). When the Commonwealth of Australia conducted extensive research into what works for Aboriginal students in their schools, they too concluded that 'the very content and status of the knowledge that is taken for granted in Western-style education may challenge and disrupt some of the foundations of Indigenous cultures. This is no small matter. Having an individual sense of "how you are supposed to be" is the most basic foundation for development and maturation, the platform for confident operation in the world' (2000, p. 143).

In Canada the 1996 Royal Commission on Aboriginal Peoples also underscored the importance of Aboriginal culture for Aboriginal students: 'Culture approaches start from the belief that if youth are solidly grounded in their Aboriginal identity and cultural knowledge, they will have strong personal resources to develop intellectually, physically, emotionally and spiritually. The ability to implement culture-based curriculum goes hand in hand with the authority to control what happens in the schools system' (1996, p. 478).

In some modest measure, the *Rekindling Traditions* project provides innovators with one way to actively support the decolonization of school science and thus nurture economic development, environmental responsibility, and cultural survival for Aboriginal peoples in Canada.

NOTES

I am indebted to the six teachers, Gloria Belcourt, Morris, Brizinski, David Gold, Keith Lemaigre, Shaun Nagy, and Earl Stobbe, whose creativity and commitment to teaching were stellar. The *Rekindling Traditions* project was made possible through support and funding from the Cameco Access Program for Engineering and Science (CAPES), the Stirling McDowell Foundations (Saskatchewan Teachers' Federation), Northern Lights School Division, Ile-à-la-Crosse School Division, Saskatchewan Education (Northern Division), and the Colleges of Education and Engineering, University of Saskatchewan.

This chapter was previously published as an article in *Canadian Journal of Science, Mathematics and Technology*, July 2002, pp. 289–304. Reprinted here with the permission of the journal and the author.

REFERENCES

Aikenhead, G.S. (1983). A retrospective account of the development of a novel curriculum in science: Prospects for change. In R. Butt, J. Olson, T. Russell, & T. Aoki (Eds.), *Insiders' realities, outsiders' dreams: Prospects for curriculum change* (pp. 124–138). Vancouver: University of British Columbia Centre for the Study of Curriculum and Instruction.

Aikenhead, G.S. (1991). *Logical reasoning in science and technology.* Toronto: Wiley.

Aikenhead, G.S. (1994). Collaborative research and development to produce an STS course for school science. In J. Solomon & G.S. Aikenhead (Eds.), *STS education: International perspectives on reform* (pp. 216–227). New York: Teachers College Press.

Aikenhead, G.S. (1997). Toward a First Nations cross-cultural science and technology curriculum. *Science Education, 81,* 217–238.

Aikenhead, G.S. (2000a). *Rekindling traditions: Cross-cultural science and technology units.* Retrieved 8 April 2002, from http://usask.ca/education/ccstu.

Aikenhead, G.S. (2000b). Renegotiating the culture of school science. In R. Millar, J. Leach, & J. Osborne (Eds.), *Improving science education: The contribution of research* (pp. 245–264). Birmingham: Open University Press.

Aikenhead, G.S. (2001). Integrating Western and Aboriginal sciences: Cross-cultural science teaching. *Research in Science Education, 31,* 337–355.

Aikenhead, G.S., & Fleming, R. (1975). *Science: A way of knowing.* Saskatoon: Curriculum Studies, University of Saskatchewan.

Aikenhead, G.S., & Huntley, B. (1999). Teachers' views on Aboriginal students learning Western and Aboriginal science. *Canadian Journal of Native Education, 23,* 159–175.

Aikenhead, G.S., & Jegede, O.J. (1999). Cross-cultural science education: A cognitive explanation of a cultural phenomenon. *Journal of Research in Science Teaching, 36,* 269–287.

Alaska Native Knowledge Network. (2001). Alaska Native Knowledge Network Web site. University of Alaska Fairbanks. Retrieved 8 April 2002, from http://www.ankn.uaf.edu.

Allen, J.A., & Crawley F.E. (1998). Voices form the bridge: Worldview conflicts of Kickapoo students of science. *Journal of Research in Science Teaching, 35,* 111–132.

Archibald, J. (1999). Hands back, hands forward: Revisiting Aboriginal voices and re-visioning Aboriginal Research. *Canadian Journal of Native Education, 23,* 1–5.

Baker, D. (1996). Does 'indigenous science' really exist? *Australian Science Teachers' Journal, 42*(1), 18–20.

Barnhardt, R., Kawagley, A.O., & Hill, F. (2000). Cultural standards and test scores. *Sharing Our Pathways, 5*(4), 1–4.

Battiste, M. (1986). Micmac literacy and cognitive assimilation. In J. Barman, Y. Herbert, & D. McCaskell (Eds.), *Indian education in Canada,* Vol. 1, *The legacy* (pp. 23–44). Vancouver: UBC Press.

Battiste, M. (1998). Enabling the autumn seed: Toward a decolonized approach to Aboriginal knowledge, language, and education. *Canadian Journal of Native Education, 22,* 16–27.

Battiste, M. (2000a). Maintaining Aboriginal identity, language, and culture in modern society. In M. Battiste M. (Ed.), *Reclaiming Indigenous voice and vision* (pp. 192–208). Vancouver: UBC Press.

Battiste, M. (2000b). Reclaiming indigenous voice and vision. Vancouver: UBC Press.

Battiste, M., & Henderson, J.Y. (2000). *Protecting Indigenous knowledge and heritage.* Saskatoon: Purich Publishing.

Bencze, L., & Hodson, D. (1998). Coping with uncertainty in elementary school science: A case study in collaborative action research. *Teachers and Teaching, 4,* 77–94.

Brandt, C. (2001). *The topography of scientific discourse: A case study of an American Indian student in the academy.* Paper presented at the annual meeting of the American Educational Research Association, Seattle.

Cajete, G.A. (1986). *Science: A Native American perspective.* Unpublished doctoral dissertation, International College, Los Angeles.

Cajete, G.A. (1999). *Igniting the sparkle: An indigenous science education model.* Skyand, NC: Kivaki Press.

Casebolt, R.L. (1972). *Learning and education at Zuni: A plan for developing culturally relevant education.* Unpublished doctoral dissertation, University of Northern Colorado, Boulder.

Cobern, W.W. (2000). *Everyday thoughts and nature.* Dordrecht: Kluwer.

Commonwealth of Australia. (2000). *What works? Explorations in improving outcomes for indigenous students.* Canberra: Australian Curriculum Studies Association/National Curriculum Services.

Costa, V.B (1995). 'When science is another world': Relationships between worlds of family, friends, school, and science. *Science Education, 79,* 313–333.

Deyhle, D., & Swisher, K. (1997). Research in American Indian and Alaska Native education: From assimilation to self-determination. *Review of Research in Education, 22,* 133–194.

Eijkelhof, M.M.C., & Lijnse, P. (1988). The role of research and development to improve STS education: Experiences from the PLON project. *International Journal of Science Education, 10,* 464–474.

Ermine. W.J. (1995). Aboriginal Epistemology. In M. Battiste & J. Barman (Eds.), *First Nations education in Canada: The circle unfolds* (pp. 101–112). Vancouver: UBC Press.

Fensham, P.J. (1998). The politics of legitimating and marginalizing companion meanings: Three case stories. In D.A. Roberts & L. Ostman (Eds.),

Problems of meaning in science curriculum (pp. 178–192). New York: Teachers College Press.

Fleer, M. (1997). Science, technology and culture: Supporting multiple worldviews in curriculum design. *Australian Science Teachers' Journal, 43*(3), 13–18.

Foucault, M. (1980). *Power/knowledge*. New York: Pantheon.

Friedel, T.L. (1999). The role of Aboriginal parents in public education: Barriers to change in an urban setting. *Canadian Journal of Native Education, 23*, 139–158.

Hampton, E. (1995). Towards a redefinition of Indian education. In M. Battiste & J. Barman (Eds.), *First Nations Education in Canada: The circle unfolds* (pp. 5–46). Vancouver: UBC Press.

Harris, J.W. (1978). Aboriginal science, Western science and the problem of conceptual interference. *Australian Science Teachers' Journal, 24*(3), 61–67.

Hodson, D. (2001). Towards a more critical multiculturalism. *Canadian Journal of Science, Mathematics and Technology Education, 1*, 117–121.

Jegede, O.J. (1995). Collateral learning and the eco-cultural paradigm in science and mathematics education in Africa. *Studies in Science Education, 25*, 97–137.

Jegede, O.J., & Aikenhead, G.S. (1999). Transcending cultural borders: Implications for science teaching. *Research in Science and Technology Education, 17*, 45–66.

Jenkins, E. (2001). Science education as a field of research. *Canadian Journal of Science, Mathematics and Technology Education, 1*, 9–21.

Johnson, M. (1992). Research on traditional environmental knowledge: Its development and its role. In M. Johnson (Ed.), LORE: *Capturing traditional environmental knowledge* (pp. 3–22). Ottawa: Dene Cultural Institute. International Development Research Centre.

Kawagley, O. (1995). *A Yupiaq wordview*. Prospects Heights, IL: Waveland Press.

Kawagley, O. (2000). Identity-creating camps. *Sharing Our Pathways, 5*(2), 4–5.

Kawagley, O., & Barnhardt, R. (1999). Education indigenous to place: Western science meets Native reality. In G.A. Smith & D.R. Williams (Eds.), Ecological education in action (pp. 117–140). Albany: SUNY Press.

Leavitt, R. (1995). Language and cultural content in Native education. In M. Battiste & J. Barman (Eds.), *First Nations education in Canada: The circle unfolds* (pp. 73–98). Vancouver: UBC Press.

Linkson, M. (1998). Cultural and political issues in writing a unit of Western science appropriate for primary aged indigenous students living in remote areas of the Northern Territory. *Science Teacher Association of the NT Journal, 18,* 90–100.

MacIvor, M. (1995). Redefining science education for aboriginal students. In M. Battiste & J. Barman (Eds.), *First Nations education in Canada: The circle unfolds* (pp. 73–98). Vancouver: UBC Press.

Maddock, M.N. (1981). Science education: An anthropological viewpoint. *Studies in Science Education, 8,* 1–26.

McGregor, D. (2000). The state of traditional ecological knowledge research in Canada: A critique of current theory and practice. In R.F. Laliberte, P. Settee, J.B. Waldram, R. Innes, B. Macdougall, L. McBain, & F.L. Barron (Eds.), *Expressions in Canadian Native Studies* (pp. 436–458). Saskatoon: University of Saskatchewan Extension Press.

McKinley, E. (1996). Towards an indigenous science curriculum. *Research in Science Educaiton, 26,* 155–167.

McKinley, E. (1998). Science curricula and cultural diversity: Are we doing enough for the aspirations of Maori? In D. Hodson (Ed.), *Science and technology education and ethnicity: An Aotearoa/New Zealand perspective* (pp. 48–58). Wellington: Royal Society of New Zealand.

McKinley, E., McPherson-Waiti, P., & Bell, B. (1992). Language, culture and science education. *International Journal of Science Education, 14,* 579–595.

McNay, M. (2000). The conservative political agenda in curriculum: Ontario's recent experience in science education. *Journal of Curriculum Studies, 32,* 749–756.

McVittie, J. (2002). Psychological constructivism and socio-culturalism in an elementary science classroom. Unpublished manuscript.

Meadows, L., Settlage, J., & Allen, N. (1999). *Windows into students' lives: Connecting with different cultures through photography.* Paper presented at the annual meeting of the National Association for Research in Science Teaching, Boston.

Michie, M., Anlezark, J., & Uibo, D. (1998). Beyond bush tucker: Implementing indigenous perspectives through the science curriculum. *Science Teachers Association of the NT Journal, 18,* 101–110.

Millar, R., & Osborne, J. (Eds.). (1998). *Beyond 2000: Science education for the future.* London: King's College, School of Education.

Mosha, R.S. (1999). The inseparable link between intellectual and spiritual formation in indigenous knowledge and education: A case study in Tanzania. In L.M. Semali & J.L. Kincheloe (Eds.), *What is indigenous knowledge? Voices from the academy* (pp. 209–225). New York: Falmer.

National Research Council [NRC] (1996). *National science education standards.* Washington, DC: National Academy Press.

Nadasdy, P. (1999). The politics of TEK: Power and the 'integration' of knowledge. *Arctic Anthropology, 36(1–2),* 1–18.

Nelson-Barber, S., Trumbull, E., & Shaw, J.M. (1996). *Sociological competency in mathematics and science pedagogy: A focus on assessment.* Paper presented to the 8th Symposium of the International Organization for Science and Technology Education, Edmonton.

Nyhof-Young, J. (2000). Action research in gender issues in science education. *OISE Papers in STSE Education, 1,* 225–231.

Ogawa, M. (1995). Science education in a multi-science perspective. *Science Education, 79,* 583–593.

O'Loughlin, M. (1992). Rethinking science education: Beyond Piagetian constructivism toward a sociocultural model of teaching and learning. *Journal of Research in Science Teaching, 29,* 791–820.

Pedretti, E., & Hodson, D. (1995). From rhetoric to action: Implementing STS education through action research. *Journal of Research in Science Teaching, 32,* 463–485.

Phelan, P., Davidson, A., & Cao, H. (1991). Students' multiple worlds: Negotiating the boundaries of family, peer, and social cultures. *Anthropology and Education Quarterly, 22,* 224–250.

Purdie, N., Tripcony, P., Boulton-Lewis, G., Fanshawe, J., & Gunstone, A. (2000). *Positive self-identity of indigenous students and its relationship to school outcomes.* Canberra: Commonwealth of Australia, Legislative Services.

Read, T. (1998). Kormilda science project. In M. Mitchie (Ed.), *Science education: Beyond the horizon.* Conasta conference proceedings (pp. 155–157). Darwin, Australia: Northern Territory University.

Ritchie, S., & Butler, J. (1990). Aboriginal studies and the science curriculum: Affective outcomes from a curriculum intervention. *Research in Science Education, 20,* 249–254.

Rodriquez, A.J. (1999). *Courage and the researcher' gaze: (Re)defining our roles as cultural warriors for social change.* Paper presented to a preconference workshop at the annual meeting of the National Association for Research in Science Teaching, Boston.

Royal Commission on Aboriginal Peoples. (1996). *Renewal: A twenty-year commitment* (Vol. 5). Ottawa: Government of Canada.

Sainte-Marie, B. (2000). *Science: Through Native American eyes.* Kapaa, HI: Cradleboard Teaching Project. Retrieved 6 April 2002, from www.cradleboard.org.

Saskatchewan Education. (1991). *Science 10: A curriculum guide for the secondary level.* Regina: Author.

Semali, L.M., & Kincheloe, J.L. (Eds.). (1999). *What is indigenous knowledge? Voices from the academy.* New York: Falmer.

Snively, G. (1990). Traditional Native Indian beliefs, cultural values, and science instruction. *Canadian Journal of Native Education, 17,* 44–59.

Snively, G. (1995). Bridging traditional science and Western science in the multicultural classroom. In G. Snively & A. MacKinnon (Eds.), *Thinking globally about mathematics and science education* (pp. 1–24). Vancouver: Centre for the Study of Curriculum and Instruction, University of British Columbia.

Snively, G., & Corsiglia, J. (2001). Discovering Indigenous science: Implications for science education. *Science Education, 85,* 6–34.

Stairs, A. (1994). Indigenous ways to go to school: Exploring many visions. *Journal of Multilingual and Multicultural Development, 15*(1), 63–76.

Stairs, A. (1995). Learning processes and teaching roles in Native education: Cultural base and cultural brokerage. In M. Battiste & J. Barman (Eds.), *First Nations education in Canada: The circle unfolds* (pp. 139–153). Vancouver: UBC Press.

Sutherland, D.L. (1998). *Aboriginal students' perceptions of the nature of science: The influence of culture, language and gender.* Unpublished doctoral dissertation. University of Nottingham, Nottingham.

Urion, C. (1999). Changing academic discourse about Native education: Using two pairs of eyes. *Canadian Journal of Native Education, 23,* 6–15.

Ziman, J. (1984). An introduction to science studies. *The philosophical and social aspects of science and technology.* Cambridge: Cambridge University Press.

PART 3

Globalization and the
Educational Response

10 Postcolonialism and Globalization: Thoughts towards a New Hermeneutic Pedagogy

DAVID SMITH

Globalization and postcolonialism are words that live in today's English lexicon like two cousins who trace their ancestry to a common stock but who arrive on the scene with very different interpretations of the family history. Postcolonialism stands in the line of 'posts' that Anne McClintock says mark a contemporary crisis in 'ideologies of the future' (1994, p. 167). Like postmodernism, poststructuralism, post-fordism, and so on, postcolonialism is involved in the work of relativizing (literally showing the interdependent relations of) the once-triumphalist Western tradition, thereby debunking any pretensions that tradition may have had about being the carrier of non-derivative pristine truths destined for universal application. This line of thinking already has a considerable body of literature associated with it (e.g., Ashcroft, Griffiths, & Tiffin, 1995; McClintock, Mufti, & Shohat, 1997; Shohat & Stam, 1994; Williams & Chrisman, 1994), so it will not be discussed in detail here, except for the way it points to a challenging of most of the core ortho-doxies in Western practices of education. How shall education proceed when its central assumptions about curricular and teacherly authority have been shown to be complicit in the subjugation of many of the world's peoples, peoples now claiming their place as interlocutors equal with anyone bold enough to make proposals about the future?

Globalization is more lately come on the scene, at least as a formal term, and generally it speaks of a particular response to a set of world conditions that found their genesis at the end of the Cold War. While some globalization theorists may have become more vocal now pre-cisely in reaction to the vacuum of cultural authority in the West that the 'post' theorists created, in general it is the assumed triumph of free-market ideology over state-sponsored economic development that is the main inspiration for globalization as a formal term. But there are other ways of understanding globalization, too, which may be more important in the long run, and some of them will be discussed here.

The literature on globalization is proliferating, and it has many dimensions. There is the work of Appadurai (1996), for example, who examines the 'cultural flows' that are part of the global landscape as a consequence of modern communications technology, media, migrations, and international financial dealings. Mittelman's (1997) collection of 'critical reflection' papers on the processes of globalization reveal such important tensions as those surrounding the identity of the nation-state in a time of transnational mega-business. King's (1997) edited book gathers wonderfully insightful pieces by people such as Stuart Hall concerning the relation of the global to the local and the nature of ethnic identity, when identity itself can be seen as fluid and problematic. Again, all of these topics have deep implications for education and teaching, to be discussed later.

First, though, a few further words about globalization itself and how one might best approach an understanding of it. Globalization is not a new phenomenon if by the term one simply means, for example, the interfusion of cultures through international trade or empire-building. In Europe, the Middle East, and Asia, one can still see traces of cultural interfusion in art, music, and architecture that go back at least to the days of Alexander the Great in the third century BCE, or to the overland silk caravans that flourished until the great sea routes to India and China were firmly established by the seventeenth century. Muslim architecture, from the eighth century on, can be clearly seen in various states of preserve over most of southern Europe, and even in parts of Latin America such as the eastern coast of Mexico. Our languages, of course, carry huge legacies of intercultural contact. English simply would not exist without Greek, Latin, Arabic, and so on. Globalization today, therefore, needs to be understood in a way unique to its present circumstances. I would like to suggest two fundamental modalities for understanding, then examine some pedagogical implications of the same.

Globalization is best understood as a kind of *imaginary*, that is, it is a construct of human imagination that serves to organize and mobilize certain forms of action in certain ways. It pertains less to any characteristic of the world in its ordinary condition than to what certain people *imagine* that condition to be, based on their desire, their theory, their ego-projection, or, say, their religious sensibility. A good example of global imaginary today might be called the *astronautical* imaginary. Space exploration has enabled most people in the world to observe televized images of Earth from the outer stratosphere. For the first time we have seen the earth as the Blue Planet, suspended in space. Such a vision, in turn, allows new kinds of wonderings, such as how a sight of such exceptional beauty could, at the same time, manage to completely conceal the human slaughter and bloodshed taking place on its surface. Or the question may arise as to why as human beings we so often seem to have such difficulty simply being at home with ourselves when so clearly we are already *at* home, on the Earth. Space exploration is a triumph of modern science, and it is precisely the distancing of Self from Others, and from one's own subjectivity in the name of objectivity, that is the core requirement of scientific possibility. So the astronautical imaginary, as part of the long trajectory of Western science, while it makes possible triumphs of one kind, in turn, also depends on a type of leave-taking, which in its most negative forms can amount to an abandonment of the particulars of life in the name of universalist claims.

German philosopher Max Scheler (as cited in Doumelin, 1976) once remarked that the history of Western civilization is the history of an endless journey 'outwards,' with the consequent evacuation of the inner life and the loss of concern for human life as lived in its detail. This is an important point, given that those who are the loudest proponents of that version of the globalization imaginary identified by Jane Kelsey (1996) as 'economic fundamentalism' often fail to recognize how their universalist vision of economic 'science' exacts violence on others. In this case, a narrow, Western-inspired theory of economic development has been taken by many authorities since the end of the Cold War to be worthy of global application, with catastrophic consequences for large numbers of the world's people. It is on this point that the term *globalization* itself needs most desperately to be identified as a kind of cultural artefact, because while it is the predominating form of globalization theory today, it is really only the latest iteration of a long-standing set of assumptions within Western culture regarding human reason as having universal form. The arguments go back to philosophers such as John Locke and Immanuel Kant in the seventeenth and eighteenth centuries, respectively, but they are also heavily implicated in the Fall and Redemption mythology of the Christian tradition, particularly its Protestant variations, which, as Max Weber (1920/1962) first suggested some 80 years ago, and R.H. Tawney (1960) some years later, are clearly linkable historically to the rise of capitalism. 'The Religion of the Market' (1997), as David Loy calls it, may be proposing itself as the next truly world religion.

To call globalization a form of human imaginary opens the possibility for that imaginary to be not only critiqued, but also revisioned when subject to influences that can reveal its limitations. It is here that the second modality of globalization comes into play, what can be termed its *facticity*.

The facticity of globalization not only names the plans and intentions of those who wish, say, to globalize markets by breaking down national and local identities; it also names all those creative strategies of resistance and recombination that people, often unselfconsciously, undertake in response to them. Youth street culture, cultural crossover, or 'world' music, alternative press media such as the journal entitled *Third World Resurgence*, mass migrations of refugees and others – all these phenomena are examples of globalization's facticity, and they speak of the thorough fluidity and irreducibility of the condition, against the determinations of those trying to assert a new 'world order.' Indeed, it is in the space between the intentions of the first group (the formal globalizers) and the actions of the second (all others) where the seeds of a potentially new form of global reality, globalization in a truer, deeper form, are to be found. It is this space 'in-between' that also marks the site of a new understanding of the work of teachers and educators for the next century. This new *postcolonial hermeneutic pedagogy*, as it may be called, has its own character and requirements, which may be briefly described as follows.

The new pedagogical hermeneutic or hermeneutic pedagogy reconfigures the work of teaching from the three basic models that have dominated the profession for the past 50 years or so – the transmission model, the pedacentric model, and more recently, the facilitator model. The first two are well understood and need little clarification here. The transmission model begins and ends with the teacher as the active knowledge expert and the student as the passive recipient of that knowledge. The pedacentric model begins and ends with the child's needs being the focus of all attention, to the ultimate undermining of any form of teacherly authority and the loss of any cultural or political address for educational work. The facilitator model is somewhat newer, a consequence of technology's rise to place of cultural dominance. The teacher is reduced to being simply the *manager* of the educational space and expected to have nothing of particular importance to say on any topic, other than being able to point the way to a good Internet site or set up project groups, manage 'behaviour problems,' and be strictly obedient to all state directives.

Because the new pedagogical hermeneutic requires of teachers first and foremost that they be *interpreters* of culture, rather than merely transmitters or managers, it is imperative that teachers be educated in such a way as to be able to speak across disciplines, across cultures, and across national boundaries. This is because the specific intention of all hermeneutic work is to bring about *understanding* (*verstehen*) between peoples and groups such that life together can precisely *be* a life, capable of sustaining human welfare in its most creative senses. Therefore, it may be more accurate to speak not of receiving an education, but of constantly being open to the means by which one can be led by life (literally, 'disciplined' from the Latin, *discipulus*) into an ever-deepening understanding of the truth of things.

Hermeneutic pedagogy is oriented by certain principles already well developed within the tradition of hermeneutics generally (e.g., Danner, 1997; Gallagher, 1994; Jardine, 1998; Palmer, 1967; Smith, 1994, 1999). These principles include: learning to attend to language as being somehow connected in its immediate uses to its etymological and time/space origins; showing the articulation between part and whole in any situation; and the capacity for creative interpretation of data in order to construct new senses of relatedness between individuals, groups, cultures, facts, and theories.

The pedagogical modus of the hermeneutic classroom is *dialogue*, in which the teacher has the capacity to interpret culture and information in such a way that students can appreciate their participation in it, as in a living stream which both flows through life and is the source of its sustenance. A hermeneutic teacher, therefore, does not just use the new information technologies as 'a tool,' but stands in a creatively critical relationship to that technology, fully aware of its capacity for misinformation, for creating addiction and other social malformations such as personal isolation, and the privatization of the knowing subject.

In its most expanded form, postcolonial hermeneutic pedagogy participates in what Pasha and Samatar identify as the core requirement of any global future, namely, 'intercivilizational dialogue' (1997). Such dialogue will require the resuscitation of what the hermeneutic tradition has always understood to be one of the cornerstones of shared human understanding, that is, a profound sense of the historically constituted nature of any current state of affairs, with the capacity for illuminating how any humanly livable future begins by acknowledging those historically derived debts and obligations that are part of any identity in the present. Consider, for example, the aspect of human migrations in the twentieth century. Walk down the streets of any major city in the Western world – London, Paris, New York, Toronto – and one of the most obvious features of the human landscape is its racial and ethnic diversity. This condition is not just a pleasant commentary on the variety of the world's peoples, however, something to be savoured in a typical multiculturalism class as decontextually illuminating the spice of life. It may be that, to some degree, but more profoundly in the hermeneutic classroom, global migrations can be taken up as a postcolonial reminder of the age of Euro-American imperialism. By the year 1945, 80% of the world's people were ruled administratively by the remaining 20%. Only by the year 1997 was the last major colonial outpost of the British empire, Hong Kong, restored to rightful hands. The postcolonial migrations, therefore, mark a feature of globalization's facticity that cannot simply be erased under a sunny interpretation of ethnic diversity, just as theorists of the new free-market globalization cannot ignore their historical complicity in the construction of the various crises of refugee migration in the contemporary context.

Symbolically, the migrations to the West can be taken as a coming home of the alter ego by which the imperial ego had constructed itself, a challenge to former colonizers to face themselves in the faces of those once defaced. The theory of endless production and commercial venturing that once made empire possible is now clearly unrepeatable given the memory that has been established. Burned within the imaginary of the formerly colonized is the memory of what it is like to have one's own traditions diminished and humiliated under an administrative arbitration not one's own, and any attempt to evade this truth for self-serving gain of a certainty will precipitate violence.

This appeal to a new heightened historical sensibility as part of a new global cultural hermeneutic is particularly important given that a central feature of the conservative version of the globalization agenda rides on a vision of the 'end of history' (Fukuyama, 1993). It is the eschatological undertone of such rhetoric that is its most disturbing feature, the belief that the time of deliberation, debate, and discussion about any shared human future is over because of the way its nature is deemed to have been already revealed in the collapse of communism, a circumstance now taken as justification for a new economic liberalism and political conservativism. The recent 'declarations' on education by organizations now claiming the unilateral right to speak for the world, such as the World Bank, the Organization for Economic Cooperation and Development (OECD), and the Trilateral Commission, all are imbued with the demand that any viable education today must serve, as its primary responsibility, the needs of a new global free market economy (Spring, 1998). And what is pedagogically required under this interpretation of affairs is a global citizenry, not educated to understand the full complexity of the his-torical construction of the present, but rather a citizenry historically amnesiated to such a degree that no further questions will be asked regarding the ultimate purpose of education. As the Conservative provincial government of Alberta declared to teachers at the start of its educational reform activity in the mid-1990s: 'You row; we will steer' (Maclean, 1995).

This sharp bifurcation of the ends and means of educational practice has intensified globally since the inauguration of administration of President George W. Bush in the United States in 2000. The administration has underwritten its foreign policy agenda with a new philosophy of naked, aggressive imperialism (Ikenberry 2002; Smith 2003), while keeping the domestic scene 'domesticated' (pacified and silent) through iron-fisted media control (Chomsky 2002). This situation has put teachers into a psychotic space because now there is a complete disconnect between the rhetoric of democracy that has undergirded the aspirational modalities of classroom practice in Western cultures for the past fifty years or so (e.g., democratically inspired pedagogy such as group work, action research projects, consensual classroom decision-making) and what is actually happening in the world, namely, a supplanting of democracy by unilateralism and heavy-handed military interventionism in the name of democracy. What now can inspire my teaching if as a teacher I can no longer assume that dialogue, for example, has any real potentiality, given that the *telos*, or end purpose of education is already predetermined in advance of that dialogue? This I believe is one of the central crises facing educators in the contemporary geopolitical context, and it centralizes the question of what is a teacher's political responsibility in a time of great political injustice and frightening ('shock and awe') abuse of political power. The answer to that question is too big to be taken up in detail here, but for teachers it must be answered from the side of teaching itself, that is, from the unique situational commitment of teaching, which is standing together with the young in the name of an always open future. Without such a stand, teaching must remain hopeless.

Indeed, it is this commitment to an open future that defines hermeneutic pedagogy in its most profound sense. The hermeneutic teacher lives in the name of human possibility, and as such, must remain vigilant at all times against those forces that would foreclose any child's ability to find a home in the world. A central challenge for teacher education programs today, therefore, must be to ensure that young teachers do not fall into a happy swoon of allegiance to the powers of darkness now embodied in the infrastructures and practices of U.S. capital. This will be a deeply difficult work, given the seductions that are so incipient in that venture, the Disneyfication of everyday life being only one example. Postcolonial hermeneutic pedagogy, in the age of globalization, keeps in mind at all times the 'underside of history' (Dussel, 1996) which is carried through the memory of colonialism to confront the lie of surface power, and to remind those who would wilfully destroy life in the name of life that for a future to be possible the sins of the past must be held in remembrance. Otherwise tomorrow may not be worth having.

REFERENCES

Appadurai, A. (1996). *Modernity at large: Cultural dimensions of globalization.* Minneapolis: University of Minnesota Press.
Ashcroft, B., Griffiths, G., & Tiffin, H. (Eds.). (1995). *The post-colonial studies reader.* London: Routledge.
Chomsky, N. (2002). *Media control: The spectacular achievements of propaganda.* New York: Seven Stories Press.
Danner, H. (Ed.). (1997). *Hermeneutics and educational discourse.* Durban: Heinemann.
Doumelin, H. (1976). *Buddhism in the modern world.* London: Colliers.
Dussel, E. (1996). *The underside of modernity: Apel, Rorty Taylor and the philosophy of liberation.* (E. Mendieta, Trans. and Ed.). Atlantic Highlands, NJ: Humanities Press.
Fukuyama, F. (1993). *The end of history and the last man.* New York: Avon Books.
Gallagher, S. (1994). *Hermeneutics and education.* New York: SUNY Press.
Inkenberry, G. (2002). America's imperial ambition. *Foreign Affairs, 81*: 44–60.
Jardine, D. (1998). *To dwell with a boundless heart: Essays in curriculum theory, hermeneutics and the ecological imagination.* New York: Peter Lang.
Kelsey, J. (1996). Life in the economic test-tube: New Zealand experiment a colossal failure. *Electronic Journal of Radical Organization Theory, 2*(1).
King, A. (Ed.). (1997). *Culture, globalization and the world-system: Contemporary*

conditions for the representation of identity. Minneapolis: University of Minnesota Press.

Loy, D. (1997). The religion of the market. *Journal of the American Academy of Religion, 65*: 275–290.

Maclean, C. (1995, 22 March). *Public address.* Sponsored by the Centre for the Study of Pedagogy and Culture, University of Lethbridge, Lethbridge, AB.

McClintock, A. (1994). The angel of progress: Pitfalls of the term 'post-colonialism.' In P. Williams & L. Chrisman (Eds.), *Colonial discourse and post-colonial theory* (pp. 291–303). New York: Columbia University Press.

McClintock, A., Mufti, A., & Shohat, E. (Eds.). (1977). *Dangerous liaisons: Gender, nation and Postcolonial perspectives.* Minneapolis: University of Minnesota Press.

Mittelman, J. (Ed.). (1997). *Globalization: Critical reflections.* New York: Sage.

Palmer, R. (1967). *Hermeneutics.* Chicago: Northwestern University Press.

Pasha, K., & Samatar, A. (1997). The resurgence of Islam. In J. Mittelman (Ed.), *Globalization: Critical reflections* (pp. 79-85). New York: Sage.

Shohat, E., & Stam, R. (1994). *Unthinking Eurocentrism.* New York: Routledge.

Smith, D. (1994). The hermeneutic imagination and the pedagogic text. In E. Short (Ed.), *Forms of curriculum inquiry* (pp. 187-209). New York: SUNY Press.

Smith, D. (1999). *Pedagon: Interdisciplinary essays in the human sciences, pedagogy and culture.* New York: Peter Lang.

Smith, D. (2003). On enfraudening the public sphere, the futility of empire and the future of knowledge after 'America.' *Policy Futures in Education, 1,* 3.

Spring, J. (1998). *Education and the rise of the global economy.* Mahwah, NJ: Erlbaum.

Tawney, R. (1960). *Religion and the rise of capitalism.* Harmondsworth: Penguin.

Weber, M. (1962). *The Protestant ethic and the spirit of capitalism.* New York: Scribners. (Original work published 1920)

Williams, P., & Chrisman, L. (Eds.). (1994). *Colonial discourse and post-colonial theory.* New York: Columbia University Press.

11 The Impact of Globalization on Curriculum Development in Postcolonial Societies

M. KAZIM BACCHUS

The Focus of Educational Programs in Colonial Societies

In discussing the factors that have influenced and will continue to influence the curriculum of educational institutions in postcolonial societies one first needs to grasp both the manifest and the latent functions of their pre-independence educational programs. Initially, the economic resources of most colonies were subject to outright pillage, and this process required unskilled and semi-skilled workers mainly for agriculture, mining, and other extractive industries; however, as production methods became more capitalized some skilled, white-collar, and professional workers were also needed. In addition, the colonizers required a small group of comprador elites to help in the administration of their colonies. These various personnel, therefore, were provided with the education and training deemed appropriate for their respective roles. But the major challenge facing colonizers was to strengthen their hegemonic control over the colonized and establish legitimacy for their authority to rule. For this, they depended partly on the repressive state apparatus (RSA) – the police, the judiciary, the militia, and the army – and on the ideological state apparatus (ISA) especially schools and other educational institutions (for a detailed discussion of how schools were used to promote colonial ideologies in different societies, see Yatta Kanu's Introduction to this volume). The challenge for the ISA was to educate and where necessary indoctrinate the colonized to accept a vision of reality, in which they continued to occupy an inferior role, both in terms of their status and the jobs they were allowed to fill. Programs of instruction were, therefore, largely focused on developing the loyalty of the colonized, providing them with practical skills, teaching them the colonizer's language, instructing them in some minor administrative roles, and preparing a few to be potential comprador elites. This also required socializing the colonized to believe in the cultural and intellectual superiority of the colonizers through efforts to denigrate their own abilities and their cultures.

This can be seen, for example, in the development of the Caribbean region where the Spanish colonizers began by destroying much of the social, political, and economic structures of the indigenous societies, exploited the region's wealth (especially its gold), and subjugated the native Indians by relegating them to the lowest position in the new social and occupational hierarchy by making them servants and slaves. The colonized were taught the skills that were needed by the emerging economy and the Spanish language, so that they could communicate with their colonizers. To ensure that the colonized perform their role as labourers, a tax was levied on them, which they could only pay by working for the colonizers. To overcome opposition to their rule, the colonial authorities used physical force supported by a process of resocialization to get the locals to accept the inevitability of their subordinate role. To achieve the latter goal priests were brought from Spain to pacify the colonized through a program of religious education. The indigenous people were taught to believe that by accepting the values and executing the wishes of the colonizer they would be laying up treasures in Heaven for themselves, thereby acquiring the prospects of a bright eternity. In an attempt to strengthen their claims of moral superiority over the colonized and to protect their own economic interests some members of the colonizing elite even suggested that the Indians did not have the moral capacity and the intellectual ability to benefit from a formal education. Others questioned whether they were rational beings, capable of living in freedom. These practices by colonizers were to dehumanize the colonized in order to allow for their more effective exploitation and the legitimization of the colonizers' own position of dominance in these societies.

When later the British seized control of some of these colonies they used similar approaches in their colonizing efforts. The introduction of the sugar industry resulted in an increased demand for unskilled and semi-skilled labour. African slaves were bought to fill this need. The new imperial elites, too, initially opposed education for the colonized, including religious education, because they assumed that if slaves were taught that all men were spiritual equals they would soon 'wish the same principle to prevail in politics' (*Colonist*, 1824) In their efforts to denigrate the black population they led them to believe that 'the buckra [whites] have a right to be master for buckra know everything but we negers [blacks] know nothing,' (Waddell, 1863, p. 35) It was even argued that blacks were incapable of learning, innately barbaric, and good for nothing.

While the colonizers continued to depend on physical restraint and punishment to keep the colonized in their place, they also recognized that this would not, by itself, produce the kind of uniform obedience that they considered necessary to ensure a constant supply of cheap labour for their plantations, especially after the abolition of slavery. Therefore, the ideological conditioning of the masses was necessary to enhance the effectiveness of the physical control mechanisms of the state in maintaining control over the population. As a result, Christianity was considered a means of reinforcing in the colonized the belief that they had to continue playing a subservient role in the new social order: The Christian denominational bodies often urged the population to 'submit yourselves to all your governors, spiritual pastors and masters and order yourselves lowly and reverently to all your betters' (Harte, 1824).

After emancipation, the imperial government made a grant to support the education or resocialization of the former slaves. But those who provided this education were instructed to encourage the free blacks to continue toiling on the sugar estates, because without their labour, 'property will perish ... the whites will no longer reside there and the liberated blacks themselves will probably cease to be progressive' (Sterling, 1835). The first colonial education adviser to the region suggested that reading and religion should be the key subjects in the curriculum, because through religion the colonized could be prevented from becoming conscious of their own independent value as rational human beings.

Later, when widespread unrest developed in opposition to colonial rule, the authorities introduced a number of changes to restore social stability. But the colonizers' continuing concern was to subdue the assertive claims of the masses, and different educational strategies were implemented to achieve this goal. The ruling elites placed great emphasis on providing the masses with practical training and a comprehensive program of agricultural education, with the aim of increasing the productivity of the local farms and, consequently, enhancing the farmers' standard of living, in an attempt to reduce opposition to their rule. An additional aim was to provide such 'practical' instruction at a very low cost by combining 'intellectual and industrial education' [so as] 'to render the labour of children available towards meeting some part of the expense of their education' (*Kaye Shuttleworth Report*). Later, the content of the primary curriculum was broadened to include English, civics, geography, and history, and taught in a manner that would lead students to see the colonizers as agents of civilization and enlightenment.

Increasing opportunities were provided for those with a better primary education to move into lower-level white-collar jobs as teachers, messengers, and policemen. Even more senior positions later became open to the colonized who had a secondary or higher education. The increased opportunities for some locals to become upwardly mobile based on their educational achievement was partly directed at getting them to believe that their societies were becoming more open to all on the basis of achievement rather than ascription. This was expected to contribute to social stability.

The education provided in the colonial hinterland of the West Indies, especially at the secondary level was almost identical to that pursued by students in Great Britain. Local students even took the same examinations set by English universities, while those undertaking studies for one of the professions received their higher education in Britain, because such qualifications were usually the only ones that were recognized in the British colonies.

As the colonies moved towards self-government and independence following the Second World War they shared a marked enthusiasm for the contribution that education could make towards their national development. In India, for example, the 1964–6 Education Commission emphatically asserted that education was a key factor in determining the level of prosperity, welfare, and security of the nation (Government of India, 1966). However, the specific cultural context in which education was provided was largely ignored, and the content of educational programs initially remained essentially unchanged. Most of these governments simply expanded and adopted the educational programs of their former colonial rulers. Later, some curriculum reforms were introduced such as adding local history and local literature to the curriculum, which was still dominated by English history and literature. But the major concern as they moved towards independence was to train future leaders by extending English-based secondary and tertiary education facilities. The assumption by the now independent or nearly independent countries was that the knowledge of their colonizers was most appropriate for their own national development.

Just prior to the independence of most of its colonies, Britain established university colleges throughout its colonial empire that were based on the British university model. They were in special relationship with the University of London, which had to approve all courses and even evaluate the learning outcomes of their students. The latent function of this relationship was to maintain British hegemonic control over these colonies by providing their new leaders with a type of higher education that would strengthen their links with the metropolis. This helped the colonizers to continue asserting their moral and cultural dominance over the colonized, even after independence, and strengthen – especially in the new elites – the beliefs, values, and attitudes that supported the colonizer-colonized relationship. For example, although studies were conducted on the sources of underdevelopment in the former colonies, researchers often used the theoretical perspectives that were developed by Western scholars based largely on experiences with their own or similar societies. This became the accepted knowledge, which these new institutions passed on to their students, and the outcome was that they tended to see their societies through the lens of their former colonial rulers. This was reinforced by the information provided in the textbooks and journals that the students used which were also produced by Western scholars.

The new leaders acquired an understanding of their societies and the world economy that was congruent with the views of their former colonizers. Furthermore, the knowledge paradigms that became acceptable to them helped to maintain and strengthen the hegemony that the colonizers had exerted over these former colonies. This did not mean that all colonial scholars were entirely restricted in their thinking by the knowledge paradigms developed by the colonizers. Some even used this knowledge to challenge the assumptions underlying the colonizers' interpretation of the realities of these societies. But these scholars were relatively few in number.

Political power initially shifted into the hands of the more formally educated members of the middle class who shared the development ideology of the colonizers, along with their views of effective governance. These individuals made up the group of comprador elites who were expected to safeguard or at least not to jeopardize the financial and diplomatic interests of the former colonizers after these colonies achieved independence. Edward Said, in commenting on this point noted that the national bourgeoisies, who were trained by the colonizers, 'in effect tended to replace the colonial force with a new class-based and ultimately exploitative one, which replicated the old colonial structures in new terms' (Said, 1993, p. 269). In Barbados, for example, Karch (1977) found that such individuals contributed to a relatively smooth transfer of power, as the country moved from colonial rule to self-government and later independence. But they also helped to ensure the continuing control of the economy by a small cohesive elite group and the continuation for many years of a system of social stratification that had emerged during the colonial era. These dependency links were further strengthened by the development assistance that the former colonial rulers along with other Western countries provided to the former colonies, often with strings attached. This usually ensured that the educational and other projects being aided were those that were supportive of, or at least not antagonistic to, the interests of the economically developed countries.

Factors Continuing to Influence Education in the Former Colonies

Independence brought wider opportunities for trade and investment to the formerly colonial nations, and this resulted in a realignment of world economic power among Western capitalist countries. The United States became a key member of this group, and its joint efforts resulted in a continuing Western hegemonic control of the former colonies through the establishment of transnational organizations such as the World Bank, the International Monetary Fund (IMF), and more recently, the World Trade Organization (WTO). These institutions virtually control the world's financial and trade activities and, as David Smith (this volume) has pointed out, this control is being aggressively extended to the field of education where demands for the alignment of curriculum with the new global economy are being made. This has tremendous implications for the developing countries (nearly all former colonies) and for the education that they need to provide for their population.

The World Bank has, within the IMF guidelines such as its structural adjustment policies, provided financing for various development projects in the former colonies. One of the unstated goals of such loans is to restrain any potential efforts by the recipients to defect from the world capitalist system. In its decisions as to what educational and other projects will receive financial support, the World Bank plays a key role in influencing the direction of development that these countries follow. This is why their officials are often referred to in the developing countries as the new colonial rulers.

The success of the World Bank and other development agencies in imposing their suggested educational reforms on the developing countries was partly because of the financial power that they wield over these countries. In addition, these countries' new leaders and planners often uncritically support the development models implicit in the Western-inspired proposals. Furthermore, any country that tries to deviate from this capitalist model of development is often punished, in one way or another, for such action. This ensures that their educational programs will continue to reinforce the servitude of mind developed during colonial days and deprive these former colonies from coming up with what might be more innovative solutions to their problems

Another important feature that has affected developments in these countries, and as a result the nature of the education that they need, is the increasing globalization of the world economy. This process is influenced by the decisions of the WTO, which are strongly influenced by the wealthier western nations. But this process, as some economists such as Lester Thurow have pointed out, is being affected by the fact that the global economy is becoming more interconnected and, in his view, is moving from unipolar to multipolar control (1996). As this happens, economic power becomes increasingly less concentrated in the hands of one or a few Western countries. In addition, the development of the world economy is becoming increasingly knowledge-based, and these two factors – globalization and the growing importance of a knowledge economy – are increasingly having an impact on the type of education that the former colonies need to ensure the economic, social, and cultural survival of their population. It is assumed that these two forces could jointly provide greater autonomy to the former colonies in determining the nature of the education they will need to provide for their population. An examination will now be made of how (1) globalization and (2) a knowledge-based world economy will affect the future of these developing countries, together with implications for the nature of the curriculum that would be most appropriate for them in the twenty-first century.

Globalization

There is currently much controversy about the effects of globalization on employment, the environment, and education in the developing countries. The goal of globalization is to achieve a greater integration of the world economy, especially in trade and the flow of capital. This involves the removal of all trade barriers between nations, and the expected outcome is a single competitive world economy. The WTO, which tries to facilitate progress towards this goal had 144 country members in January 2002, including China.

Globalization is often seen to be a key factor in achieving world economic growth and from about 1945 international trade has increased twelve-fold, with developing countries improving their share of the world market from 19 per cent to 29 per cent between 1971 and 1999 (UNDP Human Development Reports, 1999, 2000, 2001, 2002). Furthermore, the countries that have actively participated in the process have experienced a faster rate of growth than the countries that have not. But, while the relationship between increased trade and economic growth has not been disputed, it has frequently been noted that globalization has many negative outcomes, especially for poorer countries, causing commentators to remark that the economic 'science' and 'economic fundamentalism' of globalization exert violence on others (see, e.g., David Smith, this volume). In a report entitled *Does Globalization Help the Poor?* the authors suggested that 'globalization policies have contributed to increased poverty, increased inequality between and within nations, increased hunger, increased corporate concentration, decreased social services, and decreased the power of labour vis-à-vis global corporations' (Barker & Mander, 2001).

Globalization has increased the risk of environmental degradation, and with major economic decisions increasingly being made by international organizations, this process has negatively affected the local exercise of democracy. The dilemma this poses can partly be seen in the case of China, which has experienced an unprecedented rate of economic growth that, at times, has reached the equivalent of 13 per cent per year. However, it is estimated that China's entry into the WTO will result in the loss of about forty million jobs, especially among those employed in its subsidized industries. Similarly, Bangladesh, which embarked on a trade liberalization program in the early 1990s, has seen a surge in its industrial growth and its exports, as well as a fairly noticeable increase in its gross domestic product (GDP). Yet, despite the benefits derived from a more liberalized trading policy, a local economist pointed out that about 3.5 million workers were likely to lose their jobs because of the accompanying unrestricted import of foreign goods (Barker & Mander, 2001).

Another key factor affecting the former colonies has been the reluctance of rich nations to reduce their subsidies, especially in agriculture, which is often the main industry of these countries. They have also been unwilling to substantially lower their tariffs against some products from the developing countries such as textiles and establish a more level playing field in trade. The outcomes have depressed the economic conditions of the populations in these poorer countries, and partly as a result, the 2003 UNDP Human Development Report noted that over the past decade more than fifty nations have become poorer. This is especially marked in Sub-Saharan Africa, where poverty is increasing and the percentage of the population living on U.S.$1 per day has not declined during the 1990s. In addition, income inequalities on the world scene and within individual countries have been increasing over the past thirty years.

On the positive side, however, there has been a slight decline in the proportion of people living in extreme poverty, and primary school enrolments have risen worldwide from 80 per cent in 1990 to 84 per cent in 1998 (UNDP, 2001). But despite the negative outcomes of globalization for poor countries, the alternative of withdrawing from the process is not very realistic. Even Cuba has been steadily integrating into this wider economy, despite the U.S. government's trade embargo on that country. International capital flows into Cuba and its trade with Europe and Canada have increased substantially over the years.

Despite its dysfunctional aspects, therefore, globalization is an emerging reality and the only viable option that the poorer countries have is to play a more effective role in trying to influence the process, as they started to do at the WTO meeting in Cancun in September 2003. But this requires that that the citizens of these countries be adequately prepared to fully exploit the existing and emerging economic opportunities that globalization presents, able to perceive and develop new opportunities that might arise within the system, aware of those practices that are unfair to them, and equipped to put pressure on their governments to work with others to bring about changes in the world trading system to make it fairer than it is at present.

To achieve such goals the former colonies will have to improve the quality of their human resources through improved educational quality, to ensure that even if they do not always have a winning hand in international trade they can play their cards with skill and ingenuity so as not to be perpetual losers in the game. This is particularly important for small nation-states with limited internal consumption possibilities. As Darwin (1928) has observed, it is not the strongest species that survive but the ones most responsive to change, and this is also applicable to nations. This is why these countries have to better prepare their youth for the major changes in the world economy that are having an increasing social, political, and cultural impact on them. This does not imply that the task will be easy, especially since the richer countries control or strongly influence the decisions of such crucial international organizations as the WTO, the World Bank, and the IMF, which mainly serve their interests.

Towards a Knowledge-Based World Economy

The world economy is also increasingly becoming knowledge-based, and this is being ushered in by a new information age. This means that production efforts in the twenty-first century will be increasingly dependent on new knowledge, with science and technology contributing significantly to future world economic growth. The result will be a continuing shift away from the 'techno-economic' or manufacturing-based production model, which is reflected in the factory system, with its assembly line mass production that requires heavy capital inputs for machinery and raw materials and fairly large numbers of relatively unskilled labourers.

The shift is towards a new production model, which has been referred to as the innovation-mediated or knowledge-intensive production model. This model of production is less dependent on inputs of capital, raw materials, and unskilled labour and more on the application of knowledge and innovative approaches in dealing with issues and solving problems. This can already be seen in the development of industries in such fields as biotechnology, genetic engineering, artificial intelligence, and computer software. The rise of the 'Microsoft empire,' for example, originally depended on the input of knowledge and ideas, rather than on capital, and it is estimated that currently 70 per cent of an automobile's value is attributable to the knowledge embedded in its production. The increasing contribution of knowledge to the production process also has important implications for education and the creation of new knowledge through research and constantly updating the knowledge available to the population, through lifelong learning.

With the accompanying process of globalization the various phases of producing a single commodity can now be more easily carried out in different countries, thereby internationalizing what used to be national production. This becomes more possible as production also tends to be more service-oriented which makes it easier for different elements of the process to be undertaken in different parts of the world. For the developing countries to benefit from joint production enterprises, they will need an adequate supply of suitably educated personnel to undertake some of the required tasks. This is seen particularly in the field of computing science and the production of computer programs, software, and computer chips.

The new production model has also led to a realization that knowledge is not the monopoly of any particular group or groups, and therefore, efforts are being made to explore the value of the knowledge that non-Western societies have acquired over the years. As a result, ancient health practices such as acupuncture and a holistic approach to the healing process are being increasingly utilized in Western societies, while those engaged in pharmacological research to produce new drugs are more actively seeking knowledge about cures that have been used in traditional health practices. The search for the scientific basis of traditional knowledge is thus becoming more important in today's research efforts.

These developments have enormous curricular implications in the former colonies if they are to benefit more fully from globalization and the increasing use of new knowledge in the production process. Foremost, their curricula would have to prepare students to make a greater contribution towards research and development activities by strengthening the scientific and technological aspects of their educational programs. This need is evident in that, between 1987 and 1997, high-income countries had 3,127 research and development scientists and engineers per 100,000 population while in southern Asia the corresponding figure was only 152; the figure was much lower in Africa (UNDP, 2000, 2001).

The new production process demands what Reich (1992, p. 184) calls 'symbolic analysts' – that is, workers with problem-identifying and problem-solving skills who are able to acquire insights by looking at familiar problems from different and original perspectives and come up with more effective solutions to them. This is important because the emerging global economy will be replete with new and unidentified problems with unknown solutions and untried means of putting them together. The new economy will, therefore, require individuals with an inquisitive and creative outlook who are able to effectively use existing knowledge, while also creating new knowledge, to deal with existing and future problems.

The new production process requires individuals who can work with others, both nationally and internationally, in carrying out research, designing new production techniques, developing new computer software, and undertaking other production activities. Reich refers to the development of 'enterprise webs,' which require entrepreneurs from different countries to link up with each other in pursuit of their joint economic interests. Such involvement in production efforts will transcend national borders, as has happened among computer scientists in the Silicone Valley in California and those in Bangalore, which has become the centre for the creation of computer software in India.

This is being aided by the increasing ease and lower cost of worldwide communications, through telephones and the Internet. For example, between 1970 and 1990 the cost of international telephone calls fell by about 90 per cent and has continued to decline since then. But the success of such cooperative ventures needs workers who can easily relate to others from a different cultural background, highlighting the need for cross-cultural education in the school curriculum.

Other Challenges of Globalization Affecting Education in the Developing Countries

There are other outcomes of globalization that present economic, social, and educational challenges for the developing countries. One of these relates to employment opportunities. The structural adjustment policies imposed by the IMF and the World Bank, as part of their globalization or free trade policies, has produced the result that the public sector in the former colonies, which used to be their main source of wage employment, has been considerably reduced in size. These governments will no longer be able to engage in any subsidized industrial activity, and this will result in increased efforts to privatize public enterprises. This has important implications for employment in these countries. For example, individuals who were previously able to secure public sector jobs based partly on their educational credentials plus certain ascriptive characteristics are increasingly less likely to be able to do so. Large overseas private firms are already taking over local enterprises in such field as telecommunications, electricity, and even water provision, and they are introducing more sophisticated technology in their operations. This will not only reduce the number of jobs available to locals but their performance will become more important in deciding who will retain their jobs or be employed in the future.

Agriculture remains one of the major industries in the developing countries, employing up to 40–50 per cent of the workforce. Partly as a result of the environmentally deleterious effects of chemical fertilizers, more attention is being directed in the West to the use of biotechnology in food production. This stems from the increasing understanding by scientists of the genetic code and genetic engineering, which is improving or changing conventional plant-breeding techniques in order to increase output and develop new products. Furthermore, research laboratories in the West are continuing to produce new synthetic products that will gradually replace those that are grown naturally. For example, chemists now make vanilla artificially, and coconut oil is likely to be replaced by genetically engineered soya bean or rapeseed, while synthetic rubber is taking the place of natural rubber. These changes are affecting the economies of developing countries that produce such natural products. For agricultural production in the developing countries to become more efficient and cost-effective, farmers there will need the knowledge that would prepare them to use more scientifically based production methods. These developments also make it increasingly important for the former colonies to apply pressures on the richer countries to reduce their farm subsidies and throw open their markets to agricultural products and other commodities from the developing countries.

A few large corporations have been transferring some of their production activities to these countries, in search of cheap labour. But this will continue to succeed only if the countries have other attractive conditions such as a stable government and a high quality of human resources. Furthermore, to maintain their cost advantage, they will have to provide opportunities for their labour force to be continually updated in their knowledge and technical competence. Therefore, if these countries depend only on low wages to attract and retain overseas investments, they will eventually find investors moving their production to countries with even lower costs that result from the higher technical efficiency of their labour force.

The continued integration of science and communication is reducing the world to a global village. In addition to making news instantly available worldwide, the peoples of developing countries are increasingly exposed to new ideas, new commercial goods, and even to the different lifestyles in other countries. This often creates a greater restlessness, especially among the young in poorer countries, since they become dissatisfied with their own living conditions, and this fuels their desire for change or induces them to migrate to other shores. The result is a continuing depletion of the more educated human resources in the poor countries. On a positive note, the integration of science and communication, quickened by the proliferation of satellites, fibre optics, facilities for high-speed electronic transfers, computer modems, and computer software is also having an impact on the developing countries by opening up more learning possibilities for their populations. This means that knowledge is becoming more readily available to them through such mechanisms such as the Internet. The technology required to deliver this knowledge is also increasingly accessible and affordable, and some institutions are further facilitating this process. The Massachusetts Institute of Technology (MIT), for example, has decided to put all its courses on the Internet, free of cost, and the Commonwealth of Learning (COL) has been assiduously trying to improve distance learning in Commonwealth countries.

Accompanying globalization have been the increasingly 'grotesque inequalities' in wealth between the richer and poorer countries, with some poor countries becoming even poorer over the years. For example, between 1960 and 1991 the richest 20 per cent of the world's population (who live mainly in the economically more developed countries) increased their share of the total global wealth from 70 per cent to 85 per cent while the poorest 20 per cent (who live mainly in the developing countries) has seen their share fall from a meagre 2.3 per cent to a disgraceful 1.4 per cent. It has also been noted that in 1999 the total wealth of the world's 358 billionaires was equal to the combined incomes of the poorest 45 per cent of the world's population. While this has been happening, a hundred countries (most of them in Africa) with about 25 per cent of the world's population have suffered economic decline or stagnation. In seventy countries the citizens are, on average, now poorer than they were in 1980, and in forty-three countries they are poorer than they were in 1970. Similarly, the gap between the rich and the poor in most countries has not only been substantial but also widening, with the top 5 per cent of the population receiving about 30 per cent of the national income (UNDP, 1999).

Although economic deregulation has been bringing increased foreign investment and faster economic growth to some developing countries, this is often accompanied by a deepening of their rich-poor divide. As a south Asian newspaper noted a few years ago, 'the glitter of affluence among the few with their snazzy foreign cars and mobile phones' is increasingly in stark contrast to the deprived lifestyles of the more than one billion South Asians who cannot afford even the minimum daily food requirements (*Dawn*, 1955, p. 13).

There are currently more than two billion people in the developing countries who are without electricity, and they attempt to meet their needs for energy by burning coal and wood. The effect of this on the destruction of the environment has been catastrophic, and this will continue, adding to the increasing threat of global warming. In India, population growth has led to a destruction of two-thirds of the forests, and this is also happening in other countries. Furthermore, the amount of official development assistance calculated as a percentage of the donors' gross national product (GNP) has been falling and recently reached its lowest level in decades.

Another feature of many former colonies is the growing threat to the legitimacy of the state, partly because the desire of the leaders and other elites to retain their positions of dominance in these societies, often ignoring the popular clamour for more democratic political forms. The outcome is often reflected in the increasingly negative attitude of large sections of the population towards their political leadership and in an erosion of loyalty and respect for the state in general. This often results in the instruments of state governance being held in increasingly low esteem. Furthermore, in pluralistic societies, such developments have encouraged a strengthening of the ties of loyalty among members of sub-groups, often in opposition to others in the society. This has happened, for example, in Sri Lanka, Rwanda, Indonesia, India, Nigeria, Fiji, and Guyana. The outcome is intergroup conflict and increased social instability that threaten the very existence of the state and of civil society. This is happening at a time when these countries are most in need of political stability for their future economic development.

In the developing countries government support for local cultural activities is likely to diminish with globalization, since the overall philosophy of free trade is that market conditions should determine the survivability of any activity. In this context, whatever is not profitable is considered to not have any value. National governments might become unable to prevent an erosion of their local cultures, because of the cultural penetration by the richer countries through the massive export of films, music, books, and magazines. The adverse effects of this are likely to be most marked in small states with limited populations or by numerically smaller sub-groups in culturally plural societies.

Rapid population growth is another challenge faced by many developing countries. During the past forty years the world population has doubled, reaching six billion in 1999, with about half being under the age of 24 years. This figure will likely reach 8.9 billion by the middle of this century, and a whopping 97 per cent of this increase will be in the economically less developed countries (UNDP, 1999). Research evidence has shown a negative association between rapid population growth and the rate at which per capita incomes increase. Lower rates of population growth obviously allow countries to buy more time to adjust to the changing realities of the globalized economy which can improve their ability to attack poverty, reduce unemployment, universalize primary education, protect their environment, and build the base for future sustainable development.

Implications for Curriculum and Instruction in a Postcolonial Context

In curricular terms, these changes are producing many challenges for the developing countries, challenges that need to be addressed if these countries, nearly all of which had previously experienced colonial domination, are to emerge from continued domination by the rich Western nations. One major challenge is to equip students in these countries with the skills, knowledge, outlook, and vision that would prepare them to perceive more incisively the economic opportunities that are emerging from the new developments. This requires citizens equipped, through education, to question the existing popular interpretations of reality and citizens who have the research skills along with the scientific and technological training that would allow them to develop more effective and innovative solutions to their problems. The developing countries, therefore, need to expand their educational provisions, making them more inclusive, and their workers need to be able to continually update their skills and knowledge.

In terms of curricular content, the young need to be prepared in ways that strengthen their own cultural identities while learning to better relate to others from different cultural backgrounds because this is likely to equip them to engage more effectively in joint production enterprises with individuals and groups of workers from other countries. This increased cultural sensitivity would also better prepare them to work cooperatively with those from other countries to bring about a fairer world trading system. In addition, curriculum programs are required that teach the skills and attitudes needed to change the social and political structures of these countries and make their young more committed to issues such as poverty reduction and a more equitable distribution of the rewards of development, both locally and globally. Such programs would also better prepare them to work towards greater democratization of their countries by facilitating more popular involvement in the political decision-making process. This would help bring about greater political stability in these countries, a precondition for their economic development.

Derrick Cogburn, formerly regional director for the Global Information Infrastructure Commission in South Africa, has suggested that it is no longer sufficient to increase the efficiency of the existing systems of education by simply improving the quality of their various components. This is because, as he suggested, much of what is still being taught was developed to serve the economic demands of another age. As a result, students now find themselves deficient not only in knowledge, but also in the cognitive skills necessary for the evolving labour markets. Employers often complain that even university graduates from many developing countries are not sufficiently challenged to acquire new skills and assimilate new knowledge. It is suggested that 'The globalization of the economy and its concomitant demands on the workforce requires a different education – one that enhances the ability of learners to access, assess, adopt, and apply knowledge, to think independently to exercise appropriate judgment and to collaborate with others to make sense of new situations. The objective of education is no longer simply to convey a body of knowledge, but to teach how to learn, problem-solve and synthesize the old with the new' (Cogburn, 1998, p. 26).

This implies that, although the focus on science, mathematics, and social studies is important, the instructional strategies used for teaching these subjects would have to adequately prepare students for life in the emerging economy of the twenty-first century. So far, the available evidence indicates that the quality of teaching in many developing countries is low and has been declining (Lockheed & Vespoor, 1990). Some years ago, for example, Calloids (1998) and Chapman and Carrier (1990) commented on the deterioration in the quality of the education that students in these countries receive, noting that they perform poorly especially when the tasks that they face require applying knowledge to new problems (World Bank, 1985, p. 8).

This situation has deteriorated further since then, as a result of the focus on quantitative expansion of educational opportunities, which often ignores the concurrent need for qualitative improvements in instruction. In Pakistan, for example, one classroom observer noted that instruction is still predominantly teacher-centred, with teachers originating all the questions, and responses usually 'involved a simple reiteration of what she/he had just said. Chorus answers were frequently accepted and encouraged' (Allsop, 1991, p. 2). Many teachers in the developing countries are still satisfied if the students are aware of the formula, say, for calculating area and can do their sums correctly, even if they do not fully understand what the concept of *area* means. Similarly, students are taught to accept as given someone else's explanation of the reality around them, without being encouraged to make critical analyses of their own experiences and compare them with other people's interpretation of that reality. Teachers tend to encourage students to accept what is written in the textbooks rather than to challenge or raise questions about the information or the point of view expressed by the author.

The emerging globalized economy needs individuals who are inquisitive and willing to challenge traditional practices where necessary, who are prepared to grapple with ideas, not simply to regurgitate information, and who have the ability to utilize and even create new knowledge. Clearly, an education that continues to emphasize the rote acquisition of available knowledge over original thought retards the students' capacity to creatively use even existing knowledge. Instructional strategies currently used in schools need to be replaced by strategies in which teachers attempt to empower their students by helping them acquire the skills of higher- order thinking, encouraging them to question and develop alternative interpretations of reality, and teaching them how to acquire and utilize knowledge in various forms and from different sources. Above all, teachers should ensure that the experiences they provide for their students are geared towards preparing students to look critically and inquisitively at what is happening in the world around them. In other words, the new pedagogical approaches should contribute to the transformation of the conditions of marginalization, subordination, and oppression that exist in these societies (Freire, 1974). This would be somewhat akin to providing students with what Habermas refers to as critical emancipatory knowledge (1968).

The achievement of the economic and emancipatory goals proposed here will require substantial overhauling of curriculum and teacher education in the developing countries, including the retraining of practising teachers who tend to believe that their previous training will effectively serve them almost throughout their professional careers.

Such an overhauling is necessary if the unfinished business of decolonization is to be confronted and overcome.

REFERENCES

Allsop T. (1991). *A report to the Aga Khan Foundation on a visit to Karachi to assist the Task Force in Planning for the Institute for Educational Development*. Oxford, Department of Educational Studies.

Baker, D., & Mander, J. (Eds.). (2001). *Does globalization help the poor?* San Francisco: International forum on Globalization. Available at: www.parallaxonline.org. Accessed 20 June 2003.

Calloids, F. (Ed.). (1989). *The prospects of educational planning*. Paris: UNESCO IIEP.

Chapman D.W., & Carrier, C.A. (Eds.). (1990). *Improved educational quality*, Westport, CT: Greenwood.

Cogburn, D. (1998). Globalization, knowledge, education and training in the information age. *International Forum on Information and Documentation 23*(4), 23–9.

Darwin, C. (1928). *The origin of species*. London: Dent.

Dawn. (1955, 21 Oct.) Liberalization deepens rich/poor divide in South Asia. Karachi, Pakistan: Dawn.

Freire, P. (1974). *Education: The practice of freedom*. Ahlesbury: Hazell, Watson and Viney.

Government of India, Ministry of Education. (1966). *Report of the Education Commission 1964–66)*. New Delhi: Author.

Habermas, J. (1968). *Knowledge and human interest*. Boston: Beacon.

Harte, Rev. W. (1824) *Lectures on the Gospel of St Matthew*, Vol. 1. London.

Karch, C. (1977). The growth of the corporate economy in Barbados: Class/race factors, 1890–1977. In Susan Craig (Ed.), *Contemporary Caribbean: A sociological reader*, Vol. 1 (pp. 213–241). Port of Spain: College Press.

Lockheed, M.E., & Vespoor, A.M. (1990). *Improving primary education in developing countries*. Washington, DC: World Bank.

Reich, R. (1992). *The work of nations*. New York: Vintage.

Said, E.W. (1993). *Culture and imperialism*. London: Vintage.

Sterling, Rev. J. (1835). *Education of the negro population in the West Indies*, 11th May 1835. CO 318/122.

Thurow, L.C. (1996). *The future of capitalism: How today's economic forces shape tomorrow's world*. New York: William Morrow.

UNDP. (1999). *UNDP Human Development Report, 1999*. Oxford: Oxford University Press.

UNDP (2000). *UNDP Human Development Report, 2000*. Oxford: Oxford University Press.

UNDP (2001). *UNDP Human Development Report, 2001*. Oxford: Oxford University Press.

UNDP (2003). *UNDP Human Development Report, 2003*. Oxford: Oxford University Press.

Waddell, Rev. H.M. (1863). *Twenty-nine years in the West Indies and Central Africa*. London: Thomas Nelson.

World Bank (1985). *The dividends of learning*. Washington, DC: Author.

PART 4

Reimagining the Nation and National Identity in the Curriculum

12 Singular Nation, Plural Possibilities: Reimagining Curriculum as Third Space

GEORGE RICHARDSON

If a memory wasn't a thing but a memory of a memory of a memory, mirrors set in parallel, then what the brain told you now about what it claimed had happened then would be coloured by what had happened in between. It was like a country remembering its history: the past was never just the past, it was what made the present able to live with itself.

Julian Barnes (1998)

No Common Imagining

In his brilliant comic novel *England, England*, Julian Barnes reminds us of the imagined, self-serving, and, in some cases, entirely artificial character that is national identity. It has long been recognized that education plays a crucial role in that imaginative construction (Reisner, 1925; Weber, 1976; Bhabha, 1990; Smith, 1991). Until quite recently most curricula of national identity were privileged and privileging constructions that represented the nation in essentialist terms (Duara, 1996; Willinsky, 1999; Richardson, 2002b) and assumed the existence of what Benedict Anderson has called a 'common imagining' of the nation (1991). But a singular imaginary of the nation and the idea that the central task of education lies in its production have recently come under criticism from postcolonial scholars, as they point out that conceptualizing the nation in unitary terms produced curricula that privilege Eurocentrism, while marginalizing and silencing others (e.g., ethnocultural minorities, women, aboriginals, lesbians, gays) who are not perceived to be a part of the dominant narrative. The assumed coherence of the narrative of nations is belied by the fact that national curricula are created 'by powerful professors, bureaucrats, editors, publishers, and reviewers, the majority of them white males ... under the aegis of nineteenth century European notions of nationhood' and from this exclusive position emerged curricula that presented the nation as racially and culturally uniform (Mukherjee, 1994, p. 8). These singular conceptions of nation have effectively silenced the Other in face of the exclusionary pressure exerted by the weight of invented tradition. The nation, viewed as unitary narrative, thus became 'a disabling discursive category' (Gallegos, 1998, p. 233) that restricted access to the discourse of nation to the dominant class.

It would be easy to dismiss questions of colonial and racist representations in curricula, as historically bound phenomena or as cautionary tales of unacceptable practices drawn from the past; but, as scholars as diverse as Benedict Anderson, Homi Bhabha, Anthony Smith, and Partha Chatterjee remind us, the nation is at once both an imagined community and an unfinished project. As such it must project a retroactive image of stability and timelessness, while at the same time, adapting that image to the ways in which the community is changing in the present. *Nation* is much more than 'a fixed tablet of tradition' (Bhabha, 1990b, p. 2), and given the central role that education plays in the construction and maintenance of national identity, it becomes important to problematize essentialist interpretations of the nation. The question arises of how to reconceptualize curriculum in terms that do not maintain colonial structures of privilege and dominance. For Salman Rushdie, for example, the critical issue is how to create new imaginaries of the nation in the overwhelming presence of the old, thus, 'black and white descriptions of reality are no longer compatible. Fantasy, or the mingling of fantasy and naturalism offers a way of echoing in the form of our work the issues faced by all of us: how to build a new, "modern" world out of an old, legend-haunted civilization, an old culture which we have brought into the heart of a newer one' (1983, p. 62).

Drawing on postcolonial frameworks, this chapter suggests the need for new imaginaries of the nation to reconceptualize curriculum as a cultural practice. In Yatta Kanu's terms, such a reconceptualization would imply both a rigorous deconstruction of the cultural (and colonial) biases of existing curricula and a creative imagining of a curriculum that is open to 'multiple discourses, and plural assumptions and strategies' (2003; see also Kanu, this volume). In searching for ways to open up a discursive curricular space for imagining the nation as both Self and Other, one possibility is to employ postcolonial scholar Homi

Bhabha's notion of the Third Space (1990e). The third space, for Bhabha, is a dynamic interface in which cultural hybridity replaces cultural essentialism as a founding principle of the nation and in which national identity is seen to be continual and dynamic process of encounter, negotiation, and dislocation among and between cultural groups.

In an attempt to explore the curricular possibilities of the Third Space, this chapter is divided into three sections. In the first, I focus on the desire for national unity and cultural conformity that is at the root of modernist curriculum and discuss the reasons that make such a project unsustainable in postcolonial times. The next section examines Bhabha's notion of the Third Space in terms of its potential for creating a more open and inclusive imaginary of the nation and the implications that Third Space has for reconceptualizing curriculum. Using the notion of Third Space, the final section presents a critical analysis of the degree to which such postcolonial concepts as hybridity, difference, and negotiation are incorporated into recent social studies curricula in Canada.

Impossible Unity: Education and the Dream of Nation

Nations, like narratives, lose their origins in the myths of time and only fully realize their horizons in the mind's eye.

Bhabha (1990c)

One of the most striking characteristics of the modern era has been the emergence of powerful and enduring fantasy structures of national identity that ground their emotive strength and force in the legitimizing sanction of history and tradition. But, all appearances to the contrary, these structures are not timeless creations; they are the conscious creations of national elites (Anderson, 1991; Hobsbawm & Ranger, 1983). The production of what psychoanalyst Andrew Samuels has called 'the coruscating fantasy of the nation' (1993), is a historical project that required the active participation of the state for its realization. When discussing the ideal constitution for a nation-state Jean-Jacques Rousseau, for example, noted that 'la première règle, que nous avons à suivre, c'est le caractère national: tout peuple a, ou doit avoir un caractère national' (cited in Cobban, 1964, p. 319). Similarly, in their analysis of national-identity formation in capitalist societies, historians Eric Hobsbawm and Terrance Ranger described national identity as a 'manipulated and manufactured phenomenon' (1983, p. 1). Bhabha makes much the same point with his assertion that 'the first duty of the state is to "give" the nation its cultural identity and above all to develop it' (1995, p. 48). But the association of national identity with the machinery of the state implies the need for some kind of agent to generate the mythic structure of national identity that seemed and still seems so critical to the establishment of the nation as a viable entity. As already noted by Yatta Kanu and Kazim Bacchus in their respective chapters in this volume, that agent, in most countries, has been education – more precisely, schooling.

As an essential aspect in its creation, modern nationalism relies heavily on the existence of an 'education-dependent high culture' (Gellner, 1983). In *Peasants into Frenchmen,* historian Eugen Weber noted that this same high culture created the public educational systems so critical to development of the patriotism and national sentiment that Weber concludes is 'the greatest function of the modern school' (1976, p. 332). Pedagogy, for Bhabha, lies at the very heart of the national-identity construction in modern states, in which the people become 'the historical "objects" of nationalist pedagogy' designed to present the nation as a closed and timeless narrative (1990a, p. 178). In most nations, national curricula have been created to perpetuate, and in many cases manufacture, national myths for the twin purposes of grounding national consciousness in some kind of legitimizing historical tradition and garnering the allegiance of the people to the existing political status quo (Willinsky, 1998; Richardson, 2002b; Lowe, 1999). Drawing on the Canadian context, this doubled purpose was best expressed in 1926 by Canada's future governor-general, Vincent Massey, when he noted that 'in a country with so scattered a population as ours and a vast frontier exposed to alien influences the tasks of creating a truly national feeling must inevitably be arduous but this is the undertaking to which our educational systems must address themselves for by true education alone will the problem be solved. To our schools we must look for the Good Canadian' (1926, p. 6).

As the editors of *Cultural Identity and Educational Policy* conclude, the aim of national curricula is to shift the focus away from individual identity to allegiance to an 'institutionalized cultural identity' (Brock & Tulasiewicz, 1985, p. 7). In essence, the project of institutionalizing cultural identity is directed towards the construction of a fantasy of national wholeness through which the nation 'perceives itself as a homogenous entity' (Saleci, 1994, p. 15). Extending the notion of homogeneity to which Renata Salecl refers even further, the institutionalized structure of the nation has an emotive, universalist aspect. Benedict

Anderson refers to this aspect as 'a deep horizontal comradeship' that represents a symbolic space able to overcome barriers of distance and time such that 'members of even the world's smallest nation will never ... meet [nevertheless] in the minds of each lives the image of their communion' (Anderson, 1991, p. 7). As a working definition of nation, Anderson's notion of an imagined community has a particularly powerful emotional resonance because it draws on the twin aspects of equality and agency that underpin modernity and liberal democracy (Taylor, 1991; Borgmann, 1992; Beiner, 1997). But however it is constructed, the fantasy of national identity as Bhabha's 'fixed tablet of tradition' to which all the nation's peoples have equal access, and the central role of schools in its creation and transmission is unsustainable for two key reasons. The first suggests the dangers implicit in ignoring the 'impossible unity' of the national imaginary; the second highlights the importance of understanding that school curricula reflect cultural biases and speak from particular cultural locations.

The ongoing attempt to reinscribe the national imaginary as Salecl's 'homogeneous entity' is typical of the nation-building process in modern states (smith, 1991; Nairn, 1997; Brown, 2000). But, in multicutural societies, such a construct inevitably breaks down in face of its own unsustainability: 'The fact is, we are mixed in with one another in ways that most national systems of education have not dreamed of' (Said, 1993, p. 331). Furthermore, as Liah Greenfeld has observed, the concept of the 'essential nation' belies its invented nature; thus, 'there are no "dormant" nations which awaken to the sense of their nationality ... rather invention and imposition of national identity lead people to believe that they are indeed unique and as a result to become united' (1992, p. 22).

Perhaps more importantly, even when attempts are made to accommodate ethnocultural pluralism into the broader narrative of the nation, such efforts remain located firmly within totalizing fantasies of national wholeness or homogeneity and, inevitably, result in a kind of self-congratulatory cultural appropriation. In her investigation of the closure of a multicultural school in Ontario, for example, Bonny Norton Pierce cites the poignant comments of 'Maria,' an Italian Canadian student: 'A lot of commercials you see are about ethnic people. They show commercials about Canada and different ethnic people. And it's like they're trying to say, "This is an ethnic country, be proud." But then you get the people themselves in Canada who just don't look at Canada that way' (1995, p. 175). More specifically, as many scholars have noted, when they represent the changing ethnocultural composition of the nation, most curricula tend to emphasize cultural diversity rather than cultural difference (Kanpol and McLaren, 1995; Hoffman, 1996; Ghosh, 1996; McCarthy, 1998; Johnson, 2003). From a postcolonial perspective, however, an emphasis on diversity in multicultural communities can be seen as a vehicle for constraining and limiting difference; then diversity becomes 'a norm given by the host society or dominant culture that says that these or other cultures are fine, but we must be able to locate them within our own grid' (Bhabha, 1990e, p. 208). In concentrating on cultural diversity to the detriment of cultural difference, curricula neutralize the problematic aspects of living together in difference, while they maintain the comforting image of the nation as the willing recipient of the 'gift' of diversity from its minority peoples. The prevalence of this 'contributions' approach (Banks, 1996) to multicultural education is perhaps best understood in the context of Roger Collins's reminder that, in plural states, host societies view the acknowledgment of cultural difference as socially divisive (1993).

The second reason for the unsustainability of modernist curricula that attempt to create Anderson's 'common imagining of the nation' has to do with the cultural blindness implicit in representing the nation as a single narrative. Many scholars of race and culture locate the source of this blindness in Eurocentric privilege that refuses to acknowledge or interrogate its own cultural location, while employing the mechanisms that perpetuate existing patterns of dominance (Frankenberg, 1997; Kanpol & McLaren, 1995). 'Whether individual whites use these mechanisms or not is irrelevant to the outcome of the white group's superiority, and certainly the studies conducted so far suggest that most whites are socialized to employ them whether or not they actually do' (Hurtado, 1996, p. 149).

In terms of education, cultural blindness has meant the perpetuation of essentialist and racist curricula in the service of the production of a shared sense of national identity: 'Schools have always sought to instil a spirit of patriotism in the young around a common cultural legacy, and as proponents of multiculturalism have made clear, this has meant the exclusion and alienation of too many students' (Willinsky, 2002, p. 38). But the inability to see the nation in terms of its own European cultural assumptions and to understand curriculum as a cultural practice aimed at inculcating those assumptions into students becomes increasingly untenable in face of the accelerating ethnocultural diversity of the nation. The attempt to construct Anderson's essentialist 'deep horizontal comradeships,' holds less and less appeal when the nation is construed as a dynamic entity. In this regard, 'when the magic of essences ceases to impress and intimidate, there no longer is a position of authority from which one can judge the verisimilitude of representation [and] the subjectivity at work ... can hardly be submitted to the old subjectivity/objectivity paradigm' (Minh Ha, 1990, p. 82). The 'cultural construction of nationness' (Bhabha, 1990a, p. 140), which is one of the central tasks of education, can no longer afford to ignore the diverse narratives of the nation that students bring to their classrooms. As Maxine Greene has pointed out, 'a democratic community always is in the making ... there always are newcomers, always new stories feeding into living history out of which a community emerges and is continually renewed' (1996, p. 43).

The romantic fantasy of unity and communion that characterizes the modernist idea of nation is not easy to abandon. But for postcolonialist scholars essentialist concepts of nation and national identity are Western cultural constructs more associated with patterns of dominance and assimilation than with the collaborative and communal construction of the notion of 'common imagining' (Spivak, 1987; Said, 1993; Srivastava, 1996). Postcolonial scholarship rejects the current metanarrative of national identity and discuss national identity in terms of the possibilities that hybridity, difference, and negotiation represent for reconceiving the nation as narrative and performative space (Richardson, 2002b; Johnston, 2003; Kanu, 2003). The idea of nation, for Bhabha, is at best an ambivalent concept bound up in 'its transitional history [and] its conceptual indeterminacy' (1990c, p. 307), while as an intellectual *location* nation has critical importance as a site of dynamic interaction between the dominant culture and the subordinate cultures it seeks to assimilate. In the following section, I will outline how the location Bhabha refers to as the Third Space can be a curricular site where new meanings of national identity can be negotiated.

The Curricular Possibilities of the Third Space

It is in the emergence of the interstices – the overlap and displacement of domains of difference – that the intersubjective and collective Experiences of *nationness* community interest or cultural value are negotiated.

Bhabha (1994)

Homi Bhabha's 'Third Space' is an interstitial location of negotiation and hybridity: 'All forms of culture are constantly in a process of hybridity – this 3rd space between two originary moments displaces the histories that constitute it, and sets up new structures of authority, new political initiatives, which are inadequately understood through received wisdom' (1990e, p. 211).

It is important to understand that the hybridity and negotiation that distinguish the Third Space should not be confused with liberal notions of consensus and compromise. From a postcolonial perspective, national identity formation is characterized by cultural dislocation and displacement and is perhaps best seen as a 'process of enunciation of cultural difference' (Scott, 1995, p. 11). For Bhabha and others, this process makes it 'very difficult, even impossible and counterproductive, to try and fit together different forms of culture and to pretend that they can easily coexist' (1990e, p. 210). The Third Space, then, asserts the challenging notion that the 'dense particularities' specific to each group making up the nation reform and dislocate the intellectual geography of national identity in such a way that 'we see ourselves as living – and having lived – in entirely heterogeneous and discrete places' (Mohanty, 1989, p. 13). Furthermore, hybridity is not to be seen as some more democratic analogue for the reinscription of essentialist narratives of the nation that would replace the single fixed 'tablet of tradition' with multiple – but equally fixed – exemplars. Rather, hybridity suggests that the Third Space is a performative site where national culture is not merely reflected, but actively produced: 'Terms of cultural engagement, whether antagonistic or affiliative, are produced performatively. The representation of difference must not be hastily read as the reflection of pre-given ethnic or cultural traits set in the fixed tablet of tradition. The social articulation of difference, from a minority perspective, is a complex, on-going negotiation that seeks to authorize cultural hybridities that emerge in moments of cultural transformation' (Bhabha, 1994, p. 2).

But if postcolonialism refuses to accept the cultural overdetermination implicit in the nineteenth-century idea of the nation, it nevertheless suggests more open alternatives to the current formulation of national identity. While Satya Mohanty, for example, can point out how problematic national identity is in plural states, he also suggests that a less-restricting and -restrictive approach to national identity might be to examine how the difference and conflict that lie at the centre of the historical experience of all groups is essentially a shared experience (1989, p. 13). In postcolonial writing, the idea of cultural difference has been identified as a critical source of national identity (Mohanty, 1989). Both Edward Said and Homi Bhabha have emphasized that Western national identity emerges from the attempt to establish a binary relationship that requires the presence of a non-Western Other for complete realization (Said, 1979; Bhabha, 1990d). Although some observers see the process of Othering as a dangerous precursor to xenophobia and violence (Kristeva, 1993; Ignatieff, 1993); others such as Stuart Hall have shown that the internalization of the self-as-other has created (especially for the West) an open and constantly shifting boundary between West and non-West (1991). The idea that national identity represents a series of permeable and continually transgressed borders between Self and Other, between nation and foreign, effectively opens up a locus of negotiation that Gyatri Spivak refers to as a decolonized space in which the experience of colonizers and colonized must be acknowledged to be inseparable (1987, p. 259). Bhabha puts it like this: 'America leads to Africa; the nations of Europe and Asia meet in Australia; the margins of history displace the center; the peoples of the periphery return to rewrite the history and fiction of the metropolis' (1990c, p. 312).

Thus, it could be said that, in terms of national identity, postcolonialism attempts to illuminate the 'as yet unreadable alternative history' that constitutes the lived experiences of marginalized cultures (Spivak, 1987, p. 259). In this light, one particularly hopeful consequence of the destruction of the privileged position of the Enlightenment metanarrative will be the 'proliferation of discursive interventions and arguments that become the source of greater activism and a more radical libertarianism' (Laclau, 1988, pp. 79–80). These 'discursive interventions' of difference and hybridity take place within the Third Space and represent the possibility for suggesting new ways of writing the narrative of the nation in which minority discourses come to be seen as 'counternarratives of the nation that continually evoke and erase its totalizing boundaries' (Bhabha, 1990a, p. 149). In the Third Space, representations of the nation as nationalist pedagogy – as timeless, objective, and narrated text – are juxtaposed against performative and subjective acts of individual narration of the nation that take place on a continual basis (ibid.). Although the disruptive and conflictual nature of the clash of narratives that constitute the Third Space is undeniable, it is precisely this juxtaposition that creates possibilities for challenging the nation as exclusionary narrative and for narrating the nation in more open, complex, and inclusive terms. If the Third Space holds possibilities for rewriting the nation along more culturally democratic lines, the trope of the Third Space and the juxtaposition it produces hold equally hopeful possibilities for schooling where, as Kara McDonald (this volume) argues, the meaning of national identity is constantly negotiated in the interstitial spaces between formal national curricula and students' lived experiences of the nation. The Third Space, in a curricular sense, is one in which Bhabha's hybridity is performed through encounter, disruption, and transcendence. Together, these three aspects characterize the relationships between the twin narratives that constitute the Third Space, and together they offer new possibilities for reimagining the nation in the ethnoculturally diverse environments that characterize most school classrooms.

In terms of *encounter*, I refer to the notion of encountering the Other in ways that challenge the dominant cultural narrative of existing curricula. In *Re-mapping Literary Worlds* (2003), Ingrid Johnston's thoughtful study of the use of postcolonial literature in senior high school English classes, she notes that experiencing other perspectives and lived realities by reading the works of such authors as Yukio Mishima, Nadine Gordimer, Amy Tan, and Michael Ondaatje 'can challenge readers in contemporary classrooms to begin revisioning and re-mapping the world, helping them to cross cultural and political borders' in such a way that they are offered 'possibilities to engage more thoughtfully in diverse and pluralistic human adventures' (2003, p. 147; see also, Johnston, this volume).

By the notion of *disruption* I am suggesting a doubled sense of the word, through which both the dominant narrative of the nation as well as the performative narratives of its peoples are dislocated in the creation of what Bhabha terms 'a political object that is new, neither one nor the other' (1994, p. 25). In a curricular sense, disruption functions as a space of inquiry where existing identities are unsettled and new imaginaries of the nation emerge. Writing of the possibilities emerging from what she terms the 'identity clash' that typifies multicultural societies, Yatta Kanu speaks of the opportunity 'for people to define themselves in terms of new memories by which they come to know, understand, and experience themselves – memories dissociated from the old collective identities and re-imagined with another collective narrative' (2003, p. 79).

The curricular possibilities that the Third Space holds for *transcendence* are, at once, more ambiguous and more ambitious than in the case of encounter and disruption. In many respects, encounter and disruption are the natural consequences of curricula that incorporate alternative narratives of nation into their structure. Given the inevitable discrepancies and discordances that result from bringing mainstream and previously marginalized narratives together in the same curricular location, the 'identity clash' and cultural ambiguity that Kanu (this volume) refers to can hardly help but take place. But the achievement of transcendence, as a *product* of the Third Space is much less certain. For such a result to be realized, it is necessary to move beyond the 'diversity/difference' binary that tends to characterize (and divide) liberal and postcolonial thinking about curriculum. We know that the concept of cultural diversity, as applied to curricula, has meant the subtle reinforcement of the dominant narrative of the nation and the marginalization of minorities. And it is becoming increasingly clear that the assertion of cultural difference has foundered on the question of the degree to which curricula that acknowledge Mohanty's 'dense particularities' of cultural identity (1989) promote or negate the emergence of a viable civic community in plural societies. Beyond this intractable binary we need some more open imaginary of curriculum that acknowledges cultural difference yet at the same time makes community possible. This imaginary is one that 'does not involve opposing Western culture against the cultures of the non-West, but is instead founded on the principle of the heterogeneous basis of all knowledge and the need to find abiding links that connect groups across ethnic affiliations, geographic origins and locations' (McCarthy, cited in Kanu, 2003, p. 78).

The central question of whether the trope of heterogeneity has the emotive power to drive this new transcendent imaginary in face of essentialist curricula that portray the nation as a 'fixed tablet of tradition' remains unanswered. Elsewhere I have written of the difficulties that education systems in all plural societies face as they attempt to construct national identity across what postcolonial scholar Homi Bhabha has called a bar of difference (Richardson, 2002a). These difficulties and the complexities inherent in attempting to reimagine curriculum as a Third Space are perhaps best seen through examining a failed educational initiative in Canada.

Constructing the Third Space: A Cautionary Tale

What I want to emphasize ... is a particular ambivalence that haunts the idea of the nation, the language of those who write of it and the lives of those who live it.

Bhabha (1990b)

Beginning in 1993, Canada's four western provinces and three territories embarked on an unprecedented and extensive collaborative process called the 'Western Canada Protocol for Basic Education.' Their collective aim was to create common curriculum frameworks for the 'core' academic subjects. By 1999 this work was essentially complete and regional curricula had been produced for all grade levels in mathematics, English language arts, and social studies (Government of Alberta, 1999a). Of these core areas, social studies was the last to be dealt with and proved, by far, the most controversial. During the consultative process that followed the release of a draft document for the 'Social Studies Protocol,' widespread opposition to the document emerged. Indeed, this collective protest had sufficient force to result in the complete abandonment of the social studies program in the autumn of 2001, despite the immense commitment of resources, time, and money that completion of the Protocol had necessitated. Fundamentally, in terms of national identity construction, the Protocol illustrates the attempt to design a regionally based curriculum of national identity that is reflective of cultural diversity rather than cultural uniformity. In place of previous social studies curricula that tended to present national identity in more narrowly essentialist terms, the Protocol opted to speak in the plural rather than the singular. As the draft document clearly indicated, the intent of the proposed social studies curriculum was to enable students to 'appreciate and respect Aboriginal, Francophone, English language, and multiple cultural perspectives' (ibid., p. 1). But, drawing on Bhabha's theme of the ambivalence that characterizes the nation and those who live and write it, the Protocol carried with it a doubled sense of nation that betrayed the tension between a nostalgic longing for Renata Salecl's 'homogeneous entity' and the stated intent of developing a space where multiple narratives of the nation could be developed.

In describing the Third Space, Bhabha discusses both the inherent tension between the nation viewed as essentialist pedagogy and the nation seen as performance of cultural difference and the hybrid possibilities that such tension produces (1990e). A brief examination of the language that the Protocol uses to represent the four named 'perspectives' that constitute Canadian identity reveals not only the tense cultural dynamic that powers the Third Space, but also the difficulties involved in maintaining a balance between the twin narratives that constitute the space.

The Protocol and the (Re)Creation of National Hierarchies

In plural states, and especially in plural states whose demographic balance is rapidly shifting, the attempt to create Anderson's common imagining of the nation can all too easily resolves itself into a process of privilege and exclusion (Chatterjee, 1991; Benhabib, 1996; Willinsky, 1998). Or, put more directly, it can turn into a question of whether naming the official constituents of national identity creates asymmetrical power relationships between different ethnocultural groups through a reinscription of the essentialist pedagogy of the nation (Duara, 1996; Richardson, 2004).

In examining the Protocol, it is possible to see the reinscriptive process at work under the guise of the promotion of cultural diversity. Thus, the initial draft spoke of the need to be reflective of 'Aboriginal, English language, Francophone, and multiple cultural perspectives ... in creating a sense of belonging for each one of our students' (Government of Alberta, 1999a, p. 4). In stressing the need to acknowledge Aboriginal and Francophone perspectives, the Protocol performed an act of cultural redemption that retrieved the vital role that First Nations and Francophone groups played and continue to play in Canada's West and North. The nature of this redemptive function was quite clear in the section of the Protocol that described the role of social studies:

> Social Studies will enable Francophone students to assert their rights and responsibilities as fully participating French citizens of Canada.

> Social Studies will enable Aboriginal students to understand their roles and responsibilities as citizens of Aboriginal Nations and of Canada. (Ibid.)

Canadians in all four identity categories were encouraged, more generally, to 'thrive in their cultural and Canadian identity with a legitimate sense of belonging to their communities and to Canada' (Duara, 1996, p. 20).

In terms of what appears to be the special attention accorded First Nations and Francophone Canadians, it could easily be argued that these educational intents were the legitimate and logical extension of the constitutional guarantees that both groups enjoy. The difference in the language used to describe how social studies would give agency to each group is, however, particularly revealing. Thus, Francophone students were enabled to 'assert their rights and responsibilities,' while First Nations students were enabled 'to understand their roles and responsibilities.'

The difference in status and possibilities inherent in the gap between *assertion* and *understanding* represented much more than a random grammatical choice. In it was inscribed an entire history of power relations between the state and its constituent peoples that carefully established – and reinforced – a national hierarchy of cultural signification. Using the notion of Third Space, it can be said that the curricular extract cited above represents a reinscription of the formal pedagogy of the nation under the guise of an acknowledgment of the existence of different national narratives. Such a reinscription sees the people as 'objects of a nationalist pedagogy, giving the discourse [of the nation] an authority that is based on the pre-given or constituted historical origin' (Bhabha, 1990a, p. 146).

If First Nations cultures were named in the Protocol only to reinscribe their subaltern status in the national hierarchy, non-Anglophone ethnic minorities fared even worse. Throughout the document, groups described vaguely as representing 'multiple cultural perspectives,' that is minority peoples, are effectively relegated to the status of unspecified Other. This creates the strong impression that Canada's ethnocultural populations, by virtue of their assigned Otherness, have assumed the status of exotic, decentred peoples who are very much on the margins of the curricular map (Said, 1979). Nationalist discourses potently serve to legitimize some students as Canadians and, therefore, insiders and delegitimize others as outsiders and not quite Canadians (McDonald, this volume).

In opting to privilege the celebration of cultural diversity over examining cultural difference, and in reinscribing the traditional national hierarchy of the nation, the Protocol ignored understandings that national identity in plural societies such as Canada is fluid, hybrid, and evolving. But, as William Douglass indicates, '*how* as opposed to *where* [identity communities meet] is subject to constant negotiation' (1998, p. 77). In plural nations, however, the emergent conceptualization of national identity as the 'unstable, never-secured effect of a process of enunciation of cultural difference' (Scott, 1995, p. 11) has not yet achieved wide acceptance. And 'that both cultural differences and social conflict are inherent features of any pluralistic society is a perspective that remains at odds with the mainstream perspective that treats social conflict as social disease' (Collins, 1993, p. 202). This equation is founded on the modernist idea that social harmony is the ideal in pluralistic states, but harmony can easily be a mask for assimilation and repression: 'Instead of trying to reduce the existing plurality through devices like the veil of ignorance ... we need to develop a positive attitude toward differences, even if they lead to conflict and impede the realization of harmony. Any understanding of pluralism whose objective is to reach harmony is ultimately a negation of the positive value of diversity and difference' (Mouffe, 1995, p. 202). To the degree that the draft version of the Protocol emphasized the harmonious and consensual nature of constructing Canadian identity around cultural diversity – the document reminds us that one of the roles of social studies is to enable students to 'celebrate and strengthen the Canadian identity' (Government of Alberta, 1999a, p. 2) – it fell prey to the assimilationist and repressive tendencies that Chantel Mouffe and Roger Collins warn of. What is more, to the degree that it reinscribed a 'named' national hierarchy, the Protocol stepped away from creating the more open space for renarrating the nation suggested by the Third Space.

In a general sense, the effort to design a viable Western Canadian Protocol for Social Studies can be seen as a kind of cautionary tale that illustrates the complexities of attempting to reimagine curriculum as cultural practice. As one teacher noted at the consultation meetings held to review the Protocol, 'what is needed [in the Protocol] is a far more sophisticated understanding of what identity means, of the fact that in Canadian society individuals increasingly have multiple and layered identities, and of how our identities are socially and historically constructed as well as relational' (Government of Alberta, 1999b, p. 15). This same comment, I think, applies to how we need to take up curriculum reform and why we need to look beyond modernist representations of curriculum as transparent and culturally neutral.

More specifically, given an acknowledgment of the central role of culture in the construction of our own identities, new and more inclusive possibilities for reimagining the nation also emerge. These possibilities begin with the recognition that in postcolonial contexts, the hybridity, encounter, dislocation, and transcendence characterizing the Third Space offer us the opportunity to open curricula to the complex, multivocal, and ever-evolving narrative of the nation.

REFERENCES

Anderson, B. (1991). *Imagined communities: Reflections on the origin and spread of nationalism*. London: Verso.

Banks, J.A. (Ed.). (1996). *Multicultural education: Transformative knowledge and action – historical and contemporary perspectives.* New York: Teachers College Press.

Barnes, J. (1998). *England, England.* Toronto: Vintage Books.

Benhabib, S. (Ed.). (1996). *Democracy and difference.* Princeton, NJ: Princeton University Press.

Beiner, R. (1997). *Philosophy in a time of lost spirit: Essays on contemporary theory.* Toronto: University of Toronto Press.

Bhabha, H.K. (1990a). DissemiNation: Time, narrative, and margins of the modern nation. In H.K. Bhabha (Ed.), *The nation and narration* (pp. 139–181). London: Routledge.

Bhabha, H.K. (1990b). Introduction: Narrating the nation. In H.K. Bhabha (Ed.), *The nation and narration* (pp. 1–7). London: Routledge.

Bhabha, H.K. (1990c). Narrating the nation. In H.K. Bhabha (Ed.), *The Nation and narration* (pp. 306–312). London: Routledge.

Bhabha, H.K. (1990d). *The nation and narration.* London: Routledge.

Bhabha, H.K. (1990e). The Third Space: An interview with Homi Bhabha. In J. Rutherford (Ed.), *Identity: Community, culture, difference* (pp. 207–221). London: Lawrence and Wishert.

Bhabha, H.K. (1994). *The location of culture.* London: Routledge.

Bhabha, H.K. (1995). Freedom's basis on the indeterminate. In J. Raichman (Ed.), *The identity in question* (pp. 47–62). New York: Routledge.

Borgmann, A. (1992). *Crossing the postmodern divide.* Chicago: University of Chicago Press.

Brock, C., & Tulasiewicz, W. (Eds.). (1985). *Cultural identity and educational policy.* London: Croom Helm.

Brown, D. (2000). *Contemporary nationalism: civic, ethnocultural and multicultural politics.* London: Routledge.

Chatterjee, P. (1991). *The nation and its fragments: Colonial and postcolonial histories.* Princeton, NJ: Princeton University Press.

Cobban, A. (1964). *Rousseau and the modern state.* London: George Allen and Unwin.

Collins, R. (1993). Responding to diversity in our schools. In L. Castenell & W.F. Pinar (Eds.), *Understanding curriculum as racial text: Representations of identity and difference in education.* Albany, NY: SUNY Press.

Douglass, W.A. (1998). A Western perspective on an Eastern interpretation of where North meets South: Pyrenean borderland cultures. In T.M. Wilson & H. Donnan (Eds.), *Border identities: Nation and state at international frontiers* (pp. 74–91). Cambridge: Cambridge University Press.

Duara, P. (1996). Historicizing national identity, or who imagines what and when. In G. Eley & R.G. Suny (Eds.), *Becoming national: A reader* (pp. 53–71). Oxford: Oxford University Press.

Frankenberg, R. (Ed.). (1997). *Displacing whiteness: Essays in social and cultural criticism.* Raleigh, NC: Duke University Press.

Gallegos, B. (1998). Remember the Alamo: Imperialista, memory and postcolonial education studies. *Educational Studies, 29,* 232–247.

Gellner, E. (1983). *Nations and nationalism.* Oxford: Blackwell.

Ghosh, R. (1996). *Redefining multicultural education.* Toronto: Harcourt Brace.

Government of Alberta. (1999a). *Foundation document for the Western Canada Protocol for Social Studies.* Edmonton, AB: Alberta Learning.

Government of Alberta (1999b). *Response document to the Western Canada: Protocol for Social Studies.* Edmonton, AB: Alberta Learning.

Greene, M. (1996). Plurality, diversity and the public space. In A. Oldenquist (Ed.), *Can democracy be taught?* (pp. 27–44). Bloomington: Phi Delta Kappa Foundation.

Greenfield, L. (1992). *Nationalism: Five roads to modernity.* Cambridge, MA: Harvard University Press.

Hall, S. (1991). The local and the global. In A. King (Ed.), *Culture, ideology and social process* (pp. 19–40). Albany: SUNY Press.

Hobsbawm, E., & Ranger, T. (1983). *The invention of tradition.* Cambridge: Cambridge University Press.

Hoffmann, D. (1996). Culture and self in multicultural education: Reflections on discourse, text and practice. *American Educational Research Journal, 33* (3), 545–569.

Hurtado, A. (1996). *The color of privilege: Three blasphemies on race and feminism.* Ann Arbor: University of Michigan Press.

Ignatieff, M. (1993). *Blood and belonging: Journeys into the new nationalism.* Toronto: Viking Press.

Johnston, I. (2003). *Re-mapping literary worlds: Postcolonial pedagogy in practice.* New York: Peter Lang.

Kanpol, B., & McLaren, P. (Eds.). (1995). *Critical multiculturalism: Uncommon voices in a common struggle.* Westport, CT: Bergin and Gravey.

Kanu, Y. (2003). Curriculum as cultural practice: Postcolonial imagination. *Journal of the Canadian Association for Curriculum Studies, 1* (1), 67–81.

Kristeva, J. (1993). *Nations without nationalism.* New York: Columbia University Press.

Laclau, E. (1988). Politics and the limits of modernity. In A. Ross (Ed.), *Universal abandon: The politics of postmodernism* (pp. 71–83). Minneapolis: University of Minnesota Press.

Lowe, R. (1999). Education and national identity. *History of Education, 28*(3), 231–235.

Massey, V. (1926). Introduction. In C.N. Cochrane & W.S. Wallace (Eds.), *This Canada of ours* (pp. 1–6). Toronto: National Council of Education.

McCarthy, C. (1998). *The uses of culture.* New York: Routledge.

Minh Ha, T. (1990). Documentary is/not a name. *October, 52,* 77–100.

Mohanty, S.P. (1989). Us and them: In the philosophical bases of political criticism. *Yale Journal of Criticism, 2,* 7–9.

Mouffe, C. (1995). Democratic politics and the question of identity. In J. Raichman (Ed.), *The identity in question* (pp. 33–46). London: Routledge.

Mukherjee, A. (1994). *Oppositional aesthetics: Reading from a hyphenated space.* Toronto: TSAR Publications.

Nairn, T. (1997). *The faces of nationalism: James revisited.* London: Verso.

Pierce, B.N. (1995). Learning the hard way: Maria's story. In B. Kanpol & P. McLaren (Eds.), *Critical multiculturalism: Uncommon voices in a common struggle* (pp. 165–196). Westport, CT: Bergin and Garvey.

Reisner, E.H. (1925). *Nationalism and education since 1789: A social and political history of modern education.* New York: Macmillan.

Richardson, G.H. (2002a). A border within: The Western Canada Protocol for Social Studies Education and the politics of national identity construction. *Revista Mexicana de Estudios Canadienses, 4,* 31–46.

Richardson, G.H. (2002b). *The dealth of the good Canadian: Teachers, national identities and the social studies curriculum.* New York: Peter Lang.

Richardson, G.H. (2004). Nostalgia and national identity: The history and social studies curriculum of Alberta and Ontario at the end of empire. In P. Buckner (Ed.), *Canada at the end of empire* (pp. 249–267). Vancouver: UBC Press.

Rushdie, S. (1983). 'Commonwealth literature' does not exist. In *Imaginary Homelands* (pp. 61–70). London: Penguin.

Said, E. (1979). *Orientalism.* New York: Vintage Books.

Said, E. (1993). *Culture and imperialism.* New York: Alfred A. Knopf.

Salecl, R. (1994). *The spoils of freedom: Psychoanalysis and feminism after the fall of socialism.* New York: Routledge.

Samuels, A. (1993). *The political psyche.* London: Routledge.

Scott, J.W. (1995). Multiculturalism and the politics of identity. In J. Raichman (Ed.), *The Identity in Question* (pp. 3–14). London: Routledge.

Smith, A.D. (1991). *National identity.* London: Penguin.

Spivak, G. (1987). *In other worlds: Essays in cultural politics.* London: Methuen.

Srivastava, S. (1996). Postcoloniality, national identity, globalisation and the simulacra of the real. *Australian Journal of Anthropology, 7*(2), 166–190.

Taylor, C. (1991). *The malaise of modernity*. Concord, ON: House of Anansi.

Weber, E. (1976). *Peasants into Frenchmen: The modernization of rural France, 1970–1914*. Stanford, CA: Stanford University Press.

Willinsky, J. (1998). *Learning to divide the world: Education at empire's end*. Minneapolis: University of Minnesota Press.

Willinsky, J. (1999). Curriculum after culture, race, nation. *Discourse: Studies in the Cultural Politics of Education, 20*(1), 89–112.

Willinsky, J. (2002). The nation-state after globalism. *Educational Studies, 23*(1), 35–54.

13 Learning Whose Nation?

KARA McDONALD

This chapter raises ethical questions about the educational promotion of a Euro-American or Euro-Canadian notion of nationalism as a sense of belonging to the nation that has an identity of which the nationalist is proud and protective. I urge educators and students to question the authority and legitimacy of this particular concept of the nation that frames social inquiry in Canadian public schools, as well as in many other educational institutions. My intention is not to consider the future of the nation as a political or legal entity. Rather, I am concerned about the problems with the seemingly neutral nationalist discourses that underpin educational initiatives, such as to foster respect for diversity in the name of inclusion and equality. Like Richardson (previous chapter), I explore articulations of these nationalist discourses and the ways in which they serve to legitimize some students as Canadians and insiders and delegitimize others as not quite Canadian and as outsiders. This is particularly important given the renewed nationalist fervour and elaborations of Us and Them that have intensified since 11 September 2001. The time has come for educators and students to consider the ethical tensions of promoting identification with, and belonging to, the nation as propagated in Euro-American/Canadian conceptions of the nation and citizenship. In what follows, I outline why we ought to engage discursive readings of the nation that generate more ethical and relevant questions of the nation and the global.

With the unprecedented transnational movement of people, ideas, and capital, Canadian educational institutions are in the midst of an intensified coming together of different worldviews, religious differences, ethnic prejudices, intellectual traditions, and experiences and concepts of nationhood. This began with centuries of migration including, for example, the pre-Canadian and pre-American movement of indigenous peoples, the transatlantic slave trade, the importation of Indian and Chinese labour to Canada, the transportation of European convicts, and post–Second World War European migration. I argue that within this context, sustained emphasis on learning about social relations in terms of ahistorically, nationally bound cultures fosters – rather than challenges – the global nature of racism, Eurocentrism, and ethnocentrism.

These concerns emerged from my work as a high school teacher of social studies and French in Atlantic Canada. There, I grappled with how to think of my own whiteness, Scottish heritage, and economic privilege in relation to racialized and colonial histories. I wrestled with how to learn with my students about our different historical and material relationships to the nation. Compounding these dilemmas was my realization, only at this time, of the ways in which these differences found material expression in our particular and shared landscape: the Shubenacadie Residential School, only kilometres away from our Halifax school, that from 1930 to 1967 sought to strip Mi'kmaq children of their family connections, as well as their intellectual, linguistic, and cultural traditions – in an atmosphere of fear; or Halifax's black community of Africville that was literally bulldozed from view with as-yet unresolved land issues. How were we to confront the profoundly different effects of these political and economic injustices and strategies of erasure on people's lived experiences, their perceptions of their own and others' intellectual, spiritual, emotional brilliance, their sense of entitlement to, and agency in, the world? At the heart of my concern were the ways in which Eurocentric curricula, addressing socioeconomic and cultural differences within and between nations, embraced the legacies of the Enlightenment project of a Euro-classification of the world's peoples and cultures into hierarchies where the European nations, religions, and cultures were deemed to be superior to others (Eze, 1997; Shohat & Stam, 1994).

This chapter explores problems related to Euro-American/Canadian notions of nationalism, which often remain a taken-for-granted backdrop of many multicultural initiatives, reinforcing racialized inequalities and European references of cultural authority.[1] It responds to and extends Willinsky's call to pay curricular attention to 'how current notions of race, culture, and nation have been shaped by imperialism and how much of its legacy was the work of scholars and schools' (1998, p. 252). Drawing on selected postcolonial and globalization theory, I propose a discursive reading of nation that raises more ethical and relevant questions about the ways in which racism, ethnocentrism, and Eurocentrism are inscribed in nationalist and globalization discourses to produce divisions within and beyond educational communities.

By way of an outline, I explore how homogenizing nationalist discourses in the Euro-American tradition characterize students, the citizen, and the global. Drawing on examples from the British Columbia social studies curricula guidelines for Kindergarten through Grade 12, I highlight articulations of nation, culture, and difference and the associated ethical tensions that arise.[2] Although I use examples from social studies curricula particular to British Columbia, and while founding myths differ according to particular national histories, I assume that the tensions that I am identifying are at the crux of social inquiry across many educational institutions that foster learning about other people and places. First, I expose the ways in which nationalist discourses transform dramatically different experiences of the nation into a collective narrative that masks histories of genocide, forced displacement, and colonialism, and reinforces a sense of an enclosed nation with an essentialized identity. I illustrate the ways in which homogenizing nationalist discourses and celebratory multicultural discourse (1) neglect students' different histories and relations to nation-making projects and diasporic migrations; (2) mask racial hierarchies and a Euro-American cultural reference of authority that is central to the nation-making project in Canada; (3) foster Anglo-centrism and Franco-centrism; and (4) neglect an understanding of the competing linguistic, cultural, and ethnic interests and related material inequities among people that would address more directly terms and conditions of equality. I then briefly outline what I mean by a discursive reading of the nation, pointing to directions for ongoing inquiry.

Let me clarify some of my assumptions about the curricular documents on which I draw. While my analysis provides a springboard for discussion about the problems with nationalism, it does not explore the ways in which people of diverse sociocultural identities and intellectual traditions take up and negotiate related discourses, nor does it survey the nationalist discourses of the formerly colonized nations. These, too are necessary pieces for interrogating the Canadian nation-making project in more ethical ways.[3] Nevertheless, focusing on what Billig calls, the 'flagging of the nation' (1996), I focus not on extreme expressions of nation, but rather on language, constructions of nation, culture, and space that foster a nationalized and Anglo-centric consciousness of the world, often beyond the level of awareness. Influenced by Dorothy Smith's (1999) method of textual analysis, I consider the curricular documents as material objects within which to isolate and analyse how knowledge is organized to embrace social relations. My assumption is that understanding how racism, Eurocentrism, and ethnocentrism are perpetuated through seemingly neutral nationalist discourses provides a necessary basis for destabilizing them and for thinking of alternative and more ethical ways of learning about the nation and the global.

Problems with Nationalism

One problem with nationalism is the way in which Euro-American discourses transform peoples of diverse worldviews, mixed and asymmetrical cultural, ethnic, linguistic, and religious interests and traditions into a collective discourse, reinforcing a sense of nation as having an essentialized identity. For example, central goals for the British Columbia social studies curricula, Kindergarten through Grade 11, include aims for students to 'understand and prepare to exercise their roles, rights, and responsibilities within the family, the community, Canada, and the world; to develop an appreciation of democracy and what it means to be Canadian; to demonstrate respect for human equality and cultural diversity; and to think critically, evaluate information, and practice effective communication' (B.C. Ministry of Education, 2001a). These curricula acknowledge the historical and contemporary diverse make-up of, and contributions to, Canada; however, emphasis on 'what it means to be Canadian' and objectives to learn about a 'Canadian culture' and 'Canadian identity' foster assumptions of a real and neutral nation unifying its members around a common cultural identity, historical attachment to a homeland, and a consciousness of being different from other nations (Johnston, Gregory, Pratt, & Watts, 2000, p. 532). Among those who have challenged the taken-for-granted authority of nation as a collective source of identity is Edward Said, who usefully asks, 'What is a national identity made of?' (1993, p. xxv).

A problem, as Homi Bhabha (1994) argues, is that there is no homogeneous national identity, only one dependent on a discourse that transforms diverse and hybrid groups into a collective narrative. This narrative, as Benedict Anderson and Eric Hobsbawm have usefully discussed, has been socially constructed through such phenomena as daily newspapers and 'invented traditions,' including public holidays, ceremonies, school and other government institutions that generate among citizens a sense of common history, shared present, and future (Hobsbawm, 1994, p. 76). Yet, the nation, as assumed in the social studies curricular documents, is not presented to be a social construction. It is presented as a realist and essentialized entity with a 'true' national past and identity. The problem is the potential that such constructions have to erase a historically dynamic and diverse amalgam of peoples, interests, complex negotiations, notions of, and resistance central to nation-making projects: 'Where does the act of living in the everyday experience fit within this narrative?' ask Bhabha (1994, pp. 153–154). What should be of concern to educators and students, I am arguing, is the ways in which this homogenizing national narrative has acquired such legitimacy and disregard for students' varied histories and relations to Canadian nation-making projects and to diasporic migrations.

Another of my concerns is the reinforcement of a global imaginary of national boundaries beyond which lie other nations. Despite the intensified transnational flows of people, capital, and human-rights regimes, much social inquiry, including the British Columbia social studies curricula, situates students in expanding, concentric, and bounded enclosures of the family, community, nation, and then the global. Not only does learning about separate national cultures not reflect historical and contemporary transnational phenomena such as white-settler colonization of Canada, and the subsequent genocide and displacement of peoples of First Nations ancestry, but it also casts students of diverse diasporic experiences adrift from the Canada that students of European ancestry have the privilege of calling *home*. Thus, seemingly neutral questions of *Where are you from?* and *Where do you call home?* become sources of anxiety suggesting to indigenous peoples and ethnic minorities that their home must be elsewhere, that they do not quite belong to this collective national identity.

Concepts of contact, colonialism and resistance, for example, are explored in Grade 12 First Nations Studies (B.C. Ministry of Education, 2001b); however, this course is optional, and relatively few students get to take up these concepts. Instead, through the first eleven years of social studies learning, the world of bordered nations and homogeneous constructions of Canadian identity are deeply entrenched. This neglects engagement with tensions that are increasingly relevant to Canadian educational institutions, tensions related to the production of boundaries and divisions instilled by colonialism and nationalism, and the intensified and highly uneven dissolution of economic borders in the global context. How, educators and students must ask, does the implicit presence of boundaries fostered through learning about other national peoples create systems of inclusion and exclusion within educational institutions?

The tensions of producing such boundaries are raised in Himani Bannerji's powerful essay entitled, 'Geography Lessons: On Being Insider/Outsider to the Canadian Nation' (1997), where she depicts the striking contrast between the romantic construction of Canada that she experienced as a child – a Canada associated with polar bears, mythologies of the north, and 'native indians' – and her political experience as an adult of customs that cast her as alien and outsider. Bannerji's experience of a racialized nation founded on European and white norms raises compelling reasons to question the terms and effects of promoting a sense of belonging to a common Canadian identity. Although promoted in the name of inclusion, this construction of nation does not reflect Bannerji's lived cultural, economic, and political realities, nor did it equip her to deal with the potent psychological, social, and material effects of being made an outsider to this constructed Canada. Thus, important question for engaging students is not what it means to be Canadian, but rather how construction of a Canadian identity is produced and with what consequences.

A second problem with the educational promotion of nationalism relates to the ethical tensions it engenders. Missing from the curriculum is attention to the ways in which educational promotion of the nation, while mobilized in the name of unity and equality, neglects the inequalities that have been central to the Canadian nation-making project. The British Columbia Social Studies curriculum, for example, assumes a concept of nation that Benedict Anderson would call a 'deep horizontal comradeship,' despite 'the actual inequality and exploitation that may prevail' (1983, pp. 6–7). It recognizes the contributions of First Nations and all immigrant peoples to Canada, reflecting the official 1971 Canadian multicultural policy that sought to manage diversity, challenge Anglo-conformity, and deal with historical and contemporary tensions in the name of national unity (Ng, 1995; for a negation of this multiethnic approach to curriculum, see Richardson's critique of the Western Canada Social Studies Protocol, previous chapter). Yet, like Canada's official multicultural policy, educational address of these issues often emphasizes the celebratory contributions of various cultural groups to Canada, obscuring historical tensions and inequalities. The narrative of nation has involved the erasure – or what Bhabha calls a 'forgetting to remember' – of the conquests, wars, marginalizations, and exclusionary acts of symbolic and material violence that are central to many nation-making projects (1994, p. 160). National models of citizenship often were propagated in terms of belonging, membership, and entitlement to the same rights and privileges, but, in fact, rights were accorded on the basis of how the national public was defined in relation to class, gender, age, and race (Soysal, 1998, pp. 189–190). Central to this concept of citizenship was differential membership status, where 'entry was determined by the nation-state' to fill skill-gaps with immigrant labour, 'and where inequality was considered a "natural" characteristic of the social order' (ibid., p. 194).

A discursive reading of nation, as I am proposing, would draw attention to the inequalities and the Eurocentric and racial dimensions of nation-making projects that are currently absent from most social studies curricula. Discursive would include attention to the exclusionary politics, based on race, that have influenced the conditions of equality of a nation over time. It is useful for students to understand what Timothy Stanley has called an 'ideology of difference' that was historically based on a – now widely refuted – scientifically proscribed hierarchy of racialized differences (1995, p. 39). In his analysis of Canadian school textbooks from 1885 to 1925, Stanley shows how this ideology of difference characterized white people of European descent as the most civilized, active, enterprising, and intelligent race in the world, people of First Nations descent as savage and morally depraved, and people of African descent as the least intellectual, progressive, and educated (ibid., pp. 42–49). He illustrates how such assumptions served to justify an inequitable distribution of rights, labour, wages, land appropriation, and Eurocentric assimilation policies (ibid., pp. 39–40). What is particularly relevant to educators and students is to analyse the ways in which the constructions of difference among peoples have set up hierarchies of colour, intelligence, and entitlements at the psychological, social and material expense of some 'citizens.'

Attention to the racial inequalities and divisions that justified and were reinforced by policies and educational practices helps to raise ethical tensions with schools' cultivation of a sense of attachment to a shared national culture. Milloy (1999) highlights such tensions in his research on the founding assimilationist vision that underpinned Canadian residential schooling for First Nations peoples into the 1980s. As he shows, residential schooling fostering of a common national identity involved the active and deliberate replacement of some students' cultures with a dominant European culture. This included the inculcation of European values, the physical separation of children from their parents, and forced acquisition of the English or French language, which allegedly carried 'the cultures of civilization' through which European cultural assumptions were constructed to be superior and the norm of a unifying national identity (ibid., p. 25). A powerful example of the Eurocentric and racialized narrative of Canada's nation-building project is highlighted by a 1901 letter addressed to British Columbia students from Agnes Cameron, associate editor of the *Education Journal of Western Canada* and principal of a school in Victoria. Flagging the superiority of the 'Anglo-Saxon race' within Canada and of Canada within the world, Cameron characterized European values, interests, and religious beliefs as tools for a prosperous national economy and those of other cultures or races for pleasure and as deviating from that norm (1901, p. 2). This historical perspective raises important questions about how the concept of culture came to be cast as neutral despite its emergence from racialized discourses where people had to *become something else to belong* to Canada.

A critical issue for educators in considering the consequences of such exclusionary discourses is how enduring divisions are reinforced through contemporary celebratory multicultural discourses. Like the assimilation policies already mentioned, Canadian multicultural policy was legislated in the name of national unity (Ng, 1995, p. 36); however, rather than assimilating other groups to a European or more specifically a British norm, multicultural policy was conceived to instill a sense that different cultural groups have the right to be recognized and to remain separate. Rattansi argues that contemporary multiculturalism 'as it was translated into educational and political practice often conflated the question of culture with a particular understanding of ethnicity. The positive achievement of this tradition was that it allowed different communities, and their claims over their members, to be acknowledged and valued with a new, official respect. Its drawback was that a multicultural celebration of *diversity* tended to reproduce the "saris, samosas, and steel-bands syndrome." That is, by focusing on the superficial manifestations of culture, multiculturalism failed to address the continuing *hierarchies* of power and legitimacy that still existed among these different centres of cultural authority' (1992, p. 2). What is problematic is that celebratory multicultural discourses fail to acknowledge and challenge the exclusionary legacies of the nation-making project through which they themselves emerged. For example, the B.C. social studies curricula recognize the contributions of various cultural groups to Canada, yet it disregards the ways in which the advancement of a single national identity promoted British or French interests at the expense of the interests of groups that they marginalized: Multicultural discourses emphasize recognition of all cultures in the name of equality, disregarding 'racism and colonial ethnocentrism as though [visible minorities'] cultures were on par or could negotiate with the two dominant ones' (Bannerji, 2000, p. 96).

Edward Said and Simon Gikandi are among those have sought to challenge the neutrality of benevolent nationalist and multicultural discourses and to expose the Eurocentric and racialized histories of the nation through what I call a discursive reading of it. By framing the nation as 'narrative of imperialism,' they emphasize the emergence of national histories from colonial ones (Gikandi, 1996, p. 15; Said, 1993, p. xiii). This usefully exposes how imperial legacies reside in the apparently neutral categories of identity and culture that are so integral to the study of other places and peoples today. As these writers have independently argued, imperialism instituted hierarchies such as racial stratification that provided a context in which ideas of identity and difference were constituted and in which they were reproduced, elaborated, and contested through decolonization, nationalist movements, and current manifestations of globalization (Gikandi, 1996, p. 9; Said, 1993, p. xii). As Gikandi argues, 'The times we live in are both colonial and postcolonial times' (1996, p. 126). And, 'since we cannot operate outside colonialism our challenge is not to transcend it but to inhabit its central categories, to unite the histories ... to come to terms with their effects and to deconstruct their authority' (ibid., p. 46). Gikandi contends that it is not possible for the promotion of a unifying national identity to completely shed imperial traces of racism and Eurocentrism. Thus, not only must we challenge Eurocentrism by explicitly questioning the ways in which concepts of culture, identity, citizenship, and nation assume and perpetuate a hierarchy of relations (Willinsky, 1999), but we must also engage the varied and nuanced notions of culture, identity, citizenship, and nation that people of First Nations ancestry and immigrants from the formerly colonized regions of the world offer to Canadian communities.

Concepts of colonialism, imperialism, and nationalism are explored in Grade 12 B.C. social studies courses; however, with but little consideration of racial hierarchies, employing European cultural reference of authority that continues to shape people's sense of themselves and their relations with Others (B.C. Ministry of Education, 2001b, 2001c, 2001d). Traces of a Eurocentric norm emerge in curricular prescriptions such as to study an 'ethnic culture in Canada' (B.C. Ministry of Education, 2001b), begging the questions: Which groups are assumed to be ethnic? And what is the 'hidden norm' at work that affords some groups the privilege of being unaware of their ethnicity? (Cohen, 1992). Where specified in the curriculum, *nationalism* is assigned to other regions in the world such as the Middle East and India (B.C. Ministry of Education, 2001d). This may foster a sense of nationalism as an unstable condition found in the less-than-stable regions of the world (Ashcroft, Griffiths, & Tiffin, 1998, pp. 149–150). This implicitly characterizes nationalism in the West as relatively neutral and complete, masking the complex dynamics of a nation-in-the-making, as well as a norm against which other nationalist movements are measured.

A postcolonial discursive reading of the nation would draw attention to such tensions, as well as to the politics of the hyphen associated with the nation. References to the hyphenated Canadian such as Korean-Canadian or French-Canadian denote a sense of boundary that requires educational attention. Although the hyphen has been strategically used to affirm a sense of collective identity of a group and to challenge the notion of a homogeneous national identity, it is almost never used to demarcate a Scottish- or British-Canadian. The use of the hyphen, thus, not only asserts the distinct identities of the group named, but it legitimizes an often European, white, English-speaking Canadian as the unidentified norm. Like Michael Billig (1996), I advocate attention to the ways in which such utterances reinforce a deeply ingrained nationalized consciousness of Us and Them that affirms the identities of some and casts others as not quite Canadian.

Another problem with the study of essentialized national cultures is the associated production of ethnocentrism. Nationalism may be regarded as a form of ethnocentrism, 'in which cultural groups and their essential characteristics are defined by nationality, and the cultural attributes of one or more nations may be regarded as inherently superior or inferior' (Rattansi, 1992, p. 36). The B.C. social studies curricula include some attention to 'stereotyping of cultural groups [and] portrayals of Canada in mass media' and to ethnocentrism (B.C. Ministry of Education, 2001a, 2001d); however, they neglect consideration of how a predominant emphasis on learning about the 'daily life, family structure, gender roles, and artistic expression' of other nations inevitably fosters stereotypes that easily lead to the veneration of one's own culture and nation (B.C. Ministry of Education, 2001a). In his analysis of how this occurs, Said explores the close association between culture and nation and the ways in which assumptions of the superiority of one's own nation occur in part through a celebratory focus on culture. He shows how representations of distant parts of the world often embrace a concept of culture that casts other national people's lifestyles and aesthetic forms as inherent cultural differences for enrichment and pleasure. Said analyses how this concept disregards the ways in which such representations have been shaped by imperial attitudes, references, and experiences that have accompanied the institutionalization of unequal economic and social relations (1993, p. xii). Said highlights a second concept of culture that is evident in the B.C. curricula through the celebratory focus on contributions to the nation and 'each society's reservoir of the best that has been known and thought' (Arnold, cited in Said, ibid., p. xiii). Over time this has often become associated 'aggressively with the nation ... [differentiating] "us" from "them" almost always with some degree of xenophobia' (ibid.). In this sense, 'culture can even be a battleground,' where students of various nations 'who are taught to read their national classics before they read others are expected to appreciate and belong loyally, often uncritically, to their nations and traditions while denigrating or fighting against others' (ibid.).

Said's analysis of orientalism, while arguably limited in its consideration of the interrelational of dimensions such as nation, race, class, and gender, provides a powerful framework for understanding how cultural representations are inscribed with assumptions of superiority and inferiority. Useful for students, Said shows how an ethnocentric perspective develops through consideration of one's own culture as complex and 'normal,' consideration of other cultures as static, fixed, and essentialized, and through a lack of reflexivity and assumptions that knowledge produced about other national cultures is neutral or absolute, because 'ideas, cultures, and histories cannot seriously be studied without their force, or more precisely their configurations of power, also being studied' (1994, p. 5). At the core of such tensions are the ways in which differences constructed by colonial histories collide in Canada (and other nations). Sustained curricular attention to similarities and differences between separate cultures and nations neglects the historical, economic, political, and cultural relations through which racism, Eurocentrism, and ethnocentrism have emerged. The B.C. social studies curricula organize social inquiry into subsections of culture, politics, and economics, characterizing differences among peoples primarily in cultural terms (B.C. Ministry of Education, 2001e). This reflects Canada's official multicultural policy, which has framed and legislated 'equality within a Canadian democracy [and] full participation of all Canadians' through funding and programming for 'language training in English and French [and] creative encounters and interchange of all cultural groups' (Ng, 1995, p. 42). Promoting a sense of belonging to the nation on cultural terms fails to adequately address how historical and contemporary inequities emerged, the current perpetuation of inequalities on the basis of race through discriminatory immigration and refugee policies, and the terms of participation in Canada's political and economic life. Mohanty has argued that 'the goals of the analysis of difference and the challenge of race are not the proliferation of discourse on ethnicities as discrete and separate cultures. The challenge of race resides in a fundamental re-conceptualization of our categories of analysis so that differences can be historically specified and understood as part of the larger political processes and systems. The central issue then, is not one of merely acknowledging difference; rather the more fundamental questions concern the kind of difference that is acknowledged and engaged' (1990, p. 181).

More relevant to social inquiry than a focus on what seems to be neutral knowledge about isolated cultures and nations is exposure of the historical conditions through which assumptions of real or imaginary differences among peoples became institutionalized. This would include an examination of the ways in which assumptions of biological racialized differences, while now widely repudiated, came to be viewed as truth, justifying exclusionary practices associated with the nation, and remain deeply connected to perceived differences and material inequalities today. This would involve consideration of how homogenizing nationalist discourses and celebratory multicultural discourses mask different histories and relations to the nation and their relevance to discussions about current social issues such as First Nations land claims. Central to this call is the need for students to learn how knowledge is discursively constituted, how ideas and objects of inquiry such as the nation were historically situated and legitimized through institutions at particular times and places, and how associated divisions endure to reinforce systems of exclusion. A discursive reading of the nation attempts to destabilize racism, ethnocentrism, and Eurocentrism by understanding how associated assumptions of difference and inequalities are produced.

Discursive Readings of the Nation

The following is a brief outline of what I mean by a discursive reading of the nation and explanation of why this is so important for educators and students. I am proposing a two-pronged discursive reading that (1) questions the authority and legitimacy of Euro-American concepts of nation that frame social inquiry in Canadian public schools and (2) looks to alternative frameworks for thinking about social relations that more directly explore terms for inclusion and equality. At the core of this proposal is the assumption that 'knowledge is socially organized; its textual forms bear and replicate social relations. Hence knowledge must be differently written and differently designed if it is to bear other social relations than those of ruling' (smith, 1999, p. 94).

The first aspect of a discursive reading of the nation highlights the ways in which divisive colonial legacies reside in the categories of identity, culture, and difference associated with the nation. Influenced by Said (1993), Gikandi (1996), Foucault (1963/1997), Bannerji (1999, 2000), Bhabha (1994), and Willinsky (1998), this reading would expose the problems associated with Euro-American concepts of nationalism. It would deconstruct the perceived neutrality of the nation by exposing how constructions of borders and hierarchies of people were instilled by colonial and nation-making projects and how they continue to frame the ways in which we perceive social relations today. Such a reading of the nation would expose various histories and relations to the nation, inequalities and marginalizations, and a Euro-cultural reference of authority and privilege that is otherwise masked by a homogenizing nationalist discourse.

Framed by a Foucauldian historical analysis of discourse, discursive reading would explore the historical conditions and institutional practices through which the idea of a homogeneous national identity was legitimized over the past 150 years (Bhabha, 1994; Gikandi, 1996; Foucault, 1969/1997). Considering how this narrative has been constructed, how it has fostered ongoing exclusionary practices and disregarded various histories and relations to the nation helps to explain the limitations of the nation as a mobilizing concept for equality. Discursive reading would draw attention to the ways in which racism and Eurocentrism are articulated, however variously, through nationalist educational practices and everyday utterances and how such insights might be relevant to the understanding and resolution of current social issues.

In consonance with Willinsky's (this volume) notion of postcolonial supplementary moments of teaching, one objective of this proposal is the fostering of ongoing attention to the nation, including critical questions about the silences within the constructed histories and traditions of a common national identity. Particular questions to be explored with students might include: Whose traditions and whose imagined communities are fostered as the unidentified norm of homogenizing nationalist discourses? (Alarcón, Kaplan, & Moallem, 1999). How do celebratory multicultural discourses founded on the construction of so-called shared memories and culture perpetuate a sense of the triumph of one racial group over Others? (Bannerji, 1997; Willinsky, 1998). How have they masked the complex negotiation and resistance that is integral to nation-making projects? (Bhabha, 1994). Understanding how the nation has taken on the authority that it has, how educational institutions have been involved in promotion of this authority, and with what effects, would provide a basis for understanding why we should engage with social relations as framed by homogenizing nationalist discourses.

A second objective is to highlight inequalities and divisions as they are fostered through discourses of globalization. Moving beyond analysis of the social and the global in purely national and cultural terms, discursive reading would expose how difference is inscribed in political, economic, and cultural terms with social and material effects. Saskia Sassen provides a rich example of such a reading with her discursive analysis of global labour migration, there she explores how immigrants are cast as 'threatening outsiders' and how might this be challenged (1999); these questions worthy of curricular attention. Mapping the discursive field of the global labour migration of Italians and Eastern European Jews during the nineteenth and twentieth centuries, Sassen highlights how concepts of immigration, refugee, and related attitudes, values, and state processes have influenced whether immigrants are cast as 'guests' or as 'aliens.' Particularly useful for postcolonial curriculum theory is Sassen's problematization of characterizations of the global labour force, immigrant-receiving countries, and immigration processes as framed by mainstream immigration discourses; for example, she shows how the global labour force is referred to as immigrants who are often stereotyped as being from a different race or culture or ethnic group, contributing on cultural and not economic or political terms to the recipient country (ibid., p. 140). Sassen shows how countries receiving immigrants cast themselves as generous and passive recipients, isolated from political and economic systems, and as serving the immigrants' interests – and not their own. She points out that these and other assumptions suggest that the 'causes of immigration lie outside the control or domain of receiving countries' and produce feelings of immigration as a mass invasion from poor countries, without acknowledging the role of the receiving countries in making them poor in the first place (ibid., p. 151). By exposing how such assumptions have emerged from particular historical and social circumstances, how they embrace racialized inequalities, and how they obscure the current political and economic realities that govern the existence of immigrants, Sassen makes a strong case for reconceptualizing nation and citizenship in light of a racialized, gendered, and classed labour force. Her analysis begs curriculum questions such as the following: Why are migrants moving now? Who is moving (i.e., people of what racial or ethnic backgrounds)? Where are they going? What risks and tragedies are they experiencing? What jobs are migrants doing? What conditions are imposed on their entry, residence, and departure? In what ways are they denied full rights and citizenship? What and whose interests do these arrangements serve?

To challenge these divisive assumptions and inequalities, Sassen makes an argument for rewriting immigration discourses in ways that highlight immigrants' work processes and participation in the global market and the transnational processes of which countries are also a part. Drawing on research about 'how, why, and when governments, economic actors, media, and populations ... participate in the immigration process,' Sassen argues for acknowledging immigration as the highly differentiated processes that is influenced by particular historical phases, geographical locations, duration, and size (1999, pp. 1, 155). By highlighting the complex web of domestic and global forces that influence global migration, commodity production, and manufacturing, she draws attention to the crisis of *border* that continues to legitimize some immigrants as insiders and delegitimize others as outsiders. Exposing the wide range of motivations for global migration and the unequal distribution of labour that is upheld by countries including Canada, Sassen challenges the relevance of concepts such as belonging and citizenship to the promotion of inclusion. Referring to immigrants and refugees as 'today's settlers,' she seeks the necessary 'civic incorporation' of immigrants on economic, political, and cultural terms (ibid., p. 146).

Sassen's analysis opens up questions beyond the familiar realm of inquiry related to nation and culture to include the following: How do neo-liberal discourses of economic relations subsume discourses related to increasing poverty and inequality worldwide (1998, p. xxvii–xxviii)? Whose political participation and work processes are legitimized through contemporary globalization discourses? Whose are erased from view? Who does this oppress or benefit? What effects does this have for how differently located or dislocated students feel about their potential to participate politically and economically in their lives? By drawing attention to the elaborated material economic and political effects of divisions instituted by imperial and nation-making projects, Sassen has provided a useful framework for analysing and challenging racial divisions as they relate to the uneven global distribution of labour and transnational processes and systems.

Frameworks for such analysis are by no means exhaustively explored here, but they do point to important directions for ongoing empirical and conceptual research related to curriculum and social inquiry. Discursive readings of the nation and the global draw attention to the fact that nationalism, multiculturalism, and migration, for example, are not naturally occurring phenomena, but are produced and institutionalized through human activities with different psychological, social, and material effects for different people (Sassen, 1999; Ng, 1995; Smith, 1999, Bannerji, 1997). Considering knowledge as it is discursively constituted enables emphasis on the historical and social conditions through which seemingly neutral constructs such as nation have emerged to take firm hold of the social imaginary, while other ideas, perspectives, and interests and have been obscured and forgotten (Foucault, 1969/1997).

By analysing how nationalist or globalization discourses characterize peoples, priorities, political and economic actors, and differences, it is possible to consider how various and intersecting forms of oppression are perpetuated through the production of knowledge (Smith, 1999). Discursive reading moves beyond a simplistic analysis of relations of domination and subordination as a unidirectional imposition of an aggressive group's set of values or interests on a passive group. It provides a method for making visible the social relations and hierarchies that are embedded in knowledge, educational policies, and practices. A discursive reading of nation draws attention to the ways in which a homogenizing nationalist discourse subsumes inequalities, histories and relations to the nation, perpetuating divisions instilled by imperialism. Sassen's discursive analysis complements and extends this reading by considering economic, political, and cultural assumptions of globalization discourses that justify and are reinforced by a dynamic of inequality, such as that institutionalized by mainstream immigration discourses (1999). This analysis does not reject the importance of recognizing different cultural and religious values, perspectives and histories; it does reject assumptions of an essentialized nation or culture to be known, advocating analysis of the problematic aspects of such a focus of study including their relation to the institutionalization of enduring unequal economic, social, and territorial relations. Such analysis makes possible a consideration of how racism, ethnocentrism, and Eurocentrism operate discursively and how people 'enter into, and participate in, such relations in unthinking and unthinkable ways' (Smith, 1999, p. 158). If educational institutions are interested in preparing students to be active participants in their political, cultural, and economic lives through which the global is infused, and to work against imperial legacies, they must engage with the ways in which knowledge is socially organized to foster divisions, asymmetries, and exclusions. Understanding how racism and ethnocentrism are mediated through nationalist and globalization discourses will not transform these relations in and of themselves, but making them visible makes them contestable – and this is necessary for destabilizing their elaborations.

Reflections

This chapter calls for the end of fostering a sense of belonging to a nation with a homogeneous identity, and a nationalized consciousness of the world. This proposal does *not* advocate the end of educational attention to nation and its replacement with attention to globalization. Instead, it emphasizes that globalization consists of elaborated, intensified transnational processes that have emerged through histories of which colonial and Euro-nationalist movements have been a part.

The discursive reading that I am proposing challenges the widespread notion of a global-national duality as being a 'mutually exclusive set of terrains where the national economy or state loses what the global economy gains' (Sassen, 1998, p. xxvii). This assumption would disregard existing and complex global and domestic processes and perhaps foster reactionary nationalist sentiments, reinforcing systems of exclusion. As individual and membership rights previously defined on the basis of nationality are increasingly established on the basis of universal personhood through the transnational human-rights regime, nation-states are taking on new political and legal roles (Soysal 1998,

p. 205; G. Dyer, personal communication, 15 May 2000; L. Axworthy, personal communication, 10 May 2000). Such blurring of global and domestic affairs has been further reconfigured since 11 September 2001. Some spaces are opening for the pursuit of rights and solidarities at global levels; however, war, advanced by the United States in the name of 'freedom' and 'liberation' has endorsed (among other things) discriminatory antiterrorism legislation that has intensified the dangers of racial profiling and exclusionary immigration and refugee policies of nations *still* in-the-making.

What is relevant for postcolonial or anticolonial education is the need to engage new notions of membership, citizenship, and entitlement no longer rooted in assumptions of a common territory and identity, but rather of civic participation and residence. The uneven dissolution of economic borders and the intensification of global insecurities are accompanied by a reinforcement of anti-immigrant and nationalist sentiments, and real and imaginary borders along racial, religious, and political divides. This poses urgent questions for educational attention that include the following: How are these borders evoked and how are they variously articulated in different contexts within and beyond educational institutions? What constructions of difference of ethnicity, class, race, gender, sexuality are inscribed in these discourses? Whom do they benefit, and whom do they oppress? How so? Which peoples are considered first- or second-class citizens in these discourses? How might they be challenged? What if different concepts of nation and citizenship were taken up in classrooms? How might they open up spaces for different voices, art forms, spiritual and intellectual traditions, and the conversations necessary to explore the terms and conditions for equality? Such considerations provide a critical focus for educators and students to reconceptualize social relations and their communities in more relevant and inclusive ways.

NOTES

I am grateful to Yvonne Brown for her feedback on this piece, for her scholarship, friendship, and ongoing conversations about these issues. I am also thankful for the helpful contributions made by John Willinsky, Walt Werner, Leonora Angeles, Jean Barman, Jane Mitchell to earlier versions of this chapter.

1 While I acknowledge the extensive and important research analyzing the

intersections of race, gender, and class, for example, as they relate to the nation-making project and national identity formation, these considerations are beyond the scope of this chapter. For some consideration of these concerns, see Bannerji, 1997; Mohanty, 1997; Kaplan, Alarcón, & Moallem, 1999.

2 The curriculum guidelines to which I refer are included in the British Columbia Integrated Resource Package for Social Studies, Kindergarten through Grade 12 that consist of provincially prescribed curriculum learning outcomes, that is, what students are expected to know and do at an indicated grade, and suggested ideas, resources, and methods for instruction. The B.C. Ministry of Education defines social studies as 'a multidisciplinary subject that draws from the social sciences and humanities to study human interaction and natural and social environments' (2001a).

3 Roman and Stanley (1997) have taken up such questions in their analysis of Canadian Grade 7 students' negotiations of official and popular discourses of 'race' and nation. Revealing how students negotiated these in complex and unpredictable ways, they challenged educators to explore alternative discourses to multiculturalism's celebration of cultural differences. In many respects this chapter engages with that challenge, seeking new terms and perspectives with which to understand and destabilize racism, colonial ethnocentrism, and Eurocentrism.

REFERENCES

Anderson, B. (1983). *Imagined communities: Reflections on the origin and spread of nationalism.* London: Verso.

Ashcroft, B., Griffiths, G., & Tiffin, H. (Eds.). (1998). *Key concepts in post-colonial studies.* London: Routledge.

Bannerji, H. (1997). Geography lessons: On being an insider/outsider to the Canadian nation. In L.G. Roman & L. Eyre (Eds.), *Dangerous territories: Struggles for difference and equality in education* (pp. 23–43). New York: Routledge.

Bannerji, H. (2000). *The dark side of the nation: Essays on multiculturalism, nationalism and gender.* Toronto: Canadian Scholars' Press.

Bhabha, H. (1994). DissemiNation: Time, narrative and the margins of the modern nation. *The location of culture.* London: Routledge.

Billig, M. (1996). *Banal nationalism.* London: Sage.

British Columbia, Ministry of Education. (2001a). Introduction to social studies, Kindergarten to Grade 7 – rationale and approach: Social studies K–11. *Social studies integrated resource package.* http://www.bced.gov.bc.ca/irp/ssk7/rational.htm

British Columbia, Ministry of Education. (2001b). British Columbia First Nations Studies 12 curriculum: Contact, colonialism, and resistance. *Social studies integrated resource package.* http://www.bced.gov.bc.ca/irp/bcfns12/ccar1.htm

British Columbia, Ministry of Education. (2001c). History 12. *Social studies integrated resource package.* http://www.bced.gov.bc.ca/irp/his12/intro2.htm

British Columbia, Ministry of Education. (2001d). Comparative Civilizations 12: Introduction and rationale. *Social studies integrated resource package.* http://www.bced.gov.bc.ca/irp/comciv12/intro.htm

British Columbia, Ministry of Education. (2001e). The social studies K to 7 curriculum. *Social studies integrated resource package.* http://www.bced.gov.bc.ca/irp/ssk7curr.htm

Cameron, A.D. (1901, Oct.). To young British Columbians. *Victoria Daily Times.* Victoria, B.C.

Cohen, P. (1992). 'It's racism what dunnit': Hidden narratives in theories of race. In A. Rattansi & J. Donald (Eds.), *'Race,' culture and difference* (pp. 62–104). London: Open University Press.

Eze, E. C. (Ed.). (1997). *Race and the Enlightenment: A reader.* Cambridge: Blackwell.

Feinberg, W. (1998). *Common schools / uncommon identities: National unity and cultural difference.* New Haven: Yale University Press.

Foucault, M. (1997). *The archaeology of knowledge* (A.M. Sheridan Smith, Trans.). London: Routledge. (Original work published 1969)

Gikandi, S. (1996). *Maps of Englishness: Writing identity in the culture of colonialism.* New York: Columbia University Press.

Hobsbawm, E. (1994). The nation as invented tradition. In J. Hutchinson & A.D. Smith (Eds.), *Oxford readers: Nationalism.* Oxford: Oxford University Press.

Johnston, R.J., Gregory, D., Pratt, G., & Watts, M. (Eds.). (2000). *The dictionary of human geography* (4th ed.). Oxford: Blackwell.

Kaplan, C., Alarcón, N., & Moallem, M. (Eds.). (1999). *Between woman and nation: Nationalisms, transnational feminisms, and the state.* Durham: Duke University Press.

Milloy, J.S. (1999). The founding vision of residential school education, 1879 to 1920. In *'A national crime': The Canadian government and the residential school system, 1879 to 1986* (pp. 23–47). Winnipeg: University of Manitoba Press.

Mohanty, C.T. (1989–90). On race and voice: Challenges for liberal education in the 1990s. *Cultural Critique, 18*(14), 179–208.

Mohanty, C.T. (1997). Preface – dangerous territories, territorial power, and education. In L.G. Roman & L. Eyre (Eds.), *Dangerous territories: Struggles for difference and equality in education* (pp. ix–xvii). London: Routledge.

Ng, R. (1995). Multiculturalism as ideology: A textual analysis. In M. Campbell & A. Manicom (Eds.), *Knowledge, experience, and ruling relations: Studies in the social organization of knowledge* (pp. 35–49). Toronto: University of Toronto Press.

Rattansi, A. (1992). Changing the subject? Racism, culture, and education. In J. Donald & A. Rattansi (Eds.), *'Race,' culture and difference* (pp. 11–49). London: Open University Press.

Roman, L.G., & Stanley, T. (1997). Empires, emigrés, and aliens: Young people's negotiation of official and popular racism in Canada. In L.G. Roman & L. Eyre (Eds.), *Dangerous territories: Struggles for difference and equality in education* (pp. 205–233). New York: Routledge.

Said, E. (1994). *Orientalism* (2nd ed.). New York: Vintage Books. (Original work published 1978)

Said, E. (1993). *Culture and imperialism*. New York: Vintage Books.

Sassen, S. (1998). *Globalization and its discontents: Essays on the new mobility of people and money*. New York: New Press.

Sassen, S. (1999). *Guests and aliens*. New York: New Press.

Shohat, E., & Stam, R. (1994). *Unthinking Eurocentrism: Multiculturalism and the media*. London: Routledge.

Smith, D.E. (1999). *Writing the social: Critique, theory, and investigations*. Toronto: University of Toronto Press.

Soysal, Y.N. (1998). Toward a postnational model of membership. In G. Shafir (Ed.), *The citizenship debates* (pp. 89–221). Minneapolis: University of Minnesota Press.

Stanley, T.J. (1995). White supremacy and the rhetoric of educational indoctrination: A Canadian case study. In J. Barman, N. Sutherland, & J.D. Wilson (Eds.), *Children, teachers and schools in the history of British Columbia* (pp. 39–56). Calgary: Detselig.

Willinsky, J. (1998). *Learning to divide the world: Education at empire's end*. Minneapolis: University of Minnesota Press.

Willinsky, J. (1999). Curriculum after culture, race, and nation. *Discourse: Studies in the Cultural Politics of Education, 20*(1), 89–112.

Contributors

Glen S. Aikenhead is professor in the Department of Curriculum Studies, College of Education, University of Saskatchewan. His research and publications have had a strong influence on the science education policies of Canadian provinces. He is deeply committed to the research on science and technology education for Native Canadians, and his publications include *Integrating Western and Aboriginal Sciences: Cross-Cultural Science Teaching*; *Whose Scientific Knowledge? The Colonizer and the Colonized*; and *Science Education for Everyday Life: Evidence-Based Practice*.

M. Kazim Bacchus is an eminent scholar in education in developing countries. A graduate of London School of Economics, Institute of Education at the University of London, and University of California at Berkeley, Dr Bacchus has taught at all levels of education, including universities in the West Indies, the United Kingdom, and Canada. He has published widely on the social, economic, and political forces that influenced the development of education in the former British Caribbean colonies. His publications include *Utilization, Misuse and Development of Human Resources in the Early West Indian Colonies*, *Education as and for Legitimacy: Developments in West Indian Education between 1846 and 1895*, and his latest volume, *Education for Economic, Social and Political Development in the British Caribbean Colonies from 1896 to 1945*.

George J. Sefa Dei is professor and chair, Department of Sociology and Equity Studies, Ontario Institute for Studies in Education of the University of Toronto. His teaching and research interests are in the areas of antiracism studies, minority schooling, international development, and anticolonial education. He has authored, co-authored, and co-edited many books, including *Anti-racism Education: Theory and Practice; Reconstructing 'Dropout': A Critical ethnography of the Dynamics of Black Students' Disengagement from School; Indigenous Knowledges in Global Contexts: Multiple Readings of our World;* and *Schooling and Education in Africa: The Case of Ghana.*

Stanley Doyle-Wood is a doctoral candidate in the Department of Sociology and Equity Studies in Education at the Ontario Institute for Studies in Education of the University of Toronto. His area of concentration and research includes the racialization of children; the violent/violating impact of colonial relations of power as they are disseminated through knowledge production, pedagogies of alienation, imperialism/neo-colonialism, and the regulation of child bodies; antiracist and anticolonial pedagogical approaches to curriculum; and spirituality as anticolonial agency.

Ingrid Johnston is associate dean, Research and Graduate Studies, in the Faculty of Education, University of Alberta, and associate professor of English Education and Curriculum in the Department of Secondary Education. Her research and teaching interests focus on postcolonial literary studies, teacher identity, and questions of multicultural and antiracist teacher education. Her book *Re-mapping Literary Worlds: Postcolonial Pedagogy in Practice,* (Peter Lang, 2003) will appear in translation in China in 2005.

Yatta Kanu is associate professor of curriculum and instruction in the Faculty of Education, University of Manitoba. Her primary areas of scholarship include curriculum, culture, and student learning; international education; education in developing countries; teacher education; and teacher research. She has published monographs and numerous articles in these areas, including publications in *International Journal of Educational Development, Journal of Teacher Education, Canadian and International Education,* and *Journal of Educational Research* (Pakistan). She is editor of the 'International Curriculum Discourse' section of *Journal of Curriculum Theorizing* and curriculum consultant for several international curriculum reform projects. Dr Kanu has lived and taught in Sierra Leone, Pakistan, United States, and Canada.

Joe L. Kincheloe was a professor of education at the City University of New York Graduate Center and is now Canada Research Chair in the Faculty of Education at McGill University. He has written numerous books and articles on race, class, and gender and education, issues of indigenous knowledge, research and pedagogy. He is the author and/ or editor of several books including *Changing Multiculturalism; White Reign: Deploying Whiteness in America; Critical Constructivism; What Is Indigenous Knowledge?* and *Multiple Intelligences Reconsidered.*

Norrel A. London is a retired professor from the Faculty of Education at the University of Western Ontario. He has written and published extensively on colonial education and educational development and transformation in Trinidad and Tobago. His publications include *Pathways to Educational Transformation and Development: Policies, Plans and Lessons*, which is a significant contribution to the international thrust in education development in the aftermath of decolonization.

Seonaigh MacPherson is assistant professor of TESL/SLE in the Department of Curriculum, Teaching and Learning at the University of Manitoba. Her research examines issues in minority, diaspora, and indigenous language education; the globalization of English; human rights and democratic citizenship education; and linguistic and cultural education and sustainability. During the 1990s she was an English teacher and researcher working with Tibetan refugee educational programs in the Indian Himalayas. She has published in academic journals covering issues in TESL and curriculum, including *TESOL Quarterly, JCT,* and *TESL Canada Journal.*

Kara McDonald is a doctoral candidate in the Faculty of Education, University of British Columbia. She writes and researches in the areas of citizenship, national identity, and social studies education.

Ralph T. Mason is associate professor in the Department of Curriculum, Teaching, and Learning in the Faculty of Education, University of Manitoba. His interests include the reform of mathematics learning in schools, curriculum theorizing, and participatory and relational approaches to research. Along with a variety of monographs and research reports, he has published articles in journals such as *Mathematics Teacher, Journal of Professional Studies, Mathematics Teaching in the Middle Schools, Educational Technology,* and *Journal of Educational Thought.*

George Richardson is associate professor in the Department of Secondary Education at the University of Alberta. His research interests include citizenship education, national identity formation, multicultural education, international education, postcolonial theory, action research, and teacher identity formation. He is editor of the journal *Canadian Social Studies* and co-editor of *Troubling the Canon of Citizenship Education*.

David Smith is professor of education at the University of Alberta, Edmonton, Alberta. He teaches and publishes in the areas of globalization studies, curriculum theory, and religious education. Collections of his papers have been published respectively in *Pedagon: Interdisciplinary Essays in the Human Sciences, Pedagogy and Culture; Globalization and Postmodern Pedagogy;* and *Teaching in Global Times*.

John Willinsky is currently the Pacific Press Professor of Literacy and Technology and Distinguished University Scholar in the Department of Language and Literacy Education at the University of British Columbia, and a Fellow of the Royal Society of Canada. He is the author of *Learning to Divide the World: Education at Empire's End*, which won outstanding book awards from the American Educational Research Association and History of Education Society, and more recently *The Access Principle: The Case for Open Access to Research and Scholarship*. Examples of his work, including the open source software designed to improve the access and quality of research, are available at the Public Knowledge Project (http://pkp.ubc.ca), which he directs at the University of British Columbia.